PATTERNS OF DEVELOPMENT
IN LATIN AMERICA

JOHN SHEAHAN

PATTERNS OF DEVELOPMENT
IN LATIN AMERICA

Poverty, Repression, and
Economic Strategy

PRINCETON
UNIVERSITY
PRESS

Published by Princeton University Press, 41 William Street,
Princeton, New Jersey 08540
In the United Kingdom: Princeton University Press, Guildford, Surrey

All Rights Reserved
Library of Congress Cataloging in Publication Data will be
found on the last printed page of this book

ISBN 0-691-07735-5 (cloth)
0-691-02264-x (pbk)

This book has been composed in Linotron Baskerville

Clothbound editions of Princeton University Press books
are printed on acid-free paper, and binding materials are
chosen for strength and durability. Paperbacks, although satisfactory
for personal collections, are not usually suitable for library rebinding

Printed in the United States of America by Princeton University Press,
Princeton, New Jersey

CONTENTS

TABLES AND FIGURES

TABLES

FIGURES

PREFACE

In the highly charged Latin American context issues of economic strategy can seem at times of distinctly secondary importance, and at other times as matters of life and death. Conflicts over trade restrictions and government deficits in Brazil in the early 1960s, or over the money supply and wage policy in Chile in 1971 and 1972, rather pale in comparison to the gathering storms that were about to impose murderous authoritarian regimes in both of these countries. Still, the pressures that create such storms are sometimes built up, or could conceivably be moderated, by the quality of national economic strategies. It is possible in at least some cases that more coherent economic policies, adopted in time, could make such outcomes less likely. And, apart from dramatic breakdowns, differences in economic strategies have had a great deal to do with sustained contrasts such as the ability of Colombia to raise income per capita four times faster than Argentina in the last quarter century, or the anomaly of Brazil, with an income level almost identical to that of Costa Rica in the early 1970s, having a child mortality rate three times higher.

It is the differences among Latin American countries that grow most striking as one follows them over the years. More accurately, it is the interaction between common strands—common cultural and historical patterns and common pressures from the outside world—with different national responses and different kinds of change in consequence. Drastically negative results are all too common; imperfect but improving alternatives are possible too.

For particularly helpful discussions of these issues, or reading and criticizing parts of the manuscript, or for bursts of indignation at strategic points, I would like to express appreciation to Bruce Bagley, Albert Berry, Jorge Domínguez, David Fairris, Brígida García, Stephany Griffith-Jones, Jonathan Hartlyn, Brooke Larson, Nathaniel Leff, Cynthia McClintock, Michael McPherson, Oscar Muñoz, and Richard Sabot. More than twenty years ago, Colombian colleagues in the Departamento Nacional de Planeación—along with a fellow adviser, Richard Bird—helped greatly to give some of these questions initial meaning. A first-rate group of graduate students at El Colegio de México in 1970, amazingly friendly and patient, stuck to their guns in driving home concerns that never occurred to me in graduate school, but should have. In a too-brief period of research in and on Peru, Javier Iguíñiz, Jürgen Schuldt, and Raúl Torres were especially helpful. Back at home, independent-minded Williams students and an economics department remarkable for both forbearance and good ideas all contributed to raise better questions and to reduce confusion.

My wife, Denise, helped with research on issues connected with education and, by her careful reading of much of the manuscript and her unfailing sense of what matters most, did more than anyone else to direct attention to essentials. Amy Glass and Ann Montgomery cheerfully dug out problems with data and in one instance designed a statistical test that forced me to give up a cherished hypothesis. Anita O'Brien, at once eagle-eyed and understanding, did wonders to clean up the text and references. Sandy Thatcher, editor-in-chief of Princeton University Press, backed up initial encouragement for this book with just the right mixture of patience and specific advice at critical points.

A research grant from the Joint Committee on Latin American Studies of the American Council of Learned Societies and the Social Science Research Council permitted me to spend the first year of writing with the Institute of Development Studies at the University of Sussex, creating the opportunity to meet exceptionally diverse people working on issues of development in many fields, and to have a last chance to talk about these questions with that marvelously independent spirit, Dudley Seers.

Finally, three other economists who have disagreed with each other on practically everything except their deep concern for Latin America—Lauchlin Currie, Carlos Díaz Alejandro until his death in 1985, and Albert Hirschman—have been wonderfully stimulating through both their writing and many years of friendship. I would like to dedicate this book to the memories of Carlos Díaz and of Dudley Seers, to the happily very much alive and creative Lauchlin Currie and Albert Hirschman, and to Denise.

PART I

PERSISTENT ISSUES

ONE

WAYS OF LOOKING

In a world full of conflict and confusion, Latin American countries stand out for dramatic degrees of both. Blocked lives for many in contexts of increasing national and world income make for explosions or for repression more often than negotiation and widely acceptable kinds of change. Strains in basic social and economic relationships—among classes and interest groups, between objectives of economic efficiency and of social justice, and between countries and the external world—take on extraordinary intensity. This book is about reasons why poverty is so persistent and the collisions so violent, how Latin American societies are changing, and what might be done to make the changes more positive.

It is certainly not the case that these societies are frozen into a fixed pattern. Most of them have been going through extraordinarily rapid changes. Yesterday's careful explanations of why things work out the way they do, and why particular kinds of change are impossible in Latin American conditions, constantly need to be revised as counterforces break down the patterns considered to be permanent. Much of the intensity of social conflict has come from the dislocations involved in rapid change: from basically rural societies dominated by landowners toward urban dominance and high degrees of industrialization; from near-total dependence on primary exports subject to unstable world market forces toward industrial exports more sensitive to domestic costs and incentives; from earlier demographic stability first into conditions of exceptionally fast growth of population and labor force and then, beginning in the 1960s, to dramatically falling fertility and birth rates; from a mixture of personalized dictatorships and moderately open political systems under the leadership of old elites, able in most respect to keep the majority of the population out of the decision process, to a spectrum of populist, radical, ultrareactionary, and fairly open democratic societies.

Too much is going on at once to capture more than a few strands in any one search. This attempt is centered on three particular sets of issues. The first is the persistence of greater degrees of inequality than in other regions, both richer and poorer than Latin America. The second is the nature of the economic relationships between these countries and the outside world: issues of dependence, the impact of foreign trade and investment, and the evolving mixture of external help and damage. The third is the close association since the early 1960s between (a) changes toward more market-oriented economic systems with greater stress on efficiency, and (b) accompanying changes toward extreme political repression. These issues interact continuously with each other, sometimes in ways that illuminate the depth of resistance to fundamental change and sometimes, on the contrary, in ways that help bring out possibilities of doing better.

1. Diversity and Choice

Latin American studies are rich in explanations of deadlocks imposed by conflicting social forces and by dependent relationships to the outside world, demonstrating that significant change is either impossible or can only become possible by violent overturn.[1] This way of looking is so entrenched because there is a lot of truth in it. The frequency with which the promise of positive change has been aborted is discouraging. The resistances are deep. But not equally so among all countries, in all periods, and in all the dimensions that matter. Differences among the countries of the region have become increasingly pronounced since the beginning of the 1930s. They do not mean that unified explanation of persisting obstacles has lost its value, but they require greater attention to the factors explaining alternative paths. Increasing diversity underlines the possibility that the more specific details of economic and social policy choice are taking on increased importance in shaping the course of events. Positive change is not the common result, but the failure to get it may as often be due to inconsistent or misdirected policies as it is to the dominance of profound forces resistant to change.

  Some of the most influential interpretations of postwar Latin America—particularly those of Fernando Henrique Cardoso and Guillermo O'Donnell—emphasize direct causal connections among the three sets of issues central to this discussion: external dependence shapes internal forces in ways adverse for equality and for

[1] For a particularly effective statement of this view see Richard A. Fagen, "Equity in the South in the Context of North-South Relations," in Albert Fishlow et al., eds., *Rich and Poor Nations in the World Economy* (New York: McGraw-Hill, 1978), pp. 163–214.

open political systems.[2] Both Cardoso and O'Donnell reach toward differences in national experiences to clarify a common process, leaving open questions of possible variations on this process. Others have taken this line of analysis to strong conclusions: "It has become increasingly clear that transforming a society's structure and reducing its external dependence can only come about by conscious disengagement from the world capitalist economy."[3]

In Cardoso's own interpretation pressures from the outside world do not imply any predetermined common outcome: they take on varied forms in different national contexts and provoke counterpressures that differ among countries and periods. That flexibility has been criticized as a rejection of the search for a definitive governing theory, a refusal "to place theoretical limits on capitalist development at the periphery . . . a retreat from theory . . . which leaves enormous problems for those who want to go beyond *post hoc* description."[4] Exactly so. That tension between a wish to formulate universally valid principles and a wish to bring out the great variety of actual possibilities runs through all studies in the social sciences. It creates enormous problems of links between the specific and the general. But it cannot be wished away. Intellectual inquiry would be much the poorer if not inspired in some degree by the vision of a comprehensive theory that places conclusive limits on possible results, and it would also be much the poorer if any such vision were allowed to close off attention to the amazing twists and turns of reality.

O'Donnell's analytical framework postulates a common historical process in which individual societies are seen as differing mainly according to their present stage on the same path. It centers on the interactions of political and economic factors as industrialization gets under way, begins to open up new interests and bring new groups into social decisions, reaches a crucial middle stage of in-

[2] Fernando Henrique Cardoso and Enzo Faletto, *Dependencia y desarrollo en América Latina* (Mexico: Siglo Veintiuno, 1969), revised English version, *Dependency and Development in Latin America* (Berkeley: University of California Press, 1979); Cardoso, "Associated-Dependent Development," in Alfred Stepan, ed., *Authoritarian Brazil* (New Haven: Yale University Press, 1973); Guillermo A. O'Donnell, *Modernization and Bureaucratic-Authoritarianism: Studies in South American Politics* (Berkeley: University of California, Institute of International Studies, 1973).

[3] José Villamil, ed., *Transnational Capitalism and National Development* (Brighton: Harvester Press for the Institute of International Studies, University of Sussex, 1979), p. 11.

[4] Martin Godfrey, "Is Dependency Dead?" Institute of Development Studies, University of Sussex, *Bulletin* 12, 1 (1980), p. 4.

creasing strains, and then provokes authoritarian reaction. O'Donnell's analysis has been effectively criticized from many angles, but it remains highly suggestive as an attempt to clarify the origins and nature of a new kind of authoritarianism in modern Latin America, combining political repression with a stress on free markets and economic efficiency.

The particular kind of industrialization analyzed by O'Donnell is based on protection and import substitution, exemplified to an extreme degree by the countries with which he is most closely concerned, Argentina and Brazil. His research from the perspective of political science thus comes into close contact with a massive literature in economics concerning styles of development, the distortions created by import substitution, and the costs and gains of international trade. The two perspectives sometimes reinforce and sometimes collide with each other. Many of the economic studies of separate policy issues can be seen in a new and enlightening way by use of O'Donnell's analytical process, but at the same time many of them would call for recognition of development paths systematically outside his model. They do not in any sense disprove it, but they suggest the need to open it up to more alternatives.

This book attempts to construct bridges between the world of generalized interpretive models like those of Cardoso and O'Donnell and that of specific policy-oriented studies of economic development in different national contexts: on causes of inflation in Argentina, how monetary policies affect employment in Chile, how Colombian exports respond to changes in exchange rates, how changes in the structure of expenditures on education in Brazil affected income distribution in the 1960s, and so on through an ever-growing field of empirical research on detailed cause-and-effect relationships. Many such studies complement each other to build up a coherent general picture, but then many others contradict each other. Almost all are incomplete and raise new questions that need further research, and even the best of them are always being superseded by new kinds of behavior and new studies of its causes. But that is the way it should be: we need the generalizations and we also need to keep asking new questions to keep them open to a reality that does not stand still.

Latin American countries are not standing still. They are all changing, and one of the most striking aspects of change in the last forty years is how differently they have been moving. Colombia and Mexico differ in vital ways between themselves, and at the same time they differ systematically as a pair from the early postwar leaders of change, Argentina, Brazil, and Chile. All five differ in fundamental respects from Central America, and within Central America the differences between Costa Rica and El Salvador are like day and night. The causes of these differences are fascinating to explore, whether focused more on historical conditions or more on the specific policy alternatives adopted by these countries in the postwar period. Differences in behavior, and in such relatively objective measures as growth of income and changing degrees of external debt and dependence, inequality, and child mortality, add up to a strong case for the possibility of altering the course of events, even within given external world conditions, by different choices of national economic strategy. Beyond such quantitative measures, clarification of these differences may help us to understand why four of the leading Latin American countries turned into some of the most inhumanely efficient police states of the modern world while others have, so far, been able to keep evolving without that enormous cost.

2. A REFERENCE BASE OF DIFFERENT REGIME TYPES

The orientation in this discussion toward multiplicity of cases and results is to some extent moderated by use of a reference base of five different categories, listed in table 1.1 with examples of particular countries and periods. It is not that a country belongs by its nature to a particular category, or that all of them can be expected to march up from group 5 to the ultimate fate of group 1. Rather, particular kinds of regimes persist as possibilities, and countries either adopt, get pushed into, or escape from them as the pressures bearing on each country and its own responses evolve.

It would be splendid to be able to fill in examples for another category described in some such terms as "fully democratic, egalitarian, self-determined, dynamic, and peaceful." We can all dream. No actual country is a strong candidate, but some such category should be present as a conception, as a reminder not to mistake the merely bearable as a sufficient goal. If social scientists have any function it should be to point out ways to do better. But it does not help understanding to lump together all unsatisfactory conditions, countries, or even people, as more or less equivalent failures. Differences in degrees and kinds of imperfection can matter greatly.

Group 1 refers to modern kinds of authoritarian regimes based on force and oriented toward emphasis on economic efficiency: those O'Donnell termed "bureaucratic-authoritarian." That term was appropriate for the first two cases central to his analysis, Brazil

TABLE 1.1. Five Regime-Groups in Postwar Latin America, with
Examples of Countries and Periods Used in Discussion

1. Authoritarian conservative or reactionary regimes, with emphasis on market forces and economic efficiency

   Argentina 1966–70 and 1976–82
   Brazil from 1964 to 1984
   Chile since September 1973
   Uruguay from 1972 to 1984

2. Socialist or Marxist orientation

   Chile in the Allende period, 1970 to September 1973
   Cuba under Castro from 1959
   Nicaragua from 1979

3. Middle-of-the-road conservative or reformist regimes with more
   open political systems than group (1); changing balances between
   concern for economic efficiency and for social reform depending
   on particular administrations

   Chile up to 1970
   Colombia from 1960
   Costa Rica
   Ecuador from 1979
   Mexico
   Venezuela

4. Populist or radical reformist but not socialist

   Argentina under the Peróns, 1946–54 and 1972–76
   Brazil in Quadros and Goulart administrations, 1960–64
   Peru in the Velasco period, 1968–74

5. Least industrialized, usually conservative or reactionary in a more
   traditional sense than (1) or (3)

   Bolivia
   Central America except Costa Rica
   Dominican Republic
   Haiti
   Paraguay

NOTE: The English-speaking countries of the Caribbean are not included in this
discussion of Latin America.

and Argentina in the second half of the 1960s. Both of them emphasized active state management of the economy, though with a fundamental change toward more attention to relative prices and to export promotion. In contrast, the even more repressive systems of the Southern Cone in the 1970s, with strongly monetarist orientations, rejected in principle the whole idea of detailed state economic management. They were very much market oriented and repressive, but not bureaucratic. For this reason, the term used here to refer to the whole set is "market-authoritarian." In line with this distinction, the discussion here restricts the term "Southern Cone" to the monetarist cases of the 1970s in Argentina, Chile, and Uruguay, excluding Brazil. The Brazilian style of economic management was in fundamental respects different from those of the Southern Cone cases, and much more effective.

These examples of severe repression came to be seen in some analyses as the typical outcome to be expected from the breakdown of early postwar import substitution. But three have since escaped, and the outcome does not look quite as typical as it once did. The escapees may fall back, or new victims may take their places, or, just conceivably, this particular nightmare may not be repeated.

Category 2, socialist or Marxist regimes, only has one long-lasting example so far. That it has even one is to some degree surprising, considering the diligence with which the United States tries to prevent their emergence or survival. The Allende regime in Chile is placed here because the government was Marxist, though it could be placed in group 4 because the policies actually followed were close to those of the populist regimes. Nicaragua is similarly included because its political leadership has been Marxist oriented, though private ownership and production remain more important than state ownership. In some respects the contrasts among different kinds of socialist systems, and among different kinds of capitalist systems, may be at least as significant as the distinction between socialist and capitalist societies in general.

Group 5 is closer to a simple classification in terms of economic evolution: these are the countries that have moved away least from the traditional image of Latin America. They tend to stand at the low end of measures in terms of both human rights and material welfare, though their styles of repression do not match the organized modern ruthlessness of the more economically advanced market-authoritarian states. Many of these countries are in process of rapid movement too; this is a category that may have no separate meaning twenty years from now.

The distinction between categories 3 and 4 is crucial. The countries identifiable as belonging to the former group for fairly long periods have had generally conservative governments, with some periods of moderate reform, and have been able to continue industrialization without the breakdowns and crises described in O'Donnell's model. Group 4 consists of populist regimes, including the two cases central to his analysis, Argentina and Brazil. The highly elastic concept "populist," considered in chapter 12, does not necessarily mean democratic. Latin American populism can include some highly arbitrary governments, such as that of General Velasco in Peru. The meaning intended here has two components. One is that these are movements and governments that turn against many aspects of the prior status quo, particularly against prior forms of social domination, without rejecting property rights. They appeal to the dissatisfied and impatient across class lines, often with mixtures of both socialist and fascist elements, usually without any clear ideology or program. The second component is that they consistently reject reliance on market forces and conventional economic constraints: they base much of their appeal on price controls to favor urban consumers, import restrictions to protect industry, subsidies for producers, opposition to foreign investment, and government spending to favor specific groups without concern for aggregate economic balance.[5] A particularly suggestive discussion of populism published in 1965 concludes that it is "the only force on the side of reform in Latin America."[6] History suggests that this is wrong on two counts: it is not the only force for reform, and such regimes always break down.

The countries listed in category 3 do not differ from the examples of populism in group 4 by total avoidance of reforms; they differ by the separable question of attention to criteria of efficiency and consistency in economic management, not without problems but without rejection in principle of such considerations. Those that have stayed for long periods in group 3 have in general been able to pur-

[5] These characteristics are associated by Alfred Stepan with regimes he terms "inclusionary corporatism." His opposed definition of "exclusionary corporatism" fits many features of group 1 in table 1.1. The two definitions leave out (or leave as an unstated middle) group 3 in this table. Stepan, *The State and Society: Peru in Comparative Perspective* (Princeton: Princeton University Press, 1978), ch. 3, especially table 3.1, pp. 77–78.

[6] Torcuato S. di Tella, "Populism and Reform in Latin America," in Claudio Véliz, ed., *Obstacles to Change in Latin America* (London: Oxford University Press, 1965), pp. 47–74.

sue industrialization and to reduce poverty without traumatic reactions. They could break down too, even without any real reforms.
They might alternatively accomplish social improvement along with
sustained growth, or just keep going on their nonbrilliant but not
drastically repressive paths. What happens to them is partly a matter of how they are hit from the outside but more fundamentally a
matter of what economic and social policies they adopt.

3. CONFLICTING PERSPECTIVES

Interpretation of the conflicts involved in economic and social
change in Latin America repeatedly breaks out of old molds into
new analytical systems of great appeal but then, not longer thereafter, into the discovery that the new systems owe much of their
force to oversimplification and neglect of contrary considerations.
Early postwar structuralism introduced by Raúl Prebisch and the
Economic Commission for Latin America (ECLA) offered a stimulating new interpretation of the requirements of active industrialization, but it pointed economic strategy in directions that proved to
be extremely costly.[7] Dependency analysis caught vital considerations that structuralism left out but in its turn obscured so much of
the actual process of change that its own credibility has decayed
rapidly. Ultraconservative monetarism may have gained its hold in
so many countries in the 1970s partly because these influential
interpretations directed attention away from more elementary considerations of efficiency and macroeconomic balance and caused
more trouble than societies could long accept. But monetarism as a
dominant style of interpretation and action is equally likely to be
short-lived because it damages so many interests. What it leaves out,
under existing Latin American conditions, is the welfare of the majority of the people.

Each of these theoretical formulations clarifies one or several

[7] United Nations, Economic Commission for Latin America, *The Economic Development of Latin America and Its Principal Problems* (New York: United Nations, 1950),
and *Towards a Dynamic Development Policy for Latin America* (New York: United Nations, 1963); Raúl Prebisch, "Commercial Policy in the Underdeveloped Countries,"
American Economic Review 49 (May 1959), pp. 251–73; Albert O. Hirschman, "Ideologies of Economic Development in Latin America," in Albert O. Hirschman, ed.,
Latin American Issues: Essays and Comments (New York: Twentieth Century Fund,
1961), pp. 3–42; Fernando Henrique Cardoso, "The Originality of the Copy: The
Economic Commission for Latin America and the Idea of Development," in Rothko
Chapel Colloquium, *Toward a New Strategy for Development* (New York: Pergamon,
1979), pp. 53–72.

pieces of a puzzle that is larger than any of them. It is not that they are wrong and should be, one by one, disproven and consigned to the history of thought. They are each right in one or more ways and need to be included in ongoing questions of what can and should be done. The trouble comes from claims to sufficiency, from the rejection of valid opposing insights.

The initial appeal of structuralism was that it offered what seemed to be a promising alternative path to industrialization and modernization, a nonrevolutionary escape from the constraints of a style of capitalism adverse to independent growth. Failure to industrialize was blamed on free trade: imports of manufactured goods block domestic investors, and growth of traditional exports works against rising national income by driving down external prices. In the absence of redirection by the government, people go on producing more primary exports regardless of falling prices and incomes, because alternative employment opportunities in the industrial sector are kept down by the pressure of import competition. To turn away from trade would constitute an escape from a trap established by market forces. Just as free trade is a trap on the external side, concern over increased government spending as a cause of inflation should be rejected as an old-fashioned belief restricting social and economic change: inflation is not a matter of excess demand or monetary expansion but instead of limits on supply capacity, requiring increased investment for solution.

These two classic half-truths—the harmful effects of international trade and the irrelevance of demand and money as causes of inflation—are discussed in chapters 4 and 5. The more fundamental conception underlying them is that persisting economic and social characteristics of developing countries prevent the kinds of flexibility necessary to respond to market forces. Where orthodox economics assumes that changing relative prices will guide investment and productive activity in directions favorable for rising incomes, structuralism emphasizes reasons why these responses are either slow or nonexistent. The implication is that direct social action is necessary to achieve economic flexibility: market forces do not accomplish anything except to change prices and heighten inequality.

On a technical level, much of the argument can be considered in terms of elasticities of supply and demand: if both elasticities are high, if both output and sales respond rapidly to changes in relative prices, markets can reallocate resources and alleviate supply shortages rapidly, without any necessarily strong effects on income distribution either between or within countries. If elasticities are close to zero, markets will not alleviate shortages without drastic changes in relative prices, or long delays, and price changes are very likely to have strong effects on income distribution. Countless empirical studies have shown that, though elasticities vary greatly among individual products and among types of exports and imports, changes in relative prices always have effects on supply and demand, including food supplies and foreign exchange.[8] This means that structuralist prescriptions that ignore the incentive effects of relative prices often cause serious trouble, sometimes creating shortages that could readily have been prevented. But it does not mean that the whole structuralist idea is simply mistaken. The emphasis on differentially low elasticities for traditional primary products, and the idea that supply responses are in general slower and weaker (though never absent) in developing countries than in industrialized economies, are both valid.[9]

Beyond these useful reminders of real problems on the supply side, structuralist ideas are especially worth attention because of their concern for institutional restraints on production, for questions of ownership and its effects on growth and income distribution, for the frequently negative effects of market forces, and for the problem of insufficient employment opportunities. These issues would continue to have important bearing on questions of poverty and international economic policies even if the terms of trade got better all the time. In a sense, structuralism and neoclassical economics need each other: the former brings out the problems that neoclassical economics obscures, and the latter directs attention to crucial questions that structuralism leaves out. The intellectual problem with structuralism is essentially one of overgeneralization of useful insights, applying them without distinction in conditions where they are not only useless but harmful. The political counterpart is that structuralist ideas provided a package of economic policies that fitted the wishes of populist governments, became in most cases the source of their economic strategy, and consistently did them in.

[8] This issue is discussed in many specific contexts in the following chapters. The most thorough empirical study of responses to prices in a Latin American country, taking into account both direct and indirect reactions through a complete econometric model, is that of Jere R. Behrman, *Macroeconomic Policy in a Developing Country: The Chilean Experience* (New York: Elsevier North-Holland, 1977).

[9] W. Arthur Lewis, "The State of Development Theory," *American Economic Review* 74 (March 1984), pp. 1–10.

Internal relationships of classes and the state were not at all prominent in structuralist analysis. It rather followed conventional economics in postulating a relatively autonomous government capable of making decisions on economic policy appropriate to national goals. The main attention was on exploitation of the developing country as a whole by the industrialized countries, not on internal class conflicts. Dependency analysis introduced a much more realistic view of such conflicts, and particularly of the ways in which they are shaped by external forces.[10] It attacks the very idea of the nation as a separable decision-making entity.[11] National policies and the consequences that flow from them are seen as determined by the external context, by coalitions between domestic and external interests, and by preference systems that are themselves the products of external influence. In the more pessimistic versions these dependent relationships make significant social change impossible until the world capitalist system passes away. Livelier versions stress instead that dependency can take many different forms, that social change is going on all the time, and that domestic groups may play active and varied roles despite the reality of external influence.

Dependency considerations, or variants and possible replies to them, are central to this book. That is not because they are consistently accurate but because they are always relevant. The central themes and some problems with them are discussed in chapter 7. The main objection to the approach is that it obscures the reality of possible changes in degrees and kinds of dependency through better policy choices. Dependency analysis can become a negative influence on autonomy and growth when used to discredit measures to stimulate a more self-reliant style of development. This is particularly true when the perspective is used to oppose changes in financial and trade policies that could reduce import dependence, encourage industrialization through exports, and lessen the need for foreign capital.

Although orthodox economics leaves out a lot, it points correctly to the necessity of consistency between claims on output and ability

[10] Cardoso, "The Originality of the Copy"; Peter Evans, *Dependent Development: The Alliance of Multinational, State, and Local Capital in Brazil* (Princeton: Princeton University Press, 1979), and "After Dependency: Recent Studies of Class, State, and Industrialization," *Latin American Research Review* 20, 2 (1985), pp. 149–60.

[11] J. Samuel Valenzuela and Arturo Valenzuela, "Modernisation and Dependence: Alternative Perspectives in the Study of Latin American Underdevelopment," in José Villamil, ed., *Transnational Capitalism*, p. 43; Gary Gereffi, *The Pharmaceutical Industry and Dependency in the Third World* (Princeton: Princeton University Press, 1983), ch. 1.

to produce it, and between the incentives created for economic actors and the results desired. It underlines the negative effects on autonomy of exchange rate policies that discourage exports and subsidize imports, and the damage to the rural poor inflicted by industrial protection. It often helps to bring out key questions of what went wrong and what might help. But it too can obscure crucial issues. It short-circuits conflicts over control of the economic system and puts questions of social goals in the shade, as if efficiency in response to market forces were a sufficient definition of what economic policies are all about. In countries with concentrated ownership of capital and access to opportunities, its prescription of reliance on market forces may ensure long periods of increasing inequality and of pressure for authoritarian political systems to override majority preferences.[12]

Development economics, with its emphasis on disequilibrium and structural barriers to change, comes close to the ideas of structuralism but with more attention to questions of efficiency and consistency. It lacks a commonly accepted core meaning of its own, but that is the counterpart of a high degree of flexibility. The main variants in constant reference throughout this book are those associated with the classical versions of Arthur Lewis and Ragnar Nurkse on one side, and the more imaginatively suggestive, still evolving, concepts of disequilibria in the work of Albert Hirschman on the other.[13]

Marxist perspectives are not explicitly used or debated in this discussion, mainly because of ignorance of their complexities. Some of their central concerns—questions of ownership, class relationships and control of the state, the institutional framework, and external domination—are clearly crucial aspects of poverty and repression in Latin America. Marxist discussions that focus on conflicts within these societies surely come closer to what matters most than dependency analysis does: the latter's absorption with external factors can easily distract attention from the deep divisions inside each so-

---

[12] John Sheahan, "Market-oriented Economic Policies and Political Repression in Latin America," *Economic Development and Cultural Change* 28 (January 1980), pp. 267–91.

[13] W. Arthur Lewis, *The Theory of Economic Growth* (London: Allen and Unwin, 1955); Ragnar Nurkse, *Problems of Capital Formation in Underdeveloped Countries* (New York: Oxford University Press, 1955); Albert O. Hirschman, *The Strategy of Economic Development* (New Haven: Yale University Press, 1958). Hirschman, Lewis, and Prebisch have recently reviewed their own earlier ideas in Gerald M. Meier and Dudley Seers, eds., *Pioneers in Development* (New York: Oxford University Press for the World Bank, 1985).

ciety. The relationships between these two ways of thought are fascinating in themselves but go far outside the questions considered here.[14]

The consequences of Marxist government in Latin America, as distinct from the body of theory, are of direct concern in this discussion. The Chilean and Cuban examples are of great interest for their problems, and in Cuba's case for accomplishments as well. These experiences are informative in their own right, and they also bring in the role of the United States in determining the course of events. Dependency analysis captures many kinds of influence but rather downplays the roles of direct intervention and use of force. Intervention in some of its forms helps reduce poverty, and perhaps at times to lessen repression as well, but more frequently to block or reverse kinds of change that might do more. The emphasis in this book is on the economic policies of Latin American societies themselves, in the belief that they have considerable scope for choice, but it would falsify the picture to leave out of account the ways in which the United States acts to alter incentives and to foreclose alternatives.

 The links among poverty, external economic relationships, market forces, and political repression cut across all these perspectives. In a context of concentrated land ownership and restricted access to capital and to education, aggravated by rapid population growth, free markets are bound to work much more adversely for the poor than they do in either the northern industrialized countries or the developing countries of East Asia. That reality fosters intense dislike of private markets by people who care about equity. Similarly, given the desire to foster industrialization and greater self-determination, open markets allowing relatively free international trade and finance appear more as threats than as opportunities. The combination of these factors pulls those governments responsive to popular preferences into repeated conflict with efficiency criteria and considerations of macroeconomic consistency. But the understandable basis of this persistent orientation does not make it functional: it has led straight into exceptional degrees of inflation, external def-

---

[14] Cf. Gabriel Palma, "Dependency: A Formal Theory of Underdevelopment or a Methodology for the Analysis of Concrete Situations of Underdevelopment?" *World Development* 6 (December 1978), pp. 881–924; Keith B. Griffin and John Gurley, "Radical Analysis of Imperialism, the Third World, and the Transition to Socialism," *Journal of Economic Literature* 23 (September 1985), pp. 1089–1143; and especially David Booth, "Marxism and Development Sociology: Interpreting the Impasse," *World Development* 13 (July 1985), pp. 761–87.

icits and debt, and violent collisions over which groups and which goals would bear the costs of readjustment. Open political systems, responsible to popular preferences, become for many people identified with frustration and economic breakdown.

4. REGIONALISM, CULTURAL VALUES, AND ECONOMICS

To study a region instead of a particular problem within a professional discipline offers greatly enlarged possibilities for both understanding and confusion. It permits revealing comparisons among nations that have many common cultural and historical characteristics but follow different individual paths. It helps draw together ideas from normally separated intellectual perspectives and can use them to deepen each other. But it risks superficiality. Too much is going on at once, in too many dimensions, demanding professional understanding in too many directions. The approach generates temptations both to overstate the differentiating characteristics of the region and to obscure the variety of differences within it.

Edward Said's disturbing book, *Orientalism*, makes so many penetrating criticisms of regional studies that it now requires a peculiarly stubborn streak to risk another one.[15] His analysis of studies of the Orient brings out clearly the bent of writers about a region to cherish its differences from the rest of the world, whether with affection or contempt. The region becomes an object set apart from the common struggles of humanity. That tendency is visible in a good deal of writing about Latin America. Its operation harms understanding of the region itself and also gets in the way of learning from its experience about problems common elsewhere. Latin American difficulties with inflation, poverty, protectionism, repression of dissent, and practically everything else parallel similar problems all over the world. They are often worse in degree, but sometimes that looks more like a foreshadowing of trends elsewhere than something peculiarly Latin.[16]

The tendency to view Latin America as inherently prone to failure is deeply embedded in attitudes toward economic and political strategies. From the left, a common view is that the region's land-

---

[15] Edward W. Said, *Orientalism* (New York: Pantheon Books, 1978).

[16] Cf. Albert O. Hirschman, "The Social and Political Matrix of Inflation: Elaboration of the Latin American Experience," pp. 177–207 in Albert O. Hirschman, *Essays in Trespassing: Economics to Politics and Beyond* (Cambridge: Cambridge University Press, 1981), on ideas the northern countries might gain from studies of inflation in Latin America.

owners and businessmen lack ability to generate the kind of entrepreneurship necessary for autonomous economic development, so
it becomes essential to use much more direct and comprehensive
government intervention than was common in northern industrialization. From the right, an equally frequent theme is that Spanish
traditions of violent confrontation and impatience with limits mean
that popular government can only lead to disaster, or simply that
Latins expect authoritarian government and keep destroying attempts to get away from it, so there is no reason for the government
of the United States or anyone else to draw back from supporting
authoritarian regimes in the area.

These themes would not be so frequent if there were not some
foundation for them. Latin American traditions derived from the
region's Iberian Catholic heritage and its own historical experience
are distinctive in ways that can militate against economic performance and personal freedom. In particular, the strong penchant for
centralist authority embedded in Spanish political tradition during
the centuries of rule over Spanish America was firmly transmitted
to the colonies and then on to the independent Latin American
countries.[17] Neither left- nor right-wing governments in the region
can bring themselves to believe that decentralized economic and political actions can be otherwise than destabilizing. That does not
make them totally different from governments elsewhere: all of
them have a tendency to think that they have the right answers. But
in northern Europe and the United States the process of modernization and industrialization was often led by dissident religious
groups or independent businessmen acting outside or against the
preferences of the central government. The difference is perhaps
less in the tendency of governments to seek control from the center
than in the societies' sense of what is permissible for the central government and what rights are essentially individual.

High degrees of political centralization are not incompatible with
economic growth, but they run counter to individual initiative and
private entrepreneurship. If the economic system is nominally capitalist, in the sense of private ownership of most of the means of production, then a political system deeply antagonistic to decentralized
decision making creates a serious obstacle to economic perform-

[17] Claudio Véliz, *The Centralist Tradition of Latin America* (Princeton: Princeton University Press, 1980). See also Glenn Caudill Dealy, *The Public Man: An Interpretation of
Latin America and Other Catholic Countries* (Amherst: University of Massachusetts,
1977) and Howard J. Wiarda, ed., *Politics and Social Change in Latin America: The Distinct Tradition*, 2d rev. ed. (Amherst: University of Massachusetts Press, 1982).

ance. If the power and prestige of private business activity are severely circumscribed, the people who might otherwise have led economic growth are likely to put their priorities more in other
domains.

Latin American businessmen are often criticized for being too
prone to copy outside techniques and products, too dependent on
state protection, and relatively uninterested in seizing new productive opportunities. That last consideration, the possibility that people with the wealth and position that would enable them to exercise
economic leadership may simply not wish to try, can be seen in positive terms. It may be fully as rational behavior as the kind of ration-
ality expressed in capitalist entrepreneurship, just a different kind
that downgrades economic performance and profits relative to personal prestige and influence. As expressed by Glenn Caudill Dealy,
the prized characteristics of the Latin "public man" are "dignity,
generosity, manliness, grandeur, and leisure."[18] That sounds appealing, though the same qualities may come across to others as impatience, disregard for people who are not one's friends or followers, resistance to negotiation or compromise, or a tendency to locate
reality in words rather than actions. Whether regarded positively or
negatively, most Latin Americans do approach life with a different
style, and more excitement, than would be considered normal in
Massachusetts or Yorkshire. But do these absorbing differences of
life style do much to explain persisting poverty or dependence?

Within the dependency perspective a suggestive interpretation of
the characteristics of Latin American economic and social reactions
emphasizes differences from the north but explains them in terms
of external influences. Restrictions on domestic production and
trade in the colonial period, competition from more advanced industrial countries and the pull of resources toward primary production acting to discourage industrialization, along with direct
foreign investment that preempted opportunities and thereby restricted learning, all held back the growth of domestic entrepreneurial capacities. The fact of being continuously behind in all new
fields, of relying on foreign technology, undermined the ability to
initiate change.[19] This way of looking at the matter has the great appeal that it treats entrepreneurship as a variable responsive to objective conditions. It differs among countries and can be increased

[18] Dealy, *The Public Man*, p. 34.
[19] Valenzuela and Valenzuela, "Modernisation and Dependence."

or undermined, rather than being intrinsically weak in Latin America because of peculiar cultural limitations.

Economics as a discipline tends to submerge such questions. The logic of necessary consistency among economic variables is universal. If the Peruvian government keeps the price of foreign exchange too low, the country will face increasing external strains and eventual foreign exchange crisis just as surely as would any other country, even a northern imperialist power. The causal relationships between incentives and behavior cut through cultural differences. But the likelihood that a populist Peruvian government will keep the price of foreign exchange too low is raised considerably by predisposition to regard market forces as anarchic, to prefer managed trade and exchange rates intended to serve a particular conception of social order. Commonly accepted understandings act strongly to shape the choice of policies in the first place. They do not wipe out the consequences of changes in economic incentives, but they may moderate or aggravate reactions and may in particular mean that the costs of policy correctives that would have been minor in the North become traumatic in Latin America.

Although distinctive characteristics of Latin American cultures probably do contribute to the factors making successful capitalism a more difficult achievement than in the North, they do not explain the severity of poverty and the frequency of economic breakdown in the region. They impede the kinds of compromises needed for functional economic policies, and they work against the trust and respect for mutual obligation needed for both representative government and well-functioning markets. They embody a greater concern for traditional Catholic conceptions of a "just price" and "just wage," as opposed to the view that prices and wages are best left to be determined by market forces.[20] That does not mean that actual prices and wages fail to influence behavior. But it means that universal questions of conflict between moral principles and the acceptance of market forces are more intensely at issue.

5. Structure and Omissions

The three main concerns of this book—poverty, external relationships, and the association between political repression and market

[20] Alfred Stepan, *The State and Society*, ch. 1–2; John Sheahan, "The Economics of the Peruvian Experiment in Comparative Perspective," in Abraham Lowenthal and Cynthia McClintock, eds., *The Peruvian Experiment Reconsidered* (Princeton: Princeton University Press, 1983).

forces—work out in ways shaped both by common regional factors and by each country's own history and current policy responses. The structure of chapters parallels this two-sided reality: those in part I are directed to economic problems common to the region; those in part II are concerned more with the ways in which the paths of individual countries contrast with each other. Part III then tries to pull the issues back together again in terms of interacting economic and political relationships.

Concentration on central themes means leaving out much of the historical picture and many issues important for development. The discussion of long-term trends of trade and production in chapter 4 is not a schematic history of Latin American development but a review of the background of postwar attempts to transform economic structures by promoting industrialization against the forces of comparative advantage. Consideration in chapter 2 of differential access to education is not a study of educational policy in general but of particular relationships between education and poverty. Discussion of land ownership in chapter 5 deals with aspects of agriculture central to questions of poverty and trade but is certainly not a study of agriculture in Latin America. Among countries, attention is directed mainly to those in middle or relatively advanced stages of industrialization, with little discussion of those in group 5 of table 1.1. Even among the medium and higher income countries, such important and informative country experiences as those of Uruguay and Venezuela are left out of the more detailed comparisons.

Slow progress in writing this book has had the incidental value of permitting many revisions in response to belated perceptions of personal confusion and also in response to continuing changes in Latin America. Back in 1981, Argentina, Brazil, and Uruguay were locked into authoritarian systems that might well have gone from bad to worse but have instead gone away. At least for the time being! The dimensions of the external debt problems of Brazil and Mexico were not at all clear; most economists and international agencies at the time, as well as the international banks, did not seem to see any great problem on this score. We learn, but slowly. All this is a bit unnerving: almost any statement about recent changes can look out of date almost immediately. But the main intent in any case is to illuminate recurrent patterns of problems, attempted answers, failures, and occasional successes. Tomorrow will be different in many ways, not all.

Although the incorrigible habit of stating that "Latin America is" or "does" something can be noted many times, the differential character of change within the region is given more emphasis than the common characteristics. There is hardly any common problem that has not been met in contrasting ways by individual countries, with markedly different consequences. Systematic interpretation need not spill out in as many different directions as there are countries in the region, but it does need to allow for great diversity. That makes for complexity and frequent qualification. It also helps make clear that the common constraints of a difficult world do not condemn all countries to any predetermined fate: better and worse ways of responding to specific difficulties can give better or worse results.

A poem by A. R. Ammons, "The Misfit,"[21] expresses the target exactly:

> . . . not the million oriented facts
> but the one or two facts,
>   out of place,
> recalcitrant, the one observed fact
> that tears us into questioning:
>   what has not
> joined dies into order to redeem, with
> loss of singleness extends the form,
>   or, unassimilable, leads us on.

---

[21] A. R. Ammons, *The Selected Poems* (New York: Norton, 1977). Reprinted by permission of W. W. Norton & Company, Inc. Copyright (c) 1977, 1975, 1974, 1972, 1971, 1970, 1966, 1965, 1964, 1955 by A. R. Ammons.

TWO

POVERTY

> Everyone looks on progress as being, in the first place, a transition
> to a state of human society in which people will not suffer from
> hunger.
>
> —Simone Weil, *The Need for Roots*

The persistence of mass poverty in the face of evident wealth is perhaps the single most frustrating aspect of Latin American development. Economic growth has clearly raised living standards for many people, but the gains have gone disproportionately to upper income groups. In three successive estimates by the World Bank of the share of the income going to the poorest 20 percent in each region, Latin America has been the only region of the world, industrialized or developing, in which their share has persistently decreased.[1]

Absolute poverty in terms of malnutrition, poor housing, lack of access to education, and shortened life spans is at its worst in the countries with particularly low average income per capita: Bolivia, El Salvador, Haiti, Honduras, and Peru. But it remains glaring in nations at much higher levels of income, including countries with sectors as modern in so many respects as Brazil and Mexico. The first purpose of this chapter is simply to bring out individual country differences of poverty and income distribution in the dimensions of personal incomes, infant and child mortality, and education. The second is to make clear that high degrees of inequality cause greater infant and child mortality than would otherwise be likely at the same levels of national income per capita. Finally, different national policies with respect to education are given special attention as aspects of inequality, as manifestations of social purpose, and as important links in any general explanation of poverty in the region.

[1] World Bank, *World Tables*, 2d ed. (Baltimore: Johns Hopkins University Press for the World Bank, 1980), p. 461. This regional indicator for Latin America includes the Caribbean area.

1. Regional Trends and Differences
among Countries

Although inequality has been pronounced and persistent, rising income per capita in the postwar period has been accompanied by
progress in terms of many indicators of poverty, including infant
mortality, literacy, and life expectancy. Both the reality of progress
and the depth of remaining poverty are evident in rates of infant
and child mortality, shown in figure 2.1 and for individual countries
in table 2.1. In 1960, the infant mortality rate for the region was 3.6
times as high as in the industrialized countries. By 1984 the median
rate for the region was brought down by 44 percent. There can be
few more important kinds of progress. Still, the percentage reduction was less than in the industrialized countries, and the mortality
rate in 1984 was then five times that of the industrialized countries.

Much the same relationships hold for the death rate of children
from ages 1 through 4, shown in part B of figure 2.1. In 1960 this
was more than *nine* times as high as in the industrialized countries.
The main reason that this ratio between the region and the industrialized countries is worse than for infant mortality is probably that
malnutrition plays a greater role for young children than for in-
fants. This mortality rate was also brought down greatly by 1984, to
or below levels of two per thousand in eight countries. It remained
more than five times that level in Bolivia, Haiti, and Peru.

Differences among Latin American countries are so pronounced
that they point more toward individual national patterns than any
necessary regional characteristics of income distribution or poverty.
Differences between Brazil and Costa Rica for infant and child mortality are indicated by the separate dashed lines in figure 2.1. For infant mortality, the Brazilian record since 1960 is far worse than the
regional average while that of Costa Rica is much better. For child
mortality, Brazil started out 17 percent worse than the Latin American average and then in the 1960s fell further behind: the national
rate was reduced by 30 percent while the regional average came
down by 38 percent. In the 1970s, Brazil did distinctly better: the
national rate was cut by 45 percent, almost exactly the same percentage as the regional average. Costa Rica started out better than
average and then improved its relative position, reaching in 1981 a
rate of 0.8, only one-seventh that of Brazil, and among the lowest in
the world.

This contrast between Brazil and Costa Rica is not due to a higher
income level in Costa Rica. Comparisons of real income in terms of

FIGURE 2.1. Infant and child mortality rates in Latin America
compared to the industrialized countries, 1960–1981

A. Infant mortality per thousand live births

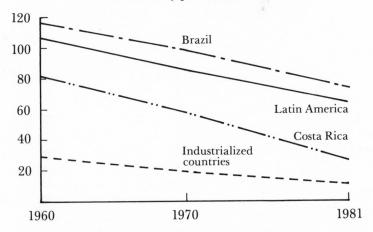

B. Child mortality (ages 1–4, mortality per thousand)

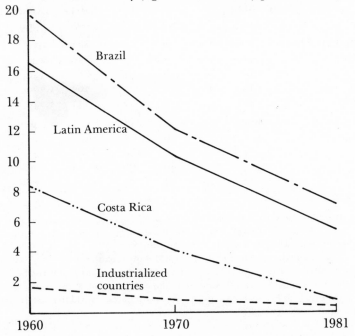

Source: World Bank, *World Tables,* Third Edition
(Washington: World Bank, 1983), vol. 2, country
tables, chart p. 144, and regional table p. 159.

TABLE 2.1. Infant and Child Mortality, 1960 and 1984, with Alternative Measures of Income Per Capita
(Countries listed in descending order of GNP per capita in 1977)

	Infant mortality (per 1,000)		Child mortality (per 1,000)		GNP per capita in current U.S. dollars		Adjusted income as % U.S. in
	1960	1984	1960	1984	1977	1984	1974
Venezuela	85	38	9	2	2,625	3,410	50.6
Argentina	61	34	5	1	1,870	2,230	46.4
Uruguay	51	29	4	1	1,449	1,980	31.1
Brazil	118	68	19	6	1,411	1,720	29.4
Costa Rica	74	19	8	(.)	1,393	1,190	23.9
Cuba	35	16	2	(.)	1,317	n.a.	n.a.
Chile	119	22	20	1	1,247	1,700	28.4
Panama	68	25	6	1	1,195	1,980	27.7
Mexico	91	51	10	3	1,164	2,040	26.5
Nicaragua	144	70	30	6	865	860	21.8
Dominican Republic	120	71	20	6	841	970	21.8
Guatemala	92	66	10	5	830	1,160	18.0
Ecuador	140	67	28	5	819	1,150	15.6
Colombia	93	48	11	3	762	1,390	19.2
Paraguay	86	44	9	2	747	1,240	13.9
Peru	163	95	38	11	721	1,000	17.6
El Salvador	136	66	26	5	589	710	14.5
Bolivia	167	118	40	20	476	540	10.2
Honduras	145	77	30	7	424	700	11.6
Haiti	182	124	47	22	230	320	n.a.

SOURCES: Mortality rates for 1960 from World Bank, *World Development Report 1984* (Washington, D.C.: Oxford University Press for the World Bank, 1984), pp. 262–63; 1984 mortality rates and GNP from *World Development Report 1986*, pp. 180–81 and 232–33; 1977 GNP from World Bank, *World Tables*, 2d ed. (Washington, D.C.: World Bank, 1980), pp. 430–32, except for Cuba. Cuban estimate is for GDP per capita from Carmelo Mesa-Lago and Jorge Perez-Lopez, "A Study of Cuba's Material Product System, Its Conversion to the System of National Accounts, and Estimation of Gross Domestic Product per Capita and Growth Rates," World Bank Staff Study no. 770, 1986. Last column as cited in note.

NOTE: Adjusted income per capita as percent of U.S. in 1974 is "Kravis-adjusted" income compared in terms of estimated real purchasing power: Irving Kravis, Alan W. Heston, and Robert Summers, "Real GDP per Capita for More than One Hundred Countries," *Economic Journal* 88 (June 1978), pp. 215–42.

purchasing power indicate that the two were approximately equal in 1970 and that Brazilian income per capita was about 23 percent higher by 1974.[2] Income does make a great difference for infant and child mortality, but it is not so much average income that counts as it is the incomes of the poor: the issue is jointly one of national income *and* its distribution.

Estimates of income per capita and of mortality rates are given for twenty Latin American countries in table 2.1. The two countries that stand out for the lowest levels of infant and child mortality in 1984, Costa Rica and Cuba, are well down from the top of the list in terms of income per capita. Costa Rica was tenth highest in terms of income in 1984; Cuba's income level is much more uncertain, but the most carefully derived estimate now available, for 1977, would place it sixth highest for that year.[3] The key explanation of their greater success in reducing infant and child mortality is that they have much lower degrees of inequality than the rest of the region. A simple cross-section regression between child mortality and average income per capita shows generally falling mortality rates with higher income, but with such a high standard deviation as to be almost meaningless. (The country observations indicate a curvilinear relationship, with more effect of rising national income on mortality rates at low income levels than in the upper ranges of income.) For a given degree of inequality, increasing income per capita certainly helps; for a given income level, more equal distribution helps just as surely.

For the region as a whole, average income per capita is much higher than in other developing regions (except for the oil export-

[2] In terms of GNP expressed at official exchange rates, income per capita in Brazil was slightly below that in Costa Rica in the middle 1970s, but this conventional measure can be misleading for many reasons, especially because of the arbitrary character of exchange rates. The last column in table 2.1, the Kravis measures comparing purchasing power, is much more appropriate (though only available for selected years): Irving B. Kravis, A. Heston, and R. Summers, "Real GDP per Capita for More than One Hundred Countries," *Economic Journal* 88 (June 1978), pp. 215–42. This is perhaps as good a place as any to admit that all such comparisons involve serious problems about accuracy and comparability of the data. Most of the statistics used in this study are based either on World Bank or Inter-American Development Bank reports because they are carefully worked out for comparability, but there is no magic way the international institutions can straighten out inaccuracies in the original sources.

[3] Carmelo Mesa-Lago and Jorge Perez-Lopez, "A Study of Cuba's Material Product System, Its Conversion to the System of National Accounts, and Estimation of Gross Domestic Product per Capita and Growth Rates," World Bank Staff Working Paper no. 770, 1986. The particular estimate used in table 2.1 for 1977 is from table 19, p. 46, explained as the most likely estimate in Appendix D.

ers of the Middle East and North Africa), but the share of the lowest
20 percent is lower than in any other region, richer or poorer. Their
share was estimated by the World Bank at 3.7 percent of total income in 1960, and at 2.9 percent for the "most recent year" available
(around 1977).[4] Both for the very poor region of Africa south of the
Sahara and for the fast-growing region of East Asia, the corresponding shares were close to 5 percent in 1960 and increased to 6.2
percent for the most recent year. To the extent that these estimates
can be trusted, the income share of the lowest 20 percent in Latin
America is less than half as high as in these other developing regions.

Improvements in welfare measures in these years owed a great
deal to rising income per capita and probably little to any lessening
of inequality. But degrees and trends of inequality differ considerably among countries. Estimates of income distribution by quintiles
in eight countries are given in table 2.2. Considering the lowest 40
percent of household incomes, their share of total income in Brazil
in 1972 was 7.0 percent. For Costa Rica in 1971, their share was 12.0
percent. For identical levels of national real income per capita (as
was approximately the case at the beginning of the 1970s), the lowest 40 percent in Costa Rica would have received on average 71 per-

TABLE 2.2. Percentage Shares of Household Income by Quintiles
for Eight Latin American Countries, Late 1960s or Early 1970s

	Lowest quintile	Second quintile	Third quintile	Fourth quintile	Highest quintile
Argentina, 1970	4.4	9.7	14.1	21.5	50.3
Brazil, 1972	2.0	5.0	9.4	17.0	66.6
Chile, 1968	4.4	9.0	13.8	21.4	51.4
Costa Rica, 1971	3.3	8.7	13.3	19.9	54.8
Honduras, 1967	2.3	5.0	8.0	16.9	67.8
Mexico, 1977	2.9	7.0	12.0	20.4	57.7
Peru, 1972	1.9	5.1	11.0	21.0	61.0
Venezuela, 1970	3.0	7.3	12.9	22.8	54.0

SOURCE: World Bank, *World Development Report 1980*, pp. 156–57.

[4] World Bank, *World Tables*, 2d ed., p. 461.

cent higher incomes than the lowest 40 percent in Brazil. It is at the low end of the income distribution that poverty kills children.

Are the poor in Latin America getting poorer? That is a very mixed picture.[5] Direct social indicators such as those cited suggest that poverty must have been decreasing, at least in terms of these important measures of welfare. And two major studies of trends for the lowest quintiles of the income distribution, where data could be obtained, concluded that there was no case during the periods studied in which the absolute income of the lowest quintiles actually fell.[6] Changes for the lowest 60 percent in the five Latin American countries included in the more recent of these studies are given in table 2.3. Three of them stood out for increasing inequality: Brazil for changes from 1960 to 1970, Mexico for 1963–1975, and Peru for 1961–1971. In these cases the lowest 60 percent of the distribution

TABLE 2.3. Changes in Shares of Income and Levels of Real Income of the Lowest 60 Percent of Income Receivers for Five Latin American Countries

		Share of lowest 60 percent			Growth rate for average	
	Period	Initial	Final	Incremental	National	Lowest 60 percent
Brazil	1960–70	0.25	0.21	0.16	3.1	1.2
Colombia	1964–74	0.19	0.21	0.24	3.1	4.3
Costa Rica	1961–71	0.24	0.28	0.34	3.2	5.1
Mexico	1963–75	0.22	0.20	0.18	3.2	2.4
Peru	1961–71	0.18	0.18	0.18	2.3	2.3

SOURCE: Montek S. Ahluwalia, Nicholas G. Carter, and Hollis B. Chenery, "Growth and Poverty in Developing Countries," *Journal of Development Economics* 6 (September 1979), table 4, p. 322.

[5] R. Albert Berry, "Predicting Income Distribution in Latin America During the 1980s," in Archibald Ritter and David Pollock, eds., *Latin American Prospects for the 1980s: Equity, Democratization, and Development* (New York: Praeger, 1983), pp. 57–84; David Felix, "Income Distribution and the Quality of Life in Latin America: Patterns, Trends, and Policy Implications," *Latin American Research Review* 18, 2 (1983), pp. 3–34.

[6] Montek S. Ahluwalia, "Income Inequality: Some Dimensions of the Problem," in Hollis B. Chenery et al., *Re-distribution with Growth: An Approach to Policy* (Oxford and New York: Oxford University Press for the World Bank and the Institute of Development Studies, 1974), pp. 3–37, especially figure 1.1, p. 14; Montek S. Ahluwalia, Nicholas G. Carter, and Hollis B. Chenery, "Growth and Poverty in Developing Countries," *Journal of Development Economics* 6 (September 1979), pp. 299–341.

received only 16 to 18 percent of the increments of national income
in these periods. But even in these cases the average income of the
bottom group increased at rates between 1.2 and 2.4 percent a year.

Such comparisons in terms of given fractions of the income distribution can help clarify what is happening to degrees of inequality, but they are treacherous bases for conclusions about changes in
poverty.[7] One problem is that they do not clarify changes over time
for specific groups. The people in the lowest quintiles at the end of
a given period need not be the same as those who were there at the
start: it could make a great deal of difference whether the bottom
quintiles in one period are mainly young families on their way up
to higher income levels or are instead mainly composed of families
permanently stuck in misery for their whole lifetimes, passing on
the same hopeless condition to their children. The first of these two
possibilities is always a factor and may often be the more important
in prosperous countries; the clues available on poverty in Latin
America suggest the depressing second possibility as the more important in this region.[8] A related problem concerns the possibility
that particular groups of people may be sinking into greater poverty
within quintiles that are gaining income. Conditions of many Peruvian peasants seem to fit this negative picture: even when national
income was rising, from 1950 to the mid-1970s, increased crowding
on poor land in the Sierra, with near stagnant agricultural production, hurt incomes of the smallest peasant producers. When this
structural factor was compounded in the 1970s and the first half of
the 1980s by singularly poor national economic policy, measures of
social welfare and especially nutrition for many areas showed progressively worsening conditions.[9]

The particular dates covered by empirical studies of inequality
and poverty can sometimes make a great difference. They would

[7] Gary S. Fields, *Poverty, Inequality, and Development* (Cambridge: Cambridge University Press, 1980). Fields gives a helpful analysis of different ways to measure poverty and recommends using the percent of families living below a fixed poverty line
at different periods. Applied to the northeast of Brazil this shows 37 percent with
incomes below the minimum wage in 1960 and 35.5 percent below the same line in
1970 (table 5.7, p. 170), a decidedly modest reduction in absolute poverty, consistent
with table 2.3.

[8] Víctor E. Tokman, "Dinámica de los mercados de trabajo y distribución del ingreso en América Latina," *Colección estudios cieplan* 3 (June 1980).

[9] Adolfo Figueroa, *Capitalist Development and the Peasant Economy in Peru* (Cambridge: Cambridge University Press, 1984), pp. 105–13; Cynthia Mcclintock, "Why
Peasants Rebel: The Case of Peru's Sendero Luminoso," *World Politics* 37 (October
1984), pp. 48–84.

not matter so much if built-in structural factors were so dominant
that they kept the degree of inequality constant, or kept changing it
in one steady direction, but that is not the general case: major
changes in either external conditions or domestic economic strategy
can significantly alter trends. Radical changes in economic strategy
imposed by conservative regimes in Argentina in 1976, Brazil in
1964, and Chile in 1973 all had powerful impacts on income distribution. For Chile, average monthly consumption of the lowest 20
percent of households in Gran Santiago fell 31 percent between
1969 and 1978. The average for the highest 20 percent increased 16
percent in the same period.[10] For Argentina the more uncertain
measure of real wages in manufacturing fell 49 percent between
1967 and 1977, while the minimum wage in agriculture fell 36 percent.[11] Whichever category included the very poorest, they surely
lost.

The Brazilian turn toward more conservative economics in 1964
similarly reduced employment and real wages in the first instance,
but then in 1967 the balance of the country's economic strategy
turned again toward promotion of growth and employment. For
the decade of the 1960s the net result was a marked increase in inequality, as shown in table 2.3. For the decade of the 1970s, with
continuing rapid growth accompanied by policies somewhat more
favorable for employment, real wages and earnings of the lowest
quintiles rose rapidly. The degree of inequality did not change
greatly but at least stopped rising: the real living standards of the
poor moved up at the same high rate as national income per capita.[12] Looking back at the picture for child mortality, where the rate
of improvement in Brazil had been below that for the region in the
1960s, it kept up with the region for the 1970s. In the educational

[10] Carlos Filgueira, "Acerca del consumo en los nuevos modelos latino-américanos," CEPAL (Comisión Económica para América Latina), E/CEPAL/IN.1, December 3, 1980, table 10, p. 80; René Cortázar, "Distribución del ingreso, empleo y remuneraciones reales en Chile, 1970–78," Collección estudios cieplan 3 (June 1980), pp.
5–25; Alejandro Foxley, "Stabilization Policies and Their Effects on Employment
and Income Distribution: A Latin American Perspective," in William Cline and Sidney Weintraub, eds., Economic Stabilization in Developing Countries (Washington, D.C.:
Brookings, 1981), table 6–4, p. 203.

[11] Tokman, "Mercados de trabajo," table 9, p. 140.

[12] Berry, "Predicting Income Distribution"; Guy Pfefferman and Richard Webb,
"The Distribution of Income in Brazil," World Bank Staff Working Paper no. 356
(1979); David Denslow, Jr., and William G. Tyler, "Perspectives on Poverty and Income Inequality in Brazil, an Analysis of the Changes During the 1970s," World
Bank Staff Working Paper no. 601 (1983).

system, prior disregard for inclusion of the poor was replaced by much greater effort to extend access to education, including to the badly neglected rural regions.

Two countries that look relatively good in table 2.3, Colombia and Costa Rica, managed in the periods covered to raise the real incomes of the lowest 60 percent of income receivers slightly faster than national income. For Costa Rica, that positive result is not surprising: it has been Latin America's closest approximation to a politically open welfare state, with no real departures since its "revolution" of 1948 (see chapter 11). For Colombia, the relatively favorable result in terms of trend is more surprising because its distribution of income has always been among the most unequal in the region; it can hardly be accused of welfare-state characteristics. What happened was partly a matter of changing economic structure and partly again a case of change in economic strategy (see chapters 3 and 11). With a change toward policies more favorable for employment creation, and with helpful background conditions permitting a good rate of aggregate growth for the 1970s, a long period of failure to raise incomes of the rural poor was replaced by a decade of real improvement. Both rural labor and unorganized urban labor at the low end gained income faster than the rise in national income per capita.[13]

In the northern industrialized countries inequality increased in the early stages of industrialization but then reached a turning point and decreased at higher income levels.[14] The study of trends in present developing countries used for table 2.3 calculates the corresponding reference level for such a turning point at about $600 at 1975 prices, when considering a turn toward a rising share for the lowest 60 percent of the income distribution. By 1975 Brazil and

[13] Miguel Urrutia, *Winners and Losers in Colombia's Economic Growth in the 1970s* (Oxford: Oxford University Press, 1985). Albert Berry and Francisco Thoumi cast some doubt on Urrutia's measures for incomes of rural labor for the first half of the 1970s, but for the period from 1976 to 1980, when the data are clearer, they similarly show a marked increase in real earnings in the rural area: "Colombian Economic Growth and Policies (1970–1984)," in Bruce Bagley and Thoumi Juan Tokatlian, eds., *Colombia Beyond the National Front* (Boulder: Westview Press, forthcoming), table 8.

[14] Simon Kuznets, "Economic Growth and Income Inequality," *American Economic Review* 45 (March 1955). Reinterpretations of the Kuznets studies in terms of current development issues have cast doubt on the generality, or necessity, of decreasing equality in the early stages of industrialization: see Fields, *Poverty*, ch. 4; and Gustav F. Papanek and Oldrich Kyn, "The Effects of Income Distribution on Development, the Rate of Growth, and Economic Strategy: Flattening the Kuznets Curve," *Pakistan Development Review*, forthcoming.

Mexico had long passed this level of income, but neither showed any evidence of a turn toward equality. Colombia and Costa Rica deserve special attention as contrasts: they do not invalidate the general picture of unusually pronounced inequality for the region, but they point to real possibilities of doing better.

2. ABSOLUTE POVERTY

Attempts to measure the number of people living in absolute poverty, as distinct from measures of income shares, require arbitrary definitions of the standard to be used. Independent studies of absolute poverty by research economists with ECLA and the World Bank have made two different sets of results available, with the former using a somewhat broader definition of requirements for a minimally decent standard of living and therefore setting a higher poverty line. But both measures may easily be regarded as too restrictive. Almost as soon as they were published they were denounced for understating the number of people living in poverty.[15]

The ECLA study used two kinds of measures. One of them, "destitution," corresponds approximately to the World Bank concept of absolute poverty. The second allows for more complex requirements, emphasizing the concept of relative poverty: families should be considered in poverty when their incomes are so low that they are cut off from effective participation in the ways of life considered normal in that society.[16] By these measures, 19 percent of the households in the Latin American countries studied were in destitution as of 1970, and 40 percent—135 million people—were below the poverty line. The measures for individual countries are given in table 2.4.

The incidence of poverty shown in table 2.4 is much greater for rural than for urban families. The most visible poverty is that in the slums of the cities, but the majority of the very poor are out in the countryside, less able to get help and less able to exert political pressure than the poor in the cities. By the ECLA measure of poverty,

[15] Fagen, "Equity in the South."

[16] Oscar Altimir, "The Extent of Poverty in Latin America," World Bank Staff Working Paper no. 522 (1982), pp. 14–18. A. K. Sen emphasizes a similar conception of poverty as including both absolute elements (nutritional needs) and relative components. For Sen, the key point at issue is each person's ability to function fully within the particular society, which must include access to the commonly accepted requirements within that society: *Resources, Values, and Development* (Cambridge: Harvard University Press, 1984), ch. 13–14, pp. 307–45.

TABLE 2.4. Estimates of Poverty and Destitution in Latin America
in Years around 1970, Using ECLA Measures

	Percentages of families below the poverty line			Percentages of families below the line of destitution		
	Urban	Rural	National	Urban	Rural	National
Argentina	5	19	8	1	1	1
Brazil	35	73	49	15	42	25
Chile	12	25	17	3	11	6
Colombia	38	54	45	14	23	18
Costa Rica	15	30	24	5	7	6
Honduras	40	75	65	15	57	45
Mexico	20	49	34	6	18	12
Peru	28	68	50	8	39	25
Uruguay	10	—	—	4	—	—
Venezuela	20	36	25	6	19	10
Latin America	26	62	40	10	34	19

SOURCE: Oscar Altimir, "The Extent of Poverty in Latin America," World Bank Staff Working Paper no. 522, 1982, table 12, p. 82.

62 percent of rural households are below the poverty line, compared to 26 percent of urban households. By the measure of destitution, 34 percent of rural families are below the line compared to 10 percent urban.[17]

Rural poverty in Latin America has been accentuated by three particular characteristics of these societies: highly concentrated land ownership, to degrees far beyond those common in East Asia or Africa; poor access to education in the rural areas; and postwar economic policies favoring urban investment. The nineteenth-century pattern of development favored landowner-exporters and

[17] These studies consistently show that a higher share of the rural population than of the urban is below any given level of income, but comparisons of the severity of poverty between rural and urban areas is always problematic in low-income countries because the characteristics of life styles differ greatly. Cf. Paul Collier and Richard Sabot, "Measuring the Difference Between Urban and Rural Incomes: Some Conceptual Issues," pp. 127–60 in Sabot, ed., *Migration and the Labor Market in Developing Countries* (Boulder: Westview, 1982).

gave highly concentrated gains in income to the large landowners. The postwar stress on industrialization went contrary to the interests of the landowners but concentrated income gains in the urban areas and continued to leave the rural poor behind.

3. POVERTY AND EDUCATION

The extremes of inequality in many Latin American countries are worse than they would otherwise have been because of prolonged failure to provide the poor with anything like equal participation in education. Inequality of income and inequality of education go together. The causation goes both ways: people with higher incomes usually make sure that their children have good educational opportunities, and the children who get more education can usually earn higher incomes with which to keep their families in advantaged positions; lower income people cannot provide as much education for their children, and the latter correspondingly earn below-average incomes in their work. If the children of the poor are left out of public education programs they are likely to be left out of economic opportunities as well, and to pass defeat on to the next generation.

Major efforts to break out of this circle of continuing inequality in the last two decades should help. But there is a strong current of distrust about what they can accomplish. As expressed by Aldo Solari, changes in societies can change the character and distribution of education, but it has never been demonstrated that changes in education can change the character of societies.[18] That position has a great deal of validity and may at the same time be seriously misleading; it is considered below after discussion of the factual record of changing educational policies in the region.

Through the first half of the twentieth century the region was split in two on educational policies. The Southern Cone countries, Costa Rica, and Cuba have long provided more nearly equal educational opportunities than the rest of the region. As of 1970, the share of the labor force with no years of completed schooling was above 30 percent for Bolivia, Brazil, and all of Central America except Costa Rica and Panama, while it was less than 10 percent in Argentina, Chile, and Uruguay (table 2.5.). These last three, with Costa Rica, stand out from the rest of the nonsocialist countries of the region both for wider distribution of education and for lower degrees of inequality in the distribution of income.

[18] Aldo Solari, "Development and Education Policy in Latin America," *CEPAL Review* (1st Semester 1977), pp. 59–91, esp. pp. 80–82.

TABLE 2.5. Percentages of the Active Labor Force with Either No Completed Years of Schooling or No More than Three Years of Schooling, in or Close to 1970

	No years of school completed	Not more than three years of school completed
Argentina	0	15.8
Bolivia	31.3	53.0
Brazil	39.2	57.1
Chile	8.2	23.6
Colombia	21.6	52.7
Costa Rica	10.8	35.2
Dominican Republic	36.5	57.3
Ecuador	24.0	44.6
El Salvador	45.4	70.0
Guatemala	50.5	75.2
Honduras	40.6	67.3
Mexico	27.1	57.4
Nicaragua	47.8	66.3
Panama	17.2	33.5
Paraguay	10.3	45.4
Peru	19.3	46.6
Uruguay	4.9	[a]
Venezuela	29.3	40.3

SOURCE: United Nations, ECLA, *Statistical Yearbook 1983*, table 38, p. 113.
NOTE: These percentages are understated to some degree because they omit small percentages of the labor force for which schooling was "not specified."
[a] Uruguayan data are not broken down separately for completion of three years or less, only for complete or incomplete primary education. As of 1970, 32 percent of the labor force had not completed primary education.

The countries that had lagged far behind in providing access to education began to make serious efforts to catch up in the 1960s and 1970s. Measures of literacy and school enrollment show impressive gains. The secondary-school enrollment ratio for the region, below both of the lower income regions of East and South Asia as of 1960, rose higher than both of them by 1981 (table 2.6). The ratio for pri-

TABLE 2.6. Regional Comparisons of Adult Literacy Rates and School Enrollment Ratios, 1960–1981

	1960	1970	1981[a]
Adult literacy rate			
Africa south of Sahara	15.7	18.5	42.9
East Asia[b]	53.2	68.3	69.6
South Asia	27.6	31.4	35.3
Latin America	64.8	72.0	79.0
Primary school enrollment ratio			
Africa south of Sahara	39.7	51.0	77.6
East Asia[b]	102.6	104.8	113.0
South Asia	56.0	67.8	73.1
Latin America	88.4	94.5	104.9
Secondary school enrollment ratio			
Africa south of Sahara	3.6	7.0	14.4
East Asia[b]	19.4	23.4	36.0
South Asia	17.4	23.9	25.2
Latin America	14.0	27.4	38.6

SOURCE: World Bank, *World Tables*, 3d ed. (Washington, D.C., 1983), vol. 2, pp. 158–59.

[a] Data as given are identified as "most recent year," which is 1981 in most cases.

[b] Data for East Asia exclude China.

mary school enrollment rose greatly too, though it remained below that of East Asia. The gains are striking, though the primary enrollment ratio of over 100 percent should not be interpreted as meaning that all children are in school.[19] A more direct measure of the proportion of children in school, for ages six through eleven, is shown in table 2.7. That too demonstrates considerable improve-

[19] See D. McGranahan, C. Richard, and E. Pizzaro, "Development Statistics and Correlation: A Comment on Hicks and Streeten," *World Development* 9 (April 1981), pp. 389–99. The enrollment ratio divides the number of children attending school by the number in the particular age group for which school attendance is legally required. An extension of the legally required period of schooling, and of the number actually attending school, can reduce the enrollment ratio by increasing the denominator (the number of children in the covered age group) more than the numerator. The enrollment ratio for Brazilian primary education fell for exactly this reason when the required period of schooling was increased from four to six years in 1965.

TABLE 2.7. School Enrollment Rates for Children between Six and Eleven Years Old, 1960, 1975, and 1980

	1960	1975	1980
Argentina	91	100	100
Bolivia	45	70	77
Brazil	48	70	76
Chile	76	100	100
Colombia	48	64	70
Costa Rica	74	95	98
Cuba	78	100	100
Dominican Republic	67	77	82
Ecuador	66	76	80
El Salvador	49	63	69
Guatemala	32	48	53
Haiti	34	39	41
Honduras	50	67	71
Mexico	58	89	94
Nicaragua	43	56	61
Panama	68	94	96
Paraguay	70	75	78
Peru	57	81	84
Uruguay	91	78	77
Venezuela	69	78	83

SOURCE: Economic Commission for Latin America, *Statistical Yearbook 1980* (Santiago: ECLA, 1981), table 35, p. 102.

ment for all countries except Uruguay, but it makes it easier to see that a great many children are still left out.

The particular children left out are those of the poor. That is true for urban as well as rural children, but particularly so for the latter. Rural poverty is both reflected and reinforced by rural school enrollments much below urban. Comparing the shares of public resources provided for education to the population shares of different socioeconomic groups, the regional ratio of expenditures to population groups in 1980 was 0.49 for farmers, 1.04 for manual workers and traders, and 2.03 for white collar workers.[20] The de-

[20] Emmanuel Jimenez, "The Public Subsidization of Education and Health in De-

gree of disproportion adverse to rural workers was higher in Latin America than in any other of the world's developing regions. And within countries, the poorer the rural area the lower its school enrollment. In Brazil in 1974 the rate for children aged seven to fourteen was 72.5 percent for the country as a whole, 55.3 percent for all rural areas combined, and 44.4 percent for the long-depressed Northeast.[21] In Mexico in 1970 the illiteracy rate for people over fifteen years old was 26 percent for the nation while in the four states with the highest rural populations (Chiapas, Guerrero, Hidalgo, and Oaxaca) the rates ran from 42 to 48 percent.[22]

Lower literacy in rural areas is mainly a result of inadequate schools, but a second cause is that the people who get above-average education are the first to move to the cities. Migration of the relatively better educated may well have a positive function for them, and for the economy as a whole, but it can also reduce potential for growth in the rural sector because it takes away the people best equipped to provide skills or to initiate new activities.[23] If migration to cities brought down the total number of people trying to live with inadequate resources in the rural areas, that would help those left behind by increasing the ratio of land to rural families. But for many countries rapid population growth is still increasing the total rural labor force despite emigration; and in some it is still increasing the total number of people left out of the educational system as well. Mexico has greatly raised expenditures on education in recent decades, but the number of people over five years old with no formal schooling increased from twenty-nine million in 1950 to thirty-one million in 1976.[24]

Although greater expenditure on primary education for the poor would help reduce poverty, a nagging question in Latin American experience, especially for education in rural areas, is its doubtful quality. Poor equipment and methods are readily visible; low quality

---

veloping Countries," *The World Bank Research Observer* 1 (January 1986), table 8, p. 119.

[21] Marcelo Selowsky, "Income Distribution, Basic Needs, and Trade-Offs with Growth: The Case of Semi-Industrialized Latin American Countries," *World Development* 9 (January 1981), p. 86.

[22] Guy Pfefferman, "Some Economic Aspects of Human Development in Latin America (with Special Emphasis on Education)," in Willem Bussink et al., "Poverty and the Development of Human Resources: Regional Perspectives," World Bank Staff Working Paper no. 406 (July 1980).

[23] Michael Lipton, "Migration from Rural Areas of Poor Countries: The Impact on Rural Productivity and Income Distribution," in Richard Sabot, ed., *Migration*, pp. 191–228.

[24] Pfefferman, "Economic Aspects," pp. 180–82.

in terms of student achievements by internationally comparable tests is evident in Latin American as in most low-income countries.[25] The quality problems include poorly trained teachers, inadequate books and materials, crowded and underequipped school rooms, national languages that are in many cases foreign to the children of Indian families, local cultural values that are foreign to the teachers, and educational bureaucracies with little interest in any curricular content actually functional for their victims.[26] Bolivia spends the equivalent of 80 U.S. cents per pupil for a year's supply of educational materials. Although Brazil spends much more, "Ninety percent of the teachers in Northeast Brazil lack pedagogical training altogether and most have little primary schooling. In 1972, 31 percent of the Northeast teaching force had not completed primary education."[27]

Brazil increased expenditures on education considerably between 1960 and 1970, but its pattern was adverse for the poor. The increases were greatest for secondary and university education, helping mainly the children of middle- and upper-income families. "The distribution of educational attainment became more unequal."[28] If the expenditures had been redirected toward primary education for all, the poor would have been brought more fully into the society, and the middle-class families deprived of public subsidies for their children would almost surely have kept up their education by private expenditures. On one side, the children of the poor get practically no education if it is not provided by the state; on the other side, public funds for higher education mainly replace private expenditures by the middle and upper income groups, adding little or nothing to human capital. The worst aspect of educational structures that emphasize higher education while many are still left out "is the social injustice which gives a few people more schooling than they need, in the hope of more eligibility for 'good jobs,' and which simultaneously deprives the many of two human rights. The first is the minimum decent schooling universally

[25] Bruce Fuller, "Is Primary School Quality Eroding in the Third World?" *Comparative Education Review* 30 (November 1986), pp. 491–507.

[26] Ibid; Solari, "Education"; Ivan Illich, *Deschooling Society* (New York: Harper and Row, 1971).

[27] Peter T. Knight, "Brazilian Socioeconomic Development: Issues for the Eighties," *World Development* 9 (November/December 1981), pp. 1063–82, statement from p. 1068.

[28] Edmar L. Bacha and Lance Taylor, "Brazilian Income Distribution in the 1960s: 'Facts,' Model Results, and the Controversy," *Journal of Development Studies* 14 (April 1978), pp. 271–97, quotation from p. 273.

agreed to be their entitlement. The second is the training and assistance which might enable them to better their lot wisely, well, and fast."[29]

Relationships between the pattern of public expenditure and the consequences for poverty and inequality involve troublesome conflicts. To spend more on inclusion of everyone works against ability to finance adequate quality for everyone in the system, and works against increases in the numbers of people with more advanced education. For a given educational budget, the social returns to higher quality education for fewer students could exceed those for more nearly equal education of larger numbers of students.[30] If the overriding objective were to increase national income, as distinct from a goal of reducing poverty within the next decade, these considerations could argue for concentrating more educational resources on fewer people. If the priority goal were instead to reduce poverty, educational policy would clearly go the other way.

To place more emphasis on primary education for those left out would surely do more to reduce poverty, but reducing the numbers who get secondary and higher education increases the relative scarcity of higher skill people and widens wage differentials. A study of the effects of such choices in Colombia in the 1970s, where secondary education increased faster than primary, shows that the wage premium in favor of higher skilled workers was reduced by approximately a fourth between 1973 and 1978: greater emphasis on secondary education helped reduce inequality.[31] This study clarifies a two-edged process. As secondary education starts to rise, those who get it move to higher income levels, increasing inequality because they move up relative to the majority of workers. But then as more people move up the balance begins to shift: when the majority of

[29] John Oxenham, "Employers and Qualifications; Brief Response," Institute of Development Studies at the University of Sussex, *Bulletin* 11, 2 (May 1980), p. 63.

[30] Jere R. Behrman and Nancy Birdsall, "The Quality of Schooling: Quantity Alone Is Misleading," *American Economic Review* 73 (December 1983), pp. 928–46; Peter J. Eaton, "The Quality of Schooling: Comment," and reply by Behrman and Birdsall, *American Economic Review* 75 (September 1985), pp. 1195–1205. Fuller, "School Quality," makes the parallel point that overcrowding of primary schools in an effort to achieve complete inclusion can reduce quality and thereby potential earnings for those low-income people who would otherwise have been given a better start. He almost suggests that the answer to this might be to delay inclusion, to continue leaving people out of primary schooling.

[31] Rakesh Mohan and Richard Sabot, "Educational Expansion and the Inequality of Pay: Colombia, 1973–1978," World Bank and Williams College (March 1985). See also Berry and Thoumi, "Colombian Economic Growth."

workers are at the higher levels, the main effect becomes one of reducing the differences among wages for different skill levels, lessening inequality. The ultimate target should be to move into this position, with secondary education abundant and capacity to raise
productivity high. But if one is concerned first about poverty, that
would call for putting the initial emphasis on primary education for
all, allowing wide differentials for skills, and delaying emphasis on
secondary education until everyone is able to participate in the
system.

A special problem in rural areas is that, since children of peasant
families can contribute something to family income by working on
the land even when very young, families face an opportunity cost of
lower current income if they keep the children in school. Improved
lifetime earnings possibilities for the child may simply be disre-
garded when immediate poverty is severe. One possible response is
to subsidize pupils and their families at the primary level in rural
areas, particularly through school lunches and health services. Experiments in Brazil show that this approach can raise rural school
attendance significantly.[32] The second is to use central government
financing to reverse local inequalities in ability to finance facilities
and pay teachers. Teachers in the rural areas are likely to be poorly
trained and so miserably paid that if they had much personal ability
they would be doing something else in the first place. In the face of
reluctance to teach in isolated rural areas, salaries should be made
higher for trained people who will work there, exactly the reverse
of the usual structure of relative pay between city and country.

Apart from questions of economic incentives, education in rural
areas of many Latin American countries involves difficult problems
of relationships to separate Indian cultures. The countries in which
the Indian peasant population is exceptionally small, especially
Costa Rica and the Southern Cone, are those that have come closest
to complete, nationwide education. That is clearly easier to do when
practically every family speaks the same basic national language in
the home. Strong attachment to native Indian languages and cultural values increases distrust of the school system by peasant families and decreases the capacity of the teachers, for the most part
non-Indian, to communicate successfully with students. Perhaps
more fundamentally, centuries of mistreatment by national governments, invariably run by people of European descent, have taught
the Indian communities to fear outside influence. From the side of

[32] Selowsky, "Income Distribution," p. 86.

the Indian communities, the kind of education they may be offered is seen as alien; from the side of the urban leaders who make the basic decisions about resource allocation, expenditure on rural education is seen as having little payoff in either political or productivity terms.

The prolonged failure of the countries with large Indian populations to accomplish anything like equal access to education for the rural sector has surely contributed to the persistence of poverty. But when educational programs are extended to rural areas their nature is crucial. Efforts to force standardized national forms of education on Indian communities can be deeply disturbing to the children involved and could wash out forever the distinctive cultural values of the Indian groups. More of the same kind of education may involve greater losses than gains. The issues involve inescapable conflicts between two valuable goals: to give children greater capacity to determine their own lives within the society as a whole, and to preserve distinctive cultural values. That is not so much a question of spending on education as it is of basic social purpose: the best course is not a matter of economic analysis but of the values of each society.

Why do so many of the people in Latin America who are concerned about inequality argue that not much can be done to alleviate it through educational policies?[33] Perhaps the most general reason is the belief that highly concentrated ownership of assets, political control by a privileged minority, and all the problems associated with dependency rule out any significant social change by a path that leaves these issues untouched. Education amounts to a kind of "reformism," which gives advantages to particular individuals but does not change inequitable structures. In addition, if one assumes that employment opportunities are determined by national economic growth and technological constraints, and that differences in levels of education serve mainly as a screening device for employers, more education for everyone would not seem to change much. When the average workers has two years of schooling, those who have four and five years gain priority in getting jobs; when the majority have six years, those with four or five, presumably as com-

---

[33] Solari, "Education"; David Barkin, "La educación: Una barrera al desarrollo económico?" *El Trimestre Económico* 38 (1971), pp. 951–93; Martin Carnoy, "Can Educational Policy Equalize Income Distribution in Latin America?" International Labour Office, World Employment Programme, Research Working Paper on Education and Employment no. 6 (August 1975); John Simmons, "Education, Poverty, and Development," World Bank Staff Working Paper no. 188 (February 1974).

petent as before, will find themselves screened out of jobs by employer insistence on the rising average.

Perhaps the main problem with this negative view is that it does not allow for the reality of increased personal potential. In its useful insistence on the importance of overall social and economic factors it slights both empirical evidence that education can raise productivity and the less definite, but still powerful, likelihood that it can enhance individual capacity to act in new directions. The people with money know that it can. They usually ensure high levels of education for their children, along with personal stimulus in the home. Many studies of the effects of cognitive learning have demonstrated that it helps raise both personal earnings and productivity, subject to the important reservation that it is not just a matter of years in school but also of educational quality.[34]

Even on the restrictive assumption of unchanging job openings, if *all* the poor were able to meet minimum standards of education, then it would cease to be the case that the poorest of them would be automatically ruled out. To take a particularly striking example, employment in jobs paying over one minimum wage in Brazil increased twice as fast as the working age population between 1960 and 1978, but the rate of increase of such employment for those with less than four years schooling was only one-third as great as for those with more than four years.[35] To have brought everyone up over four years might not have increased the rate of growth of total employment, but it would have reduced a significant inequality of participation in that growth.

The most costly side of inadequate access to education in Latin America is that those who are left out will spend their whole lives with a lower capacity to respond to or to create new opportunities than they would otherwise have had. Education is not so much to provide specific work skills—they are mostly gained on the job rather than in school—as it is a means to enhance individual capacity to act. Farmers with more schooling adopt improved production techniques more rapidly, know better how to get credit or get attention to their problems, and are more likely to see, or to initiate, new opportunities outside of agriculture. Theodore Schultz, reviewing

[34] George Psacharopoulos, "Education, Employment, and Inequality in Less Developed Countries," *World Development* 9, 1 (January 1981), pp. 37–54; M. Boissiere, J. B. Knight, and R. H. Sabot, "Earnings, Schooling, Ability, and Cognitive Skills," *American Economic Review* 75 (December 1985), pp. 1016–30; Jimenez, "Public Subsidization of Education," table 10, p. 123.

[35] Selowsky, "Income Distribution," p. 86.

extensive research on these questions, concludes that the most important value of education is its contribution to the "ability to deal with disequilibria."[36]

The reason that the poor get left out of decent access to education is not that the societies themselves lack resources to provide it. Middle and upper income groups do their best to hold down tax revenue and at the same time push effectively to get more secondary and higher education, as highly subsidized as possible, for their own children. Generalized good will toward the poor gets squeezed out by what appears as a lack of resources, after everyone else has done their best to make sure there is little left. That is, of course, not a peculiarly Latin American trait. And it clearly can be changed in Latin America itself: when one of these societies is thoroughly changed as in Cuba and Nicaragua, one of the first reforms is a determined drive to extend primary education to everyone.

Persistent poverty cannot be explained in any adequate way by failures in education, but this fact should not be allowed to obscure the point that more nearly equal educational opportunities could do a great deal to help many of the individuals involved. When new opportunities do open up, the poor are always the last to respond. People with relatively little formal education are less likely to have the personal confidence to take independent action of any kind, to learn about new opportunities, or to be able to learn quickly how to handle any new jobs they may find. It is not that schooling transforms societies: it is rather that it can lessen the burden of personal defeatism.

4. CUBA AS A CONTRASTING EXAMPLE

Direct measures of education and health in Cuba are reasonably comparable to other countries, but data on income levels and distribution are scarce and difficult to interpret. Cuba does not report, or apparently even calculate, national product in any way comparable to the members of the World Bank. The estimate of Cuban income per capita in 1977 that is given in table 2.1 comes from a special study that gives several alternative estimates reached by different methods of combining incomplete information: it is probably the closest anyone can come with current information. It is also far higher than previously reported estimates by the World Bank,

[36] Theodore W. Schultz, "The Value of the Ability to Deal with Disequilibria," *Journal of Economic Literature* 13 (September 1975), pp. 827–46.

which would have placed the country's income level down in the lower third for the region, rather than sixth highest.[37] But in any case, it seems clear that Cuba's health statistics are outstanding relative to its level of income; Costa Rica is the only close parallel. As of 1977 Cuba had the lowest infant and child mortality rates and the highest life expectancy in the region. As of 1984 its infant mortality rate was still the lowest, and its child mortality rate one of the two lowest, equal to Costa Rica. The contrast with the richest country, Venezuela, is stark: in 1984 Venezuela had more than double Cuba's infant mortality rate.

Primary education for the poor was one of the first priorities of the postrevolution Cuban Government. The prerevolution base had been one of the best in Latin America, which is not to say that it was very good. It had the typical rural-urban difference: roughly 20 percent of urban children were left out, and 50 percent of the rural.[38] The new regime increased primary school enrollment by about two-thirds between 1958–59 and 1962–63 and used a crash program to locate and teach illiterate adults.[39] As shown in table 2.7, Cuba was in 1975 one of the three countries in Latin America with complete school enrollment for children between six and eleven.

Secondary education stagnated and university enrollments fell while the drive to provide complete primary school coverage was continuing. That must have imposed serious costs of scarcity in ability to handle higher-skill activities, and it may have slowed up growth. But in the 1970s secondary and university enrollments began climbing too. By 1976 secondary education covered half of the

[37] The World Bank estimate for GNP per capita in 1978 was $810 per capita, with a negative growth rate (-1.2 percent) for the period 1960–78. Mesa-Lago and Jorge Perez-Lopez, "Cuba's Material Product System," arrive at much higher estimates for the level of income by 1977 (the most recent year they include), and positive growth rates from 1965 to 1977. The Bank does not defend, or even explain, its earlier estimates: they were always regarded as very rough, but it was difficult to tell how rough until this new study was made.

[38] Richard Jolly, "Education," pp. 161–280, in Dudley Seers et al., *Cuba: The Economic and Social Revolution: Moving Toward Socialism* (Chapel Hill: University of North Carolina Press, 1964), p. 170. See also Arthur MacEwan, *Revolution and Economic Development in Cuba* (New York: St. Martin's Press, 1981), pp. 74–81. Jorge L. Domínguez, *Cuba: Order and Revolution* (Cambridge: Harvard University Press, 1978), p. 25, notes that Cuba's aggregate school enrollment ratio was the highest in Latin America during the Machado presidency.

[39] Domínguez, *Cuba*, table 5.10 and pp. 165–73; Jolly, "Education," p. 181. Jolly raises good questions about the quality and the opportunity costs of the crash program of education in 1961, while emphasizing the positive achievement in terms of breaking through to provide new opportunities to the poor.

school-age population, and university enrollment had reached, at 10.8 percent of the relevant age group, nearly double the enrollment ratio prior to the revolution.[40] Cuba thus reversed the order of priorities in Brazil in the same period: it followed the sequence best suited to equalize opportunity, probably at a considerable cost in terms of restraint on growth of skills in short supply, while Brazil was placing the emphasis on advanced and technical education, with the stated purpose of answering demands for skills and the accompanying effect of leaving out the poor.

The differences between Cuba and the rest of Latin America in terms of health and education are partly explicable by the fact that the Cuban Revolution started out from what was for the region a relatively high level of welfare. As of 1960 the infant mortality rate was already the lowest in the region, and life expectancy the third highest (behind Uruguay and Argentina). But it would be a mistake to assign all the credit for the country's high comparative levels in 1984 to its prerevolution position. If the measures for Cuba are compared to the median for all the countries listed in table 2.1, the degrees of superiority for infant and child mortality are both slightly more pronounced in 1984 than they were in 1960. It is particularly striking that the country's high performance on these basic measures of welfare was maintained in the postrevolution years when national production and income apparently did not grow as rapidly as the Latin American average. In contrast to most of the region, Cuba has had much less difficulty in reducing poverty than in achieving growth of income per capita.

5. CONCLUSIONS

Simply as a factual description, it seems clear that welfare standards of the poor have been raised considerably in most countries in the last quarter century, in the sense of such fundamental measures as child mortality, education, and life expectancy. The reductions of infant and child mortality have been sufficiently rapid to make a great deal of difference to the youngest generation but not fast enough to reduce the high ratios between these Latin American mortality measures and those in the industrialized countries. It is particularly sobering that on the former count fourteen of the nineteen countries listed in table 2.1 other than Cuba still had in 1984

[40] Carmelo Mesa-Lago, *The Economy of Socialist Cuba: A Two-Decade Appraisal* (Albuquerque: University of New Mexico Press, 1980), p. 165.

higher infant mortality rates than Cuba did back in 1960. Ten of the countries had higher levels of child mortality in 1982 than Uruguay did back in 1960. There is nothing intrinsic in the average income levels of these countries that dictates such miserable conditions: it is much more a matter of unequal opportunity and unequal incomes.

Against the general picture of long-term improvement in basic measures of welfare, there have been contrary deteriorations in particular regions and countries, some of them well known and surely many others yet to be documented. Living conditions for many Peruvian peasants deteriorated seriously in the 1970s and early 1980s, because of a combination of adverse structural factors and singularly unhelpful economic policies. The squeeze of the poor in Chile under its post-Allende repressive regime is another striking example, in this case of a deliberately anti-egalitarian economic strategy. Both Chile and Peru are of course capitalist, market-oriented economic systems. But then so are Colombia and Costa Rica, which did much better in the same period. It is hard to see how anyone would want to defend Latin American versions of capitalism in general on the basis of this record, but the differences among particular national versions deserve careful attention because they are enough to result in greatly different consequences for the people who most need help.

THREE

EMPLOYMENT AND EARNINGS

People who care about avoidable poverty in Latin America tend to split in two camps, which need not work against each other but often do. One emphasizes investment, creation of employment opportunities, and macroeconomic management; the other, such questions as the distribution of land ownership, foreign influence, social barriers to mobility, differential access to education, or use of the political system to stack the cards in favor of special privilege. Both sides are right, except when they disdain the other.

The real situation might by now be much better if the side emphasizing investment and employment did not so often allow these valid concerns to direct attention away from, or to oppose, intervention intended to correct structural obstacles or to provide direct help to the poor. It might also be better by now if the side emphasizing more direct corrective action did not so often ignore negative effects on employment creation and macroeconomic balance. This chapter emphasizes questions of employment, in the belief that they are fundamental in the majority of Latin American countries. Later chapters try to do justice to the other set of considerations, which are even more fundamental but may not accomplish much if employment opportunities remain inadequate.

1. CHANGING EMPLOYMENT CONDITIONS, EXCESS LABOR, AND THE LEWIS MODEL

Economic growth normally creates new employment opportunities, but the rate at which it does so can be insufficient to be any real help. If a great many people are stuck in activities in which their productivity and earnings are very low, while rapid growth of population keeps feeding in new workers searching for land or employment, market pressures will keep working against wages even though national income is rising. Increases in incomes will then go mainly to property owners, and any increases in wages mainly to those workers with special skills, increasing inequality by leaving the majority behind. Unless and until labor becomes persistently scarce, the operation of uncontrolled markets may keep on indefinitely increasing inequality.

The hopeful side is that the rate at which employment opportunities are created can be raised by choices of national economic policy. During the last five years in which Colombian economic strategy was oriented toward import substitution as the basis of industrialization, from 1962 to 1967, employment in manufacturing grew only half as fast as production; with major changes in economic policies from 1967, the growth of employment in manufacturing speeded up to 80 percent of the rate of growth of production for the next decade, itself almost half-again higher than before.[1] Such a change means that more people can move up to relatively stable employment at wages that, though low compared to those in the industrial countries, are normally high enough to bring them out of severe poverty. Faster growth of opportunities for productive employment can be a particularly powerful way to help the poor.

Development economics has been strongly marked by, and constantly attacked for, the concept of "excess labor": the idea that countries in the early stages of development are characterized by massive underemployment in traditional activities, in the sense of work that yields low products and low income, alongside a minority of workers who earn higher incomes in modern-sector activities. The general idea of excess labor at incomes so low they may fall below subsistence is one of the most venerable in economics, given great attention by the classical economists and revived by W. Arthur Lewis in his 1954 model of growth "with unlimited supplies of labour."[2] But for neoclassical economics the term has no meaning: increases in the labor supply relative to land and the stock of capital may drive down the marginal productivity of labor and therefore wage rates, but workers are never "excess' in the sense of being left out of the normal operation of labor markets. Poverty has many causes, and low productivity is one of the most important, but it is not a problem of lack of employment.

Crucial issues of economic strategy are involved in these conflicting interpretations. If excess labor is a persisting reality then a market economy may leave many people out of the process of growth. Increasing investment and national income may not even trickle down: they may not decrease poverty at all. The opportunity cost of

[1] Albert Berry, ed., *Essays on Industrialization in Colombia* (Tempe: Arizona State University, Center of Latin American Studies, 1983), table 2.20, p. 68.
[2] W. Arthur Lewis, "Economic Development with Unlimited Supplies of Labour," *Manchester School* and *Theory of Economic Growth*.

labor will be low and employment created by import restrictions a net gain, not a loss of efficiency: the strategy of import substitution should raise income. Similarly, fast growth of aggregate demand should be safe, and consistently desirable, because productive capacity is available waiting to be activated. On the opposite understanding, if markets are integrated in the sense postulated by neoclassical economics, everyone is included in the process of growth, investment can normally be expected to raise the demand for labor and wage rates, labor has a real opportunity cost so industries that require protection to cover high costs probably reduce national income in real terms, and it is always necessary to be careful about raising demand because there is no great reservoir of underutilized productive capacity embodied in excess labor.

Which view is right? That depends on the actual situation in the particular country. The Lewis view is almost completely irrelevant to Argentina, which has no peasant class and has for most of its history been better characterized by labor scarcity; it is at the same time a reasonable approximation to conditions in Peru, with many peasants in the Sierra who have never participated in gains in national income and may be sinking into deeper poverty each decade. Neither the Lewis model nor the neoclassical interpretation can be considered logically necessary, but both are real possibilities. How does one measure or test the actual conditions in particular cases? That is not a clear-cut process yielding answers to which everyone must agree. Most people who have studied labor-market conditions in Mexico have emphasized the persistence of large-scale underemployment, and the need to speed up the rate of economic growth to keep employment rising even fast enough to absorb new entrants to the labor force, but a particularly thorough new empirical study concludes just the opposite.[3] The International Labour Office carried out a massive group research project demonstrating that Colombia at the beginning of the 1970s had profound problems of unemployment and underemployment, and then an impressive study of wage trends showed that real wages were rising well for unorganized workers with little or no bargaining power to help them.[4]

Before plunging into details of how one might go about judging for oneself among such contradictory assessments, it might help to clarify the main lines of the Lewis model. It has provoked a host of

[3] Peter Gregory, *The Myth of Market Failure: Employment and the Labor Market in Mexico* (Baltimore: Johns Hopkins University Press, 1986).
[4] International Labour Office, *Towards Full Employment: A Programme for Colombia* (Geneva: ILO, 1970); Urrutia, *Winners and Losers.*

valid objections—it leaves out some absolutely vital issues—but it directs attention to significant questions that get buried by analysis presuming the equilibrium conditions of a fully integrated economy. It helps organize objections almost as well as the points Lewis intended to make.[5]

The concept of excess labor intended is not a matter of open unemployment. The presumption is that everyone has to find some work to do, as peasants or employees or by inventing jobs themselves, but that there are not sufficient opportunities for regular employment in modern-sector jobs paying above-subsistence wages. Employers in that sector pay wages above income levels prevailing in the rest of the economy in order to draw in and hold the labor force they need, and they limit their hiring to the number of workers it is profitable to hire at this wage level. For Lewis, two points were central. One is that the pressure of additional labor seeking regular jobs keeps wages in the modern sector from rising. This means that gains in income go chiefly to employers as profits, enabling them to finance a rising rate of investment. The other is that this investment gradually clears up excess labor by creating new jobs, until the economy reaches a "turning point" at which labor becomes scarce and earnings begin to rise in all sectors of a more fully integrated economy.

Lewis invited more criticism than necessary by postulating a zero marginal product for workers in traditional fields, and by the implication that their earnings could not rise until a definite structural change is accomplished by reaching the critical turning point through increases in modern-sector employment. Empirical studies have consistently show that the marginal productivity of labor in traditional activities is greater than zero everywhere examined.[6] Less consistently, many studies of countries with large shares of the labor force in traditional activities have shown that their earnings can rise right along with national income in some periods (though they may often fall back in other periods, or rise less rapidly than national income per capita). Such findings effectively contradict any

[5] Gustav Ranis and John C. H. Fei develop much more explicitly the role of population growth and the process of change within agriculture, significantly extending the Lewis model, in "A Theory of Economic Growth," *American Economic Review* 51 (September 1961), pp. 533–65. Keith B. Griffin, *Underdevelopment in Spanish America* (London: Allen and Unwin, 2d ed. 1971), pp. 19–31, criticizes the Lewis approach mercilessly, and the whole idea of dualistic growth models in the process.

[6] Lyn Squire, *Employment Policy in Developing Countries* (New York: Oxford University Press for the World Bank, 1981), especially ch. 4–6.

pure form of the Lewis model, but they do not disprove the main points intended. Marginal products and earnings of labor in agriculture and traditional small industry and services are invariably below those in the modern sector. The presence of a great deal of labor in low-income activities can exert continuous pressure against increasing wages for unskilled workers even with positive marginal products in all fields. Wage rates may be stagnant for a decade or more at a time, because the labor supply outruns demand for workers while national income is rising. The core problem is still profoundly important in some countries, if not in all. Still, the issues become matters of degree rather than presence versus absence of excess labor, and conclusions either way become matters of debate in each country and period.

Historical studies of Latin America in the nineteenth century more often suggest labor scarcity than the contrary. Scattered indicators of rural earnings bring out periods in which they increased and others in which they fell, not simple stagnation. The ratio of land to labor was fairly high compared to Europe or Asia, and population growth was much more moderate than it became in the twentieth century. Landowners often found it difficult to get enough workers and used their influence to promote legislation authorizing varied forms of forced labor, tying workers to particular estates. Where Indian families with shared access to land were for a long time able to continue accustomed ways of life with little need to seek outside employment, as in the Peruvian highlands, they were pushed steadily toward wage employment under pressure from people seeking private ownership of the land and from governmental policies working to reduce separation from the national society.[7]

In the twentieth century, prior demographic equlibrium changed toward rapid population growth in many countries, though much less so or not at all in the Southern Cone. The rate of population growth in Colombia from 1850 to 1900 was 1.1 percent a year; it doubled to 2.2 percent from 1900 to 1930 and continued rising to 3.0 percent for the 1960s. Brazil's rate of population growth went from 1.8 percent a year for 1850–1900 to 2.9 percent for the 1960s; El Salvador from 1.7 percent to 2.9; Guatemala from 1.0 to 2.8; and

[7] Florencia E. Mallon, *The Defense of Community in Peru's Central Highlands: Peasant Struggle and Capitalist Transition, 1860–1940* (Princeton: Princeton University Press, 1983).

Peru from 1.4 to twice that rate.[8] The increases were achieved
mainly by advances in medical techniques helping to reduce mortality rates: an immense gain in terms of health and life expectancy
but without the accompanying economic and social changes that
had helped to bring birth rates down along with mortality rates in
the countries industrializing earlier.[9] The resulting phase of exceptionally rapid population growth may itself be changing now, as discussed below: starting in the early 1960s fertility rates began to
come down significantly. But as of the beginning of the postwar period the dynamics of labor markets were commonly adverse to
workers, in the sense that the labor supply was growing fast relative
to opportunities for employment. Particularly in the poorest countries, population pressure on the land was steadily increasing.

Much of the support for protection and industrialization came
from the conviction that they could reduce poverty by providing
new employment opportunities, before anyone ever heard of the
Lewis model. The model did not invent an unreal problem, or cause
the adoption of policies to promote industrialization, but it provided a splendid fit for structural analysis and the strategy of import
substitution. The model and the strategies had a highly desirable
target, but both overshot by downplaying opportunities to increase
real incomes in traditional activities, particularly agriculture, by investment and technological change raising productivity in these
fields. They went astray by overstressing industry as the main hope
for change. The model goes wrong in another respect by suggesting
a near-automatic turning point, given patience and a steady emphasis on investment. The conception that the turn is bound to
come may obscure the crucial possibility that the forces sustaining
inequality could go on indefinitely, generation after generation.

2. Measures of Progress, or the Lack of It

Considering those countries in which persistent poverty has been
most pronounced, outside of Costa Rica and the Southern Cone,
progress in reducing it by creation of new opportunities for productive employment might be measured in many different ways.

[8] Nicolás Sánchez-Albornoz, *The Population of Latin America: A History* (Berkeley:
University of California Press, 1974), p. 169, for the earlier periods; table 3.2 below
for the 1960s.
[9] Alan B. Simmons, "Social Inequality and Demographic Transition," pp. 85–110
in Archibald Ritter and David Pollock, eds., *Latin American Prospects for the 1980s*
(New York: Praeger, 1983).

Relevant indicators might include changes in the numbers of workers remaining in agriculture, changes in the number of people classified as self-employed or unpaid family labor, trends in wages of unskilled workers, or wages outside of industrial employment. Each possible indicator has its own ambiguities. A decrease in the number of families depending on agriculture can be a particularly useful clue of improving conditions, though an increase would not necessarily indicate deterioration. Increases could be consistent with falling rural poverty if new land is becoming available fast enough, if investment in agriculture is high and well directed to keep raising productivity, if the rural labor force has the advantage of decent education to favor their mobility and productivity, or if industrial production is relatively decentralized and creates nonfarm employment opportunities in rural areas. All these conditions have contributed to favorable trends for rural incomes and equality in the more successful East Asian countries; few of them have been anywhere near as helpful in Latin America.

One of the main regional differences in this respect is the poor record of many Latin American countries in providing opportunities for education in rural areas, as discussed in chapter 2. Another, surely related, is that the East Asian pattern of dispersed industrial production, which helps so much to provide nonfarm earnings possibilities in rural areas there, has not been common in Latin America. "In Colombia, for instance, non-agricultural income's share [of the total rural family income] has fallen from 15 percent to 10 percent during the last thirty years compared with a rise from 30 percent to 50 percent in Taiwan."[10] In Peru as of the end of the 1960s, thirteen of twenty-four departments had either no recorded industrial production at all or, at the highest, no more than one percent of the national total of industrial value added. The urban concentration of Lima-Callao accounted by itself for no less than 74 percent of the country's industrial value added.[11] In such a context, with few alternative earnings possibilities in rural areas, an increase in the number of people in agriculture is highly likely to signal increasing poverty.

Between 1960 and 1980 all Latin American countries reduced substantially the percentages of their labor forces remaining in ag-

[10] Gustav Ranis and Louise Orrock, "Latin American and East Asian NICs: Development Strategies Compared," pp. 48–66 in Esperanza Durán, ed., *Latin America and the World Recession* (Cambridge: Cambridge University Press, 1985), quotation p. 61.

[11] World Bank, *Peru: Long-Term Development Issues* (Washington, D.C.: World Bank, 1979), vol. 3, p. 383.

riculture, as shown in table 3.1. But the absolute number of people working in agriculture nevertheless increased in fourteen of the twenty countries. These included all the lower income countries in the region as well as some of those with middle and higher per capita incomes. Between 1960 and 1984 the labor force in agriculture increased 23 percent in Bolivia, 48 percent in the Dominican Republic, 52 in Ecuador, 62 in El Salvador and Guatemala, 79 in Par-

TABLE 3.1. Percentage Shares and Total Number of Labor Force Remaining in Agriculture, 1960–1984

	Percent in agriculture		Thousands of workers				Change in total, 1960–1984	
	1960	1980	1960	1970	1980	1984	Number	Percent
Argentina	20.0	13.0	1,583	1,520	1,399	1,352	− 231	− 14.6
Bolivia	61.0	50.0	782	796	909	964	+ 182	+ 23.3
Brazil	51.9	38.2	11,720	13,800	14,572	14,719	+ 2,999	+ 25.6
Chile	29.8	18.4	746	685	678	669	− 77	− 10.3
Colombia	51.5	27.4	2,430	2,340	2,106	2,047	− 383	− 15.8
Costa Rica	51.6	35.1	193	224	268	281	+ 88	+ 45.6
Cuba	38.9	23.3	885	799	692	647	− 238	− 26.9
Dominican Republic	66.6	56.1	586	704	820	865	+ 279	+ 47.6
Ecuador	57.5	44.4	810	962	1,135	1,227	+ 417	+ 51.5
El Salvador	61.6	50.4	502	617	754	812	+ 310	+ 61.6
Guatemala	66.9	54.9	802	999	1,211	1,297	+ 495	+ 61.7
Haiti	82.8	66.6	1,891	1,730	1,933	1,999	+ 108	+ 5.7
Honduras	70.1	62.6	417	536	680	760	+ 343	+ 82.3
Mexico	55.1	36.0	5,964	6,665	7,204	7,269	+ 1,305	+ 21.9
Nicaragua	61.8	42.8	302	316	352	372	+ 70	+ 23.2
Panama	50.8	34.5	178	215	226	228	+ 50	+ 28.1
Paraguay	56.0	48.9	308	382	498	550	+ 242	+ 78.6
Peru	52.5	37.3	1,644	1,719	1,901	1,978	+ 334	+ 20.3
Uruguay	20.7	11.9	209	165	133	124	− 85	− 40.7
Venezuela	35.1	18.0	863	795	857	863	0	0

SOURCES: Food and Agricultural Organization, *Production Yearbook 1972*, vol. 26, pp. 19–20, for 1960 data; *Production Yearbook 1984*, vol. 38, pp. 66–68, for all other data.

aguay, and 82 in Honduras. These are countries with great poverty
in agriculture: increasing numbers in that sector make the situation
worse than it otherwise would have been.

The negative pressure of increasing numbers in agriculture has
been offset to varying degrees by bringing new land under cultivation. In Brazil, from 1969–71 to 1982, arable land increased nearly
50 percent faster than the rural labor force.[12] Even though land
ownership concentration probably increased, the labor/land ratio
turned in a direction that should help reduce rural poverty. Of the
countries cited above that experienced large increases in the agricultural labor force, Bolivia and Paraguay also managed to raise
their arable land areas relative to the labor force. The most unfavorable cases in terms of this relationship were the Dominican Republic, Ecuador, El Salvador, and Guatemala, for all of which the increase in arable land was less than half that of the labor force.

Colombia was one of the few countries outside of the Southern
Cone in which the agricultural labor force actually fell between
1960 and 1984, by 16 percent. In the perspective suggested here,
that change was for the better: it favored rising real incomes for
those who stayed in agriculture, and probably meant that those who
moved to the cities were able to gain higher-income alternative employment. It was achieved mainly by a rare combination of circumstances: a good rate of growth from 1967 to 1980, and a redirection
of economic policies focused on making the growth process more
employment-creating. But it is also true that the movement out of
agriculture was speeded up by negative factors: by increasing rural
violence in the 1970s, both from active guerrilla movements and
from military repression trying to eliminate them, and by the government's decision in 1973 to abandon land reform efforts. That
decision may well have contributed to the strength of the guerrilla
movements in this period, as well as to discouragement about future
opportunities in agriculture.[13] Still, the decrease in agricultural employment must have been for the most part both a sign and a cause
of progress in reducing poverty: a response to better employment
opportunities outside agriculture, and a factor contributing to the
rise of rural earnings in this period.

Although Brazil has not yet managed to reduce the number of
workers in agriculture, growth rates of rural labor show a suggestive

[12] United Nations, Food and Agricultural Organization, *FAO Production Yearbook*,
vols. 34 and 37, for 1980 and 1983 (Rome: FAO, 1981 and 1984), table 1, pp. 48–50.
[13] See discussion in chapters 6 and 11.

difference between the 1960s and the 1970s. National economic growth was weak from 1960 to 1967, and for that decade as a whole the agricultural labor force increased by 17 percent. But in the 1970s, with faster aggregate growth and more attention to employment, the increase in the agricultural labor force was cut down to 7 percent. Given good incentives for agricultural investment and exports and a rapid increase in the total of arable land, the lower rate of increase in rural labor proved to be consistent with a fairly rapid increase in rural earnings. As in Colombia, a real breakthrough seemed to be in the making: surplus labor was being cleared up.

Movement out of agriculture would not be much of an achievement if migrants to the cities could not find jobs, but research on migrant experience shows that is not typical. They usually find employment quickly: open unemployment is more identified with educated urban workers than with unskilled migrants.[14] The kinds of jobs they find, in activities termed "urban informal" or "urban subsistence," typically involve a step up from rural poverty but not up to the income levels prevailing for regular employment in the modern sector.[15] Indicators of degrees of progress, if any, need to take into account what is happening in such activities as well as in agriculture.

Changes in the numbers of people classified as self-employed, as unpaid family labor, or as domestic servants give a rough indication of trends in employment conditions for urban as well as rural unskilled labor. These heterogeneous categories include both desirable jobs and activities of very low productivity and earnings. More productive societies would increase particular kinds of self-employment but would greatly reduce the total in this category. Alejandro Portes has worked out a comparison of trends for these groups in Latin America between 1950 and 1980 and those in the approximately corresponding period in the United States, 1900 to 1930. In the United States the total of self-employed, unpaid family labor and domestic servants was equal to 51 percent of the labor force in 1900 but was brought down to 31 percent by 1930. In Latin America their share of the labor force was 47 percent in 1950, and it was brought down only slightly, to 42 percent, by 1980.[16]

[14] Squire, *Employment Policy*, ch. 7–9, pp. 98–132.

[15] Ibid., and William E. Cole and Richard D. Sanders, "Internal Migration and Urbanization in the Third World," *American Economic Reveiw* 75 (June 1985), pp. 481–94.

[16] Alejandro Portes, "Latin American Class Structures: Their Composition and

The service sector is often considered to be something of a dumping ground for surplus labor coming into the city slum areas and unable to find regular employment. The conception is easy to understand, with so many people acting as self-appointed parking guards on city streets, spending hours to collect infinitesimal tips from the people rich enough to have cars to park, while others negotiate with local organizers for rights to ransack city dumps. But there are many different kinds of service activities, including income-elastic "new" services such as independent professional consulting, government employment, and repair work in fields requiring technical skills. At the other end are the "old" service jobs, which few people would enter if they had alternatives and many will leave as employment conditions improve, particularly in household services and petty trade. A sample comparing the proportions of these two categories of services for industrialized and for developing countries as of 1960 shows that the higher income countries had on average 9 percent of their labor forces in "new" services and 5.5 percent in "old"; for the less developed countries the averages were 4 percent for the positive category and 8 percent for the "old."[17] Mexican economists frequently argue that increases in service employment are proof of deteriorating employment conditions. The argument unduly slights the positive component but has a real foundation: the share of the labor force in the more positive group of service activities was 1.2 percent at the time of this study, while that in the "old" services was 9.3 percent.

A particularly thorough attempt, by Peter Gregory, to dissect data on categories of employment arrived at a cautious conclusion that the quality of employment in most developing countries was improving up to the early or middle 1970s, not deteriorating.[18] For one of the lower income Latin American countries included, the Dominican Republic, the data show clearly positive trends through the early 1970s: the numbers in self-employment and unpaid family labor both went down, and growth rates for employment in sales and services were below that in nonagricultural production activities. But the other low-income countries mostly go the other way. In

Change during the Last Decades," *Latin American Research Review* 20, 3 (1985), table 5, p. 29.

[17] Squire, *Employment Policy*, pp. 136–37.

[18] Peter Gregory, "An Assessment of Changing Employment Conditions in Less Developed Countries," *Economic Development and Cultural Change* 28 (July 1980), pp. 673–700, and "Employment, Unemployment, and Underemployment in Latin America," *Statistical Bulletin of the OAS* 2 (October-December 1980), pp. 1–20.

El Salvador, Guatemala, and Paraguay, employment in services and in sales grew faster than employment in nonagricultural production; in Ecuador and in Peru it grew faster in sales (though not in services) than in production.[19] The generally positive picture of employment trends in this study is convincing for most countries other than the low-income Latin American cases, and for the Dominican Republic, but is more doubtful for the rest.

Still another indicator of what is going on, perhaps the least ambiguous provided that the data can be trusted, is the path of real wages for workers outside the organized industrial and mining sectors. Positive trends for their earnings would strongly suggest improving labor market conditions. The problem is the scarcity of dependable information: all data on earnings and income are open to considerable doubt, but those for real incomes in agriculture and services are particularly difficult to establish. The most systematic multicountry measures of rural earnings available, by the Regional Program for Employment in Latin America and the Caribbean (PREALC), include estimates for actual wages in agriculture for only five countries, along with minimum wages and other indicators for ten others.[20] For various subperiods between 1965 and 1980, seven of the fifteen countries show fairly clear trends of rising real wages in agriculture, five show downtrends, and the others are either constant or show contradictory results by different indicators (cf. table 3.2). Brazil and Colombia are among the cases of increasing real wages in the 1970s, consistent with the evidence of a decreasing agricultural labor force in Colombia and with the greatly slower increase in Brazil in that decade. El Salvador, Guatemala, Honduras, Nicaragua, and Peru all show falling real wages. This dispersion of results suggests exactly the same interpretation as the measures of employment: there is no pronounced general trend for the region as a whole either toward massive continuing deterioration or toward strong improvement, but agricultural earnings have been deteriorating in particular countries where the rural labor force is still increasing rapidly.

Evidence of a major rise for real wages in Colombian agriculture in the 1970s makes a strikingly hopeful contrast to prior stagnation: real wages of landless agricultural workers had failed to increase at

[19] Gregory, "Employment and Underemployment," table 2, p. 11.

[20] PREALC, *Mercado de trabajo en cifras, 1950–1980* (Santiago: PREALC, Oficina Internacional de Trabajo, 1982), table II-3, pp. 149–51. These and other indicators of wages are discussed in section 5 below.

all in the three decades from 1935 to 1964.[21] As of 1964, wages of blue-collar workers in manufacturing were three times those of agricultural workers. But as the number of workers in agriculture began to go down real wages in that sector rose: Miguel Urrutia estimates that they increased 50 percent between 1970 and 1979, while real wages in manufacturing were almost unchanged. Another study of the same period by Albert Berry and Francisco Thoumi points out a change in the method of reporting data that makes measures for the first half of the 1970s uncertain, though their results for the clearer period from 1976 to 1980 also show a marked positive trend: real wages went up by 22 percent in these years. Unhappily, extension of the data to 1984, when aggregate growth practically stopped, shows that they fell back 19 percent, wiping out the gains of the last half of the 1970s.[22]

In the urban sector, Urrutia's study identifies unskilled workers in construction and domestic servants as the lowest paid categories. Average wages for construction workers increased more slowly than national income per capita in the course of the 1970s, but those for unskilled helpers rose more rapidly than wages for skilled workers. Real wages in services fell in the early years of the decade and then began to rise from 1974. If the special sample for workers in Bogota can be trusted, one of the most positive indications of all is that earnings of women working as maids increased from 12 percent of average earnings for all male workers in the city as of 1973 to 42 percent by 1977.[23] One would like to believe it.

The complexities of attempts to assess labor market conditions in these countries are brought out particularly well in Peter Gregory's controversial study of Mexico.[24] He focuses on employment and wages for the workers in unorganized fields, both rural and urban, who constitute a substantial fraction of the lower half of the income distribution. His main conclusions run squarely contrary to earlier

[21] Urrutia, *Winners and Losers*. The earlier stagnation of real earnings in Colombian agriculture is documented in R. Albert Berry and Miguel Urrutia, *Income Distribution in Colombia* (New Haven: Yale University Press, 1976).

[22] Berry and Thoumi, "Colombian Economic Growth."

[23] Urrutia, *Winners and Losers*, table 3, p. 20.

[24] Gregory, *Myth of Market Failure*. Brígida García makes a good case for a more reserved view about labor market conditions in Mexico, giving particular attention to increases in the category of the self-employed in the industrial sector. Her analysis helps to bring out the fundamental uncertainties of the data: "Desarrollo capitalista y absorción de fuerza de trabajo en México: La dimensión regional," paper presented at the Third Reunion on Demographic Research in Mexico, Mexico City, November 1986.

studies pointing to worsening employment conditions, especially in the period of "stabilizing growth" from 1956 to 1970 (see discussion in chapter 11). Gregory demonstrates convincing reasons to doubt that conditions were deteriorating, either in the sense of a worsening balance among kinds of employment or failure of wages for unorganized workers to keep up with those in urban industry. In urban labor markets desirable structural change has been shown by faster employment increases in production activities and in the better-paid side of services than in sales or domestic service. In agriculture, although the labor force continued to grow between 1940 and 1970, the area of land under cultivation grew even faster.[25] In this picture, the Lewis turning point seems to have been passed several decades back.

Although this new research on Mexico helps to clarify real improvements it leaves open a good deal of room for differences in emphasis and for doubts about the future. Given the earlier heavy imbalance in service activities toward the "old" services, as noted above, the fact that the higher-paid side has been growing more rapidly than the low is better than the contrary, but the fact that the latter is still *increasing* is important too. At Mexico's level of income per capita, and especially at the end of the 1970s when employment growth was exceptionally rapid, the fact that the number of household maids was still increasing by 3 percent a year can scarcely be seen as a positive sign: it should by then have been possible for women to leave the field, not enter it. In agriculture, as Gregory notes, the positive contribution of increasing land under cultivation and falling ratio of labor to land up to 1970 took place only in the higher-income rural areas favored by public investment; in the poorer regions the ratio of labor to land kept on increasing. Even in the former areas it may no longer be possible to keep adding to land under cultivation at any reasonable cost: arable land increased only 2 percent between 1970 and 1983, while the agricultural labor force rose 9 percent.[26] More generally, if three decades of extraordinarily rapid aggregate growth (1940 to 1970) failed to reduce a degree of inequality that is one of the highest in the world, the trend so far can hardly be regarded as a success story.

All of these indicators add up to a mixed result of real progress in some countries and periods but deterioration in others. For the three decades up to 1980, the positive changes were made chiefly by some, though by no means all, of the countries in the middle and

---

[25] Gregory, *Myth of Market Failure*, ch. 4.
[26] UN, FAO, *FAO Production Yearbook*, 1984, vol. 38, pp. 50–52 and 66–68.

upper income ranges; for the poorest, negative changes were more nearly the rule. For the latter, it is hard to see how conditions can be improved greatly without drastic reorientation of economic policies and of land ownership conditions as well. For the semi-industrialized countries, the mixture of results, as opposed to any evidence of generalized deterioration, suggests that even moderate changes in the specific policies that shape incentives in this domain could make the balance turn more positive.

3. Aspects of Population Growth

Growth of population in excess of the growth of productive employment can add greatly to the pressures making poverty worse, and it has surely done so in many Latin American countries.[27] Attempts to promote family planning as a means to restrain population growth, and thereby to help reduce poverty, were for a long time handicapped by opposition coming from both the traditionalist side, including some of the leadership of the Catholic Church, and the radical left. The opposition is still there, but behavior of families has changed radically while the debates have been going on. Fertility rates and family size began to come down fast in some countries in the 1960s, and the changes gathered momentum in the 1970s.

Colombia is rightly regarded as one of the more conservatively Catholic countries in Latin America, and it had until the early 1960s a well-deserved reputation for high birth rates and family size. Based on 1960–64 data, a woman living through the normal childbearing age span had on average 5.4 children.[28] But about that time both lay groups associated with the medical profession and parish-level priests began to provide information about the possibilities of birth control. Neither the Church nor the government adopted any public position in favor of birth control; it was rather a quiet process of providing information and moral reassurance. The results demonstrated that Colombian women were ready to change behavioral patterns. The birth rate peaked during 1960–64 and fell by a third in the next decade. Birth rates also fell rapidly in Chile and Costa

[27] Nancy Birdsall, "Analytical Approaches to the Relationship of Population Growth and Development," *Population and Development Review* 3 (March and June 1977), pp. 63–102; William W. Murdoch, *The Poverty of Nations* (Baltimore: Johns Hopkins University Press, 1980); Squire, *Employment Policy*, ch. 15, pp. 177–93.

[28] Joseph Potter, Myriam Ordóñez G., and Anthony Measham, "The Rapid Decline in Colombian Fertility," *Population and Development Review* 2 (September and December 1976).

Rica in this period, and then in the course of the 1970s they began
to come down significantly all through Latin America.[29]

Low incomes, and in particular rural poverty, are usually associated with high birth rates: for the rural poor, children begin to contribute to family income when very young, and in later years they
provide the only source of support for older parents when they are
unable to continue working. Rising income levels usually reduce
such economic pressures to have children, and rising opportunities
generally encourage reductions of family size. These factors have
operated in Latin America but more slowly than in other regions: a
contrary influence retarded the transition. A possible explanation
of this differential behavior is that families in many countries have
been held in low-productivity rural occupations, and therefore
maintained behavior normally corresponding to much poorer
countries. Rising incomes for urban families have had little bearing
on the life opportunities and the reproduction patterns of the rural
poor.[30]

Where the growth of the labor force begins to slow down this
should help to reduce poverty, but in some countries such slow-
downs may result more from deteriorating economic or political
conditions than from the expression of new behavioral preferences.
Emigration caused by a deteriorating economy and repressive political regime was significant in both Chile and Uruguay in the
1970s. The most striking mass emigration of all has been from
Cuba. This outflow—like the emigration from Chile—certainly suggests large-scale dissatisfaction with existing conditions. For the
other countries the changes in demographic trends are for the most
part evidence of something closer to voluntary changes of behavior
in response to falling death rates, urbanization, and changing values. They point in a positive direction, toward a lessening of the
pressures making for persistent poverty.

4. INCOME DISTRIBUTION, CONSUMER PREFERENCES, AND OUTPUT COMPOSITION

High rates of population growth would not eternally postpone the
turning point toward lessening inequality and poverty if openings
for productive employment could be increased fast enough. In
Lewis's formulation this was mainly a question of the rate of investment. In postwar Latin America that did not turn out to be the core

[29] Ibid., p. 518; Murdoch, *Poverty of Nations*, table 2-12, p. 55; Simmons, "Demographic Transition."
[30] Murdoch, *Poverty of Nations*, pp. 60–65.

problem. Investment remained fairly high relative to national income in most countries, but too much of it took the form of capital-intensive, labor-saving technology: employment increased far more slowly than the capital stock.[31]

Disappointingly slow growth of employment has been explained in many different ways, some of which collide with each other in terms of their implications for desirable policy. Structuralist explanations put the blame either on historical conditions of income distribution and the consumption preferences of upper income groups or on technical characteristics of modern industry, dependency theorists on the behavior of multinational firms, and orthodox economics on the incentives acting on choices of producers. Problems with incentives include artificially low prices for the foreign exchange needed to buy imported capital equipment, subsidized credit and tax advantages for purchases of machinery, and wage pressures acting to encourage labor saving. Each of these competing explanations has enough solid support to reassure believers that they need look no further, but no one of them is really sufficient: policies based exclusively on any one version would leave out too much that matters.

The structuralist case has been explained with unusual clarity and force in Sylvia Ann Hewlett's study of Brazil, *The Cruel Dilemmas of Development*.[32] She traces the historical roots of the problem to the high concentration of income and property ownership established in the colonial period and fortified in the nineteenth century. During the long period of relatively free trade, up to the depression of the 1930s, the upper income minority used its growing income primarily for the purchase of imported consumer goods while the majority of the population constituted the market for home-produced "wage goods." When the leading countries of Latin America began to foster import substitution in the 1930s, the first industries that came into being to replace prior imports were almost inescapably focused on products identified with the demand patterns of upper income groups. National structures of production changed toward consumer durable goods characteristic of consumption patterns in

[31] Patricio Meller, "Enfoques sobre demanda de trabajo: Relevancia para América Latina," *Estudios cieplan* 24 (June 1978).

[32] Sylvia Ann Hewlett, *The Cruel Dilemmas of Development: Twentieth Century Brazil* (New York: Basic Books, 1980), See also David Felix, "Interrelations Between Consumption, Economic Growth, and Income Distribution in Latin America Since 1800: A Comparative Perspective," in Henri Baudet and Hen Van der Meulen, eds., *Consumer Behaviour and Economic Growth in the Modern Economy* (London: Croom Helm, 1981).

the industrialized countries. Whether the new industries were initiated by domestic entrepreneurs or by foreign firms, they normally
adopted the methods of production in use in the industrialized
countries, methods which had often been developed specifically to
save on high-wage labor in the countries of origin. The pattern of
demand for inputs of these new industries therefore focused on
complex modern equipment, usually itself imported, and on labor
with specialized skills rather than unskilled workers.

Such patterns of final demand and input requirements are self-
reinforcing: expenditures of higher income groups foster the
growth of industries that have a structure of input requirements
biased toward need for the capital and skills of people with higher
incomes. Given highly concentrated distributions of income, the
preferences of these groups have a disproportionate influence on
the structure of final demand. As in so many other respects, existing
patterns of behavior keep repeating themselves. What, if anything,
might make it possible to break out of this circle?

One possibility is that the growth process itself could work gradually to raise the earnings of the labor force as a whole and favor
rising demand for mass-market wage goods likely to be more labor
intensive. That seems to have been happening in Brazil and Colombia, at least during their sustained expansions from 1967 to 1980,
but there is nothing automatic about the result. With a highly elastic
supply of labor and concentrated ownership of assets, growth of national income works more to keep the structure of demand pulled
toward the products that can be purchased by higher income
groups. If the pattern of growth is to be changed under such conditions, it needs to be shaped by selective policies to alter incentives
in ways favorable for employment creation. Consumer demand patterns could be altered by taxes and subsidies, producers' choices of
technology could be reoriented to some degree by making capital-
intensive methods more expensive, and final demand could also be
altered both by governmental spending patterns and by specific institutional changes. Growth of employment is not something technically predetermined: it is at least in part a function of the character of national economic policy.

5. Wage Policies and Employment Opportunities

Conflicts among desirable but contradictory objectives are particularly acute in dealing with wages. A healthy development process
should surely include rising real wages for all workers. In addition

to the direct importance of rising wages for living standards, it is hard to imagine a democracy able to survive for very long if property incomes keep going up but wages do not. A pattern of strikingly contrasting trends is bound to foster violent pressures for change, and countermeasures to repress change. A democratic society cannot stay that way long if its people split between groups who insist on drastic change and groups who will not accept it.

Many of the people concerned with national economic policies in the early postwar years made the goal of raising wages a major theme. Besides being a natural objective in its own right it promised a way to create a broad coalition of interests favorable for change: it could bring a growing urban labor force into the political arena on terms likely to minimize class confrontation because all the participants would be gaining at the same time.[33] That goal clearly has great appeal but it needs to be weighed against the possible cost: raising wages too rapidly can hurt the poor and block the whole economy. It matters a great deal how fast they are raised and whether they go up equally for all workers or only for particular groups.

In Argentina, the early postwar champion for wage increases, real wages of industrial workers were raised more than 60 percent from 1946 to 1949, while GNP per capita increased only 4 percent.[34] This did help create an urban coalition in favor of industrialization, but not for long. The wage increases raised demand for consumer goods so much more rapidly than output could be increased that imports were pulled in at a high rate. At the same time, potential exports of meat and wheat were redirected into domestic consumption. External deficits rose swiftly to levels that could not be financed. And since part of the increase in wages came out of the real income of the people who were not in the industrial sector, the process heightened social conflict and opposition to industrialization itself. The coalition in favor of industrialization came apart quickly, as a result of strains that could have been avoided if the rate of increase in wages had been more nearly consistent with the growth of output.

Apart from the question of the overall rate of wage increase, a crucial distinction is necessary between (a) increasing wages for those particular workers who have regular jobs in preferred activi-

---

[33] O'Donnell, *Modernization and Bureaucratic-Authoritarianism*, ch. 2.

[34] Carlos F. Díaz Alejandro, *Essays on the Economic History of the Argentine Republic* (New Haven: Yale University Press, 1970), table 133, p. 538.

ties such as mining, industry, or government and (b) increasing earnings for workers who either have no regular employment or are unable to move out of occupations with productivity and income levels much below those of regularly employed workers in the modern sector. Separately higher industrial wages encourage firms to choose more labor-saving kinds of technology than they otherwise would have, limiting employment growth for those left out.

The Argentine example in the 1946–49 period of rapidly rising wages for industrial workers was followed at first in some other countries, but it has not been the general pattern since. Considering the record from the mid-1950s to the early 1970s, Richard Webb concluded that urban wages in the usual case increased at approximately the same rate as property incomes instead of either shooting up ahead of profits or staying down on the floor as suggested by the Lewis model.[35] His data comparing real wages in manufacturing to the growth of output per capita are shown in the first two columns of table 3.2, along with similar measures for the 1970s. For the earlier period, 1956–1972, real wages of industrial workers increased in all thirteen of the countries included. In four of them, including post-Perón Argentina, the rates of wage increase were lower than those of GDP per capita. In eight others, industrial wages outpaced GDP per capita; in three cases—Chile, Colombia, and Peru—by a ratio of more than two to one. Then, in the second period shown in table 3.2, from 1970 to 1980, the picture goes the other way. Real wages in the industrial sector decreased in eight of the fifteen countries included. In all eight cases of falling real wages, GDP per capita was increasing. Industrial workers were certainly not privileged recipients of rising relative incomes in this decade.

Two distinct patterns are visible in those countries in which industrial wages rose very little or fell in the 1970s. In one set of countries, agricultural wages went up and reduced the degree of inequality within the wage structure; in the other, agricultural as well as industrial earnings went down sharply. Rural wages rose more rapidly than industrial in Brazil, Colombia, Costa Rica, and Ecuador, and more rapidly than GDP per capita in Colombia and Costa Rica. That pattern is distinctly more favorable for reduction of poverty than the contrary of stagnant rural earnings in the presence of rising industrial wages. The two countries in which rural wages took

[35] Richard C. Webb, "Wage Policy and Income Distribution in Developing Countries," in Charles R. Frank and Richard Webb, eds., *Income Distribution and Growth in the Less-Developed Countries* (Washington, D.C.: Brookings, 1977).

TABLE 3.2. Changes in Real Wages Compared to Changes in Gross Domestic Product Per Capita, 1956–1972 and 1970–1980

	Annual percentage rates of change					
	1950s to early 1970s		1970 to 1980			
	1	2	3	4	5	6
	Real wages, manufacturing 1956–72	GDP per capita 1959–71	Real wages Industry	Agriculture (avg)	(min)	GDP per capita
Argentina	0.5	2.6	−5.5		−7.3[a]	0.8
Brazil	2.3	3.1	4.5	5.2[a]		6.0
Chile	4.6	2.1	1.0		1.1	0.8
Colombia	4.7	1.9	−0.2	4.0		3.3
Costa Rica	0.5[a]	2.2[a]	2.3		4.3[a]	3.0
Dominican Republic	3.6	1.0	−1.0[a]			4.3
Ecuador	4.1	1.8	5.0		5.4	5.7
El Salvador	—	—	−0.7		−1.6	0.2
Guatemala	1.8	2.1	−4.5		[b]	2.7
Mexico	3.8	3.9	1.4		2.4	3.8
Nicaragua	7.1	3.5	−3.0[a]		−2.8	−1.5
Panama	5.5	4.7	[b]		3.1	3.0
Peru	4.1	1.8	−1.4		−0.7	
						0.8
Uruguay	—	—	−7.2	−4.5		2.5
Venezuela	2.7[a]	0.6[a]	0.6[a]			1.5

SOURCES: Columns 1 and 2 from Richard Webb, "Wage Policy and Income Distribution in Developing Countries," in Charles R. Frank, Jr., and Richard C. Webb, eds., *Income Distribution and Growth in the Less-Developed Countries* (Washington, D.C.: Brookings Institution, 1977), table 2, p. 241; columns 3–5 from PREALC, *Mercado de Trabajo en Cifras, 1950–1980* (Santiago: Oficina Internacional de Trabajo, 1982), cuadro III-3, pp. 149–51; column 6 from Inter-American Development Bank, *Economic and Social Progress in Latin America, 1984 Report* (Washington, D.C.: IDB, 1984), table 3, p. 420.

[a] Estimates for these countries are for shorter intervals within stated periods.

[b] Contradictory indicators; no dependable estimate.

steep plunges, alongside sharply lower industrial wages, were Argentina and Uruguay, two of the countries taken over during this decade by highly conservative authoritarian regimes. These joint wage decreases in both industry and agriculture were testimony above all to a determined political drive to favor incomes of property owners and to reduce the power of labor. They were not in any sense a simple return to market forces ironing out distorted wage patterns.

Downward pressure on wages in general, as distinct from equalizing changes, was defended in the Southern Cone countries by the argument that whenever there is a great deal of unemployment or underemployment falling real wages could reduce it by encouraging firms to substitute labor for other factors of production. Unemployment, in this view, is evidence that wages are too high relative to productivity. That argument has a sufficient logical basis to deserve consideration but it can go seriously wrong. Trends of wage increases exceeding the growth of productivity may truly be adverse for growth of employment, and they were in some countries in the early postwar years. But to apply the same logic to an effort to restore employment in conditions of macroeconomic contraction is at the least pointless and may easily make things worse. If a government uses macroeconomic deflation of demand to force down wages and prices, wages may go down but the net consequence is bound to be falling, not rising, employment.[36] If the dominant goal of national policy is to raise employment, a necessary part of the solution is to bring aggregate demand up to the level of productive capacity, rather than drive demand down to force wages down. The possibility of wage levels adverse for employment is real, and an important consideration for long-term strategy, but it is totally inappropriate for short-run policy in the midst of recession.

For some structuralists, even the idea of any long-run change in employment prospects through changes in wages relative to other factor costs is a dubious proposition: methods of production are seen as technically determined and relatively inflexible. In that view, wage rates could go below subsistence before the economy would arrive at full employment by this route. The process of adjustment

---

[36] Alejandro Foxley, *Latin American Experiments in Neoconservative Economics* (Berkeley: University of California Press, 1983), emphasizes the contrast between Brazilian success in raising employment by combining concern for relative prices with promotion of aggregate demand, and the Chilean result of rising *un*employment after real wages were reduced.

would be through starvation. Adam Smith and Thomas Malthus saw this possibility, and they were right.

In principle this is an empirical question, and many studies have tried to answer it. They consistently show that the degrees of variability in response to changing factor prices are greater than zero, though in many activities not very high. Some lines of production, particularly in new industries, have relatively fixed technologies regardless of factor prices; more traditional kinds of manufactured goods often allow for widely different ratios of employment to output.[37] One of the best of these empirical studies, examining the engineering characteristics of a long list of industries, reached the conclusion that, in the countries studied, there was no significant room for increasing employment by decreasing wages. But this was not because of totally inflexible methods of production, it was because differences in wages among these countries had already led to different techniques of production absorbing as much labor as could efficiently be employed.[38]

Given that the logic of variable factor proportions is valid in many, though by no means all, activities, rates of growth of industrial wages exceeding growth of productivity probably do slow up increases in employment. As an indication of the possible magnitudes involved, a study of wages and employment in five semi-industrialized Latin American countries for the period 1963–1972 concluded that the rate of growth of employment in the industrial sector in these countries could have been raised from its actual 3.6 percent to something between 5 and 7 percent a year, if the rate of growth of real wages had been held to a range of 2 to 3 percent a year instead of its actual average growth of 3.7 percent.[39]

If one wanted to design a wage policy solely concerned with employment creation, it probably should be the kind envisaged in the Lewis model: real wages in the modern sector would not rise until unskilled labor becomes scarce. But any target of constant real wages within a process of rising national income is probably unten-

[37] Meller, "Enfoques"; R. Albert Berry and Richard Sabot, "Labour Market Performance in Developing Countries: A Survey," *World Development* 6 (1978), pp. 1199–1242; Henry J. Bruton, "Economic Development and Labor Use: A Review," in Edgar O. Edwards, ed., *Employment in Developing Countries* (New York: Columbia University Press, 1974).

[38] David Forsythe, Norman S. McBain, and Robert F. Solomon, "Technical Rigidity and Appropriate Technology in Less Developed Countries," *World Development* 8 (May–June 1980), pp. 37–98.

[39] Selowsky, "Income Distribution," pp. 78–79.

able in an open political system responsive to majority preferences. A democratic system must be able to include the majority of workers in the gains of growth in most years, at least as long as national income is growing. That should be consistent with rising employment provided that the society can reach some understanding on sustainable rates of wage increase. A possible guide would be to allow or to promote increases at the rate at which income per capita rises, but not faster than that until market forces act to generate more rapid increases for unorganized labor in traditional activities. Such a rule could result either in more inequality (of urban wages relative to profits), or more equality (by bringing up the incomes of the very poor more rapidly). A tighter rule against wage increases might be more favorable for employment growth, or a faster rate of wage increase more favorable for political cooperation; an open society would have room to choose alternative viable solutions according to public preferences. But it is hard to see how an open society could be maintained unless economic strategy includes rising wages and also keeps the increases within the limits of possible growth of production.

6. Conclusions: The Ideology of the Employment Model

Limits on the rate at which people can move out of low-productivity occupations and rapid growth of the labor force have been among the most potent factors acting to aggravate inequality and poverty in Latin America. If the rate of growth of productive employment could be raised and kept above that of the labor force this could gradually turn market forces in the direction of rising real incomes for all workers. Economic growth alone may fall to do it. Growth without adequate employment opportunities can leave the majority of the people out of the picture. In some countries, it has.

The Lewis model helps clarify some of the most important features of Latin American development, but it also puts some of them out of focus. It overstresses the importance of industrial investment as opposed to investment in agriculture, treats inequality as a natural and in a sense desirable aspect of economic growth for long periods, and implies that everything will eventually be corrected by market forces. It suggests that things will work out well in the long run if existing inequities are accepted and the institutional structure is left intact. A particularly strong critic of the whole approach,

Keith Griffin, attacks it for many reasons but perhaps especially because it directs attention away from what matters most. "The essence of development is institutional reform."[40]

It is certainly true that the Lewis model directs attention to issues of resource allocation and investment rather than institutional change, and it is in this sense a conservative approach to analysis of development. But the analysis contains significant clues about desirable economic policy for any regime that wishes to reduce poverty, in particular the importance of employment creation. Especially in the poorest countries, opportunities for productive employment have not been growing fast enough to keep up with the growth of the labor force: the situation is deteriorating in the sense of failure to move toward the turning point of the Lewis model. But in the 1970s Brazil and Colombia were, by policies favoring employment creation along with sustained growth, able to start a long-delayed process of bringing up real incomes of labor in agriculture. That does not mean that structural changes such as redistribution of land ownership, better education in the rural areas, or more egalitarian tax systems lose relevance. They could all be important contributors to reduction of poverty and of inequality. But the goal of institutional reform should not be allowed to block attention to incentives favorable for creation of employment opportunities, because that could be a powerful way to reduce poverty while contributing to the possibilities of growth as well.

[40] Griffin, *Underdevelopment*, p. 49.

FOUR

EXTERNAL TRADE, INDUSTRIALIZATION, AND ECONOMIC GROWTH

Structures of production and trade are intimately bound up with questions of how each society is run, by whom, for what purposes. Relatively open international trade, the basic orientation of Latin American policy from the mid-nineteenth century up to the 1930s, can and did help to raise national income. But it differentially favors the incomes and the influence of exporters, who in nineteenth-century Latin America were primarily the owners of large estates and mineral resources. Given concentrated ownership of the resources used for exports, their growth can increase concentration of income, leave out the poor, and work against diversification of production. Exports in general, regardless of effects on income distribution, can also pull societies away from their own distinctive values toward those of the outside world. In the nineteenth century that last consideration was often regarded favorably, in the belief that greater contact with the outside world would pull Latin America away from Iberian-style centralization and scholasticism toward the cultural and technical vitality of northern Europe. The more conservative side in the nineteenth century, born again as the more radical perspective in recent decades, takes the contrary way of looking at the same issues: an open economy and multiplication of contacts with Europe and the United States are seen as a sellout, as acceptance of domination by external values.

Rejection or at least severe limitation of trade gained wide support during and following the depression of the 1930s. The depression demonstrated to everyone that countries dependent on primary exports could be pushed back into poverty by adverse changes in the world economy, immune to national control. That blow greatly reinforced persistent pressures from local industrial interests to increase protection against imports, and from the modernizing side of these societies eager to escape from economic and political control by conservative landowners. Looking back, it is hard to see how these mutually supporting pressures could have been resisted. But it is easy to see how they could, as they did in many countries, lead down a self-defeating path by building structures of production dependent on inputs of production supplies, capital goods, and foreign technology, while turning away from exports and weakening the ability to earn the foreign exchange needed to pay for the inputs required by this style of growth.

The problem was not the goal of industrialization, or modernization, but the mixture of inconsistent pressures created by the particular form of the process. Where national economic strategies were better designed—or were forced into more viable compromises by conflicts among domestic interest groups—the process worked moderately well. And where economic strategies were revised to deal with problems as they became clearer, the countries concerned made distinctly better headway than the rest, both in economic terms and in avoidance of drastic political reaction.

1. GROWTH LED BY PRIMARY EXPORTS

Relationships with the external world have been something of a plague for Latin America ever since Columbus. Spain destroyed well-organized prior societies and tied down production and trade of the colonies in the sixteenth and seventeenth centuries for its own intended benefit. In the late eighteenth century both Spain and Portugal adopted more active policies of trade promotion, though still very much under their regulation. That brought out a pattern of internal conflict highly suggestive of issues two centuries later. Legally regulated trade was conducted by designated merchants or trading monopolies, adept at using governmental rules to ensure their own profitability. They saw themselves as the defenders of orderly local markets and production, against the destabilizing pressure of landowners who wanted to break out to sell freely in external markets.[1] The landowning export interests, in conflict with governmental restrictions and with the interests of those benefiting from the system of controls, neatly foreshadowed the positions taken by landowners in the Argentina of Perón in the late 1940s, fighting against a new system of trade control designed to foster industrialization.

In the first decades after independence, conflicts over questions of trade control remained very much alive, with the political balance swinging back and forth between a liberal side seeking a more open system and a conservative side trying to protect more self-contained

[1] Claudio Véliz, *The Centralist Tradition of Latin America* (Princeton: Princeton University Press, 1980), ch. 6.

economies. The relatively stagnant world economy in this period did not exercise any strong pull toward expansion of exports. But the context changed greatly in the middle of the nineteenth century as the industrial revolution in Europe and North America began to raise incomes there more rapidly and to create strong markets for raw materials. Rising demand for their primary products then pulled Latin America toward exports and the domestic political balance toward domination by landowner-export interests.[2]

Economic and political dominance by landowner interests in most countries of the region was backed up intellectually by arguments against Iberian-style social and economic regulation, in favor of greater reliance on market forces and especially on free trade. The juxtaposition of a highly selective class interest with the case for free trade based on the principle of comparative advantage naturally led everyone who favored industrialization (or simply hated the dominant landowning class), to detest the ideas of free trade and comparative advantage. That persisting identification of export-led growth with landowner interests turned out to have high costs in the years following World War II: it acted to discredit and delay strategies that would have permitted steadier growth through increasing *industrial* exports.

International trade should help raise national income by directing productive effort toward greater output of goods that have higher value outside the country than they would in a closed internal market, and by moving productive resources away from those activities for which domestic opportunity costs are higher than the costs of getting the same goods through imports. That principle first came to be accepted as a guide to policy in England in the same period that Latin American countries gained their political independence. For England, its adoption meant that the country's industrialists could count on low-cost imports of raw materials and on freedom to pursue markets for the industrial products in which they led the world, while domestic agricultural producers were constrained by foreign competition and rural workers were driven into urban labor markets. For Latin America, as for the United States at the time, it meant instead that agricultural and mineral producers gained from production for world markets while manufacturers were forced to cope with competition from more advanced European producers.

[2] E. Bradford Burns, *The Poverty of Progress: Latin America in the Nineteenth Century* (Berkeley: University of California Press, 1980).

Rising exports of primary products certainly did generate good rates of increase in national income. Argentina's output per capita probably increased about 1.5 percent a year between 1850 and 1900, and the growth rates of Mexico and Chile were not far behind.[3] Carlos Díaz Alejandro estimates Argentina's income per capita in 1880 at about $470, expressed in 1970 dollars. That was probably higher than income per capita in Italy at the time, and higher than per capita income in most developing countries a century later. His estimates for Argentina and Brazil indicate that both countries were able to triple their income per capita between 1880 and 1930. In both countries, fairly substantial industrial sectors developed in response to growing national markets, some of it aided by spasmodic protection and some without any protection at all.[4]

These rates of growth for the leading countries were similar to those in Europe in the same periods. They were probably higher than typical for the smaller Latin American countries, especially those for which export production was under foreign ownership. Cardoso and Faletto make a useful distinction between those countries in which the production of exports was predominantly under domestic ownership, particularly Argentina and Brazil, and those in which foreign investors owned the property and gained much of the income from exports.[5] The former not only retained a larger share of export earnings but also, perhaps more importantly, gained more capacity to organize production and to deal with changing markets.

Considering the period from the 1870s to the 1930s, Prebisch and ECLA thought that it was possible to identify a trend of progressively worsening terms of trade for primary exports, holding down

[3] David Felix, "Consumption, Economic Growth, and Income Distribution."

[4] Carlos Díaz Alejandro, "No Less than One Hundred Years of Argentine Economic History Plus Some Comparisons," in Gustav Ranis and Robert L. West, eds., *Comparative Development Perspectives: Essays in Honor of Lloyd Reynolds* (Boulder: Westview Press, 1984), table 4, p. 331, and Díaz Alejandro, *Essays on the Economic History of the Argentine Republic*, pp. 273–68. Díaz Alejandro emphasizes the use of protection in Argentina, but Nathaniel Leff gives more stress to Brazil's ability to industrialize in sectors not given protection, including production of capital equipment for domestic industry: *The Brazilian Capital Goods Industry, 1919–1964* (Cambridge: Harvard University Press, 1968), pp. 134–142.

[5] Cardoso and Faletto, *Dependency and Development*, introduction. They characterize Argentina and Brazil as dependent but with the kind of "dependency where the productive system was nationally controlled," as contrasted to "enclave" economies. The Argentine case does not fit the picture quite as well as Brazil because foreign ownership was dominant for the packing houses involved in meat exports.

the growth of Latin American income by transferring the gains of rising productivity to the industrialized countries. The argument was based on a valid presumption, that structures of demand move away from basic primary products toward industrial as incomes rise, and was backed up by statistical analysis believed to demonstrate a persistent adverse trend. But the logic was incomplete and the statistical demonstration did not stand up well to more systematic examinations.[6] The argument took a strong hold anyway, perhaps because it supported a widespread wish to promote industrialization. It could be interpreted as a slightly out-of-focus way to direct attention to a real contrast in world market trends: the *volume* of industrial exports has in most periods grown much faster than that of the basic primary exports. This contrast in terms of quantities does not have quite the same ring of taking away income from Latin America by adverse price changes, but it still means that industrial exporting is the more promising market. A strategy of redirecting the structure of production toward industrial exports (and toward those particular primary products that have relatively high income elasticity of demand) could have done a good deal to raise the rate of economic growth. To join in the growth of world exports for such products would have been a rewarding improvement; to withdraw from trade in favor of redirecting production to the home market was a very different response, throwing away valuable opportunities.

Growth of traditional primary exports in the nineteenth century had positive effects on national income but probably did not help much if at all to reduce poverty. Exporting made the domestic prices of agricultural products and of land higher than they would have been in a closed economy. An export boom for food products means almost inescapably that domestic food prices rise too, with regressive effects similar to the imposition of a selective tax on food. If land ownership is widely dispersed, or if labor is so scarce that increased agricultural production for exports drives up wages, then

---

[6] Charles P. Kindleberger, *The Terms of Trade: A European Case Study* (New York: MIT and Wiley, 1956); and Theodore Morgan, "The Long-run Terms of Trade Between Agriculture and Manufacturing," *Economic Development and Cultural Change* 8 (October 1959), pp. 1–23. A more recent examination using ingenious methods of dealing with interpretation of the data has come closer to support of the ECLA finding for the originally debated seventy-year trend up to 1938, though it also concludes that the hypothesis does not fit the postwar years: John Spraos, "The Statistical Debate on the Net Barter Terms of Trade Between Primary Commodities and Manufactures," *Economic Journal* 90 (March 1980), pp. 107–28.

trade may decrease inequality of income. It probably did not in Latin America: real earnings of rural labor rose in some periods and fell in others, but land ownership and earnings from exports of primary products were highly concentrated.[7]

Such conflicts between positive effects of primary exports on growth of national income and negative effects on the poor have been highly important in Central America in recent years. Land previously used for peasant production under rental or crop-sharing agreements, or simply left in undergrowth and at least potentially available for subsistence farming, were brought into modern commercial production at a rapid rate in the 1950s and 1960s, primarily for cotton and meat exports. The change was a response to new technical possibilities on the production side, particularly insecticides and new fertilizers, combined with credit from international institutions, technical aide in upgrading quality, and help through improved access to the U.S. market. The growth of export earnings was spectacular, and the accompanying development of local industries in processing exports and providing inputs was striking as well. But at the same time thousands of peasant producers were displaced by changes in access to land, especially by a switch to demands for cash rentals at the high rates reflecting the increased value of land in production for exports. The market worked powerfully to squeeze out low-value uses of land, and to squeeze out low-income producers in the process. The problem was that there were not nearly enough higher-income places to go: between displacement of small producers from agriculture and rapid population growth it is very likely that the numbers in absolute poverty increased all through the export boom, and even more likely that these pressures contributed significantly to the increasing violence in the region.[8]

It is not necessarily the case that new primary exports have adverse effects on the poor. That is an unlikely outcome with labor-intensive new exports such as flowers, or possibly with high-value fruit exports, with seafood, or many other activities that can provide

[7] Land ownership is discussed in chapter 5 below. Díaz Alejandro explains the negative effects of export booms for food products, both for questions of access to land and for food prices, in "Latin America in the 1930s," pp. 17–49 in Rosemary Thorp, ed., *Latin America in the 1930s: The Role of the Periphery in World Crisis* (New York: St. Martin's, 1984). See also Díaz Alejandro, "Open Economy, Closed Polity?" in Diana Tussie, ed., *Latin America in the World Economy* (New York: St. Martin's, 1983).

[8] Robert G. Williams, *Export Agriculture and the Crisis in Central America* (Chapel Hill: University of North Carolina Press, 1986).

new earnings opportunities with little or no opportunity cost in withdrawing land from small producers. It would also not be the outcome where small owners themselves produce for export so that the advantage of higher earnings is widely spread. It would be a potentially costly mistake to discourage primary exports in general. But for many technical and ownership conditions actually encountered in Latin America, growth of particular primary exports can be seriously detrimental to the poor.

On the import side, trade helps to hold down prices and to discourage high-cost production. It can be especially helpful for the poor if it provides the products they need at low cost, particularly food. In Latin America, it did not help much. At least up to the import substitution period of the 1930s, imports were chiefly manufactured consumer goods purchased by middle and upper income groups: their main direct effect was to raise living standards of higher income groups by increasing supplies and holding down prices of the goods more important to them than to the poor.

The general conclusion that the character of Latin American trade in the nineteenth century was more favorable for the rich than for the poor does not depend on any assumption of deteriorating terms of trade: the poor might have been better off if prices of food exports had been lower and prices of imported consumer goods had been higher. The conclusion depends more on the concentration of land ownership and the elasticity of labor supply. Those conditions varied greatly among countries. In Argentina, land ownership was less concentrated than in most other countries and labor was not in surplus. Immigration was encouraged to provide additional labor, but even then Argentina developed a less unequal distribution of income than most of the rest of the region.[9] Different patterns of land ownership acted in other countries to alter the consequences of trade. In Colombia and Costa Rica, as contrasted to Brazil and El Salvador, the coffee exports important to all of them were produced mainly by small farmers: the same export crop helped to lessen inequality in the first two countries and probably to increase it in the latter two.[10] Costa Rica's combination of available

[9] On the role of immigration, see Díaz Alejandro, "No Less than One Hundred Years." Differences in income distributions cannot be compared in any dependable way for this period, but when the necessary date became available for recent years they showed Argentina to be less unequal than most of the rest of Latin America: see table 9.1 below.

[10] William Paul McGreevey, *An Economic History of Colombia, 1845–1930* (Cambridge: Cambridge University Press, 1971), pp. 196–99.

land and scarce labor, with no significant Indian population to exploit made it one of the least unequal of all the Latin American countries.[11]

In addition to its direct effects on incomes, international trade can be a powerful stimulus to learning about the ideas, markets, technology, and life styles of the outside world. That can be viewed as a positive process of learning and broadening, and it was seen in this way by Latin America's dominant elites in the nineteenth century.[12] Philip II in the days of Spain's imperial power saw it differently, as a threat of corrupting foreign influence. He tried to shut out not only competing commodities but books and ideas as well.[13] In a sense, modern criticism of dependence takes much the same view: external contact is seen as reinforcing attachments not only to foreign goods and technology, but to the capitalism and materialism from which Latin Americans need to be sheltered.

It is certainly true that a strong orientation toward imported products and technology can be costly. David Felix has contrasted consumer behavior in Mexico from 1895 to the 1920s, before the days of import substitution, with that of Japan in the same period. His results show that as industrialization proceeded, Japanese demand remained more firmly attached than Mexican to traditional artisan and small-industry products. Despite much lower tariffs on imports in Japan than in Mexico, the latter's consumption pattern was the one that turned more in favor of imports. In Mexico, employment was driven down in the craft sector faster than it increased in the modern sector. In Japan, "the craft sector was a technologically progressive sector, with rising productivity and real wages, not a technologically stagnant employer of last resort."[14]

Nations and groups within them surely do differ in degrees of attachment to traditional products and life styles. The point made by Felix is an important aspect of Latin American dependence and supports the structuralist position that relative prices may be of secondary significance in explaining consumer and producer behavior.

[11] Mitchell A. Seligson, *Peasants of Costa Rica and the Rise of Agrarian Capitalism* (Madison: University of Wisconsin, 1980). "Peasants found that because of a scarcity of manpower they could sell their labor for a high price to coffee plantation owners. Those who chose to reject this alternative could do so only because they had another: farming the virgin farmlands off the meseta" (p. 154).

[12] Burns, *The Poverty of Progress.*

[13] J. H. Elliot, *Imperial Spain, 1469–1716* (London: Edward Arnold, 1963), especially ch. 6. Foreign books were banned in 1558 and all Spanish books required prior licensing. In 1559 Spanish students were forbidden to study abroad.

[14] Felix, "Interrelations."

It complements another important consideration in the case of Japan, namely, that the Japanese did not allow foreign investment for production within the country. The two considerations reinforce each other, both expressing a behavioral pattern that was favorable for Japanese autonomy and economic growth. But it does not follow that Latin America would have done much the same if trade had been shut off in the nineteenth century. The area's culture would surely have remained close to Europe in any case. Greater isolation might have fostered brilliantly independent thought and technical change, or it might have fostered a more stagnant society by shutting off the stimulus of new ideas. It is impossible to be sure, but the experience of Spain after Philip II suggests that the latter outcome might be the more likely.

Although patterns of influence are clearly important, the propensity of Latin American countries to favor imported industrial products may have been more fundamentally a consequence of domestic inequality. The majority of the people of the region—probably the whole Indian population as well as the non-Indian peasants and landless rural labor—must have remained attached to traditional products: they had no alternative. But they counted for little in consumer markets because they had so little income. Only a minority of Latin Americans could enter markets for imported consumer goods, and their preferences dominated total spending. If their preferences had been oriented more toward domestic products that would have been helpful, but the basic factor was the high degree of inequality, which made their preferences so dominant.

2. The 1930s and the Adoption of Import-Substituting Industrialization

The world depression of the 1930s cracked the foundations of the primary export model and drove Latin America toward intensive import substitution as a response to the collapse of earnings from exports. The initial impact of the depression forced down incomes throughout the region, but in many countries national measures to cope with the collapse began to favor recovery with a greater component of industrial activity than ever before. Díaz Alejandro distinguishes two groups of countries in terms of more passive and more "reactive" policy response during the depression. Argentina, Brazil, and Chile were the most active. The Central American countries along with Cuba, Mexico and Peru were among the more passive. "Colombia, as usual, had an intermediate set of policies."[15] Activist policies included both direct barriers to imports and, in contrast to the following period of deliberate import substitution, aggressive devaluation. In the deflationary context of the 1930s the devaluations did not provoke offsetting domestic inflation. For 1930–34, compared to 1925–29, prices of imports were raised greatly relative to domestic alternatives, creating powerful incentives to shift demand away from imports toward domestic production.

With exchange rates and import barriers acting together to redirect demand for manufactured goods to the domestic market, manufacturing production began to rise much more rapidly than gross domestic product. Furthermore, industrial growth in the 1930s and through the Second World War was labor intensive, raising employment rapidly, because it did not rely on imports of foreign machinery and equipment. The availability of imported capital goods was restricted as well as that of consumer goods. With strong market demand but limited access to imported equipment, domestic producers adapted productive capacity in ways appropriate to their own managerial capacities and to the availability of labor. Some of the countries achieved exceptionally high rates of gain in total factor productivity.[16] The combination of domestic technology and high demand proved to be a recipe for a fairly healthy process of import substitution. But that was not the recipe used by the more active countries after the end of the war.

As world trade became open again after 1945, the Latin American countries that had established a great deal of new industrial capacity sensibly resolved to keep the process going. Argentina and Brazil were the leaders in what became a widely followed path of protection and state promotion to keep industrializing through import substitution. This could be seen as an extension of the preceding response to the 1930s, but there was one costly difference. Imports of consumer goods were still restricted but industrialists were allowed, or even encouraged, to import the most modern possible kinds of capital equipment. With that change, import substitution fostered increasing technological dependence and became much less helpful for employment.

The main features of the import-substitution strategy included:

[15] Díaz Alejandro, "Latin America in the 1930s."

[16] Henry J. Bruton, "Productivity Growth in Latin America," *American Economic Review* 57 (December 1967), pp. 1099–1116. See the comments and partial revision of the measures in this study by Constantine Michalopoulos, "Productivity Growth in Latin America: Comment," *American Economic Review* 58 (1968), pp. 435-39.

(1) protection applied to consumer-manufactured goods but much less if at all to capital equipment, in order to hold down the costs of producers' goods; (2) differential exchange rates or retention of overvalued rates also intended to keep down costs of imported equipment and production materials; (3) tax incentives and direct subsidies to encourage investment; and (4) fixed low interest rates for the same purpose.[17] Industrial investors were sheltered and supported without regard for their costs of production. But the strategy was broader than mere support for industrialists. Public-sector spending and promotional activity increased greatly as well. In Argentina especially, and to a lesser degree in Brazil, the government supported increases in urban wages and greater organization of labor. The influence of professional classes and especially of civil servants gained markedly. It was not so much a one-dimensional triumph of industrial interests as a general shift of power to the urban sector, especially to organized groups, at the expense of previously dominant primary export interests. And, to a great extent, at the expense of the unorganized poor.

The strategy of import substitution to stimulate investment and industrialization got results. Arthur Lewis had suggested that the key to sustained economic growth would be to get the share of total product used for investment up from something on the order of 6 percent of 12 percent. He was wrong about that being a sufficient key, but in fact the Latin American regional average of investment to GDP reached 18 percent in 1955 and 22 percent by 1970.[18] The latter ratio is well above the historical average of the northern industrialized countries (though not up to such exceptional cases as Japan and the Soviet Union). Rates of growth of industrial production are shown in table 4.1. They speeded up from 4.0 percent a year for 1950–1960 to 6.3 percent for 1965–1970 and remained high until world contraction and external debt problems slowed the region abruptly from 1980. These rates of increase exceeded those of the industrialized countries from 1960 to 1980, though they do

[17] Werner Baer, "Import Substitution and Industrialization in Latin America: Experiences and Interpretations," *Latin American Research Review* 7, 1 (1972), pp. 95–122; Henry J. Bruton, "The Import-Substitution Strategy of Economic Development: A Survey," *Pakistan Development Review* 10 (summer 1970), pp. 123–46; Albert Hirschman, "The Political Economy of Import-Substituting Industrialization in Latin America," *Quarterly Journal of Economics* 82 (February 1968), pp. 2–32; Ian Little, Tibor Scitovsky, and Maurice Scott, *Industry and Trade in Some Developing Countries* (Oxford: Oxford University Press for the OECD, 1970); Joaquin Muns, *Industrialización y crecimiento de los paises en desarrollo* (Barcelona: Ediciones Ariel, 1972).

[18] World Bank, *World Tables*, 3d ed. (Baltimore: Johns Hopkins University Press for the World Bank, 1984), vol. 1, p. 501.

TABLE 4.1. Manufacturing Production in Latin America Compared to Other Regions: Growth Rates and Shares of Manufacturing in Gross Domestic Product, 1950–1981

A. *Annual rate of growth of manufacturing production, percent*

	1950–60	1960–65	1965–70	1970–77	1970–81
Latin America	4.0	5.2	6.3	5.8	4.8
Africa	—	8.3	7.1	5.6	6.6
East Asia	—	5.1	11.3	11.6	12.9
South Asia	6.4	8.7	4.0	4.3	4.2
Industrialized countries	6.1	5.7	5.7	2.8	2.7

B. *Manufacturing production as percent of gross domestic product*

	1960	1970	1977	1981
Latin America	20.8	24.2	26.5	20.7
Africa	11.5	13.2	13.2	8.0
East Asia	16.0	19.6	20.7	32.7
South Asia	13.1	13.6	15.5	16.4
Industrialized countries	28.7	27.1	27.0	20.4

SOURCES: World Bank, *World Tables*, 3d ed. (Washington, D.C.: World Bank, 1983), vol. 1, pp. 487 and 510, for all except 1970–77 growth and 1977 structure of production; 1977 data from *World Tables 1980*, pp. 372–73 and 390.

not match the spectacular rise that began in East Asia in the middle 1960s.

Manufacturing production constituted 20.8 percent of GDP in Latin America as of 1960, considerably above the share in all other developing regions but well below the ratio of 28.7 percent for the northern industrialized countries. In the next twenty years the difference disappeared: by 1977 the share of manufacturing was practically equal in Latin America and in the industrialized countries, at 27 percent. When the shares fell on both sides in the recession of 1981 they fell equally, to just above 20 percent in both cases. Apart from cyclical variations, the long-term trend of demand in all countries gradually moves away from primary toward industrial products in the early stages of growth, and then at higher income levels more toward increasing shares of expenditures on services. The share of manufacturing in GDP in Latin America caught up with the northern countries both because it was growing in Latin America and because the structure of demand in the north had moved more toward services. But differences in trends of demand are not the whole story. For East Asia, the striking rise in the manufacturing share of total output was much more a matter of success in exporting industrial products. By 1973 exports of manufactures equalled 40 percent or more of manufacturing output in South Korea, Singapore, and Taiwan, but less than 5 percent for Argentina, Brazil, and Mexico.[19] One of the most costly aspects of the import-substitution strategy in Latin America was that it worked against industrial exports and held the growth of manufacturing down to the rate of growth of domestic demand.

Official measures of manufacturing as a share of GDP for individual countries show a range of almost three to one in 1955 and again in 1977, with Argentina's manufacturing share at 29.4 percent and Honduras at 10.3 percent in the former year, and Argentina still highest at 36.5 percent with Bolivia lowest at 12.9 in 1977. But there is a problem with these measures, especially for Argentina: they are systematically distorted by protection. Restrictions on competing imports allow industrial producers to raise their prices above outside levels, making the domestic ratio of industrial to agricultural prices higher than that prevailing in world trade. Such changes in relative prices make the share of industrial production in GDP, valued at domestic prices, higher than it would be for the same physical volume of output in a more open economy. Argentina's national accounts show manufacturing to be 31.3 percent of gross domestic expenditure in 1958, but if production had been valued at world prices this ratio would have been only 22.5 percent.[20]

3. Costs of Import-Substitution Strategies as Implemented

The central problems with the strategy as used in Latin America were that it fostered production methods adverse for employment,

---

[19] Bela Balassa, "Export Incentives and Export Performance in Developing Countries: A Comparative Analysis," *Welwirtschaftliches Archiv* 114 (1978), table 1, p. 36. See also Gustav Ranis, "Challenges and Opportunities Posed by Asia's Superexporters: Implications for Manufactured Exports from Latin America," in Werner Baer and Malcolm Gillis, eds. *Export Diversification and the New Protectionism* (Champaign: University of Illinois for the National Bureau of Economic Research, 1981), pp. 204–30.

[20] Little, Scitovsky, and Scott, *Industry and Trade*, table 2.12, p. 73.

hurt the poor, blocked the possible growth of industrial exports, encouraged high-cost consumer goods industries while impeding vertical integration, and accelerated multinational entry into domestic industry. The difficulties were to some extent inherent in the desired transition from a primary export economy, but they were magnified by particularly costly methods. Individual countries demonstrated by their very different degrees of departure from criteria of economic efficiency the scope for holding down, or for aggravating, the strains of the process. Two indicators of such differences in degree are given in table 4.2: levels of protection for industrial producers of consumer durable goods, and the extent to which subsidies through negative real interest rates were used to reduce the relative cost of capital equipment, and so to favor capital-intensive methods of production.

TABLE 4.2. Comparisons of Tariff Rates and Real Interest Rates for Six Countries at the End of the 1950s

	Average tariffs and charges for semimanufactured and durable consumer goods (percent) 1957–59	Excess of rate of inflation over reference rate of interest (average percentage points) 1958–60
Argentina	139	17.5[a]
Brazil	143	21.0
Chile	96	8.4
Colombia	48	3.5
Mexico	58	2.0
Peru	25	1.2

SOURCES: Rates of inflation from International Monetary Fund, *International Financial Statistics*, 1972 Supplement, using indexes of the cost of living; central bank discount rates from ibid. except for Argentina; Argentine interest rate from Banco Central de la República de Argentina, *Memoria anual, 1960* (Buenos Aires, 1961); tariff rates from Santiago Macario, "Protectionism and Industrialization in Latin America," *Economic Bulletin for Latin America* (March 1964), table 5, p. 75.

[a] The interest rate comparison for Argentina is for 1960 only, using the Treasury bill rate for 360 days. All other interest rates are averages for 1958–60, for the central bank discount rates.

Of the countries listed in table 4.2 all except Peru were at the time following strategies of import substitution. (Peru still had a relatively open economy at the end of the 1950s, then moved to high protection a decade later.) Although all the others were in a sense trying to do the same thing, the table makes clear that Argentina and Brazil stood out for much more aggressive degrees of protection and interest rate subsidies than Colombia and Mexico. Argentina and Brazil themselves differed in many ways not brought out by the table: although national strategies penalized primary exporters severely, the degree was much greater in the former. Besides protection, the methods included steep taxes on exports and the use of multiple exchange rates designed to take away income from exporters while subsidizing imports of industrial equipment. A natural result of these differences was that Argentina encountered foreign exchange difficulties more quickly, and in more severe degree, than Brazil. On the positive side, Colombia and Mexico remained in relatively close touch with world prices. When policies emphasizing industrialization for the home market became clearly untenable, Colombia and Mexico could move toward export promotion with much less trauma than Argentina and Brazil.

Since the first purpose of the strategy was to promote faster industrialization, it was natural to use subsidized credit and other means of reducing equipment costs for investors, but these policies worked against the interests of the underemployed because they favored adoption of the latest and most labor-saving foreign technology. Preferences of producers are biased toward labor-saving technology in any case: machinery does not go on strike or seize the factory. But when the preference operates to destroy employment opportunities in a low-income country, the appropriate response of economic policy is to make foreign machinery and the use of credit more expensive relative to the cost of labor. The policies adopted went in exactly the wrong direction.

Incentives favoring imports of capital goods also acted to discourage actual and potential domestic producers of capital equipment. The structure of industrial output was pulled in the direction of consumer goods rather than capital goods. Methods of production were pulled toward techniques relying more on capital and energy, and on specialized managerial and labor skills, than on unskilled labor. It was almost as if the system had been designed to increase demand and earnings for the people with capital and with access to education: to aid selectively the people with prior advantages.

Investment by foreign firms for domestic production was encouraged by restrictions on exports to the country, by the offer of protected markets, and by the fact that the upper income groups dominant in domestic markets wanted the consumer goods familiar to firms in the more industrialized countries. The conception of what was needed focused on the volume of investment and not on who the industrialists were. As dependency considerations came more to the fore, the multinationals came to be blamed for distorting the structure of production. They surely did add their own pressures to accentuate the distortions but the incentives were already there: they took advantage of a system that fostered costly choices by domestic and foreign producers alike.

For exporters of primary products, the strategy acted to discourage both production and exports by reducing the real income that could be earned from exporting, and the resources available to them for investment. In a sense, that was part of the purpose: to shift resources from the primary to the industrial sector. But it also meant holding down the country's earnings of the foreign exchange needed to pay for the equipment and supplies imported by the industrial sector. That handicap could have been resolved by stepping up industrial exports, but the same set of incentives worked to limit them as well. Protection raised the earnings possible from sales in the domestic market, and indirectly acted to raise the cost of production, while doing nothing to increase earnings from exporting. With the value of foreign exchange kept down by overvalued currencies, incentives to export were minimal. This balance of policy expressed a preference for more inner-directed development, less dependent on foreign markets, but it acted to restrict the rate of growth of each industry to the rate of growth of domestic demand and left the industrial sector unable to help finance its own import requirements.

As of the beginning of the 1960s the export structures of all the middle-income Latin American countries were badly out of balance with their structures of production: they remained almost entirely primary-product exporters even though they had developed substantial industrial sectors for sales to domestic markets. This imbalance responded to the structure of incentives stated above: it was not in any sense intrinsically impossible to export manufactured goods from new industrial sectors in developing countries. As of 1962, when Latin American exports of industrial products were only 5 percent of total exports, the lower income countries of East Asia, with smaller ratios of manufacturing output to GDP, had

achieved manufactured exports equal to 25 percent of their total
exports (table 4.3). When Latin American countries switched over
more toward export promotion themselves, it also worked for them:
the ratio of manufactures to total exports climbed to 22 percent by
1980.

Differences between the structures of production and of exports
are shown for seven countries in table 4.4. There is no reason to ex-

TABLE 4.3. Manufactured Goods as Shares of Total Commodity
Exports for Latin American Countries and East Asia, 1962 and
1980 (percent of total exports)

	1962	1980
Latin America and Caribbean	5.1	22.2
East Asia, excluding China	25.5	47.0
Argentina	3.2	23.2
Bolivia	—	2.7
Brazil	3.2	38.6
Chile	3.7	20.2
Colombia	3.4	20.3
Costa Rica	9.5	34.3
Cuba[a]	5	5
Ecuador	1.8	2.7
El Salvador	8.3	35.3
Guatemala	7.3	24.2
Honduras	2.0	12.5
Mexico	15.6	39.6
Nicaragua	2.3	13.8
Panama	2.8	8.9
Paraguay	11.4	11.3
Peru	1.0	17.0
Uruguay	4.4	38.2
Venezuela	6.1	1.7

SOURCE: World Bank, *World Tables*, 3d ed. (Washington, D.C.: World Bank, 1983),
vol. 1, pp. 519 and 521, for all except Cuba.

[a] Cuban ratios are for 1960 and 1980, from World Bank, *World Development Report
1983*, p. 166.

TABLE 4.4. Comparative Shares of Manufactured Products in
Exports and in Domestic Production for Seven Countries,
1960 and 1980

	1960			1980		
	1 Percent of exports	2 Percent of GDP	3 Ratio (1)/(2)	4 Percent of exports	5 Percent of GDP	6 Ratio (1)/(2)
Argentina	4	32	0.1	23	25	0.9
Brazil	3	26	0.1	39	27	1.4
Chile	4	29	0.1	20	21	0.95
Colombia	2	17	0.1	20	22	0.9
Costa Rica	5	14	0.4	34	20	1.7
Mexico	12	19	0.6	39	24	1.6
Peru	1	24	0.04	16	27	0.6

SOURCES: Column 1 from World Bank, *World Development Report 1981*, pp. 150–51;
columns 2 and 5 from *World Development Report 1982*, pp. 114–15, except for Argentina and Brazil, which are from *World Development Report 1983*, p. 153; column 4 also
from *World Development Report 1983*, pp. 166–67.

pect that the percentage of manufacturers in exports should match
exactly the percentage of manufacturing in total output: countries
with exceptionally good natural resources will normally have lower
shares of manufactured exports than countries without such primary products. This is a good part of the reason why the Latin
American shares are so much lower than those of East Asia. But
when such industrialized economies as Argentina and Brazil cannot
get manufactured exports higher than 3 or 4 percent of the total it
is indicative of grossly distorted incentives. What could be done was
shown clearly enough after their economic strategies were turned
away from extreme protection toward export promotion. As of
1960, the share of manufactures in total exports was for both of
these countries only one-tenth as high as the share of manufacturing in output; by 1980, the manufacturing share in exports was almost equal to that in production for Argentina and was higher than
the manufacturing share in production for Brazil, Costa Rica, and
Mexico. That structural transformation was a major step forward,
which had been unduly delayed by the earlier strategy.

To stress the prior bias against industrial exports, and the gains from removing it, is not meant to suggest that primary exports are unimportant or undesirable. Growth rates would have been higher, and dependency possibly less, if the total foreign exchange earnings from all exports had been kept higher, reducing the need for external credit. But in some respects industrial exports do have more positive connotations than traditional primary products. One of the most important is that attention to industrial export markets keeps producers in closer touch with changes in products and technology, in a better position to learn about new possibilities that can be carried back into higher productivity and improved product quality. Another consideration is that industrial exports do not, like basic agricultural exports, compete for land use and put additional pressures on the rural poor. Finally, they face higher average world elasticities of demand than the traditional primary exports, though not necessarily for more diversified agricultural products. Old-line exports such as coffee, copper, and sugar have weaker market prospects than many newer exports such as flowers, fruit, and seafood.[21] Primary products also differ among themselves with respect to degrees of labor intensity, as do industrial. All exports are not equal. To stay with the traditional basic commodities and neglect diversification is the least promising strategy of all.

The process of import substitution was originally expected to lessen the need for exports by reducing the ratio of imports to national income. This hypothesis turned out to be valid for the first few years of active substitution policies, but then it became extremely difficult to get the ratio down further. New domestic production meant new requirements for machinery and imported intermediate products. That effect would have been difficult to avoid in any case, but the degree could have held down by using exchange rates set at levels making foreign exchange expensive, to force firms to search for less expensive domestic inputs. Keeping the cost of imported inputs down worked systematically to maintain demand for imported equipment higher than it need have been. The "im-

[21] Income and price elasticities for groups of Chilean exports as estimated by José de Gregorio bring out this pattern of differences: world income elasticities of demand for total exports excluding copper are approximately twice as high as the same elasticities when copper is included; the long-rung price elasticity of demand for copper is estimated at 0.14, that for industrial products collectively at 1.77, and for diversified agricultural and seafood products 3.56. "Comportamiento de las exportaciones e importaciones en Chile. Un estudio econométrico," *Colección estudios CIEPLAN* 13 (1984), pp. 53–86, cuadros 1 and 2.

port intensity of import substitution" proved to be far higher than expected, and higher than necessary.[22]

Shortages of foreign exchange became a way of life for most countries pursuing import substitution, but degrees of strain varied among them according to the extent to which their particular policies penalized exporters. Argentine policy under Perón pushed measures adverse to the primary sector further than anywhere else, almost as if the intent were as much to punish landowners as to move resources to the industrial sector. In Brazil and Mexico agricultural producers retained somewhat more influence on policy decisions and were able to hold down the bias of incentives. These countries did not have nearly as much trouble as Argentina with maintenance of primary exports in the early postwar years, or with foreign exchange restraints on growth. For the decade 1950–1960 the growth rate of total Latin American earnings from exports was 4.4 percent a year, and that of Argentina only 1.2 percent.[23]

All these criticisms of the costs of import substitution as practiced suggest that different methods could have done a good deal to lessen the resulting problems. It is not the general idea of entering new lines of production to replace imports that is the essence of the difficulty. It is rather the particular set of distortions built into the way the leading countries tried to implement the strategy that did them in. These distortions were far from accidental. They reflect punitive domestic strategy aimed against landowners, a deep-rooted aversion to international trade that worked against promotion of industrial exports as well as primary, and the natural pressures of industrialists seeking both protection in their own interests and low-cost access to imported equipment.

4. Growth of Output Per Capita

The costs of import substitution as practiced bore down more on employment opportunities, inequality, and dependence than on rates of growth of output per capita. The regional record for increases in output per capita compares fairly well to the rest of the world except for the Asian "super exporters." Output per capita increased 90 percent between 1960 and 1980.[24] In the worldwide

[22] Díaz Alejandro, "On the Import Intensity of Import Substitution," *Kyklos* 18 (1985), pp. 495–511.

[23] World Bank, *Work Tables 1980*, pp. 329 and 381.

[24] Inter-American Development Bank, *Economic and Social Progress in Latin America, 1985 Report* (Washington: IDB, 1985), appendix table 3, p. 388.

recession of 1980–84, it went back down by 9 percent. That period of retreat made Latin America's relative performance look less good: although growth slowed down greatly in all regions it remained positive for both East Asia and the industrialized countries, while turning negative in Latin America.

Table 4.5 gives national growth rates by subperiods from 1950 up to 1980, and measures of the decreases from 1980 to 1984. Considering individual countries, Argentina and Brazil were in the 1950s the leaders in use of protection for industrialization, but the effects on their growth in this decade were markedly different: Argentina's rate of growth was pitiful while Brazil's was outstanding. The strategy itself was clearly not fatal: the interesting question, discussed in detail in chapter 8, is what were the main differences between these two leading cases? From 1960 to 1965 it was Brazil's turn to look weak while Argentine began to move more positively. That relative success in Argentina, particularly for the second half of the 1960s, points to real capacity more often submerged by poor economic strategy, though it also raises difficult questions of the political and social costs involved in this period.

Brazil recovered its pace of growth in the second half of the 1960s too, and then continued a highly impressive performance up to 1980. The positive change in terms of growth in the second half of the 1960s can be ascribed in part to a turn away from import substitution toward export promotion. But, as in Argentina, that change was only one aspect of a reorientation that had drastic social and political consequences. For both of these countries, as for Chile and Uruguay, reversal of the mistakes of import substitution had extraordinarily high costs in human terms.

Chile does not match the general pattern of regional growth rates at all well. Its growth rate was slightly below that of the region in the earlier years and then, despite its own improvement, fell even further below the region in the second half of the 1960s. For Chile, the second half of the 1960s was a critical period in which moderate reform including some degree of income equalization was accomplished, along with export promotion, but in which inflation soon forced a retreat. The dramatic swings of the early 1970s, first to radical social change combined with excess demand, and then to extremes of deflation and reliance on market forces, both worked badly in terms of economic growth: real income per capita grew less than 1 percent a year for the 1970s as a whole, then fell even more steeply than the average for the region in 1980–84. In this case, and again in Argentina from 1976, a reversal from import substitution to extreme market orientation proved to be disfunctional.

TABLE 4.5. Growth Rates of Gross Domestic Product Per Capita, 1950–1984

	Percentage rate of growth per year				Ratios	
	1950–60	1960–65	1965–70	1970–80	1980/60	1984/80[b]
Latin America[a]	1.9	2.0	3.4	3.4	1.91	.91
Argentina	0.9	2.1	3.2	0.7	1.40	.87
Bolivia	—	2.7	2.2	1.8	1.49	.73
Brazil	3.6	1.0	5.4	5.9	2.51	.91
Chile	1.8	1.6	2.4	0.8	1.33	.89
Colombia	1.5	1.3	3.0	3.6	1.87	.99
Costa Rica	—	1.5	3.6	3.0	1.84	.89
Dominican Republic	2.1	1.6	3.8	4.3	2.02	.99
Ecuador	—	—	1.1	5.7	2.08	.93
El Salvador	1.5	3.6	1.3	0.8	1.40	.83
Guatemala	0.8	2.4	2.8	2.7	1.68	.85
Haiti	—	−1.2	−1.2	3.0	1.23	.90
Honduras	−0.3	1.4	1.9	1.5	1.39	.89
Mexico	2.5	4.0	4.4	3.5	2.02	.94
Nicaragua	2.7	7.2	1.5	−2.4	1.17	.93
Panama	2.0	4.8	4.7	3.0	2.36	.97
Paraguay	0.2	1.3	1.9	5.3	1.88[c]	.95
Peru	2.9	3.2	0.5	0.8	1.40	.86
Uruguay	0.8	−1.4	2.7	2.5	1.42	.83
Venezuela	3.8	3.7	1.8	1.1	1.43	.83

SOURCES: World Bank, *World Tables*, 3d ed. (Washington, D.C.: World Bank, 1983), pp. 486–88, for first three columns; Inter-American Development Bank, *Economic and Social Progress In Latin America, 1985 Report* (Washington, D.C.: IDB, 1985), appendix table 3, p. 388, for last three columns.

[a] Region includes Caribbean area.

[b] 1984 figures are preliminary estimates by IDB.

[c] IDB does not give 1960 measure for Paraguay; the estimate in this table is from growth rate given by World Bank in World Bank, *World Development Report 1982*, p. 111.

Peru provides an interesting contrast in timing too, in this case with a pattern that fits most of the critical comments about import substitution. In the early postwar years, up to the late 1960s, the country remained relatively open, with little deliberate promotion of industry (cf. table 4.2). The country's growth rate in this period exceeded the regional average by a fairly wide margin, both for the 1950s and for the first half of the 1960s. But from 1968 national policy moved abruptly toward extreme protection. The growth rate turned up very briefly and then turned down again, very decisively. The really depressing problem is that when subsequent economic policy was reversed toward export promotion and greater concern with efficiency, an initial improvement in economic performance was soon followed by a new relapse.

The pattern of growth rates in Colombia almost exactly reverses the timing in Peru. Its rate of economic growth was distinctly below the regional average from 1950 to 1965. Like Brazil, though in a less dramatic way and without intensified political repression, the country shifted over more toward export promotion and lessening protection. The growth rate doubled in the second half of the 1960s and then rose further in the 1970s. The country's improving relative performance continued in the much more difficult 1980–84 years: while output per capita fell 9 percent for the region as a whole, the decrease for Colombia was only 1 percent.

The unhappiest side of the estimates in table 4.5 is that the poorest countries fell even further below the regional average income level from 1960 on. As of 1980, the six poorest countries—those with per capita incomes below one thousand dollars measured in 1980 dollars—were Bolivia, El Salvador, Haiti, Honduras, Nicaragua and Peru. Not a single one of them managed to grow at the regional average rate between 1960 and 1980. In fact only one of them, Bolivia, managed to grow at even half the regional average rate. When regional income per capita fell between 1980 and 1984, none of the five did distinctly better than average, and three of them did distinctly worse. Compared to the regional fall of 9 percent, Peru's income per capita fell 14 percent, El Salvador's 17 percent, and Bolivia's 27 percent.

5. Better Economics and Worse Problems

It is easier to pile up valid objections to protection and import substitution as an industrialization strategy than to find constructive ways out of it. Most of the countries that went too far with this strategy eventually switched away from it in ways that would appear to be appropriate: toward more promotion of exports, and particularly of industrial exports; toward exchange rates and interest rates more appropriate for employment creation, more likely to reduce reliance on capital-intensive and overly import-dependent kinds of production; toward better incentives for agricultural production; and toward a more coherently selective vision of industrialization. These changes had a lot to do with improvement of growth rates for both production and employment in Brazil and Colombia but worked out much less well in other countries. In Chile and for a time in Argentina they involved real setbacks to employment and to industrialization, as well as increased poverty and extremely high costs in terms of political and social repression. A reorientation of development strategy was necessary, but why did it so often prove to be so bitter?

Exactly what went on in particular cases is examined in the country chapters below, but in general terms it is clear that the basic policy reorientation away from import substitution can go seriously wrong. It can set back industrialization, if tariff reduction is not accompanied by promotional policies to keep industrial growth going. It can set back employment, if the effort to drive down inflation is pushed to degrees holding domestic demand far below productive capacity. It can certainly intensify conflict between the government and the urban labor force, or between the government and the great majority of the population. Change toward a strategy of industrial exports is favorable for employment, but if urban wages have under protection gone too high to permit external competition an export orientation creates great pressure to drive them down. And that exceptionally difficult tension is by no means the only one. Taking away protection damages many industrial interests too; making foreign exchange more expensive hurts those industries that depend on imported equipment and supplies; reducing government deficits to hold down inflation hurts both those who must pay higher taxes and those who lose sales or subsidies; and so on across a long list of problems. Harmful economic policies don't come out of the blue in the first place; they come out of pressures for advantage, and advantages once gained are not lightly given up.

Is it reasonable even to suggest that good management could accomplish this transition in ways likely to moderate social conflict? That is one of the most difficult questions of all: a general reorientation of economic strategy means that there are bound to be losers in the years immediately following the change, and they are bound to fight back if they can. The experiences of countries switching away from import substitution bring out more painful problems than examples of clean success. But it has not been so far a story of unrelieved disaster. Some countries have managed to make the policy turn without political and social relapse, and all of them have surely learned something of what they need to avoid. The details of what particular countries have done should provide good clues: some changes have had clearly positive effects, others have reduced some problems while creating new ones, and still others have just plain gone wrong. Granting, even insisting, that each country must find its own path in the face of its individual constraints, these diverse experiences suggest at least potentially open paths toward a less unequal and more sustainable kind of development.

FIVE

INFLATION, EXTERNAL DEFICITS, AND
IMF STABILIZATION PROGRAMS

High rates of inflation and repeated foreign exchange crises are particularly striking manifestations of the intense economic and social conflict in the region. Although they can develop from many different causes, and be dealt with in many different ways, the core problem for both has been the difficulty of reconciling claims of competing interest groups. That difficulty is universal; northern industrialized countries fail often too. The difference in Latin America has only been that an important subset of the region has foundered on it so often, to such extraordinary degrees.

The subset of countries that have had the most systematic problems of repeated inflation and external deficits—problems which keep being repeated for continuing reasons rather than those due to erratic factors or revolutionary changes—have been among the middle and higher income group with fairly broad social participation, not those with older-style repressive systems. Ultraconservative governments with little interest in popular preferences can squash opposing claims readily: the few whose preferences matter can live well with inflation kept down by forcing the rest into line. Governments that are more concerned with raising living standards for the majority as well as the need to provide incentives and resources for investment have a harder time making all claims fit within realistic limits.

It is not impossible to succeed fairly well, just difficult. The difficulty has led to arguments that the best course is to accept inflation as a normal counterpart of growth rather than risk either economic stagnation or political repression in an effort to stop it. The problem with that idea is that the cost of failure to keep inflation from rising is so high: when it accelerates it becomes profoundly irritating to everyone, conveying a sense that a society that cannot restore control has somehow lost its inner coherence. There must be selfish forces at work—labor unions, or capitalists, or imperialists, or the government itself—manipulating the economic system to steal one's hard-earned income. Economic analysis may suggest that little harm is being done when prices and wages rise at similar rates, but that does not do much to lessen the edge of uncertainty and antagonism added to daily life as well as to business decisions. Inflation is one more straw that can turn people into vengeful militants.

Analysis of inflation and external deficits took a distinctive turn in Latin America by identifying the villains as (1) persisting structural conditions of underdevelopment, as distinct from monetary factors, and (2) negative pressures from the world economy, inherent in the imbalances between industrialized and developing countries. Such structuralist interpretations have the great appeal of treating inflation and external deficits as issues that involve profound economic transformation, rather than simple technical questions of monetary restraint. They also have the disadvantage of deflecting attention from perfectly feasible responses that might have made these problems a good deal less costly. The opposite extreme interpretation, the "monetarist" side of a long series of debates, treats government deficits and monetary expansion as the villains, to be cut down without any great attention to possible costs. This is an old debate but worth reviewing because the people who make decisions on economic strategy repeatedly adopt one or the other of these positions, as if one were right and the other wrong, despite evidence that neither one works well. A successful strategy requires escape from both of these crippling misconceptions.

The present chapter considers successively: (1) regional inflation and the great differences in inflation rates among countries; (2) the controversy between monetarists and structuralists over causation and remedies; (3) external deficits and the character of IMF stabilization programs in the region; (4) the external debt crisis of the 1980s; and (5) connections between these economic issues and political repression.

1. REGIONAL INFLATION: DIFFERENCES BY COUNTRY AND BY PERIOD

When Latin America first gained a reputation for exceptionally high inflation, in the 1950s and 1960s, only five countries were actually involved: rates of inflation for the majority were not greatly different from the outside world. One of the five with exceptionally high inflation for a time, Bolivia in the first half of the 1950s, was going through a revolution; once the postrevolution government settled down the inflation did too (at least until the 1980s). The other four cases of exceptionally high inflation were a familiar special set: Argentina, Brazil, Chile, and Uruguay. Their inflations were not due to revolution or any other one-time special cause: they were caused by common pressures that continued to operate until the four countries became the victims of market-authoritarian reaction.

Developing countries in general have on average somewhat higher rates of inflation than industrialized countries, but they vary a great deal among themselves: nothing in the nature of economic development makes high inflation inescapable. Developing countries in Asia have usually had lower average rates than those in Latin America, though in the 1960s the majority of the Latin American countries had such low rates that they kept the two regional averages fairly close. Using the IMF category of "non-oil developing countries," the Asian group had an average inflation rate of 15.6 percent in the 1960s while the Western Hemisphere group averaged 20.3 percent (table 5.1). This moderate difference widened greatly in the 1970s as the rate in Asia came down to 9.3 percent while the Western Hemisphere rate speeded up to 38.7 percent. In the 1980s the two groups look as if they belonged to entirely different worlds: in 1980–85 the Western Hemisphere rate reached 107 percent a year while that for Asia came down to 7 percent.

Two very different sets of problems have been responsible for the higher rates in Latin America, one applying mainly to 1960–80 and the other mainly to the 1980s. In the 1960s and 1970s the four particularly high cases were primarily consequences of internally generated inflationary pressures, individual country issues rather than a regional matter. In the 1980s high rates of inflation have been much more of a regional problem, more related to world economic and financial conditions, though still variable in effect according to the policies followed in individual countries.

In the second half of the 1970s, measured rates of inflation in many countries were understatements of the degrees of domestically generated inflationary pressure. This was a period of easy and abundant international credit, encouraging recourse to external borrowing to finance rising imports. Many countries held down their rates of inflation by allowing excess demand to spill over into excess imports: the import surplus was used both for growth and as a way of holding down domestic price increases. But then external credit tightened at the end of the 1970s, as monetary policy in the United States became much more restrictive and reinforced a similar line of policy in England. Interest rates began to rise rapidly in real terms, the restraint on world demand hurt export markets and

TABLE 5.1. Annual Rates of Inflation by Country, 1960–1985
(Compound percentage rates of increase of consumer prices)

	1960–70	1970–80	1980–84	1984–85
Argentina	19.6	38.1	290.2	672.1
Bolivia	5.5	18.8	251.7	11,748.0
Brazil	47.6	35.2	132.5	227.0
Chile	29.1	130.4	19.0	30.7
Colombia	11.2	21.1	21.9	24.0
Costa Rica	2.3	10.8	40.2	15.1
Dominican Republic	1.9	10.4	11.4	37.5
Ecuador	4.5	12.6	27.4	28.0
El Salvador	0.7	10.7	12.8	22.3
Guatemala	0.8	9.6	4.8	18.7
Haiti	2.8	10.7	8.7	10.6
Honduras	2.4	7.8	7.8	3.4
Mexico	2.7	16.6	61.4	57.7
Nicaragua			28.7	219.5
Panama	1.3	7.0	3.8	1.0
Paraguay	3.3	13.1	13.5	25.2
Peru	9.3	30.2	89.1	163.4
Uruguay	44.1	64.2	38.7	72.2
Venezuela	1.0	8.4	11.0	11.4
For comparison:				
IMF index for world	4.0	11.0	13.1	13.7
IMF indexes for nonoil developing countries				
(a) Asia	15.6	9.3	7.0	6.6
(b) Western Hemisphere	20.3	38.7	95.9	163.6

SOURCE: IMF, *International Financial Statistics, 1983 Yearbook* and October 1986, p. 73.

the terms of trade for primary exports, and debt service became much more difficult. When Mexico came to the point at which it could no longer meet scheduled payments on its debt, in 1982, the world of international finance suddenly went into reverse. Net new credit became extremely scarce and the whole region was forced to reduce its use of resources abruptly. That meant a drastic reduction in domestic supplies of imports, accompanied in many cases by sharp devaluations in an attempt to stimulate export earnings. The sudden rise in rates of regional inflation was in the circumstances probably unavoidable. But the higher rates in this period are no longer evidence of weak domestic restraint: they are instead the consequence of a dramatic effort to restore balance under very difficult external conditions.

The last column of table 5.1 shows some fantastic new highs in rates of inflation in 1985. The worst cases were Argentina, Bolivia, Brazil, Nicaragua, and Peru. The situation in Nicaragua, under military attack and blocked from access to some of the main sources of international credit, is clearly in a different category from the other cases. The other four have in common one striking new feature: they all managed to initiate nonorthodox stabilization programs in 1985 or 1986 that succeeded, at least initially, in bringing down greatly the wild rates of the former year. The changes involve too many different questions in each country for comprehensive discussion here, but some of the key features are noted at the end of section 3, and some of the special characteristics of the Peruvian program are considered in chapter 10.

2. MONETARISTS AND STRUCTURALISTS

New ways to think about inflation were greatly stimulated in early postwar Latin America by the intensity of inflation itself.[1] But new ways of thinking are not to everyone's taste. In this context they provoked stern reaction from believers in more traditional monetary-fiscal analysis. The more traditional side in Latin America got stuck with the label "monetarist," although this greatly oversimplifies a position that was essentially an argument for reliance on market forces as opposed to state-led development. The antimonetarist side, the "structuralists," emphasized chiefly that persistent problems on the side of supply mean that the price system does not work well in Latin American conditions, and that these difficulties make it impossible to achieve growth without accepting inflation.[2]

[1] Albert Hirschman, "The Social and Political Matrix of Inflation: Elaborations on the Latin American Experience," pp. 177–207 in Hirschman, *Essays in Trespassing*.

[2] Werner Baer and Isaac Kerstenetsky, eds., *Inflation and Growth in Latin America* (Homewood: Irwin, 1964), especially the statements by W. Arthur Lewis (criticizing the idea of inevitability), and Dudley Seers (on the structuralist side). See also the articles by Roberto de Oliveira Campos, David Felix, and Joseph Grunwald in Albert

This debate was nominally focused on inflation, but it was the underlying conflict over the desirability of relying on the price system, and the question of who gains and who loses if a society allows its economy to be shaped by market forces, that gave the arguments their edge. They were at once ideological and technical. On the technical side they translate into such issues as the elasticity of supply in the agricultural sector, or the response of exports to changes in the price of foreign exchange. They can also be readily translated into the terminology of more recent Northern debates over supply-side economics: the meaning, if any, to the concepts of full employment and of excess demand, the relevance of expectations and of different "policy regimes" for central bank behavior and for labor markets, and in general what if anything can be done to achieve full utilization of productive potential without inflation. Both the earlier Southern version and its current Northern variants combine dense forests of ideology with small clearings carved out by empirical research.

Monetarist explanations of inflation in Latin America had little trouble identifying causal factors. High rates of growth of the money supply and of government deficits have in most cases been closely associated with high rates of inflation.[3] Given the absence of well-developed capital markets, government deficits are in most cases financed by borrowing from the central bank, raising bank reserves and the money supply. If a government keeps down its expenditures and the central bank correspondingly keeps down its additions to the monetary base—as the more conservatively run Central American countries used to do most of the time—the countries do not normally have high rates of inflation, whether they speak Spanish or not.

The structuralist answer to the preceding has two key themes: it may be necessary to accept some inflation as the price of any decent rate of growth of output because the elasticity of supply is relatively low in many fields of production, particularly agriculture, and once a high rate of inflation has been established any attempt to eliminate it by monetary restraint will stop growth without doing much to stop

Hirschman, ed., *Latin American Issues*, and Dudley Seers, "Inflation: The Latin American Experience," Institute of Development Studies at the University of Sussex, Discussion Paper 168 (November 1981).

[3] Robert Vogel, "The Dynamics of Inflation in Latin America, 1950–1969," *American Economic Review* 64 (1974), pp. 102–14; "Comments" by Roger Betancourt and by Edmund Sheehey, and reply by Vogel, *American Economic Review* 66 (September 1976), pp. 688–98.

the inflation. In this view, the root problem is on the side of production and pricing: structures of production are so inflexible that even moderate rates of growth of demand are bound to provoke specific shortages and rising prices. If the money supply is not increased fast enough to keep up with these inescapable price increases, then growth will be choked off.[4] Argentina and Brazil and the other countries that took forceful measures to stimulate development were bound to have high rates of inflation for some time because that is a necessary characteristic of growth in conditions of inelastic supply; more conservatively run countries may serve as examples of how to avoid inflation, but the method is essentially to accept persisting underdevelopment.

The structuralist arguments of the late 1950s might be seen as anticipating a major change in Northern macroeconomic analysis. At the time of the debate in the South the dominant version of macroeconomics, following Keynes, explained both inflation and unemployment primarily in terms of aggregate demand. Given an initial problem of unemployment and idle productive capacity, increases in spending by government or by private investors will stimulate production and employment, with no inflationary effect, until the economy reaches a position of full employment. This assumes that complementary inputs of all kinds are in adequate supply, that production is restrained only because firms cannot count on markets for increased output. This vision leaves little room for problems coming from the side of supply, or for government intervention except to maintain adequate demand. The structuralists, not unlike later supply-side economists in the North, argued instead that there are many kinds of supply constraints other than labor, and that inflation can arise either from increasing demand or from interruptions to supply even in conditions of unemployment. Instead of a clear cutoff position at full employment—below which it is safe to increase demand without inflation—supply is always inelastic and increases in demand will always exert upward pressure in prices.

Simplified diagrams can cause their own confusions, but the difference between the Keynesian macroeconomic model and the structuralist position might be clarified by risking one. In panel A of figure 5.1, D_1 is the initial aggregate demand curve, intersecting an

[4] Susan M. Wachter's econometric tests to identify the direction of causation brought out a complex picture, supporting the monetarist interpretation in some cases but the structuralists in others, according to particular countries and periods examined: *Latin American Inflation: The Structuralist-Monetarist Debate* (Lexington: Lexington Books, 1976).

FIGURE 5.1. Alternative versions of aggregate demand and
supply relationships

A. Conventional macroeconomic model

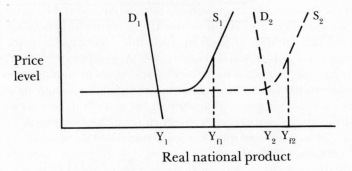

B. Structuralist version

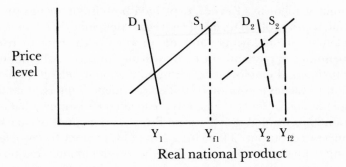

C. Effect of devaluation on the aggregate supply curve

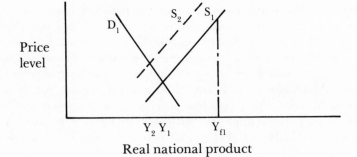

aggregate supply curve S_1 at the level of national product Y_1. In the Northern macroeconomic version, the supply curve is relatively flat, implying constant prices, up to the level of output corresponding to a critical minimum level of unemployment, Y_{f_1}. The reasoning is that industrial production can be raised or lowered without greatly changing unit costs, while wage rates will not begin rising significantly (above their prior trend), unless unemployment falls to its critical minimum level.[5] Aggregate demand can move to the right in the shortrun as far as Y_{f_1} without stimulating inflation. Then as time goes by, as investment and technological change raise productive capacity, the aggregate supply curve moves rightward, represented by the new curve S_2. Aggregate demand and production can grow at the same rate as the supply curve shifts out, without any necessary rise in prices. Prices will start heading up only if demand moves too fast: if the aggregate demand curve begins to intersect the supply curve on its vertical slope, where wages start rising more rapidly and production bottlenecks begin to appear. The critical point in all this is that there is one safe upper limit to rates of growth of aggregate demand: below that limit potential output is being wasted but above it inflation will accelerate.

In panel B of figure 5.1 the structuralist variant is depicted as one in which the supply curve rises steeply at levels of output far below any position of labor shortage, because of increasing costs and spreading bottlenecks, even while many specific activities still have room to expand production. Supply elasticity is always low, even with a great deal of unemployment. The central policy objective is not so much to ensure adequate demand as it is to move the aggregate supply curve outward and to make it more flexible: to *create* the kind of elasticity that Keynes, dealing with the industrialized countries, took for granted.

Structuralist ideas tend to wipe out any conception of an identifiable limit of productive capacity, and therefore any clear meaning to the idea of "excess demand." There are always some shortages,

[5] The basic Keynesian model and its many complications are explained in leading macroeconomic textbooks such as Rudiger Dornbusch and Stanley Fischer, *Macroeconomics*, 3d ed. (New York: McGraw-Hill, 3d edition, 1984), and Robert J. Gordon, *Macroeconomics* (Boston: Little, Brown, 1984). For Keynes, the critical minimum level of unemployment was the point of "full employment." More recent versions reject the possibility of full employment without inflation and use instead such concepts as the "natural" or "normal" rate of unemployment to define the upper limit for aggregate demand without inflation. A near equivalent explanation of the macro system in structuralist terms is Lance Taylor, *Structuralist Macroeconomics* (New York: Basic Books, 1983).

some inflationary pressures, and some room for increasing national income. Inflation might be kept low by keeping output down to levels such as Y_1 in the shortrun, and then moving cautiously to higher levels such as Y_2 as capacity increases, but this solution would involve a continuing waste of possible output. On the graph, the waste of potential in each period is indicated by the difference between Y_1 and Y_{f_1}. That lost opportunity would mean lower rates of investment and slower growth than if inflation were accepted. Inflation will rise if aggregate demand is moved nearer to Y_{f_1}, but this is because of supply inflexibility rather than monetary expansion or excess demand. Given increasing prices, the money supply must be increased fast enough to keep up liquidity and to maintain demand in real terms; monetary expansion is a consequence of inflation, necessary to allow growth of demand and production, rather than the cause.

Structuralist explanations of reasons for low elasticity of supply included a number of doubtful assertions that have not stood up to empirical research but also a good many others that vary from plausible to convincing. One argument, which probably had more validity prior to the twentieth century than it does now, was that large landholders are more interested in holding land for status purposes than for production and do not respond to strong markets any more than they can within the limits of familiar methods and minimum effort. This kind of behavior may have been common in earlier Latin American history but does not seem so now. The dynamism of Brazilian agriculture after improvement of incentives for its growth from the mid-1960s on, and of large commercial estates in Mexico from 1940 to the 1960s, are two of the more dramatic demonstrations that there is nothing inherently feeble about large landowners in Latin America. But it remains true that short-run supply elasticity in agriculture is normally lower than in industry everywhere, and that agriculture accounts for a greater share of economic activity in Latin American economies than it does in the industrialized North.[6] An additional problem is that the smaller landowners have such low incomes that improving markets may lead them to increase consumption of their own output, holding

---

[6] Relative inelasticity of agricultural production is emphasized (to the point of serious overstatement), in Solon Barraclough, ed., *Agrarian Structure in Latin America* (Lexington, Mass.: Lexington Books, 1978). Bruce Johnston and John Mellor note that it is a general worldwide characteristic: "The World Food Equation," *Journal of Economic Literature* 22 (June 1984), pp. 531–74. For econometric tests of many other structuralist propositions see Behrman, *Macroeconomic Policy*.

down increases in deliveries to urban consumers. It is not that agricultural output cannot increase—it can grow reasonably well in
most Latin American countries if incentives are kept positive and
appropriate infrastructure is provided—but it is still likely that
when incomes increase rapidly, demand for food will outrun increases in supply.

Structuralists arguments often focused on agriculture but they involved many other issues, always with an element of validity but
often with a tendency to see difficulties as impossibilities. For both
agriculture and industry the absence of a developed capital-goods
sector means that machinery necessary for expansion or reorientation of output must be imported, but imports may be blocked by
lack of foreign exchange. For the whole economy, weak educational
systems with limited access for the poor mean that labor skills are
not diversified and workers are not readily able to learn rapidly.
And industrialists little accustomed to either commercial or technological change may not act quickly in response to new opportunities.

This range of arguments might be summarized as a position that
underdevelopment is a condition of inflexibility on the supply side:
of low productivity that can only be increased by direct action to
change the persisting factors that keep it low. For the structuralists,
it was necessary to change the conditions of land ownership, reduce
dependence on imports of manufactured goods, curtail freedom
for producers to raise prices in the absence of increased costs, and—
for some of the less conservative spirits—break away from reliance
on private investment and ownership in the industrial sector. The
analysis called for land reform, import substitution, price controls,
and a greatly expanded public sector.

While all these arguments point to real problems, structuralism is
simply wrong when it leads to disregard of any role of excess demand in causing inflation and external deficits. From the perfectly
correct perception that there is always some idle capacity in some activities, often a great deal of labor ready to move into new employment opportunities, and some chance to stimulate investment by increasing the pressure of demand against existing capacity, this way
of thinking leads to the indefensible conclusion that it is almost always helpful to increase total spending. Since the limits of productive capacity have some give in them—they do not constitute a brick
wall or a perfectly vertical aggregate supply curve—why not push
harder and grow faster?

Repeated experiences have given a treacherous kind of support to belief in the likely gains of rapid increases in aggregate demand. In Argentina at the beginning of Perón's government, from 1946 to 1948; in Cuba in 1959–60; in the first two years of expansion under Velasco in Peru; and in Chile during the first year of Allende's government, the economic systems responded to increased demand with remarkable increases of output. At first, but not for long. Initial positive response turns quickly toward problems for food supply, then for more and more raw materials, then for almost everything as inventories are run down, skilled labor becomes hard to find, and even unskilled labor begins to seem scarce. After twelve to twenty-four months, the domestic supply response to further increases in demand heads toward zero: if there is any further response on the supply side it comes from increased imports or reduced exports, or both. What happens is that the normal flexibility in any capitalist economy, sometimes increased by prior deflation or recession, first allows a rapid response to increased demand and then runs out. The critical testing point for every radical-populist government is usually its second year: does the government then begin to slow down rates of increase in spending or, deluded by the sight of everything expanding at once, does it keep both feet on the accelerator? Cuba under Castro put on the brakes. Perón, Velasco, and Allende did not.

Concepts that deride or neglect the problem of excess demand are bound to cause trouble. But structuralist arguments still have important things to say. They direct attention to the consequences of ownership patterns and help break down the barriers between such questions and more conventional analysis of markets. They also serve to underline the likelihood that the flexibility of supply is lower than it need be because of such fundamental weaknesses as limited access to education, social and racial barriers to opportunity, and cultural-historical patterns of behavior that have long made it easier to get rich through political and personal favors than through risk-taking investment. Producers will respond to incentives but they may demand a lot of incentive for relatively little action: the path to growth by reliance on private markets without major structural changes is very likely to fortify inequality and special privilege.

3. EXTERNAL DEFICITS AND IMF STABILIZATION PROGRAMS

Foreign exchange crises have been the most frequent direct causes of interruptions to growth, or in the worst cases prolonged paraly-

sis, in postwar Latin America. They can come mainly from the outside, as in the generalized credit contraction and debt impasse of the
1980s, or from the inside. The debt problems of the 1980s are discussed in the following section; the present section is concerned
with internally generated crises and with the IMF programs intended to force corrective action.

External deficits on current account (an excess of imports over
exports, as distinct from the overall balance of payments including
capital flows) can be normal and healthy aspects of any development
process. In a well-ordered world additional resources would be provided to low-income countries on a regular basis by either loans or
grants, permitting higher rates of investment for given standards of
living, or jointly higher consumption and investment, than would
otherwise be possible. In terms of national accounts, the excess of
imports over exports permits the total of consumption plus investment plus government spending—"absorption," or total domestic
use of resources—to exceed total production. Stated positively, an
import surplus should help development. Alternatively expressed,
an import surplus means that the country is using up more income
than it is producing.[7]

Even considered in its positive role as a contribution to domestic
supply, a deficit still raises an implicit question: why not supply domestic needs from production rather than excess imports? Two
general ways to answer the question point to central issues involved
in disputes with the IMF when crises break out. One is that the economy may be operating close to the limit of its productive potential,
raising output as fast as capacity can be increased: the deficit measures an excess of aggregate demand over *possible* output. In such
conditions, to reduce the deficit requires cutting consumption or investment or both. The second directs attention to the structures of
production and demand rather than aggregates. If the specific components of demand going directly or indirectly into imports are too

[7] For discussion of the debates over IMF policies, it might help to put this set of
relationships in algebraic terms. With Y = total output, A = absorption of goods and
services by domestic spending, M = imports, and X = exports, the basic national accounting identity is:

$$Y = A + X - M,$$
$$\text{or} \quad (M - X) = A - Y.$$

Deficits on current account mean that absorption exceeds production, but that need
not mean that it is necessary to cut down absorption to correct them: it may be possible to reduce them by increasing production. The requirement is to reduce the difference between absorption and production.

high relative to the share of output going into exports, a country may have an external deficit at levels of output far below the limits of productive capacity. In such a case, to reduce the deficit requires changing the structures of demand and production but not necessarily any decrease in consumption or investment.

Even if the outside world economy does not change at all, if there is no external impact to make things more difficult, a deficit can be turned into a crisis either by raising demand too fast relative to capacity or by structures of demand and production that generate increasing deficits short of capacity. A deficit becomes a crisis when either domestic borrowers or foreign lenders become convinced that deep trouble lies ahead: that economic breakdown or devaluation are becoming so likely that they had better get money out of the country as fast as possible rather than bring more in. Exactly when it becomes time to move is a matter of judgment; fortunes can be made or wiped out, and often are. There is no general rule. But if everyone sees that aggregate demand is rising much faster than output—if Peru's external deficit on current account starts moving up from 2 percent of GNP to 5 percent to 10 percent—somewhere along that path new credit will become excruciatingly difficult to get. When it does, the logic of initial imbalance leaves little room to move: if the import surplus can no longer be financed in normal ways, either domestic absorption will be forced down or an emergency lender has to be found. Up in Washington, of all places, the IMF stands ready to be consulted.

From the point of view of the government concerned, the existing levels of consumption, investment, and government spending are necessary responses to real objectives: the problem is that external finance is no longer available to meet firm requirements. The point of view of the IMF is less easy to state. Critical versions suggest an institution lying in wait to get control of the nation's economic policies and reshape them in a monetarist, market-oriented, conservative model. More positive versions emphasize the original function of the Fund: to provide emergency credit to help countries avoid drastic contraction threatened by temporary problems, and technical advice on how to get the deficit under better control if the problem seems likely to be more than temporary. In between, perhaps the most common criticism of the Fund is that it applies a standard package of remedies to all countries whether it is appropriate or not, leaning to the side of deflation for financial safety whether it is really needed or not.[8]

[8] Roberto Frenkel and Guillermo O'Donnell, "The 'Stabilization Programs' of the

The key elements in the usual set of Fund prescriptions are monetary restraint and devaluation: the first to cut down excess demand
and the second to reorient the structures of demand and production away from imports and toward exports. Monetary restraint is
intended to reduce inflationary pressure, to release productive capacity to make possible greater exports, to hold down demand for
imports, and possibly also to restrain capital flight. The Fund usually recommends targets expressed as limits for monetary expansion and as schedules for reduction of government deficits. In many
negotiations recommendations have come to include limits on wage
rates, to restrain consumption and to hold down production costs.
If the currency is being devalued while wage rates are held down in
nominal terms, this implies a cut in real wage rates, and likely conflict over the degree. Depending on the particular situation the recommendations may go much further into detail on tax structures,
subsidies, import controls, and related questions, all leaning in favor
of opening up market forces, of cutting down controls and subsidies. Governments never need to accept all this passively, but it is
undeniable that once caught in foreign exchange crises they begin
to have to share authority with the IMF over details of national economic strategy.

Three major questions are involved in conflicts over the Fund's
usual conditions for new credit: (1) the necessity of reducing consumption and investment; (2) the necessity and the costs of devaluation; and (3) the Fund's orientation toward elimination of controls and subsidies in the interest of promoting more open markets.
The first two aspects of the Fund's approach are in many cases exactly what is needed; in some cases not. The third is less of a logically
necessary part of stabilization policy than a set of preferences about
the nature of a country's development strategy.

First it should be recognized that the Fund's prescriptions of ①
monetary restraint and devaluation are often fully appropriate.
The kind of case that warrants this approach might be exemplified
by Argentina under the first Perón government, with national pol-

International Monetary Fund and Their Internal Impacts," in Richard D. Fagen, ed.,
Capitalism and the State in U.S.-Latin American Relations (Stanford: Stanford University
Press, 1979), pp. 171–216; William R. Cline and Sidney Weintraub, eds., *Economic
Stabilization in Developing Countries* (Washington, D.C.: Brookings, 1981); Gerald D.
Helleiner, "Lender of Early Resort: The IMF and the Poorest," and John William-
son, "On Seeking to Improve IMF Conditionality," both in *American Economic Review*
73 (May 1983), pp. 349–58; Tony Killick, Graham Bird, Jennifer Sharpley, and Mary
Sutton, "The IMF: Case for a Change in Emphasis," pp. 59–81 in Richard E. Fein-
berg and Valeriana Kallab, eds., *Adjustment Crisis in the Third World* (New Brunswick:
Transactions Books, 1984).

icy used to raise total government spending and wage rates rapidly at the same time: inflation was internally created both from the side of aggregate demand and by pushing up the aggregate supply curve. Domestic spending greatly exceeded output, with the difference supplied by excess imports. To provide credit to keep up an external deficit of this type would do no more than postpone, through increasing external debt, the necessity to bring absorption back down to fit productive capacity.

Sometimes other cases also seem clearcut, such as that of the dramatic Mexican increase in spending from 1978 to 1982, outrunning by far even a high rate of growth of export earnings from oil. But deflation would be the wrong remedy, slowing up growth and increasing poverty needlessly, if the country concerned had considerable underutilized productive potential. The solution would still be to stimulate exports, but that would not require reducing internal demand. The problem in practice is that ability to expand production is almost always open to some degree of doubt in countries for which there is no clearly defined capacity limit, in which high levels of underemployment are chronic, and in which there may be many particular industries unable to use capacity fully even under the best of conditions.

To reduce a trade deficit requires cutting the excess of absorption over production. That might be done either by reducing spending or by increasing production (see note 7). The IMF sometimes seems to *identify* external deficits with excess demand requiring deflation, giving little attention to the possibility of increasing output instead. That is particularly inappropriate when negotiations are carried out in conditions of recession, as they have been in several Latin American countries in the 1980s. After problems with external finance have forced down production for several years it can hardly be said that the economy is up against limits of capacity requiring further reduction of spending.[9] The case can be complicated in many ways, in particular when production is blocked by lack of foreign exchange to import necessary specific inputs. Absent credit to continue importing in the first place, it is true that the economy cannot expand. But to provide credit should then permit increasing total

[9] Discussions of deflationary pressures imposed on Brazil in 1982–83 brought out this issue particularly well. See Carlos Díaz Alejandro, "Some Aspects of the 1982–83 Brazilian Payments Crisis," and following comments in *Brookings Papers on Economic Activity* 2 (1983), pp. 515–52, especially the defense of the IMF position in comments by Richard Cooper and the contrary comments of Rudiger Dornbusch.

production and not require reduced spending. In such conditions economic policy should be expansionary rather than contractionary.

The second set of issues concerns devaluation. It is sometimes rejected for doubtful reasons, but there is no denying that it involves a host of problems. A common but usually wrong argument is that it is not likely to raise export earnings and so cannot really help. Provided that its effects are not quickly washed out by increases in domestic costs to a degree matching or exceeding the rate of devaluation, it can be counted on to raise earnings for industrial exports, and often for diversified primary products, though it may not help at all for major primary commodities such as coffee, copper, oil, or sugar.[10] The reasons for the differences are partly matters of differences in elasticity of supply, which is normally higher on the side of industrial products than primary, and partly matters of inelastic demand for traditional primary products. In the early postwar years it made sense to doubt the response of exports because they were precisely the kinds of primary commodities for which positive response is least likely. To stick with the same position when the countries are or could become industrial exporters is to miss a fundamental change in structure and in resulting possibilities. Two recent demonstrations by Argentina and Brazil reinforce the evidence of detailed research studies: under pressure to strengthen export incentives in the debt crisis, Argentina raised the dollar value of its exports by 10 percent in 1983 and 11 percent more in 1984; Brazil by 9 percent in 1983 and 23 percent in 1984.[11]

The structures of Latin America exports in the early postwar period made successful devaluation particularly difficult. Marcelo Diamand has given a good explanation in terms of what he describes as "unbalanced production structures."[12] If a country has a strong comparative advantage on the side of primary products, and industry is oriented mainly to the domestic market at protected prices above world levels, devaluation will raise incentives for po-

[10] Richard Cooper, "Currency Devaluation in Developing Countries," *Princeton Essays in International Finance*, no. 86, June 1971; Jere Behrman, *Macroeconomic Policy*; Sebastian Edwards, "The Exchange Rate and Non-Coffee Exports," appendix D in Vinod Thomas et al., *Combining Macroeconomic and Agricultural Policies with Growth: The Colombian Experience* (Baltimore: Johns Hopkins University Press, 1985); José de Gregorio, "Comportamiento de las exportaciones."

[11] IDB, *Social and Economic Progress, 1985 Report*, table I-7, p. 29.

[12] Marcelo Diamand, *Doctrinas económicas, desarrollo e independencia* (Buenos Aires: Paidos, 1973), and "Overcoming Argentina's Stop-and-Go Economic Cycles," in Jonathan Hartlyn and Samuel A. Morley, eds., *Latin American Political Economy: Financial Crisis and Political Change* (Boulder, Colo.: Westview Press, 1986).

tential agricultural exporters but may not for industrial: if their prices are too far out of reach of competitive levels even a major devaluation up to an equilibrium exchange rate may leave them unable to compete in external markets, while acting to raise their costs. Increases in the cost of living, if not matched by money wage increases, will contract demand for industrial products at the same time as costs rise, forcing the industrial sector to contract and raising urban unemployment. Positive response is far more difficult than for an industrialized economy: where industries are actively competing in world markets they gain immediately from devaluation and can usually increase output rapidly in response. Devaluation can raise employment and earnings quickly, and should stimulate the whole economy, because of the difference in the initial structure of production and trade.

Diamand's argument fits readily into macroeconomic analysis in terms of the behavior of the aggregate supply curve. As illustrated in panel C of figure 5.1, devaluation shifts the aggregate supply curve upward, moving the economy to a higher price level while deflating aggregate demand in real terms. If monetary expansion is held down to restrain inflation, devaluation is very likely to be contractionary. If monetary expansion is allowed to offset the contractionary effect of the shift in the supply curve, continued inflation is hard to stop. The analysis helps considerably to explain why IMF-type stabilization programs in Latin America have a much poorer record in achieving price stabilization than they do on the side of improving external balance.

The effect of devaluation on inflation is a universal logical relationship, not a problem peculiar to Latin America, but Diamand's analysis helps connect this macroeconomic behavior to the domestic structure of production. If the industrial sector is so far over on the side of comparative disadvantage that it does not respond to devaluation by increasing exports, the country can be badly stuck. But a lot depends on economic management in each case. Diamand's evidence comes directly from Argentine experience, which is an extreme example rather than a norm.[13] In Brazil, Colombia, and Mex-

---

[13] Even in the particularly troublesome Argentine cycles of the 1950s and 1960s, econometric tests of the effects of devaluation suggest that the resulting increases in prices offset no more than half of the degree of devaluation. See Carlos Díaz Alejandro, *Exchange Rate Devaluation in a Semi-Industrialized Country: The Experience of Argentina* (Cambridge: MIT Press, 1965), and Richard Mallon and Juan Sourrouille, *Economic Policy Making in a Conflict Society: The Argentine Case* (Cambridge: Harvard University Press, 1975).

ico devaluations have had some inflationary repercussions but not
to a degree wiping out their effectiveness in stimulating exports.
One of the major reasons for such differences is that the structures
of production in these countries were not twisted as badly as that of
Argentina. Some industries remained or were brought into close
contact with world prices so they could respond successfully to devaluation by increasing exports. The problems are tougher than in
East Asia, but there is nothing inherent in Latin American development that makes answers impossible.

The most difficult problems with devaluation are not so much external as internal. In particular, a determined effort to hold down
inflationary repercussions almost inescapably involves conflict over
sharing the burden. The degree of wage restraint is a key issue. If
money wages rise by the full percentage of devaluation then nothing at all is accomplished. The net result is just a higher price level.
But to apply restraint need not mean that living standards of workers must be driven down in real terms: that is more a question than
an automatic result. If the initial context is one in which demand
clearly exceeds productive capacity it is probably necessary to reduce real wages and consumption, at least initially. The compensating possibility in this case is that employment and production may
resume an upward trend and real wages can come back up if exports actually rise, as has been the usual case when inflationary reactions are restrained. The initial negative impact does not need to
be anything like a reduction in real wages fully equivalent to the degree of devaluation. Consumption can be brought down in part by
higher taxes on sales, or property, or nonwage incomes, instead of
placing all the burden on wages.

If the external problem is structural rather than a matter of excess demand, if the deficit is too high even at levels of output below
capacity, it should not be necessary from a macroeconomic view-
point to cut real wages at all. It would still be necessary to hold cost
increases for exports below the full proportion of devaluation, but
that could be done by using subsidies to reduce their costs without
cutting real wages, or alternatively wage cuts could be matched by
transfers to workers (or lower taxes on them), keeping their standard of living up while also stimulating exports. Such options and issues of the distribution of burdens and gains are separable from the
question of whether or not to devalue in the first place. If an overvalued currency is handicapping growth by blocking export possibilities, devaluation can help employment by getting the country out
of the impasse. Concern for real wages can then be answered by off-

setting measures; it should not rule out correction of an exchange rate adverse to growth.

③ The third set of issues concerning IMF stabilization programs is their strong orientation against controls and subsidies, in favor of reliance on market forces. If any one aspect of that set of policy preferences deserves special reconsideration it is the pressure exerted to eliminate subsidies intended to support consumption by the poor. The reason for such pressure may be more than a matter of orientation toward markets: subsidies add to government deficits and inflation when they are not covered by taxation. The evident answer is that increasing taxes or reducing other forms of government expenditure could get at the same macroeconomic problem without deepening poverty. It is the deficit that is the problem, not the subsidy. It may be that constant IMF opposition to subsidies comes from repeated failure to get governments to raise taxes to balance them, or it may be that subsidies sound like bad things in general, but it would be a welcome sign if the balance of IMF recommendations were changed to give greater weight to alternatives of macroeconomic adjustment that did not bear down directly on the poor.

The more general opposition of the Fund to all kinds of controls and subsidies can help clear up specifically damaging restraints that retard supply response (perhaps most importantly the use of price controls at the producer level for food), but such opposition to controls can be pushed to extremes that would almost wipe out capacity for independent national economic management. A good example of what amounts to an uncompromising prejudice against intervention has been brought out in connection with the stabilization program in Mexico in 1976.[14] It is not easy to see why this predisposition needs to be part of a stabilization program. The explanation probably does not lie within the Fund itself: it is rather that the main industrialized countries dominate the policy orientation of the Fund and push it consistently toward the open markets they consider to be desirable. The incentives operating on the Fund as an institution are stacked on the side of protecting interests of investors within the developing country, for placing much of the adjustment burden on real wages, and for pushing national economic strategy in the direction of more market-oriented, less internally managed styles of development. A highly conservative set of preferences, de-

[14] Laurence Whitehead, "Mexico from Bust to Boom: A Political Evaluation," *World Development* 8 (1980), pp. 834–64.

fensible in many ways but still essentially those of financial interests, leads often to actions particularly adverse for lower income groups. This policy orientation is not in any sense a necessary condition of successful stabilization.

When adjustments have to be made, particularly when domestic absorption has to be cut, the main question is how the costs are shared. The frequent failures of stabilization programs testify to the fact that the strains can become unmanageable. But it is at least conceivable that a government with some capacity for leadership could negotiate shared adjustment, acceptable because it is not flagrantly inequitable. If that can be done, spirals of inflation and ineffective devaluation can be broken without worsening the distribution of income.[15] This should be most nearly feasible when the economy is operating below productive capacity and inflation is more a matter of expectations, plus interacting devaluation and resulting price increases, than a matter of excess demand. In this kind of context—in conditions that have been termed "inertial inflation"—it should not be necessary to drive anyone's real income down: it should be possible by collective restraint to bring down price increases without reducing real wages or employment. Exactly this kind of consideration has been an important element in the initial success of the unorthodox stabilization programs adopted in 1985 and 1986.

Four of the countries with the most wildly accelerating inflation in 1985 managed to slow it down remarkably in 1986: Argentina with its "Austral Plan," Bolivia with a more traditional approach by monetary restraint plus wage restraints, Brazil with its "Cruzado Plan," and Peru with a complex policy combination discussed briefly in chapter 10.[16] In Argentina, Brazil, and Peru, the programs included a strong element of price control, plus changes toward more import controls rather than toward liberalization. Particularly in Brazil and Peru, the programs aimed at increasing employment and real wages rather than at contraction. In both cases, wages were raised to higher levels and then held, while price increases were blocked. The

[15] Oscar Muñoz, "Hacia la reindustrialización naciónal," in Alejandro Foxley et al., eds., Reconstrucción económica para la democracia (Santiago: CIEPLAN, 1983), pp. 297–348, esp. pp. 315–20.

[16] On experience with attempts to stop hyperinflation, and a discussion of the Plan Austral in Argentina, see Rudiger Dornbusch and Stanley Fischer, "Stopping Hyperinflations Past and Present," National Bureau of Economic Research Working Paper no. 1810 (January 1986). On the breakdown of the Cruzado Plan in Brazil, see Eliana Cardoso A. and Rudiger Dornbusch, "Brazil's Tropical Plan," National Bureau of Economic Research, Working Paper no. 2142 (February 1987).

first effect was to raise mass purchasing power, spending, and production. As output increased, the rate of inflation came way down.
The short-run advantages of this approach over an alternative of
contraction seem evident. The question is, How quickly does the
balance among policies change as the economies near productive
capacity and imports begin to rise more rapidly? Most past experiments of this kind have worked well for a year or slightly longer, but
have not been reoriented in time to avoid breakdown. That is exactly what happened in Brazil, the only country in which output was
rising rapidly when the program was adopted, and the one that
came nearest to its capacity limits; the Cruzado Plan broke down at
the end of 1986. The other countries still had room, and need, to
keep output growing. They should be able to keep on expanding
longer without going beyond the limits of their productive capacity,
but they also need to keep the collapse of the Cruzado Plan in mind
as a warning of the need to reorient policies as the limits are ap-
proached. It may help that these countries now have democratic
governments: a democracy may not be able to force real wages
down in the style of authoritarian governments, but it may have a
compensating advantage of ability to appeal for cooperation, if costs
and gains are shared in reasonably equal ways.

4. EXTERNAL DEBT

The normal flow of individual country stabilization programs involving the IMF suddenly turned into a flood at the beginning of the
1980s, as tighter monetary policies in the industrialized countries
drove up interest rates and checked new lending all over the world,
demand stopped growing, and prices of many raw material exports
fell steeply. Latin America was hit by a generalized debt crisis, rain-
ing on authoritarian governments and democracies alike. The crisis
may have helped undercut acceptance of the authoritarian regimes
at the beginning of the decade, but it also created intense pressures
on the established democratic societies and on the new democracies
that began to replace authoritarian governments in Argentina, Brazil and Uruguay. It has been a peculiarly perverse time to force so
many governments to override public preferences by drastic reduction of real wages and contraction of demand. They have all done
so, but that does not mean that they are out of the woods.

The debt crisis can be seen as yet another demonstration of dependency. First, rising oil prices increased costs of energy imports

for most countries of the region, and then a drive by international banks to relend the surplus earnings of the oil exporters greatly eased borrowing conditions, jointly encouraging a higher rate of borrowing simply to keep going on development paths that the countries themselves had not greatly changed. Second, monetary restraints applied in England and the United States for domestic reasons drove up interest costs on external debt, worsened export markets, and simultaneously cut down the flow of new credit. The borrowers' side played its role too: Argentina and Chile stimulated borrowing abroad by combining high internal interest rates with overvalued currencies, Mexico plunged into an incredible round of rising government deficits and splurge of imports, and Colombia showed by restraint on its external deficits and borrowing that governments can still make independent choices. The generous way to put it is that most countries had good uses for additional finance and sensibly took advantage of increased offers on good terms, only to be cut off without warning by external changes. A less generous view is that many of them lost sight of an important reality, that more is not better when it comes to borrowing.

The concept of a desirable target for external borrowing is elusive but potentially helpful. For developing countries, a deficit on current account financed by capital inflow is normal and can be helpful but also has negative counterparts in several dimensions. One of the most important is that it increases dependence, on imports in general, on foreign capital equipment and technology, and on the good will of the governments or financial institutions providing the credit. On the level of resource use, continued borrowing means a rising claim of interest costs on current output and export earnings, a share of production that can no longer be used for consumption or investment but simply goes out of the country. The cost may well be worthwhile, if the borrowing permits a greater increase in productive capacity than needed to pay the interest, but then there is a second-level financial problem: debt service normally requires foreign exchange, so borrowing will lead to a foreign exchange impasse unless the resources borrowed can be used to raise earnings by enough to cover rising service payments.

The criterion of overall resource use points to a possible though insufficient guideline: not to let external debt rise faster than national output. A safer guideline would be to keep interest obligations from rising relative to foreign exchange earnings. By either of these two tests, Latin American borrowing in the 1970s was too high. The ratio of net debt to GDP increased from .18 in 1973 to .32 by 1980 and .41 by 1981.[17] That increase was not far out of line with worldwide borrowing by developing countries in the period: some of the dynamic East Asian countries also ran up high ratios of debt to GDP, without getting into crises when financial conditions tightened. The reason for the difference is that they achieved such high ratios of exports to national product that debt service did not outrun their capacity to earn foreign exchange. Latin America did not borrow a great deal more relative to output but far more heavily in terms of interest obligations relative to export earnings.[18] For seven countries studied in detail by the Inter-American Development Bank, annual interest on external debt increased from 12 percent of export earnings in 1974 to 37 percent by 1981.[19]

Particular countries began to show such signs of strain that commercial lending slowed down or stopped for them before any recognized general crisis. Peru had gone deeply into debt and come under restraint from the mid-1970s, commercial lending to Costa Rica fairly well stopped by 1979, and Chilean financial institutions began to crack by 1981. But the general turning point did not come until August 1982 with the Mexican government's admission that, despite greatly increased oil export revenue, it could not get enough new credit to keep up service on existing debt. As lenders backed off everywhere, seeking shelter, conditions came close to a 1930s-style world financial panic. Two institutions came to the rescue: the Federal Reserve of the United States and the International Monetary Fund. They helped put together an emergency loan package for Mexico and began to organize methods of dealing with what has become a steady series of new emergencies. The Federal Reserve also took a positive step for the whole world by reversing the process of monetary contraction, which had put the brakes on in the first place, and began to stimulate growth of U.S. bank reserves and lending.

From that point the international financial institutions and the governments of the industrialized countries took on a limited but surprisingly flexible role in providing flows of new credit and putting constant pressure on the private international banks to resume lending, even though the banks would individually have preferred

[17] Ricardo Ffrench-Davis, "The External Debt Crisis in Latin America: Trends and Outlook," in Kwan S. Kim and David F. Ruccio, eds., *Debt and Development in Latin America* (Notre Dame: University of Notre Dame Press, 1985), table 7, p. 146.

[18] Jeffrey D. Sachs, "External Debt and Macroeconomic Performance in Latin America and East Asia," *Brookings Papers on Economic Activity* 2 (1985), pp. 523–64.

[19] IDB, *Social and Economic Progress, 1985 Report*, table I-2, p. 22.

to call in their loans and batten down the hatches.[20] Compared to an alternative of allowing private financial markets to work freely all this has been an immeasurable improvement. On the other hand, none of these institutions or governments has accepted any idea that they have any obligation to share the burden of adjustment to excessive debt by actually writing any of it off, or subsidizing interest, or guaranteeing net new flows of credit sufficient to permit resumption of economic growth at anything like prior rates. The process remains instead one of continuous renegotiation as new emergencies arise, with many compromises but a general attitude that the debtors are the ones who must straighten things out. The creditors seem determined to keep debtors on a short leash subject to constant check, despite the evident strains of the process and the costs in terms of deepening LDC hostility.[21] This approach could easily be read as demonstrating that what the financial institutions and governments care about is avoiding collapse of the banks or the world financial system itself, not particularly about growth in the developing countries.

On the side of the debtors, the impact has been and remains severe. Investment plunged everywhere, unemployment increased, real wages and social services have been cut severely, and some governments have been so preoccupied with the debt and need to seek new credit that actions in other directions have been almost paralyzed.[22] Still, a good many positive moves have been accomplished. Tax systems have been strengthened to reduce government deficits, a good deal of sheer waste which seemed unimportant before has been cut out, imports of luxury consumer goods have been generally tightened, capital flight has been brought under better control in some countries, and new exports have been greatly stimulated. By 1984, production began to recover at moderate rates in most countries, and at its more usual high rate in Brazil. But the beginnings of renewed expansion in Mexico seemed to be deepening its underlying problems. Despite all the contractions of wage levels, employment, investment, and government services, the debt is still rising, the near-term outlook worsening, and tensions rising to a de-

---

[20] Albert Fishlow, "Revisiting the Great Debt Crisis of 1982," in Kim and Ruccio, eds., *Debt and Development*, pp. 99–132.

[21] Rudiger Dornbusch, "Policy and Performance Links Between LDC Debtors and Industrial Nations," *Brookings Papers on Economic Activity* 2 (1985), pp. 303–56.

[22] IDB, *Social and Economic Progress, 1985 Report*, gives a careful quantitative account of the contractionary process and beginnings of revival.

gree that would have torn things apart already in most other Latin
American societies.

In a sense, the immediate cost of the crisis has been met. Rates of
domestic absorption that were running further and further above
national product have been forced down much closer to or below
current GDP, by varying combinations of export growth and import
reduction on the external side, and by drastic reductions of investment and lower real wages on the internal side. That enormous
shock should not need to be repeated. But continuing constraint
may be harder to live with than emergency tightening. Unless the
debts are somehow cut down, interest charges will continue to eat
up such high shares of current earnings that any sustained growth
of investment may be nearly impossible.

Starting from such tight constraints, the efforts by international
financial institutions and governments to provide more credit and
stimulate more private lending certainly have positive connotations.
They have helped greatly to avoid worse contraction. To increase
the level of new lending would go beyond that to help restore better
growth rates. But there are some negative connotations involved
too. One of them, discussed in later chapters, is that much of the
added lending comes along with a firm push toward the particular
kinds of internal economic strategies favored by the IMF and the
United States: for private enterprise, free entry and good treatment
for foreign investors, and against regulation or subsidies for social
purposes. Lenders are convinced that all this is desirable; borrowers
are forced into a corner where choices are tightly constrained.

If new lending does not return to earlier proportions, that might
in the long run be more desirable than if it did. The character of
growth under more restrained financial conditions might be healthier than that in the past. If reliance on external equipment and technology is reduced by a combination of more restricted external
credit and higher real prices of foreign exchange, the pressures for
a more independent style of development will be greater than before. Most of the semi-industrialized countries should be capable of
developing efficient lines of capital goods, if they concentrate on
those appropriate for their resources and do not try to spread across
the whole spectrum. The capacity to develop diversified exports has
been demonstrated for many of these countries, including significant capital goods exports in the case of Brazil. Relief from the high
costs of past borrowing could be a great help, but a return to high
rates of new borrowing could lead to worse problems in the future.

5. STABILIZATION AND REPRESSION

It is no accident that the most inflation-prone Latin American countries—Argentina, Brazil, Chile, and Uruguay—have also been notable for the frequency of their foreign exchange crises and became those hardest hit by modern totalitarian reaction. The same tensions that made inflation so difficult to deal with worked against the ability to keep democracies functioning. First in Brazil, following the military coup of 1964, then in even more drastic versions in Chile and Uruguay after 1973, and Argentina from 1976, regimes that suppressed political freedom and human rights and implemented terrorist programs to eliminate suspected supporters of all kinds of left-wing causes explained their purposes in terms of restoring social discipline, returning to free markets, and ending the scourge of inflation. "Economics as a system of discipline" took on new meaning in these devastating contexts.[23]

The evident association between exceptionally high rates of inflation and subsequent extremes of political repression can be interpreted in very different ways. A simple conclusion might be that stabilization policies should be applied forcefully to beat down inflation, whatever the costs in terms of lost growth, before it reaches levels destroying democratic systems. A contrary interpretation is that people can learn to live with inflation as long as it does not actually lower their living standards, but unmanageable pressures will build up if tough stabilization policies force direct confrontation in an effort to stop it. Fears for democracy in the early 1980s have been focused more on dangers from overly strict stabilization than on those of inflation. In a world in which nothing is ever really safe, which course is more dangerous: to let inflation continue or to apply strict stabilization policies to force it down?

Albert Hirschman's interpretation of these issues is particularly suggestive.[24] On one side, he warns against the political dangers of hyperinflation of the runaway type which has caught Argentina several times, which immediately preceded the military coup in Brazil in 1964, and which reached record levels in Chile under Allende. On the other side, he argues that in some contexts it is more dan-

[23] The phrase is taken from the title of an article by Adolfo Canitrot, "Discipline as a Central Objective of Economic Policy: An Essay on the Economic Programme of the Argentine Government since 1976," *World Development* 8 (1980), pp. 913–28.

[24] Hirschman, "Matrix of Inflation," and "The Turn Toward Authoritarianism in Latin America and the Search for Its Economic Determinants," pp. 89–135 in Hirschman, *Essays in Trespassing*.

gerous to try to beat down inflation than to accept it. Where growth under conditions of distorted structures of production creates inflation, but real incomes of all social groups are increasing, none of them is likely to tear apart the political system just because of rising prices. If the government accepts some inflation it can avoid head-on confrontation with labor over wages, or business and landowners over taxes. Price and wage claims that are excessive in nominal terms can be accepted in the process of social bargaining, leaving it up to the inflationary process to scale them down in real terms. The tensions adverse for democracy are greatest when all sides come to see the issues in terms of using force to keep everyone else into line.

Hirschman considers that the ill-fated efforts of the IMF and the United States through its aid program to force deflationary policies on Brazil in the late 1950s helped derail an unusually successful growth process and led to the political and economic breakdown of the early 1960s.[25] A critical Brazilian policy option in 1967 supports the same view. After the military government, which took power in 1964, had driven the inflation rate down from about 90 to 30 percent through an intense contractionary program, it opted against IMF preferences to accept the remaining inflation and return to expansion. At first the results in terms of political repression were no better, and for a time even worse, but as economic growth continued at high rates the country was able to start back toward a more open political system. Increased space to answer competing economic claims does not in any sense guarantee a more open political system but it can help if a society tries to move in that direction. The economic path taken in Brazil might be compared to the contrary choice under the Chilean military regime, where obsession with driving down inflation created extremely high levels of unemployment, reduced consumption of the lower 40 percent of the population, set back industrialization, and has so far left a political impasse with no sign of any return toward democracy.[26]

It is not easy for a nonauthoritarian government to keep a coherent balance where deep division in public preferences work against clear-cut response to new problems. Costa Rica in the period 1978–1982 provides a spectacular example. It is Latin America's most fully open democracy, and had for a long time achieved above-average economic management but when faced with a collapse of coffee export earnings in 1978 the system proved for a time incapable

[25] Hirschman, "A Dissenter's Confession," pp. 102–103.
[26] Foxley, *Latin American Experiments.*

of any effective response. The president wanted at first to implement full IMF-style open economy correction but was forced to back down precisely because all major groups—industrial and agricultural producers, importers and exporters and financial interests, consumers and private-sector workers and public-sector employees—were able to defend themselves effectively. The government did not manage to find any consistent path, or to stick to agreements made with the IMF about what to do.[27] Investment, GDP, employment, and real wages were driven down sharply as external negotiations failed. The indecision and degree of economic deterioration were at least as bad as the breakdown that immediately preceded military intervention in Brazil in 1964. But in contrast to Brazil, attachment to an open society outweighed pressure for drastic solutions. The cost of this prolonged impasse was severe, in terms of both inflation and external debt, but as of 1985 the case for tolerance seemed reasonably well validated: after four years of confusion a new elected government introduced policies that soon began to bring down inflation and to promote economic revival.

A popular majority can be wrong, but so can an unpopular minority. The authoritarian governments of the Southern Cone, for all their emphasis on stopping inflation, had no brilliant record of success. Is the problem essentially that systematic national characteristics make inflation particularly intractable in these countries? Three hypotheses suggest that they have been—for reasons that are in part historically given but at least in part problems that may be moderated by better economic policies—more inflation-prone than most of the rest of Latin America.

Hypothesis number one: it is easier to control inflation in societies in which the main economic groups are not at each others' throats for other reasons, as they have been in Argentina since the first Perón government turned urban-rural conflict into channels of mutual destruction. Strategies of economic growth that aggravate conflicts among groups maximize the difficulties of macroeconomic balance.

Hypothesis number two: the degree of labor militancy developed in Argentina, Chile, and Uruguay prior to the authoritarian takeovers made the control of inflation more difficult than elsewhere, in

[27] Eugenio Rivera Urrutia, *El Fondo Monetario Internaciónal y Costa Rica, 1978–1982* (San José: Departamento Ecuménico de Investigaciones, 1982); Juan Manuel Villasuso, "Foreign Debt and Economic Development: The Case of Costa Rica," pp. 175–87 in Antonio Jorge, Jorge Salazar-Carillo, and René Higonnet, eds., *Foreign Debt and Latin American Development* (New York: Pergamon Press, 1983).

particular because it meant that any relatively liberal government was torn to pieces if it tried to impose wage restraint. That militancy had its positive side in protecting workers against arbitrary action adverse to them, and in pushing the societies toward more social concern than might otherwise have been likely, but it certainly made inflation more difficult to control. The alternative need not be suppression of labor; it could conceivably be one of incorporating labor into decision-making processes, in exchange for restraints on wage increases to keep them consistent with the productive capacity of the economy. Such incorporation may be impossible in some countries, because of either recalcitrance by property owners or unwillingness to accept limitations from the side of labor. But if it could be done in any of these countries it would not only make the control of inflation easier; it would lesson the dangers of renewed repression.

Hypothesis number three: the disconnection between domestic prices and world price levels fostered by the more extreme cases of protected industrialization in the early power war years was a major factor both in creating external deficits in the first place and then in making correction through devaluation more inflationary and less effective than it would otherwise have been.

6. Conclusions

Most cases of extreme inflation and repeated external deficits in Latin America can in a superficial sense be explained either by excess demand relative to productive capacity or by structural imbalance in the sense of excessive import requirements for production relative to exports. At a deeper level, these problems grew out of the stresses of trying to change old-style underdeveloped countries, with a great deal of inequality and little diversification of production, into more modern industrial societies. The strains of transition came mainly from efforts to transfer income and power away from landowner-exporters to the industrial sector, against the resistance of a long-privileged conservative class to sharing political power, aggravated by impatience for rapid change on the part of reform-minded people in all sectors.

These inescapable conflicts were greatly heightened in some countries by early postwar policies turning urban-rural conflict into a state of warfare pitting workers and industrialists against landowner-exporters. They were also made more difficult than necessary by kinds of economic analysis that disdained questions of macroeconomic balance as if they were somehow irrelevant to the real issues of structural change. No country could escape the strains of transition, but many proved able to escape both high rates of inflation and extreme political repression. They did it partly by avoiding head-on social conflict of the Argentine variety (or by backing away before it went too far), partly by avoiding extremes of protection and policies adverse to primary exports, partly by adopting policies favorable for industrial exports, partly by correcting the price of foreign exchange at steady low rates rather than by the shock process of large devaluations, and partly by keeping tighter limits on monetary expansion and government spending.

Criticism of IMF stabilization programs has at times been wildly exaggerated: the basic themes of monetary restraint and devaluation are often exactly what is needed. But it is true that the Fund often calls for reductions of consumption and real wages even in those cases where the problem is structural and not a matter of excess demand, and sometimes goes beyond recommendations directly relevant to stabilization by insisting that countries give up all kinds of controls and subsidies as a matter of general principle. Stabilization policies could often be oriented more toward growth of output than contraction: negotiations over adjustments to external debt in the 1980s have usually taken place in conditions of excess capacity and high unemployment, but in this period the Fund went in the wrong direction toward tighter conditions of monetary restraint than in the late 1970s. When reductions of consumption are necessary they could be directed more toward higher income groups by measures to tax them while protecting consumption of necessities. A penchant for reductions of real wages, and opposition to subsidies for consumption by the poor, increase inequality when that is in no sense necessary for stabilization.

When countries achieve growth without excess demand they can avoid the imposition of external preferences. When they lose macroeconomic balance external credit can be a great help, but it is totally arbitrary to condition such help on measures that make the distribution of income more unequal in those countries.

SIX

OWNERSHIP I: LAND

Questions of property ownership are much closer to the center of the stage in Latin America than in the United States: that is one of the main manifestations of frustration over the ways that the Latin economies function. But does ownership have much to do with the capacity of an economy to function well? Economic analysis rather suggests that it does not. It is possible to study a great deal of economics without ever encountering a serious question about ownership. The core of the subject is a logical system that treats capital and land as factors of production to be analyzed by universally applicable techniques without regard to who owns them. This drive toward principles applicable anywhere, regardless of ownership systems, is appropriate and often successful for questions of allocative efficiency and national income. For many other questions, such as hunger or national autonomy, it is not. For analysis of the conflicts of development in Latin America it leaves out too much.

1. WHY OWNERSHIP MATTERS

The normal assumption in conventional economics is that a nation's laws, and the policies set by its government, determine the rules for permissible behavior by business firms and the incentives to invest and produce. The normal assumption in radical economics is the reverse: the laws that are adopted and actually enforced, and the policies chosen by governments, are dominated by preferences of property owners in the first place. Both views capture aspects of a reality that differs greatly among countries. It is surely not true that influence flows only in one direction, from the state to the firms or the contrary. The process is much more likely to involve a circular flow in which both control of the means of production and control of the state involve conflicting interests reacting back and forth on each other. Changes of ownership, from private to public or back, from foreign to domestic or the contrary, are both subject to national policies and significant in determining what policies are chosen.

Ownership of productive resources carries special weight within the decision processes of a society and thereby helps shape the character of its development. The fundamental reason for disproportionate influence is that what property owners do about investment, production, financial flows, and community relationships can greatly affect the welfare of everyone in the society and help implement—or demolish—any intended government program. That does not mean that property owners are either unified in their preferences or able to force the society to accept all of them. Conflicts of interest among property owners are common and often crucial for policy choices: conflicts between landowners and industrialists, between export-oriented and protected industries, between producers of consumer goods who want cheap imported capital equipment and producers of capital goods who want protection, and so on through an endless list. Some want to stay in the world economy and some want out; some want active government favors and some prefer a weak, poorly financed government; some want increasing purchasing power for workers to buy their products and some prefer tight restraint on wages. Such differences provide plenty of openings for movement by any governments that actually wish to bring other interests into the picture. The underlying question is whether government itself represents only the interests of property owners or is also concerned with the welfare of urban labor, of landless rural labor, of the poor who may not be in the labor force at all, and of the country as a whole.

Much of Latin American economic policy can best be explained by assuming that governments normally concentrate on defending the more powerful ownership interests in any given period: landowners in the nineteenth century, protected domestic industrialists in the early postwar period, and in some countries more recently the interests of externally oriented industry. But by no means all significant changes in economic policy can be explained in such simplistic terms. Different ownership groups change in their preferences and in their relative weight, urban labor often makes itself heard, landowners are not dead yet, and even peasants sometimes make a dent on current policy preferences. Beyond the group pressures, some government leaders have forceful ideas of their own that break out of readily explicable patterns of influence by particular interests. No Colombian ownership group drove President Betancur to concentrate his interests on achieving a truce with rural guerrilla movements; no Mexican drove President López Portillo to increase taxes on capital relative to labor. Peruvian landowners seemed to be able to dominate Peruvian politics up to the mid-1960s, but a leftist military regime swept them away in a thorough land reform in the next few years. Ownership isn't everything.

The chances that ownership will dominate choices of economic strategy should normally be less if the political system of the country allows all social groups to have access to information and to bring their anxieties to bear on the government. That is not to say that the interests considered in making policy choices are certain to be more diversified if the society is democratic. Democracies can be undercut by keeping many of the poor in ignorance through educational systems that do not effectively extend to rural areas; or by differential access to financing for elections and for influencing administrators; or by using the threat of military intervention to rule out particular candidates or parties or ideas. Even societies that achieve widespread participation and manage to avoid military intervention are rarely able to come close to reducing the role of property owners to the equivalent of "one vote per person."[1] Latin American societies do not come close at all. Democracies are exceptionally difficult to maintain, and even those that work relatively well rarely reach out to the whole range of social interests. The voices of property owners come through with heightened force because the societies have not generally achieved wide political participation and because ownership itself is extraordinarily concentrated.

In addition to its bearing on choices of national policy, the pattern of ownership can make a great deal of difference for the economic consequences of any change in constraints or incentives. Land ownership structures and their relationships to the ways the Latin American economies function have always been an important part of structuralist arguments, partly because of consequences for production and partly because of their effects on rural poverty. The two kinds of concern are not exactly parallel. Agricultural production might be raised greatly without having much effect on rural poverty, if ownership of land is highly concentrated. Conversely, policies favorable for agricultural production are more likely to reduce rural poverty if ownership is more nearly equal.

Poverty is practically inescapable where arable land is scare relative to the rural labor force. But it is also true that for any given availability of land, poverty could be minimized by dividing the land equally. The actual pattern of ownership in most Latin American

[1] See especially the illuminating analysis by Charles Lindblom in *Politics and Markets: The World's Political-Economic Systems* (New York: Basic Books, 1977).

countries is highly concentrated: the great majority of rural families are forced down to much smaller land holdings, and deeper poverty, than would be the case with more equal ownership. Many individual families escape by moving out of agricultural production, either by seeking urban employment or by nonagricultural production within the rural sector. But such possibilities depend to some degree on possessing at least minimal skills of reading, writing, and counting: they are held down in many of the countries by weak systems of education in the rural areas. Preferences of large property owners had much to do with this weakness: the landowners who dominated local decisions were rarely interested in rural schools for their own children, and they saw rural education either as an unnecessary expense for children of peasants or even as a possible danger for control of local labor.[2]

Concentration of land ownership can make a great deal of difference for the effects of international trade. Primary exports serve to raise national income much as international trade theory suggests, but they may do little to reduce poverty, or may in some conditions make it worse. The reason they did little historically to reduce poverty was that highly concentrated land holdings meant that increasing incomes from primary exports went to very few people. Small subsistence farmers may have gained from higher domestic prices due to exports, and from increasing demand for rural labor, but the bulk of the gain went to the large landowners. Rising national income from increasing primary exports may even worsen poverty if increased incomes of the large landowners enable them to bid up the price of land and reduce its availability for subsistence producers. If reduction of poverty had been the dominant social goal, free trade under these conditions would probably have been blocked.

Coffee exports from Colombia and from prerevolution Nicaragua provide a good example of the differences flowing from ownership patterns. For both countries, coffee has long been the leading primary export. In Colombia, coffee production is carried out mainly by independent small landholders. Periods of good export earnings result in widely spread gains. It is true that the gains do not reach the poorest rural people without land, but they are much more widely distributed than they would be if production were organized in large commercial plantations under concentrated ownership. In Nicaragua before its revolution, coffee production was

---

[2] F. LaMond Tullis, *Lord and Peasant in Peru: A Paradigm of Political and Social Change* (Cambridge: Harvard University Press, 1970).

efficiently carried out in very large plantations, most of them owned
by Somoza and his close associates. Years of good export earnings
helped them buy up more of the country and build up assets abroad
in case of hurried departure. The same trade policies, with the same
commodity exports, had considerably more inegalitarian implications because of the ownership structure.

Keith Griffin and Jeffrey James emphasize another aspect of
ownership concentration as part of a general argument that incre-
mental policies to lessen inequality cannot succeed without asset redistribution. In countries in which the poor are truly hungry, any
program to raise their living standards by such means as transfer
payments or public sector employment will immediately stimulate
expenditure on food. If food production cannot be rapidly increased, as it usually cannot, prices will rise swiftly. That may transfer real income back from the poor to the producers and sellers of
food. If food production is concentrated, then income will promptly
be reconcentrated.[3] This is a complicated and uncertain question,
examined in section 4 below; it is a matter of trade policy as well as
ownership, but the latter is certainly relevant.

Ownership patterns in the industrial sector can of course matter
too. Between ownership of industry by foreign as opposed to domestic firms, one significant variable discussed in the following
chapter is the effect on domestic research and development: foreign-owned firms are much more likely to concentrate research activities at their home-country headquarters than to promote them
within the host country. If there is to be any significant learning
through research efforts inside a developing country it is crucially
important to have some domestic-owned firms within the sectors in
which research is feasible.[4]

Apart from differences between foreign and domestic ownership, the degree of concentration can make a considerable difference in the ways markets operate. When a market consists of a small
number of sellers they may be able to exploit buyers and to impede
changes favorable for efficiency. Northern industrialized countries
have long recognized the issue and have sometimes acted on it by
laws permitting the government to block proposed ownership concentrations, or even to take existing firms apart. Such attacks on
ownership structures have sometimes been criticized on the ground

---

[3] Keith B. Griffin and Jeffrey James, *The Transition to Egalitarian Development* (New
York: St. Martin's, 1981). This and the following chapter owe a special debt to this
stimulating book.

[4] Peter Evans, *Dependent Development*.

that it is in most cases difficult for any small group to achieve effective market control under open conditions of entry for new firms, especially with relatively free trade allowing import competition. For the United States, there is plenty of room to argue about the matter. For Latin American countries, concentration of ownership in most modern industries is far higher. The role of the connected family group, of a few conglomerates that combine banking and industrial interests and reach across many fields, is much more important than in the industrialized countries.[5] Competition from imports may serve as a restraint in those countries that allow it, but where small groups of producers are particularly powerful they are particularly able to shape policies of protection in their favor. The power of concentrated ownership is exercised with much less public information, behind greater import protection, within legal systems that contain practically no antitrust restraints to hold back abuse. Those differences are not accidents: the concentration itself provides the political force to minimize restraints on its use.

2. LAND OWNERSHIP AND LAND REFORM

The special tensions of land ownership in Latin America come from juxtaposition of two extremes: large numbers of rural people in deep poverty, with little or no land, in the face of concentrated ownership in large holdings to degrees not matched in any other region of the world. But should rural poverty be regarded as a result of inadequate access to land or instead as a result of insufficient opportunities for alternative employment? From the latter point of view it is not crucial to change land ownership, because even if nothing can be done about it rural poverty could be gradually alleviated by increasing both rural and urban nonfarm employment.[6] That view is

---

[5] Nathaniel H. Leff, "Industrial Organization and Entrepreneurship in the Developing Countries: The Economic Groups," *Economic Development and Cultural Change* (July 1978), pp. 661–75, and "Entrepreneurship and Economic Development: The Problem Revisited," *Journal of Economic Literature* 17 (March 1979), pp. 46–68.

[6] Two of the economists most familiar with Colombian agriculture and the Colombian economy as a whole, Lauchlin Currie and R. Albert Berry, have neatly bracketed the two sides of these issues: Berry emphasizes land ownership structure and Currie instead the importance of getting excess people out of farming through rapid employment growth. See Berry, "Farm Size Distribution, Income Distribution, and the Efficiency of Agricultural Production: Colombia," *American Economic Review* 62 (May 1972), pp. 403–408; Berry and Miguel Urrutia, *Income Distribution in Colombia*; Currie, *Accelerating Development: The Necessity and the Means* (New York: McGraw-Hill, 1966).

surely correct in the sense that creation of employment opportunities can help greatly, and may in some countries provide an adequate solution, but this possibility is no reason to rule out concern
for ownership of land. In many countries there are far too many
people backed up in the rural sector relative to new openings for
nonagricultural employment. As shown in table 3.1, the farm labor
force is still increasing in many countries, though not all. Creation
of nonfarm employment opportunities may not help enough to
keep the situation from worsening. To make land holdings less unequal could be a direct and powerful way to lessen rural poverty.

    As of 1950, the largest 9.5 percent of all farm land holdings in
Latin America included 90 percent of the land.[7] Latifundia, defined
as estates employing more than twelve permanent workers, constituted only 1.3 percent of total farms in Colombia but included 49.5
percent of all farm land. In Guatemala, only 0.1 percent of farms
were in this size range, but they held 40.8 percent of the farm land.[8]
Minifundia, defined as holdings too small to enable a family to get
out of poverty if dependent on their agricultural production, accounted for 64 percent of all land holdings in Colombia but only 5
percent of the land, and close to 90 percent of all farm holdings in
Ecuador, Guatemala, and Peru. In these last three countries in the
mid-1960s less than 10 percent of all farm units were classified as
family farms, large enough to enable a family to earn incomes above
the poverty line from their own farm. That proportion was higher,
though still less than a majority (between 39 and 49 percent of all
farm units), in Argentina, Brazil, and Chile.[9]

    The owners of minifundia, along with completely landless rural la-
bor, provide the work force available for the large landholders and
for nonfarm rural employers. The incomes of those who own small
farms may often be determined more by the wages and the amount
of work they can find in such employment than by their earnings
from production on their own land. But employment opportunities
themselves depend in part on the structure of ownership: high de-

    [7] Thomas F. Carroll, "The Land Reform Issue in Latin America," pp. 161–201 in
Albert Hirschman, ed., *Latin American Issues: Essays and Comments* (New York: Twentieth Century Fund, 1961), data from p. 165. For a comparison of degrees of concentration in Latin America to other regions, see Shlomo Eckstein et al., "Land Reform in Latin America: Bolivia, Chile, Mexico, Peru, and Venezuela," World Bank
Staff Working Paper no. 275 (April 1978), ch. 1.

    [8] Celso Furtado, *Economic Development of Latin America* (New York: Cambridge Uni-
versity Press, 2d ed., 1976), p. 75. See also the extensive date on land owernship distribution in Solon Barraclough, ed., *Agrarian Structure in Latin America*.

    [9] Barraclough, *Agrarian Structure*, table 2-1, p. 16.

grees of concentration work against use of labor because the large land holdings are operated with much more capital and land-intensive methods than the small, using much less labor per hectare.[10]

Although it is evident that rural poverty could be lessened by dividing land more equally, that fact does not make it get divided. It does not often get divided by public policy decisions because large landowners have a significant voice in determining those decisions. It does not get divided by market forces because subsistence producers and landless rural labor are not often able to buy land, and because commercial operators of large estates are usually able to gain advantages of privileged access to credit as well as political influence. Even reform governments concerned with the land hunger of the rural poor may be held back by fear of the economic consequences of redistribution for output and especially for export earnings. For those who emphasize economic growth as the surest way to lessen poverty, land reform can appear as a danger rather than an opportunity. If market forces act in the first place to drive producers toward the most efficient use of land, doesn't that imply that expropriation and redistribution would be likely to reduce efficiency?

The likely effects of land reform on output depend very much on the character of the reform and the historical context in the particular case. But one of the best-established empirical relationship in studies of agricultural development is that output per hectare is usually higher on small than on large farms.[11] That relationship is due to several factors, including especially the more intensive use of land in smaller holdings. Small farmers use all of their land, put in much more labor time per hectare, and may also exert more active

[10] Berry, "Farm Size Distribution"; Berry and William R. Cline, *Agrarian Structures and Productivity in Developing Countries* (Baltimore: Johns Hopkins University Press, 1979); Keith B. Griffin, "Systems of Labour Control and Rural Poverty in Ecuador," pp. 172–220 in Griffin, *Land Concentration and Rural Poverty* (New York: Holmes and Meier, 1976). Griffin argues that large landholders in Ecuador, facing semi-isolated local labor markets, hold back employment to keep down wages and to keep the bargaining position of workers weak.

[11] See especially Berry and Cline, *Agrarian Structures*; Peter Dorner and Don Kanel, "The Economic Case for Land Reform: Employment, Income Distribution, and Productivity," ch. 3 in Dorner, ed., *Land Reform in Latin America: Issues and Cases* (Madison: University of Wisconsin, Land Tenure Center, 1971); Eckstein et al., "Land Reform," pp. 113–20; and the data for output per worker and per hectare in seven Latin American countries in Barraclough, *Agrarian Structure*, table 2-6, pp. 26–27. The separate study of land structure in Colombia by Berry, "Farm Size Distribution," p. 406, indicates that holdings in the range between five and ten hectares have the highest social productivity; those under three hectares have lower yields, and those above ten have steadily decreasing returns per hectare as size increases.

personal effort under pressure to raise output when the depth of poverty of the family depends so much on the result. Larger land holdings leave more land idle but apply more capital equipment and purchased inputs per hectare on the land they actually use. For particular crops, such as cotton and sugar, large landholders may also gain significant economies of scale; for more diversified basic foods, the beans or potatoes or other traditional peasant foods, diseconomies of scale may be more important and the comparative advantage is rather on the side of smaller farms. Output *per worker employed* is normally higher on the large farms because of their higher ratios of capital and land per worker, but output per hectare is greater on the smaller farms. Where labor is abundant but land is scarce, total output is maximized by getting as much as possible per unit of land, not by using large farms and reducing the use of labor.

Albert Berry and William Cline have calculated estimates of how much total output could increase in eight different countries or regions, with known production techniques, if land were more equally divided. They estimated the possible gain in output to range from 10 percent in Pakistan as of 1960 to nearly 80 percent in Northeast Brazil as of 1973, with intermediate values of 25 percent for Brazil as a whole and 28 percent for Colombia.[12]

Mexican agriculture constitutes an apparent exception to the general rule that output per hectare is relatively low on large farms. A major reason for that is precisely that the giant estates dominant before the revolution of 1910 were greatly cut down in size either in the revolution or during the major redistribution of land under President Cárdenas in the 1930s. The share of total crop land held by large estates was cut from 70 percent as of 1923 to 29 percent by 1960.[13] Many estates remain fairly large: the nominal limit of 100 hectares was allowed to go as high as five hundred hectares under special provisions. The owners were in most cases able to hold on to their best land and responded to the new situation by focusing more effort on maximizing income from that remainder. They often achieve higher value of output per hectare than the smaller farm units, and they have raised output per hectare more rapidly since 1940, partly by concentrating on particular crops for which economies of scale are significant. Land reform plus assurances to remaining owners against further expropriation "transformed, on a

---

[12] Berry and Cline, *Agrarian Structure*, table 5-1, pp. 132–33.

[13] Eckstein et al., "Land Reform," table 3, p. 13; see discussion pp. 11–14 and 36–42. Susan R. Walsh Sanderson, *Land Reform in Mexico: 1910–1980* (Orlando: Academic Press, 1984).

significant national scale, a class of owners of very large traditionalist latifundia, accustomed to easy income without innovation, into
a group suddenly reduced in their holdings but still able to muster
substantial resources and recover their economic position by improvement in their farming methods."[14]

The large estates that remain concentrate chiefly on standardized
crops for export, leaving to smaller producers the more diversified
production of basic food for the domestic market. Since the two
kinds of agriculture are aimed at distinct markets, relative output
value and income depend to a considerable degree on Mexican policy with respect to international trade and exchange rates: an in-
ward-looking strategy with low value of foreign exchange favors the
relative earnings of small holders producing mainly for the home
market, while a stress on export incentives favors the large landholders. Mexican strategy was for a long period focused on the export side, providing stronger incentives and more help through
public investment to the larger landowners. That was unfavorable
for equality but worked well for agricultural production. From 1940
to 1960 output increased at an annual rate of 4.6 percent, double
the rate for Latin America as a whole.[15] Both the reduced sector of
large farms and the smaller holdings created through redistribution
performed better than the prerevolution system of extremely large
haciendas.

Why should redistribution of land by expropriation give better
economic results than reliance on market forces? It might not, if the
existing distribution were the result of a long period of adaptation
to market pressures driving producers toward the most efficient
possible scales and techniques of farming. But if the initial conditions are in large measure an expression of historical inheritance
patterns, in some cases tracing back to land grants of the colonial period and in many to nineteenth-century power struggles, with large
estates held together by families concerned at least as much with social prestige and political power as with commercial production,
then the element of efficiency considerations buried in all this may
be almost invisible. Where initial land holdings were radically disrupted by revolutionary reforms, as in Mexico, the greatly reduced
postreform estates proved to be far more consistent with efficient
economic performance than the prior structure of private ownership. In most of Latin America at the start of the postwar period, the

[14] Eckstein et al., "Land Reform," p. 39.
[15] Ibid., p. 26.

distribution of land holdings had little to do with any tests of efficiency through economic performance.[16]

As the materialistic twentieth century has worn away at noncom-
mercial values, the nonmarket considerations in land use have gradually faded in importance relative to commercial objectives. Increasing orientation toward economic returns has moved large
landowners toward greater efficiency. But significant barriers still
hold back any thoroughly efficient redistribution of ownership. In
particular, large landholders can always get more and cheaper
credit than small, and they are often favored on the side of costs by
policies permitting cheap imports of the equipment and current inputs important to them but not to the labor-intensive small producers. Large landholders could obtain higher incomes per hectare
even if they were less efficient. But that consideration in terms of
price distortions is probably only a minor part of the picture. The
owners of large estates are much better placed to have public roads
built where they want them, infrastructure oriented to their needs,
and laws both enacted and interpreted to their benefit.[17] The cards
are all stacked in ways to favor earnings of the larger estates, and to
make them better able to buy additional land, even when they are
not to the most efficient producers.

Although more equal distribution of land would be likely to raise
agricultural production in most Latin American countries, land reform through legal processes in capitalist economies would seem to
be a most implausible expectation. Still, it has not been totally
blocked. Industrial interests as well as concern for social reform favor breaking away from systems dominated by large landholders.
These preferences helped to accomplish some moderate reform
programs in the 1930s, and in the early 1960s the United States
added both encouragement and financial support under the Alliance for Progress. The reasons included a mixture of real concern
to lessen poverty with the hope that land reform could convert potentially revolutionary peasants into rural landowners with a stake
in the preservation of property rights. That combination of objectives had strong appeal for moderate reformers, and for policy
makers in the United States during the immediate aftermath of the
Cuban Revolution. Chile, Colombia, Ecuador, Peru, and Venezuela

[16] Cf. the discussion of Peruvian highland estates in Tullis, *Lord and Peasant*, and
the historical background in Barraclough, *Agrarian Structure*, ch. 1.

[17] Cf. Barraclough, *Agrarian Structure*, pp. 114–20.

all enacted land reforms through normal legal processes in the late 1950s and early 1960s.[18]

Some of these gradualist reforms made headway for a time, though all fell far short of their objectives. In Peru the widely supported reform legislation of 1964 was almost totally blocked by landowner opposition. The pressure broke through a few years later but only after the civilian administration, which had failed to accomplish anything, was overturned by General Velasco's left-wing military government. In Chile, Eduardo Frei pushed through a fairly substantial reform, redistributing approximately 10 percent of all agricultural land after carrying through a constitutional reform to authorize appropriations of property, but this still left a sense of defeat because the scale fell far short of his stated goal.[19] In Colombia, the democratic reform took on real life for a time in the 1960s, given strength by Carlos Lleras Restrepo both before and during his presidency. As in so many other domains, Colombian political leadership seemed exceptionally able to combine cautious conservatism with the capacity for genuine change.[20] But in this field that capacity broke down. As the land reform program began to gain momentum, it woke up dormant peasant frustrations and incited increasingly active reform groups. They began to seize land illegally and to organize to assert stronger political pressures. That process upset many moderate reformers and discredited President Lleras within his own party. The land reform agency lost support and the whole operation was buried shortly after the end of his term, to be replaced by programs of rural investment and community development that did not challenge ownership conditions.

Merilee Grindle concluded from the Colombian experience that it shows the power of Latin American elites "to manage and exploit the pressures for change to arrive at solutions which preserve traditional structures and positions of dominance."[21] The experience

[18] Carroll, "The Land Reform Issue"; Merilee Grindle, *State and Countryside: Development Policy and Agrarian Politics in Latin America* (Baltimore: Johns Hopkins University Press, 1986).

[19] Robert R. Kaufman, *The Politics of Land Reform in Chile, 1950–1970* (Cambridge: Harvard University Press, 1972); William Ascher, *Scheming for the Poor: The Politics of Redistribution in Latin America* (Cambridge: Harvard University Press, 1984), ch. 7.

[20] Thanks to Albert Hirschman the Colombian case became celebrated as an example of reformist progress by indirect and patient methods overcoming traditional resistances; see his "Land Use and Land Reform in Colombia," pp. 93–158 in Hirschman, ed., *Journeys Toward Progress: Studies of Economic Policy Making in Latin America* (New York: Twentieth Century Fund, 1963).

[21] Merilee Grindle, "Whatever Happened to Land Reform? The Latin American

looks in most respects like a telling example of refusal to allow fundamental change. But Albert Hirschman, ever able to bring out positive signs in events that to others appear to be defeats, found a decade later that the spirit of the rural activists remained very much alive, transformed into production cooperatives and associations helping peasants get credit and political attention. In that view, it is misleading to conclude that "a social movement that has not achieved its preordained objectives, such as the movement for agrarian reform in Colombia, is an unqualified failure. . . . The social energies that were aroused in the course of that movement did not pass from the scene even though the movement itself did. These energies remained, as it were, in *storage* for a while, but were available to fuel later, perhaps very different, movements."[22]

3. RADICAL LAND REFORMS

The legislated land reforms of the 1960s were consistently held within narrow limits, but more radical authoritarian or revolutionary overturns of land ownership structures have often been potent. The first big land reform in Latin America was at the heart of the Mexican revolution. That bloody struggle and its aftermath of reform in the 1930s changed ownership greatly. The Bolivian revolution of 1952 was not initially concerned with land issues, but when peasants launched their own direct and violent action to take over the land it led to an unusually thorough reform.[23] The Cuban revolution of 1959 was followed by profound changes in land ownership, in this case mainly by creating state farms to replace prior private ownership. The authoritarian reform under Velasco in Peru starting in 1969 was more peaceful but did not accomplish much for reduction of rural poverty, for reasons discussed below.

Long-term effects of land reforms depend a great deal on their purposes and nature in each case. In Mexico an objectives of lessening social protest by redistribution, or by accepting land seizures, has been offset in most periods by a strong concern for keeping up agricultural exports to provide foreign exchange earnings. Public investment in support of agriculture has gone mainly to the larger

Experience," University of Texas at Austin, Institute of Latin American Studies, Technical Papers Series no. 23 (1980), p. 31.

[22] Hirschman, *Getting Ahead Collectively: Grassroots Experiences in Latin America* (New York: Pergamon Press, 1984), pp. 55–56.

[23] Ronald Clark, "Agrarian Reform: Bolivia," pp. 127–64 in Dorner, *Land Reform*; Eckstein et al., "Land Reform," pp. 42–50.

export producers, not the beneficiaries of the reforms. In Peru a central objective was to foster cooperatives, to avoid both market-oriented individualism and Soviet-style collective farming. In Cuba and to some extent in Nicaragua, policy has been mainly directed toward state farms, allowing some private producers but not fostering cooperatives. In both these cases the initial emphasis on state farms was subsequently lessened: Cuba began to adopt cooperatives in the late 1970s, along with a new role for private markets, while Nicaragua began to respond more to pressure from peasants for individual ownership. How well have these different approaches worked in comparison with each other?

In Mexico, redistribution was enormous but far from complete. It created a dualistic system: many more peasants participated in land ownership while at the same time commercial agriculture on the large northern estates was shielded from thorough redistribution.[24] On the side of social stabilization, the increase in small-scale ownership worked to lessen pressures for radical change in the rural area. The peasants have usually provided a force for stability, of support for the ruling government party even when its policies have not been oriented to their interests. On the side of output, the country achieved much better results than the rest of Latin America for a long time, from 1940 to the early 1960s. Rapid industrialization was managed without adverse incentives hurting agricultural production and exports; instead, high rates of investment in agriculture helped achieve good rates of aggregate growth. But then in the course of the 1960s this process ran into increasing trouble.

At least two major changes acted to break down the previously stable course of Mexican agricultural development. One was that public sector investment in rural areas began to slow down. The other was that rapid population growth outran the rate of migration to the cities: continuing increases in landless agricultural labor generated new pressures for redistribution. By 1960 Mexico had more landless rural families than it had prior to the revolution of 1910; the combined proportion of landless families and *minifundistas* had been reduced to 37 percent of rural families by 1940 but by 1960 it was up to 48 percent.[25] The Mexican government, in its classically compromising style, responded by modest new programs of redistribution, and by accepting some illegal land seizures, while at the

[24] Alain de Janvry, *The Agrarian Question and Reformism in Latin America* (Baltimore: Johns Hopkins University Press, 1981), pp. 123–31, and Merilee Grindle, *State and Countryside*, pp. 61–67 and 99–104.

[25] Eckstein et al., "Land Reform," table 6, p. 17.

same time trying to reassure the owners of the large estates that they would remain immune. But even a limited turn back toward redistribution in the 1970s undermined the confidence of the large landholders in the security of their position. The previously strong growth of Mexican agricultural production slowed down greatly.

In the late 1970s food exports fell while imports climbed. Even the ancient Mexican staples, corn and beans, came to be supplied increasingly by imports. The change was partly a matter of rising domestic demand and partly one of limits on the supply side. In addition to the effects on demand of population growth and rising incomes under the impact of the oil boom in this period, the two reformist administrations of the 1970s promoted consumer subsidies of basic foods intended to improve nutrition of the poor. On the supply side they both made positive moves as well: they turned away from the costly prior practice of holding down prices at the producer level and began to raise public spending in support of rainfed production by small producers as well as irrigation. But despite the combined effects of increasing demand and more public support, the response on the supply side could not keep up with the growth of demand. That could be explained by the high rate of growth of consumption, by its structure, by competition between domestic supply and exports, by natural resource limits (especially water), or by all these factors together. Rose Spalding compares the main competing explanations, placing special emphasis on the power of upper-income groups to pull land into use for animal feed crops and meat production, and for fruit and vegetable crops, at the cost of staple foods.[26] The importance of that consideration does not rule out concern for natural resource limits, population pressure, and export objectives. When Mexican economic growth resumes, the conflicts over land and water use, and over trade policy for agriculture, seem almost certain to intensify.

In contrast to the Mexican attempts to balance private commercial agriculture on large estates with elements of land redistribution, in a system allowing political pressure from all directions, the land reforms in Cuba and in Peru simply swept away the large private landholdings by decree, without compromises in the name of protecting commercial export agriculture. Cuba left some private ownership for small holdings, subject to marketing through state chan-

[26] Rose J. Spalding, *The Mexican Food Crisis: An Analysis of the SAM*, Center for U.S.-Mexican Studies, University of California at San Diego, Research Report Series, 33 (1984). Susan Sanderson, in *Land Reform*, puts primary emphasis on population and resource limits (p. 123): "poor land, scarce water, and too many people."

nels, but converted the large holdings to state farms. The Velasco government in Peru eliminated large private estates but avoided both distribution to individuals and the use of state farms. The central theme was to develop cooperative production without state ownership. Expropriated land was sold on nominal terms to the permanent workers on the former large estates. The results of these very different reforms in Cuba and Peru were strongly conditioned by everything else going on in these societies, and of course by great differences in their natural conditions for agriculture, but they cast considerable light on the inherent characteristics of the two strategies.

The Peruvian land reform removed a long-standing source of inequity and at the same time destroyed the remaining power of large landowners to hold back economic and social change. But it has been criticized for two failures: lack of attention to rural poverty and negative effects on production.[27] The first of these criticisms is fully justified. The reform essentially helped only the prior permanent workers on the large estates, leaving out both landless rural labor without permanent employment and the small holders who had earned a good share of their income by working seasonally on the estates. It left out the great majority of the rural poor. It also gave some groups of workers control of estates with high income potential while giving others land unlikely to yield decent incomes. In terms of degrees of inequality there was some gain from wiping out the highest incomes at the top of the former structure, but new inequalities were introduced by the character of the reform itself.

The agricultural cooperatives in Peru have had a mixed record in their ability to organize production. Cooperatives involved in highland crop production did not do well at all, though an offsetting factor was that output on small individual side holdings rose greatly compared to prereform results.[28] Cooperative sheep-raising operations turned out more positively, and on the relatively modernized coastal sugar estates the results for production were also reasonably good. Cynthia McClintock's studies of particular cooperatives in the

[27] José María Caballero, "Sobre el carácter de la reforma agraria," *Latin American Perspectives* 4 (Summer 1977), pp. 146–59; Cynthis McClintock, *Peasant Cooperatives and Political Change in Peru* (Princeton: Princeton University Press, 1981); Cristobal Kay, "Achievements and Contradictions of the Peruvian Agrarian Reform," *Journal of Development Studies* 18 (January 1982), pp. 141–70; Tom Alberts, *Agrarian Reform and Rural Poverty: A Case Study of Peru* (Boulder: Westview Press, 1983).

[28] Eckstein et al., "Land Reform," pp. 50–60 and 68–71.

highlands make clear that the changes were very uneven.[29] Those with a better resource base in the first place, and thus greater earnings opportunities, were often able to generate more active interest in group effort because it paid off. The poorer cooperatives with less scope for increasing group incomes remained inefficient because workers put all their attention on private plots of land and side activities.

The growth of agricultural output has been exceptionally low in Peru for a long time and was not improved by the land reform. Food output per capita failed to grow at all from 1955 to 1967, rose briefly in 1970 with the first stage of the reform, and then fell fairly steadily. It was back down to the 1955 level by 1974, and it kept on going down through the rest of the decade.[30] Total agricultural production in 1981 was only 10 percent above 1970, which looks feeble compared to increases of 49 percent for South America as a whole or 70 percent for Brazil.[31] The postreform stagnation in Peru might be blamed in part on problems of organization and incentives in the cooperatives: group farming in cooperatives has given relatively weak results, compared to family farms, almost everywhere.[32] But that cannot be the whole story, because the cooperatives involved less than half of the agricultural land, and at least those in highland sheep-raising and sugar production on the coastal estates did raise output fairly well. Cynthia McClintock emphasizes two other factors: (1) very poor and deteriorating soil conditions in the highlands, and (2) adverse government policies, including the use of price controls which turned the internal terms of trade against agriculture, and misdirection of public investment toward showcase large projects rather than the small-scale irrigation improvements vitally needed in the highlands.[33]

[29] McClintock, "Peasant Cooperatives," ch. 8.

[30] Alberts, *Agrarian Reform*, pp. 12 and 207; Kay, "Achievements and Contradictions," p. 161.

[31] United Nations, Food and Agricultural Organization, *FAO Production Yearbook*, 1981 (Rome: FAO, 1982), p. 77.

[32] John Mellor and Bruce Johnston, "The World Food Equation," pp. 558 and 562–63.

[33] McClintock, "Why Peasants Rebel: The Case of Peru's Sendero Luminoso," *World Politics* 37 (October 1984), pp. 48–84, and "After Agrarian Reform and Democratic Government: Has Peruvian Agriculture Developed?" in F. LaMond Tullis and W. Ladd Hollist, eds., *Foods, the State, and International Political Economy: Dilemmas in Developing Countries* (Lincoln: University of Nebraska Press, 1986). Alberts, *Agrarian Reform*, underlines the continuity of neglect of the rural sector in the years preceding the land reform, during the Velasco period, and afterward.

Comparing Peruvian agricultural production since the land reform to the results with state farms in Cuba makes the Peruvian system look less bad. As shown in table 10.1, the total output of Cuban agriculture fell by nearly a fourth in the first three years of the revolutionary government. It got back up to the 1959 level by 1965, but then went down once more. Fourteen years after the revolution, in 1973, it was still below 1959.[34] Peru's participant-managed cooperatives may not be as effective production units as individual small farms but they look better than the Cuban state farms. The comparisons with Cuba goes the other way with respect to reduction of poverty. The state farms in Cuba offered equal employment opportunities for everyone at nationally standard wages, eliminating the Peruvian problem of people just left out of the reform. Both systems probably lost a good deal of potential for increased output, as compared to equalized individual ownership, but in Latin America that latter solution remains to date only a dream.

Nicaragua after its revolution left private agriculture in place except for the large estates that had belonged to Somoza and his closest supporters. The expropriated estates were turned into state farms on the Cuban style, partly as a matter of government preference for collective ownership and partly to keep the land in production of export crops: it was expected that distribution to individual peasant producers would cause a shift out of exports into food production for domestic consumption, reducing earnings of foreign exchange. That preference, intensely debated from the start, gradually gave way to increasing pressure from peasants for redistribution to them as individuals. Beginning in 1982 national policy became more eclectic, promoting both more cooperatives and more individual distribution: the government did not follow the Cuban insistence on staying with state farms as an ideological necessity. The results for production from 1980 through 1984 were mixed, with good growth for most domestic crops but not for the basic exports, coffee and cotton.[35] That difference could be read as an indication of better performance by individual producers than by the state farms, though the comparison may be unfair: the export crops have been those most affected by deliberate disruption of planting

[34] See discussion in chapter 10.

[35] Joseph Collins et al., *What Difference Could a Revolution Make? Food and Family in the New Nicaragua* (San Francisco: Institute for Food and Development Policy, 1982); Carmen Diana Deere, Peter Marchetti, S.J., and Nola Reinhardt, "The Peasantry and the Development of Sandinista Agrarian Policy, 1979–1984," *Latin American Research Review* 20, 3 (1985), pp. 75–109 (crop production data given in table 4, p. 86).

and harvesting, and killing of rural workers, by the counterrevolutionary guerrillas sponsored by the United States.

Does land reform have any future in Latin America? Alain de Janvry's thorough analysis of Latin American agrarian problems gives powerful reasons for doubting it.[36] In his view, legal appropriation of private land for redistribution is possible only in periods of transition from political dominance by landowners to dominance by urban industrial interests: the latter may side with reform when landowners are seen as blocking policies favorable for industrialization, but they turn away from it once that obstacle loses significance. This interpretation in terms of class interests fits the semi-industrialized countries well but raises some doubts. One concerns the countries not nearly so industrialized, such as Ecuador and most of Central America. These countries might yet prove to be live arenas of conflict over land reform, partly because of de Janvry's own basic point: landowners still have great power within the societies and may be seen by urban industrial interests as impediments to adoption of policies needed for a more viable process of industrialization.

In addition to that consideration, reasoning in terms of a two-way class struggle between landowners and industrialists tends to obscure possibilities of change led by the rural poor. That kind of change may not be eternally impossible. Bolivian peasants took the issue in their own hands thirty years ago and succeeded. The necessary condition of success was that the government at that time was responsive to popular preferences and supported change rather than initiate massacres. The main question may be less a matter of class dominance than one of the degree and kind of political participation in the society. Where democratic systems are possible, and significant fractions of the population become sufficiently aware to make their voices heard, it would seem most unlikely that pressures for land reform could remain suppressed. Guatemala did have a brief experience of democracy in the late 1940s and early 1950s, and a major reform was initiated by a government sympathetic with the rural poor. The program was not blocked by internal class relationships: it was only reversed by a military invasion sponsored by the United States to overturn the democratic government.[37] The obstacle may not be so much any unanswerable condition of de-

[36] de Janvry, *The Agrarian Question*, ch. 8, pp. 255–68.
[37] See discussion in chapter 13.

pendent development, or the blocking power of conservatives within open legal systems, as it is the use of political repression.

Another variable that may become crucial in some countries concerns the number of people stuck in low-productivity agricultural activities. Where escape from rural poverty through increasing alternative employment begins to succeed, in the sense of reducing the number of people in agriculture and raising their real incomes, that is bound to take the steam out of demands for land reform. This may be the main structural factor underlying the turn away from reform in Colombia: uneasiness of the elite about increased political activism might not have carried the day if the main problem were clearly getting worse. By the same token, even a semi-industrialized country dominated by industrial interests may be forced back into struggles over land reform if landless rural labor keeps on increasing, as in Mexico. The ultimate question may be more a matter of success or failure in providing nonfarm employment, and that is a question that may be reopened anywhere if creation of new employment opportunities is either chronically too slow or brought to a halt by failure to maintain economic growth.

4. Food Prices, Land Ownership, and Trade Policy

Circular causation from ownership to income flows and back to asset distribution is particularly striking when applied to issues of food prices, supplies, and land. Three of the main questions are: (1) the effects of policies of "cheap food" to aid urban workers and industrialization; (2) promotion of exports and its possible effects in pulling land out of production for domestic food; (3) the consequences for food prices, and through them for income distribution, of reform efforts to raise the standard of living of the poor. Griffin and James insist that "The distribution of assets is unquestionably the primary determinant of the distribution of income and of the process by which incomes are generated. Neither the former nor the latter can be altered fundamentally without a change in the ownership and control of productive wealth."[38] Is that right?

The first of these policy issues, the use of price controls or subsidies to provide "cheap food" for urban consumers, has come up repeatedly under reform governments of many different varieties. One question is whether or not such policies actually do make food

[38] Griffin and James, *The Transition*, p. 37.

prices lower than they otherwise would be. Price controls may not be effective at all, if black markets immediately take over, but even if they are enforced they may reduce the food supply by worsening incentives for production. If large landowners are mainly concerned with export markets anyway, as in Mexico, it should not much matter to them; in that case it is the smaller rural producers who lose incentives and income. If large landowners are mainly suppliers to the domestic market then controls will hurt them, and may reduce inequality of income, but are also likely to discourage food production for the domestic market. The poor of the country are almost bound to lose: anything that reduces the supply of food hurts them most of all. But this common problem is not so much a question of land ownership patterns as it is one of production incentives to all food producers. A possible answer is to introduce subsidies to keep the price of food down for the urban poor while keeping up receipts of producers in order to keep up supply. That method raises a problem of macroeconomic imbalance if the subsidies are not covered by taxes: then the ultimate question is not so much the pattern of ownership as where the taxes are placed, on property owners or on workers and the poor.

The second set of issues over food prices concerns exports. Economic policies structured to encourage primary production for exports may pull land away from production of subsistence foods for the domestic market. The exports provide foreign exchange earnings that could in principle be used to import more food: if Chilean landowners export wine instead of selling fruit on the domestic market, or if Mexican owners of large estates concentrate on selling strawberries and tomatoes to the U.S. market rather than corn in Mexico, that is because the export market value is greater than the domestic market value of food output from the same land. National income is raised by the process and net food supply could be increased. But for those concerned with poverty that is not a sufficient answer. The question is, what happens to the gains in income through exporting?

In one conceivable kind of situation the logic of comparative advantage, to export agricultural production when it pays better than food for the home market, should certainly be accepted: if the government is actively concerned with the domestic food supply and will be able to use the foreign exchange earnings from exports to pay for increased imports of basic foods. In such a context, which might apply to an egalitarian reform regime, this is exactly the policy that would best serve the poor: it would maximize incomes by trade along lines of comparative advantage and use the gain to meet their needs. But this is not often the context in Latin American countries. If the earnings from food exports go to wealth landowners who use the foreign exchange for their next shopping trip to Paris, the net result of drawing more land into export production will be to decrease the real incomes of the poor.

If it is small producers who get the export receipts, and they themselves are on the borderline of poverty, then the balance could fall either way. Some of the poor win and others lose. For this issue, unlike the first question, the structure of ownership could make all the difference. If the export earnings go to large landowners and are kept by them, a government interested in reduction of poverty might well want to limit the operation of comparative advantage. The objection to this course is that it would hold down the growth of real national income, and thus hurt the poor and everyone else in the longer run. The objection is valid: within the constraints of concentrated land ownership there is no good solution. The optimal remedy would be exactly what Griffin and James argue to be necessary, to redistribute land ownership more equally. With such a change the country could follow comparative advantage to get maximum national income with much less possibility of negative effects on poverty.

The third set of issues concerns the possible offset to income redistribution that could occur if rising incomes of the poor lead to rapidly increasing food prices, diverting real income back to landowners. The basic presumption that a significant rise in incomes of the poor would increase the demand for food and change the structure of relative prices has a convincing foundation for a closed economy. The marginal propensity to increase food consumption in response to rising income is very high for the lowest income groups in all developing countries and falls steadily for higher income groups.[39] Transfers of any given fraction of national income from rich to poor are bound to increase total demand for food. Given the likely condition that domestic food production cannot be increased rapidly, increased demand will begin to drive food prices up. But then why not solve the problem temporarily, pending increased food production, by importing additional supplies?

Griffin and James discuss this possible solution through trade but

[39] Ibid. pp. 17–20; John W. Mellor, "Food Price Policy and Income Distribution in Low-Income Countries," *Economic Development and Cultural Change* 27 (October 1978).

conclude that it cannot provide an answer alternative to changes in ownership. They point to the breakdown of food distribution in Chile under Allende as a specific example of the general argument; effective redistribution in the first place led to exactly the kinds of food shortages and price increases that they argue to be inescapable, followed by black markets and increasing bitterness against the government.[40] They are certainly right that the problem was crucial for the Allende regime, and that recourse to imports did not provide a solution. Food imports were increased on a large scale: by 86 percent in volume terms during 1971. And, somewhat contrary to the underlying thesis that food supply is normally inelastic, domestic output increased 27 percent between 1971 and 1973.[41] But all that was totally insufficient to deal with the demand pressure unleashed by income redistribution, which gives some indication of how much demand for food by low-income groups is normally pent up.

The upper limit on the supply side came from inability to finance increasing imports on a scale sufficient to meet the increase in demand. But that is not exactly a consequence of the structure of land ownership: it is a much more a matter of the ability to supply exports, plus the possibilities of borrowing. In this particular case opposition by the United States to extension of external credit for Chile acted to make the foreign exchange situation worse than it might otherwise have been. The more general problem is that, when domestic demand far outruns productive capacity, the possibility of raising foreign exchange through added exports is almost nonexistent. The essence of the problem for Chile was a degree of stimulus to demand far too great for any economy to answer adequately. If real wages increase 10 percent in a year it may be possible to meet the increase in demand for food, but to raise them more than 40 percent in one year created an impossible situation.

Conflicts between interest in raising national income through exporting and interest in keeping an adequate supply of food in the domestic market could be eased if the composition of exports could be shifted more toward industrial products. Raising industrial exports could help finance increasing food supplies, rather than take food away. This means that export incentives become part of food supply policy. Rapidly rising real wages in the dynamic East Asian

[40] Griffin and James, *The Transition*, pp. 82–86.
[41] Ibid. Steffan de Wylder, *Allende's Chile: The Political Economy of the Rise and Fall of the Unidad Popular* (Cambridge: Cambridge University Press, 1976), ch. 7.

export economies in the 1960s and 1970s depended fundamentally on this solution of shifting to industrial exports, as opposed to backing away from trade. The strains in Chile were much too severe for any short-run solution by this path, but a sustained orientation in this direction could set up far better conditions of short-run flexibility to deal with food prices in the course of egalitarian reform, or any other context.

5. CONCLUSIONS

Concentrated ownership of land does not prevent economic growth, but it fosters inequality of income to degrees far beyond any levels to be expected in a well-functioning market system. When such concentration is the rule in economies dependent on primary exports as the leading growth sector, this factor alone can account for high inequality both directly through concentration of current earnings and indirectly through economic policies, dominated by landowner preferences, which run against industrialization and creation of alternative employment opportunities. The semi-industrialized countries have for the most part passed through the long stage of landowner domination, but the poorer countries have not, and the pressure of excess labor in agriculture in these countries is probably still worsening.

Some of the basic presumptions of economics need serious qualification for countries with such ownership conditions. The full sense of comparative advantage works only if the society can channel the gains in export earnings back into food supplies as well as resources for investment: if they go mainly into current consumption for a minority, the case for exporting is feeble.

A possible answer to the preceding problem, and to many other built-in conflicts in market-oriented development, would be to restructure incentives to foster more industrial exports and reduce reliance on land-based primary products. Such exports could provide *support* for a program of redistribution, rather than work against reduction of poverty. It would be great if such a reorientation were accompanied by thorough land reform, but between the determined opposition of the conservative side and the urban focus of most reform governments the possibilities of the latter look low in the extreme. And even where an unexpected reform government breaks through and actually does carry out major changes in land ownership, as in Peru, that is just the beginning of the story: that major reform did not accomplish much of anything for reduction of poverty, or for production. Weak results for agricultural production and food supply under Peruvian cooperatives as under Cuban state farms certainly suggest that relatively equal distribution to individual families is a better bet than either. They do not mean that land reform itself is bound to be adverse for growth: relatively equal ownership combined with reasonably favorable incentives for those who produce food would surely yield good results for output as for reduction of poverty.

SEVEN

OWNERSHIP II: MULTINATIONALS,
PUBLIC ENTERPRISE, AND DEPENDENCY

Where is this division of labor to end? and what object does it finally serve? No doubt another may also think for me; but it is not therefore desirable that he should do so to the exclusion of my thinking for myself.

—Thoreau, *Walden*

Industrialization has changed many of the relationships between Latin American countries and the outside world but has not brought with it any great increase in degrees of national autonomy. How much does that matter, and in what ways? From some points of view, it may matter at least as much or more than economic growth: to be subservient to outside control may be the worst aspect of underdevelopment.[1] One of the most crucial questions is the way in which external influence conditions internal possibilities: does it restrict these countries to such a narrow range of choices that it prevents change toward more participatory societies? How much room is there to move, and what moves might conceivably increase autonomy?[2]

The best versions of dependency analysis help a great deal to bring out two-way reactions between external pressures and internal preferences. The worse postulate a kind of helplessness that grossly misrepresents the vitality of Latin American societies and leads to ster-

[1] It is always a treacherous business to try to say what the goals of others really are. Stephen D. Krasner, *Structural Conflict: The Third World Against Global Liberalism* (Berkeley: University of California Press, 1985), argues that the leading goal of developing countries is to gain power over events, including collective power to reshape the world economic system. Dependency analysis suggests that any such idea of a single shared goal is likely to be misleading: it may be true that many people put great value on such objectives, but others in positions to influence choices may regard greater national autonomy more as a threat than a promise.

[2] Gary Gereffi, *Dependency in the Third World*, points out that the very idea of changing degrees of dependence within capitalism is rejected as meaningless by those who consider that socialism is the only answer. If the opposite of dependence is socialism, different degrees of dependence within capitalism have so significance; if the opposite is autonomy, changes in degree may mean a great deal.

ile debate about why nothing can be done. Many choices open to these societies could have lessened dependency in the earlier phases of industrialization and could do more in the years ahead. It is not that dependency analysis is wound up with imaginary problems or mistaken about the depth of external influence. But ideas need to keep moving if they are to have any hope of dealing accurately with reality, and reality includes a great deal more action by domestic groups, following their conceptions of both social interests and their own, than the analysis usually recognizes.[3] By mistaking much of the picture, the analysis can suggest response in directions likely to deepen rather than lessen dependency in the future.

The particular aspects of dependence considered here are: (1) in what ways it may be deepened or on the contrary reduced by interactions with the world economy, apart from specific influences associated with multinational corporations; (2) relationships between multinational firms and national economic strategy, treated as a two-way matter in which changes in that strategy can alter the behavior of the firms; (3) public enterprise as a potential instrument for governments seeking to get away from dependence on foreign investment; and (4) conflicts between incentives for effective economic performance and the wish to defend autonomy.

1. External Orientation and Room to Move

Concepts of dependency keep moving as the world moves, and rightly so. The particular problems emphasized keep changing because the problems themselves get transformed, while the sense that something fundamental is wrong remains very much alive. The process is like a series of battles in which dependency analysts identify a real problem, doubters pull together evidence that it can be managed if appropriate actions are taken to resolve it, and while they are doing so new versions of dependency move on the highlight new issues. There is no reason for the process ever to stop: problems will never be in short supply. But is there some persisting core to dependency analysis, something that sets it apart from a general conviction that the world is a frustrating place? Exactly what is the fundamental continuing wrong?

[3] Dudley Seers, ed., *Dependency Theory: A Critical Reassessment* (London: Francis Pinter, 1981); David G. Becker, *The New Bourgeoisie and the Limits of Dependency: Mining, Class, and Power in "Revolutionary" Peru* (Princeton: Princeton University Press, 1983); Peter Evans, "After Dependency"; and David Booth, "Marxism and Dependent Sociology."

Two aspects of the analysis seem central: that the kinds of capitalism possible in market-oriented developing countries are limited, crippled versions of what is possible in the older industrialized countries, and that the limitations can only be surmounted, if at all, by coming as close as possible to eliminating contact with the industrialized countries. The basic weaknesses at issue are the inability of Latin American countries to achieve widespread participation in decision making and in the gains of growth, and the frequent cases of blockage or breakdown when particular governments try to move outside existing patterns toward significant social change. Gary Gereffi and Peter Evans put it too strongly, but still understandably: "It would appear that the band of acceptable policy is exceedingly narrow and that the penalties for straying outside it are strict and swift. . . . The semi-periphery is simply not free to explore a welfare-oriented version of capitalist development."[4]

To what extent is this interpretation valid? That depends on what it really means. On one level it is simply wrong. Any government that actually wishes to establish a more egalitarian strategy of development, and understands what it is doing in terms of economic cause and effect, can do a great deal to change such fundamental factors as the national patterns of production and consumption, land ownership, taxation, and use of state-owned firms. The two fundamental doubts concern volition—or influence over the government—and ability to use appropriate policies. Dependency analysis focuses on the first and rather neglects the second: it helps to explain why so few Latin American governments try seriously to break out of dependency constraints, but it fails badly as a guide for the few that do try.

Four themes common to much of dependency analysis are closely connected to the central questions in this book: (1) the costs of the kind of dependence on primary exports that early postwar industrialization policies were intended to break; (2) the frequency of foreign exchange crises, forcing countries to take orders from external creditors, and in particular putting them under pressure to reduce social programs; (3) the fact that reorientation toward industrialization through exports, which offers a possible release from foreign exchange constraints, also works against independent national choice of structures of production and consumption; and (4) the

---

[4] Gary Gereffi and Peter Evans, "Transnational Corporations, Dependent Development, and State Policy in the Semi-Periphery: A Comparison of Brazil and Mexico," *Latin American Research Review* 16, 3 (1981), pp. 52 and 54.

ways in which an emphasis on international trade may favor multi-national relative to domestic firms, and favor orientation of domestic policies in ways adverse for labor and for social reform.

Dependence on primary exports clearly did involve high costs. It left the economy open to violent shocks from changes in external demand, accentuated inequality, and favored political dominance by landowner-exporters, opposed to industrialization as well as to social reform. The remedy, in the early postwar version of withdrawal, was to turn away from export promotion and to block imports of everything not essential for domestic production. The strategy certainly helped speed industrialization in the first years but as implemented it created more dependence than it corrected. The methods adopted left out the poor, encouraged excessive dependence on foreign technology and foreign ownership, and relied too much on external credit rather than promotion of industrial exports. The old dependency was reduced but newer aspects were worsened: a process of structural transformation that would have been difficult at best was made more costly than necessary by the methods used to answer the perceived problem.

The particular weakness in the chosen strategy that most often brought growth to a halt was the common inability to generate the foreign exchange earnings necessary to pay for imports of capital equipment and production materials. That imbalance greatly increased influence exercised by external creditors and by the domestic financial interests linked to them. The imbalance might have been avoided by promotion of industrial exports if combined with avoidance of excess demand. Particularly in Brazil and Colombia for the decade from 1967 that response worked well to earn foreign exchange and to speed industrialization. It also promoted a rapid rise in employment and even rural incomes.

For those who want no part of the world economy, industrial exports are just as bad as primary. They still mean exposure to shocks from the outside, to bargaining pressures from importing countries, and to disproportionate domestic influence by those industrialists who are exporters. They may mean more directly than in the case of primary exports that domestic price and wages have to be lined up with external market values. But do these legitimate concerns outweigh the probable gains? Industrial exports ordinarily provide employment without pulling land away from domestic food supply, foreign exchange to keep up growth without the subservience of going deeply into debt, and enhanced possibilities for domestic producers to learn more about technological advances and about how to produce more efficiently. What kind of independence would be gained by opposing such opportunities?

It is true that growth led by industrial exports does not by itself get countries out of the woods with respect to external deficits, or constitute a storm shelter from changes in external economic conditions. The whole region was set back badly in the first half of the 1980s by adverse external factors, first stopping growth and then exerting great pressure to reshape internal economic choices to fit the preferences of the United States. Monetary contraction beginning in England and followed by the United States in 1978, and the ensuing world recession, badly hurt Latin American exports and made credit tighter everywhere. The other side of the picture is that those developing countries that had established strength in industrial exports came back up fast. Those countries in Latin America with the worst debt problems did their part in creating them: it was not the external economy that forced the Mexican government to run internal deficits on the order of 15 percent of gross national product, or the Chilean government to freeze an overvalued exchange rate. Colombia did not follow the pattern of the others in the 1970s but instead accumulated foreign exchange reserves; it did not fall into the debt trap and has not been forced into contraction by pressure from the IMF. That difference is an aspect of decreased dependence, as a consequence of economic policies appropriate to reduce it.

A more troublesome question about promoting industrial exports is that this strategy creates pressures pulling domestic prices and wages into line with external markets and values. If the country follows a highly open system, with few constraints on imports, domestic prices must be aligned with external prices. That would rule out such objectives as reducing poverty by keeping down relative prices of basic foods consumed by the poor, or reducing inequality by maintaining high relative prices for consumer durable goods important to upper income groups. But there is no need to follow the logic that far: imports of luxury consumer goods can be held down by imposing high internal taxes along with high tariffs on such products, and consumer prices of basic foods for the poor can be held below world prices by subsidies. Countries that follow a nearly complete open-economy prescription, as Chile did in the late 1970s, cannot maintain independent internal price structures. Brazil, Colombia, and Mexico have instead kept many elements of separation permitting national choices at the same time as they actively promote industrial exports. That orientation may to some extent limit the growth of industrial exports, but it has the counterpart advantage of leaving more space for internal choices with respect to structures of production and distribution.

The fourth theme cited above, that an open-economy orientation favors multinationals over domestic firms and works against domestic social reform programs because of a perceived need to favor foreign investment, is perhaps the most important. The questions should be split in two: an external orientation in the sense of promoting industrial exports and the role of multinationals in shaping policy choices by national governments. In general, an orientation toward exports favors *some* multinationals, those that are or become exporters, and hurts those producing only for the protected domestic market. The implications of this distinction are discussed in the following section. The second set of questions concerns the effects of multinationals on domestic economy policy. The problem is not so much that multinationals dictate domestic policies as that governments lean over backward to attract the firms by trying to ensure "a favorable business climate." That mild-sounding term may mean anything from reasonably civilized treatment of investors to laws against strikes, or even repression of domestic labor organizations, of popular dissent, and of democratic institutions. Foreign firms themselves are rarely likely to insist on repressive measures, and may even avoid countries where stability seems to depend on them, but they avoid signs of turmoil even more assiduously. If a government puts high priority on reassuring foreign investors, it is more likely to lean toward holding back on social reform actions and toning down dissent than otherwise would be the case. The case for participation in the international economy is strong on the side of promoting industrial exports but extremely doubtful on the side of encouraging foreign investment.[5]

The very concept of national choice raises difficult questions; the special value of dependency analysis is not that it answers them but that it directs attention to them. A nation does not "choose" whether to accept or to alter dependency relationships. A nation is not a decision-making entity. National policies respond erratically to evolving conflicts of interests within the country and to the influences coming from outside. In the illuminating interpretation of Brazilian and Mexican experience by Gereffi and Evans, there is no external

[5] Carlos Díaz Alejandro, "Delinking North and South: Unshackled or Unhinged?" in Albert Fishlow, ed., *Rich and Poor Nations in the World Economy* (New York: McGraw-Hill, 1978).

villain but instead a network of influences uniting domestic business and government with the preferences of foreign firms and governments, toward shared goals of modernization and economic growth.[6]

A pervasive kind of pressure is self-generated by the belief that external credit will be denied and foreign investment will stop if radical social policies seem likely. A radical or even moderately reformist government can be viewed as such a threat that foreign investment will pull back and capital flight start even before the government actually does anything. Many domestic interest groups are so dismayed at such prospects that they are ready to accept authoritarian measures to suppress popular choice, without any necessary push from the outside. That does not mean that they always win the day: reformist governments can often gain support from major sectors of the business community, and many business leaders themselves would prefer moderate reform to confrontation and the risk of political breakdown. In such divided contexts a lot depends on the negotiating skill of the particular government, and a lot on the particular external context. If outside governments are doing their best to promote trouble, they will succeed.

Although shared preferences to put investment first often work against social reform measures, they are not the whole picture. Where countries have some channels of expression of popular preferences, they create more pressure toward reforms as means of keeping the basic lines of the society intact. Reforms can be desired even by conservatives if they are seen to lessen the dangers of radical alternatives. If an all-out revolution is considered to be the only meaningful kind of change, then it is true that such a solution will never be peacefully accepted. But if the issue is instead action against poverty, or greater control of multinationals, or more progressive taxation, then any or all of these lines of change could be followed without making the sky fall down. What is fairly certain to be explosive is not what Gereffi and Evans state—the possibility of exploring "a welfare-oriented version of capitalist development"— but instead the possibility of eliminating private ownership.

Moderate reformist governments able to take some steps in directions of social reform and reduced dependency have been fairly frequent. Some of them have made some headway; when they have broken down, the problem has usually been misjudged economic policies (especially excess demand and insufficient attention to ex-

6 Gereffi and Evans, "Transnational Corporations," pp. 31–64.

ports) rather than any stone wall established by external forces. Even radical reformist governments, including the belligerently antidependency regime of Velasco in Peru, usually have at least several years running time before opposition grows to the point of stopping them. If they functioned well in the time available, the odds in favor of stopping them would be much lower. Most of the time it is the nonworkability of domestic choices that do such governments in.

If nonconformist governments that wished to reduce dependency were able to pay attention to policy choices favorable for productive employment, efficiency, and exports, they would last longer and would accomplish more. But nonconformist governments are not likely in the first place if the circle of decision making in the country is narrowly restricted to existing business and military leadership. The chances of reducing dependency might be raised if Latin American political systems became more democratic, not just in the sense of holding elections but in providing education and information to help make all groups aware of the issues and able to participate effectively in the political process. The condition of dependency itself works against open political systems but clearly does not make them impossible in all Latin American countries. The quandary, or circle of mutually offsetting possibilities, is that conservative governments that pay great attention to efficiency are not often interested in either social reform or reduction of dependence, while governments more prone to combat in terms of social policy are also prone to adopt nonfunctional economic policies. Latin America needs, but does not often get, governments that are concerned with both social reform and coherent economic performance. If and when that combination of objectives comes together, autonomy could be built up gradually through more effective response to the specific problems that keep setting the countries back.

2. ECONOMIC ASPECTS OF MULTINATIONAL FIRMS IN THE INDUSTRIAL SECTOR

It must be more than an accident that the Latin American drive toward industrialization in the 1945–1980 period coincided almost exactly with a leap of corporate vision in the industrialized countries from the domestic to the world economy. The timing of the two changes might be explained in part as a consequences of technological advance: the explosion of multinational firms on a world scale would not have been possible without the innovations in communications and transport of these years, and these same innovations helped link Latin American industries much more closely to external technology than was possible before.[7] The coincidence might also be explained in terms of joint repercussions to the depression of the 1930s and the consequent shift toward greater social regulation in the United States: just as the depression stimulated Latin American efforts to escape from dependence on primary exports, it stimulated changes in outlook in the United States that led many firms to look much more seriously for opportunities to expand abroad.[8] Yet another factor is that in this period the United States became for a time the dominant world power: as the country took the world for its domain in a new way, its corporations moved outward and helped carry the ideology of markets, profit, investment, and economic growth. Whatever one's preferred themes, the fact of immediate relevance is that foreign ownership, foreign technology, and foreign influence became deeply embedded in a Latin American industrialization process totally misinterpreted as a means to gain greater national autonomy. Small wonder that dependency analysis, when it came, found much to work on.

Multinationals do not all have identical consequences. Their effects on poverty and political repression depend to some degree on the context and policies of the particular country and to some degree on the corporations' motives for investment in the country. Among countries, Peter Evans suggests a useful clarification: multinationals in the industrial sector have only limited interest in the poor and small countries; they concentrate on those that have relatively large internal markets and are at least semi-industrialized.[9] In Latin America, their economic weight has been greatest in Brazil and Mexico. The size of these markets, combined with political conditions considered most of the time to be favorable for foreign investment, makes these countries leading targets. At the same time, it has given them more than usual bargaining power to affect what the firms do. Similarly, smaller countries that are able to achieve growth of income through successful economic strategies then become more interesting to the multinationals and simultaneously better able to bargain with them.

Bargaining power is only one aspect of the question, and some-

---

[7] Raymond Vernon, *Storm over the Multinationals: The Real Issues* (Cambridge: Harvard University Press, 1977).

[8] Richard Newfarmer, ed., *Profits, Progress, and Poverty: Case Studies of International Industries in Latin America* (Notre Dame: University of Notre Dame Press, 1985).

[9] Evans, *Dependent Development*, pp. 292–314.

times not the most important. Which kinds of firms come to which country, and what they do, also depends on the structure of economic incentives established in the countries. Within the general objective of making profits, a corporation may come to a country mainly to build up its market there, or mainly to move part of its production process there in order to reduce costs. In the first case the firm is rarely interested in exporting, and not primarily concerned with utilizing the country's own factor of production. On the positive side, it may well favor national policies of industrialization because its own markets are enlarged in the process. In the second case the firm is less interested in the growth of the domestic market but much more likely to concentrate on using the factors of production in the country that are relatively low cost. In a context of labor surplus, that means it is more likely to establish labor-intensive lines of production and to choose methods of production that generate domestic employment.

Multinationals that aim at sales in the domestic market are often producers of brand-name goods for higher income urban consumers; those that come to the country to take advantage of low labor costs are more likely to create employment and to earn foreign exchange. If the national government's objectives were oriented toward serving the interests of the higher income people in the more modern sectors of the economy, the first kind of firm would be a natural ally. The set of policies favorable for attracting such firms would be tariff protection against imports, subsidies reducing the costs of capital equipment, and overvalued exchange rates to hold down costs of imported equipment. If the objective were instead to reduce poverty, the second kind of firm would be more likely to help. The set of policies appropriate to attract such firms would be exactly the opposite. By far the more common form of investment by multinationals in Latin American industry is the first kind, aimed at domestic sales in a protected home market. That result fits the initial postwar mixture of national policies to promote import substitution, and it presumably reflects what the governments involved most wanted to accomplish. If they wished to change the balance more toward reduction of poverty, they could do so by changing the structure of incentives accordingly.

Potentially positive roles of multinationals include the vitally important ability to create new kinds of productive employment, permitting more people to move out of poverty, and that of stimulating domestic activity and capacity for change by introducing new ideas and skills. They can in fact have such effects, but the positive side may easily be swamped by the damage they do. A particularly important concern is that foreign investment may foreclose opportunities for domestic investment and learning, by moving into new fields that domestic firms could have entered or by taking over existing domestic firms and eliminating independent national management.

Albert Hirschman has made a particularly effective case for the belief that the more nearly industrialized Latin American countries have reached a level of entrepreneurial capacity which could permit them to enter new fields more rapidly if openings were not preempted by foreign investors: they have by now gone well past the early stages of industrialization in which domestic potential for entry in new fields is so weak that the countries need to reply on foreign investors.[10] That judgment applies somewhat unequally among countries: it fits Brazil and Colombia much better than Bolivia or Central America. But the actual flow of foreign investment has been particularly high toward the more advanced countries, which need it least, because these are the countries in which market opportunities and the necessary skills are most evident. Furthermore, it has not always taken the form of creating new firms that domestic entrepreneurs were unable to establish: takeovers of existing firms have been common.[11] Takeovers do not normally involve weak or mismanaged domestic companies but are on the contrary aimed at the most dynamic national firms showing evidence of ability to provide leadership. They selectively curtail independent growth of the best national firms.

The fact of a takeover need not mean a net economic loss. The foreign firm has to pay for the acquisition, which puts financial resources under national control to some degree. It may well have technological capacities, or marketing information, that permit it to increase the value produced by the existing firm, to speed up its growth and increase its contribution to national income. That kind of effect is clearly both possible and uncertain; it depends on just what the former local owners might have done and what new foreign owners do. But another kind of effect is fairly certain whichever way the balance goes with respect to national income: local entrepreneurs who might have developed their own capacities in independent managment of a growing firm are converted either to

[10] Albert O. Hirschman, "How and Why to Divest in Latin America," *Princeton Studies in International Finance*, no. 76 (November 1979).

[11] Newfarmer, ed., *Profits, Progress, and Poverty*, ch. 2.

hired management acting under others' direction or to retirees contributing nothing. The capacity for self-sustaining growth of national entrepreneurial ability is likely to be lessened.

The outstanding twentieth-century example of a country that came out of underdevelopment to a powerfully independent role in world competition, Japan, points to the great potential advantage of *not* allowing any significant foreign investment.[12] Foreign firms were at one time active in Japanese industry, including U.S. automobile firms until the Japanese changed their policies to exclude them in the 1930s, but the country's industrialization has been carried out almost entirely by domestically owned firms. The experience argues in favor of a position similar to that of Hirschman for Latin America. But one important additional consideration is that Japan did not simply block foreign investment; it created an extraordinarily active program of study and purchase of foreign technology and of government support for guided investment programs by domestic firms. The key was not a simple exclusion of foreign firms: it was the country's phenomenal effort to foster domestic learning and entrepreneurial capacity.[13]

It would take a heroic leap of faith to conclude that Latin American countries might, by excluding foreign firms, duplicate the kind of drive to competitive strength shown by Japan. But it is not at all impossible that they could make some headway in this sense if they imposed the right kinds of restraints and incentives on foreign investment. What lines of national strategy might go in positive directions, and what are the chance that such choices might actually be implemented?

One key to better results would be to refuse to permit takeovers of existing firms unless they are smaller producers within industries that have strong domestic leadership. That could block some potentially productive takeovers, but it would surely pay off in preserving more national capacity for entrepreneurial growth and for competition as well. The problems in deciding which kinds of proposals to accept and which to reject would be closely similar to those encountered in antitrust actions in the United States aimed at blocking an-

---

[12] Saburo Okita, "Causes of Rapid Growth in Postwar Japan and Their Implications for Newly Developing Countries," in Saburo Okita, *The Developing Countries and Japan: Lessons in Growth* (Tokyo: University of Tokyo Press, 1982).

[13] Miyohei Shinohara, Toru Yanagihara, and Kwang Suk Kim, "The Japanese and Korean Experiences in Managing Development," World Bank Staff Working Paper no. 574 (1983); Chalmers Johnson, *MITI and the Japanese Miracle* (Stanford: Stanford University Press, 1982).

ticompetitive mergers. Such a policy would require above all a government convinced that preservation of domestic management is desirable.

A second helpful strategy would be to make it costly for foreign firms to import capital equipment and inputs for current production, so they would have more of an incentive to search for domestic suppliers and for techniques of production that require domestic labor. That implies an active exchange rate policy to make sure that the price of foreign exchange does not fall relative to domestic production costs. If the country also has a high level of protection on imports of manufactured goods in general, it should resist demands of foreign firms to import their own equipment duty-free, even if it is an intrafirm transaction. That is to say, imports should be made costly for the foreign firms on the same terms, for the same reasons, that they should be made costly for domestic firms.

A third line of policy would be to refuse to allow high degrees of protection on the end products of the foreign firm. High protection raises profitability for sales to the domestic market: it constitutes a tax on consumers, increasing earnings for foreign firms even if they fail to contribute value added as measured in terms of international prices. The tax on consumers then becomes a source of foreign exchange loss. "Transfer pricing" is often the vehicle used by the firm to get such earnings out of the country without taxation, by overstating its costs, but this particular accounting technique is not the basic problem. Transfer pricing would be of little or no significance if tariff protection for the firms were held down in the first place. To hold down protection would discourage entry by some multinationals, specifically by those that cannot make profits selling at competitive world prices. If such firms do not come in, so much the better for the country.

A combination of high prices for foreign exchange with more limited tariff protection on end products sold to consumers (or alternatively with high domestic sales taxes to limit profits on such goods) would increase incentives for those firms that are interested in exports and decrease them for those firms interested only in sales to the domestic market. That combination should be favorable for the balance of payments, both through increased export earnings and decreased import requirements. Earnings from exports might be difficult to capture by taxation, but at least they do not constitute profits taken out of the country's own real income by high-priced domestic sales under protection. And the foreign firm that is primarily interested in exporting will almost by definition be more concerned with use of low-cost domestic inputs; in a labor-surplus country that points to employment-creating products and technologies. Such possibilities fit closely the experience of Singapore in the last twenty years, with high rates of growth of national income and real wages coming in large part from active foreign investment directed to industrial exports.[14]

Such measures to change the character of foreign investment through generalized incentives could help correct some of the most evident economic problems associated with multinationals. Direct administrative techniques could help too. Colombia and the other Andean Pact countries managed to cut down considerably on restrictive clauses imposed by multinational parents on local branches, on overinvoiced imports, and on excessive royalty payments.[15] Mexico applies conditions of shared domestic ownership in most fields, Brazil excludes foreign firms from some industries considered to be particularly important for development of national entrepreneurship, and Korea has strengthened its capacity for growth by requiring foreign firms to direct most or all of their output to exports.[16] Many countries have speeded up the process of learning by nationals through quota systems requiring early promotion of domestic employees into skilled and executive roles.

More generally, Peter Evans argues that local capacities for research and development, for the kinds of learning that can do most to lessen dependency in the future, can be raised if national bargaining power can be applied to require more joint ownership than multinational firms themselves prefer.[17] The firms usually want to keep technological information to themselves because it is the basis of their current earnings advantages and of their own future bargaining position. If the firm is a leader in a particularly important field it may be able to resist pressures to share control and allow access to research, but when products are more standardized or national technological capacity increases, control of access to technology can be made more a matter of bargaining. In Evans's study of

[14] Augustine Tan and Ow China Hock, "Singapore," pp. 280–309 in Bela Balassa, ed., *Development Strategies in Semi-Industrialized Economies* (Baltimore: Johns Hopkins University Press for the World Bank, 1982).

[15] Constantine Vaitsos, *Intercountry Distribution of Income and Transnational Enterprises* (Oxford: Clarendon Press, 1974).

[16] On Brazil, see Evans, *Dependent Development*; on Korea see the section by Kwang Suk Kim in Shinohara et al., "Japanese and Korean Experience," and Larry E. Westphal, Yung W. Rhee, and Garry Pursell, "Korean Industrial Competitiveness: Where It Came From," World Bank Staff Working Paper no. 469 (1981).

[17] Evans, *Dependent Development*, pp. 172–212.

Brazil, the bargaining position of local firms and of the government improved steadily through the country's period of exceptionally rapid industrial growth in the years after 1967 and has been used to accomplish major changes in the degree of national control.

Aggressive national bargaining can be helpful to open up greater possibilities for domestic research and learning, but this is no reason to neglect the use of general economic incentive to shape the behavior of firms. If national policies make it pay foreign firms to undertake the kinds of actions that are wanted for employment or exports or domestic learning, if they make it less profitable to concentrate on production of luxury goods for upper income domestic groups and costly for them to use import-intensive techniques, behavior will change in desired directions. Degrees and forms of dependency can often be changed by the quality of choices within the limits open in each country.

3. PUBLIC ENTERPRISE

Conditions of dependency might in principle be changed by development of state-owned firms in the fields particularly preferred by foreign investors. Such firms play a major role as investors and producers in many developing countries, creating a three-way division of ownership among domestic private firms, multinationals, and public enterprise.[18] They could conceivably be used as an instrument of social change, for such purposes as locating production in backward regions, developing low-cost products for basic needs, promoting worker participation in management, or building up national research and development capacities. In practice, they are used much more often to complement private enterprise, carrying out activities that are necessary for the shared goal of industrialization but that private investors do not want to undertake themselves. Analysis of dependent development explains this common behavior as evidence of constraints on national choice: public firms cannot be used as instruments of social reform because that would weaken possibilities of capital accumulation and lead to withdrawal

[18] Leroy P. Jones, ed., *Public Enterprise in Less Developed Countries* (New York: Cambridge University Press, 1982); Jones, *Public Enterprise and Economic Development: The Korean Case* (Seoul: Korean Development Institute, 1975); Malcolm Gillis, "The Role of State Enterprise in Economic Development," *Social Research* 47 (Summer 1980), pp. 248–89; John Sheahan, "Public Enterprise in Developing Countries," ch. 6 in Geoffrey Shepherd, ed., *Public Enterprise: Economic Analysis of Theory and Practice* (Lexington, Mass.: Lexington Books, 1976).

of investment by multinationals. In this view, public enterprise can help implement development but cannot serve to reduce a kind of dependency that restricts social change.[19]

As participants in production and investment, public firms have both advantages and disadvantages. From the point of view of diversification and growth, a special advantage they offer is that they can be used to invest in new lines of production that private firms are unlikely to enter. That includes particularly the kinds of production activities for which capital requirements are high relative to the size of the firm. Private investors in the high-risk environment of most developing countries have understandable reasons to emphasize the safety of the familiar, to bias investment toward the known and the protected rather than the new and uncertain. In such conditions, public investment can implement useful projects that might otherwise be long delayed. But the readiness of public firms to carry out investment spending can lead to trouble too. They do not pay as close attention as private firms do to holding down costs, or respond as flexibly to preferences of buyers. They are not as likely to pay close attention to changing market conditions and are particularly unlikely to seek out new kinds of export markets.

As compared to multinationals, both public and private domestic firms are at a disadvantage in knowledge of up-to-date technology, international markets, and world supply conditions. They are also at a disadvantage in some fields because they do not ordinarily have established market positions based on patents and brands comparable to those of the multinationals. For activities concentrated on international trade and finance, and for the preferences of high-income domestic consumers, the multinationals have most of the advantages. For lower income domestic consumers, and in general for products that have more stable technologies, they may well be at a disadvantage. Each of the three types of firm thus has particular advantages that give it a role within a "triple alliance," in a mixture of collaboration and competition with each other.[20]

[19] The position is central to the analysis in Evans, *Dependent Development*. See also the more sweepingly negative statements in Immanuel Wallerstein, "Dependence in an Interdependent World: The Limited Possibilities of Transformation Within the Capitalist World Economy," *African Studies Review* 17 (April 1974), pp. 1–26, and Muzaffer Ahmad, "The Political Economy of Public Enterprise," in Jones, ed., *Public Enterprise*, pp. 49–64.

[20] Evans, *Dependent Development*; Brian Levy, "The Industrial Economics of Entrepreneurship and Dependent Development," Ph. D. dissertation, Harvard University, 1983.

Differences among countries in the use of public enterprise reflect both the realities of economic openings and differences in political-social forces.[21] The most coherent early example of public enterprise as a means of shaping development was the Chilean Corporación de Fomento de la Producción, CORFO. More than just a vehicle for particular investments, CORFO "marked the social decision that the state should assume leadership in conducting the process of industrialization and transformation of the structure of production."[22] Oscar Muñoz explains the institution as a direct consequence of the political transformation by which the Popular Front of 1938 gained the presidency and reoriented Chilean economic strategy toward the conception of the state as entrepreneur. From its inception in 1939 until the military overturn of 1973, CORFO provided the government with an instrument to negotiate from a position of strength with private investors, both domestic and foreign. Naturally, the organization was cut back to a very restricted role, though not eliminated, when the market-authoritarian regime took power in 1973.

Not all conservative governments have been adverse to the active use of public enterprise. Its role has been particularly strategic in conservatively run Brazil, as in the more erratic conservative-plus-populist Mexican system, and it has been consistently important through many changes of regime in Argentina.[23] One part of the explanation for its use under many market-oriented governments, as long as they are not obsessed with distrust of state action in the economy, is that they can see ways to use public firms to raise investment and diversify production, in support of private firms and without any intention of conflicting with them. Another part of the explanation is that public firms can be expressions of nationalism,

[21] The systematic economic reasons for similar patterns of public enterprise across countries despite differences in ideologies are emphasized in Leroy P. Jones and Edward S. Mason, "The Role of Economic Factors in Determining the Size and Structure of the Public Enterprise Sector in Mixed Economy LDCs," in Jones, ed., *Public Enterprise*.

[22] Oscar Muñoz Gomá, *Chile y su industrialización: Pasado, crisis y opciones* (Santiago: CIEPLAN, 1986), p. 74. See discussion pp. 22–24 and 71–92.

[23] Werner Baer, Isaac Kerstenetzky, and Annibal V. Villela, "The Changing Role of the State in the Brazilian Economy," *World Development* 1 (November 1973); José Roberto Mendonça de Barros and Douglas H. Graham, "The Brazilian Economic Miracle Revisited: Private and Public Sector Initiative in a Market Economy," *Latin American Research Review* 13, 2 (1978), pp. 5–38; Thomas J. Trebat, *Brazil's State-Owned Enterprises: A Case Study of the State as Entrepreneur* (Cambridge: Cambridge University Press, 1983).

and favored for that reason by regimes that are conservative in terms of social policy but at the same time strongly nationalistic. Even the military government in Brazil, for all its concern to be on good terms with international investors, used public firms increasingly in fields preferred by multinationals: in the course of the 1970s the relative weight of multinationals in the industrial sector was steadily reduced by rapid expansion of the public firms.[24]

Since public enterprise can play important roles in diversifying investment and conceivably in increasing autonomy, its own quality of performance becomes highly significant. If it is persistently misdirected or badly run, it undermines development and autonomy by wasting resources. On these counts, Latin American public enterprise has not been strong. It has been prone to waste resources through excessively capital-intensive technology and inefficient operation. An extensive international comparison of public firms showed that in financial terms, Latin American firms look weaker than those in Africa and Asia.[25] It is true that the performance of public firms cannot be judged adequately by measures of financial profit: they are sometimes intended to accomplish other objective and are often subject to more effective price control and other direct restraints than private firms. But consistently weak financial results, in the absence of special social achievement, suggests that public enterprise as actually used in Latin America may increase dependency by weakening economic performance.

The degree to which public firms pay attention to questions of efficiency depends greatly on the goals of the particular national government.[26] When Peruvian public enterprise was launched on a large scale in the Velasco government the main purpose was to increase the role of the state, not to fuss about efficiency. The generals given command of the state firms used them as vehicles to provide jobs, develop strategic regions, build personal empires, or whatever else seemed to them most useful, without great concern for what all this did to the Peruvian external debt or national product. When the Brazilian military went the other way in the 1960s, to raise efficiency as a means of raising national growth, the Brazilian state firms made

[24] Gereffi and Evans, "Transnational Corporations"; Hewlett, *The Cruel Dilemmas of Development*, ch. 6.

[25] Andrew H. Gantt II and Guiseppe Dutto, "Financial Performance of Government-Owned Corporations in Less Developed Countries," International Monetary Fund, *Staff Papers* (1968), pp. 102–42.

[26] John Sheahan, "Differences in the Roles and Consequence of Public Enterprise in Developing Countries," Williams College Research Memorandum no. 80 (1981).

a notable shift toward profit making and provision of a higher share]
of their own investment needs, tightening up much as a private cor- ↓
poration tightens up in conditions of adversity. In Argentina, public]
firms go through cycles in such matters: when a populist govern-↓
ment is in office the public firms spend freely and greatly raise the
number of workers they use per unit output; when the opposite
kind of government comes in, behavior goes in the opposite direction, toward minimization of cost.[27]

Market-authoritarian regimes are more likely than populist governments to exert pressures on public firms to avoid waste, and to
contribute to growth by covering their own costs rather than running deficits. They are, of course, most unlikely to use public firms
for purposes of social reform. In more democratic regimes the interest in using them for social purposes is normally greater, but unhappily that orientation often comes along with disregard of efficiency. The typical populist use of public enterprise is mainly to run
the firm at a loss in order to subsidize sales and to hire more workers
even if they add nothing to output. For those countries with oil production the standard behavior of state oil firms is to sell oil products
at prices far below their value as exports, and thereby to subsidize
the wealthy minority who have automobiles. The same practice also
increases the relative profitability of energy-intensive production
processes in industry and works against creation of employment opportunities. Subsidizing sales of oil products may be intended in
part to help the poor, by reducing costs of public transportation, but
the evident solution for such a target is to subsidize bus transportation directly and stop wasting national resources to raise the real
income of the rich. Similarly, the use of public firms to raise employment could have a positive element, if labor is used as an alternative to import-intensive machinery, but when it neither saves imports nor adds to output it mainly serves to lower national income.
There are always some positive elements in the objectives intended,
but to run public enterprise at a loss is rarely an effective way to
reach the objectives.

Social use of public enterprise does not need to get tangled up
with waste and special privilege. What is necessary is to separate out
the costs of intended social functions, to cover these specific costs by
subsidies from the budget, and then to direct the firms to aim at prof-

[27] Adolfo Canitrot, "La experiencia populista de redistribución de ingresos," *Desarrollo Económico* 15 (October–December 1975), pp. 331–51.

its on their operations as producers of commodities.[28] That is the
kind of approach normally used for public enterprise in Europe,
and it can work. It emphasizes close attention to costs and to value
of output. It would require that payments to managers as to workers
be consistent with their alternative earnings in other activities. Even
a public firm directed toward social functions can become a liability
when its managers and workers use it mainly to raise their own
standard of living. In the absence of restraints from owners concerned with profits, effective performance requires active external
supervision.

Apart from Brazil and Mexico, public enterprise has not played
as active a role in the semi-industrialized countries of Latin America
as it has in the more dynamic East Asian economies. The difference
might reflect the greater relative influence of the United States in
Latin America: the Japanese example in Asia, and the more open
attitude of English traditions toward public ownership, make the
Asian context more favorable to acceptance of public enterprise.
But beyond that difference in attitudes, it may well be that public
enterprise is intrinsically less suited to Latin American countries.
The essence of the institution is that it is open to wider goals than
direct market performance: it can take on many different possible
functions according to the goals transmitted to it in the particular
society. To perform well in any sense at all requires that the goals be
fairly well defined. "Public enterprises will be more efficient instruments of policy in countries where there is broad consensus as to
what goals are important than in countries wracked by continual
conflict."[29] It is not surprising that they have functioned less well in
Argentina than in Japan or Norway. But that difference should
lessen, in Argentina as in all of Latin America, to the extent that national economic strategies become more coherent.

The main problem with public enterprise in Latin America is less
one of incompetence than it is one of relating means to goals. Conservative governments confine its use too narrowly, while populist
and reformist governments are prone to misuse it by paying too little attention to avoidable waste. That problem of lost opportunity
falling between the two kinds of misdirection is a common theme in
this book in many connections. It may apply with special force to the

---

[28] The classic statement and application of this principle is the French "Nora Report," Comité Interministeriel des Entreprises Publiques, *Rapport sur les entreprises
publiques* (Paris: La Documentation Française, 1968).

[29] Brian Levy, "A Theory of Public Enterprise," *Journal of Economic Behavior and Organization*, forthcoming.

use of public firms. They could play a far more useful role, as instruments of social change and also as contributors to economic growth, if they were used by a reform-oriented government able to see that efficiency is a means toward its own goals.

4. DEPENDENCY ANALYSIS AS CREATIVE CONFUSION

Something powerful in human nature drives people with good ideas toward imperialistic formulations, trying to explain practically everything in terms of one concept. Dependency analysis has gone this way in some of its versions, losing any distinctive meaning in the process. The more compelling versions are those that focus on the question of exactly how external influences limit or bias internal choices, without trying to rule out the significance of differences in national conditions and policies. By this path, they serve as an important correction to a basic weakness in much economic analysis. That core problem with economic analysis is the presumption that nations (or individual people, or corporations, or governments) choose to do what they do in response to self-determined preferences.

That conception of self-determination is fairly dubious even for individuals, but in the absence of accepted alternatives it gets stretched to include decisions by governments and countries. It is a presumption loaded with implicit values, some of them very appealing. It fits democratic theory, respect for individual rights, and the case for noninterference in the affairs of other countries. To argue that it is simply wrong—that people and whole societies do not know what is best for them and need to be straightened out—can lead to a kind of intellectual authoritarianism. And yet, all of us do make choices that damage ourselves. People, like countries, are tangles of mutually contradictory wishes whose implications they do not fully understand. For Argentina, explanations of conflict in terms of competing group interests are only half the story, at best: incomplete understanding of what will actually serve each group's interests, once repercussions on the society as a whole have begun to work out, plays a vital role too. Both aspects together mean that even relatively free domestic choices of economic strategy can and often do damage the society as a whole.

External influences may do good as well as harm. On the personal level, external messages may make things worse if they twist preferences in the interests of others to the detriment of one's self. But they may also be essential for any responsible behavior. Individuals who listen only to themselves are unlikely to contribute positively to others, or to thrive themselves. And so with nations. Influences from outside may often be unambiguously negative, but they may at times serve to enlarge understanding. The fact that they come from outside is not a sufficient basis to qualify them as undesirable.

The most useful clue from dependency analysis is that national decisions are made by particular groups and coalitions and need not represent in any way the preferences or the real interests of the majority of the people in the country. It would be a costly misapplication of dependency criteria to identify all contact with the outside world as an actual or potential disaster, to try to cut such contact off regardless of its positive or negative character. Ideas of foreign origin are often good ideas; products of foreign origin may really raise domestic living standards; technology from abroad may help raise incomes of the poor; external markets can provide income and increased employment; contact with the outside can widen personal awareness and capacities. The negative possibilities emphasized by dependency analysis are real too. There is plenty of room for debate about exactly which are positive and which are harmful relationships. Which external contacts are desirable can only be judged in a meaningful way if the majority of the people in the country are able to know what is going on and to take part in the decisions.

PART II

NATIONAL PATTERNS
OF RESPONSE

EIGHT

EARLY INDUSTRIALIZATION
AND VIOLENT REACTION:
ARGENTINA AND BRAZIL

Argentina and Brazil, along with Chile, were the leaders of Latin American industralization in the first years of the postwar period. With fairly well-established industrial sectors at the start, and wide public support, they led the way toward further industrial growth through protection and direct government promotion. But the way proved to be traumatic. All three developed new kinds of economic and social strains, and all relapsed, at different crucial points, into intense political repression. From a sufficient distance, they fit a somber common picture. Examined more closely, the patterns of their responses, and the consequences, differ considerably. Can these differences illuminate future choices, either for them or for other countries?

The two societies differ greatly in the nature of their labor markets and class structures. Brazil started the postwar period with a great deal of persistent underemployment in both rural and urban sectors, consistent with the Arthur Lewis model of excess labor. In contrast, Argentina had a much more integrated economy and society, little persistent underemployment, wide access to education, and less inequality (table 8.1). It came closer to the conditions presumed by neoclassical economics: all factors of production were scarce and valuable in market terms.[1] That greater integration did not make things easier. It reduced the scope for increasing national income by incorporating the underemployed, and it raised the costs of misallocating resources. Generalized resource scarcity aggravated conflict between the urban industrial sector and landowner-exporters, because increased allocation to one side almost inescapably implied absolute losses for the other. In a sense, some of Argentina's economic strains may have derived from a case of mistaken identity: it was so much outside the usual model of under-

[1] Carlos Díaz Alejandro, "One Hundred Years."

developed countries that policies conceivably useful for them were for it inherently nonfunctional.

1. FROM PROSPERITY TO DEEP TROUBLE: THE HIGH PERIOD OF IMPORT SUBSTITUTION

Both Argentina and Brazil built up substantial industrial sectors prior to the 1930s.[2] Domestic producers rather than foreign dominated export production, and the long-term increase of their earnings encouraged the gradual growth of manufacturing for the domestic market. This process accelerated in the 1930s and 1940s as access to imported manufactured goods was cut back, first by the collapse of external demand and export earnings and then by restricted supplies from the industrialized countries during the war. As early as 1950 fully a fourth of the Argentine labor force was employed in manufacturing (table 8.1). The proportion was much lower in Brazil, but with a population three times that of Argentina the absolute size of its manufacturing sector was even larger.

When the two countries adopted more deliberate policies to promote import substitution in the early postwar years, the consequences were mixed in both cases, but the mixture was much more negative in Argentina than in Brazil. The difference was due to contrasts in both their economic structures and their policies. Both followed the same general policy objective, to divert resources into industrial capital formation by protection and subsidies that changed relative prices and earnings in favor of industry, acting as a tax on primary producers. But the degrees and overall balance of costs and gains differed considerably.

Argentina under Perón, from 1946, went far beyond any necessary diversion of resources away from agriculture, taking away from primary exporters about half of the real income they would have received at current prices in the period 1946–49. The method was a combination of differential exchange rates adverse to exporters and the use of a marketing board to capture much of remaining export receipts. William Ascher describes the methods well; he explains the procedure as a rare example of successful redistribution.[3] Where real wages of urban workers had increased at the same rate as GDP per capita from 1943 to 1946, in the next three years they were raised 62 percent, far outpacing the increase of 4 percent in real in-

[2] Díaz Alejandro, *Essays*; Nathaniel H. Leff, *Underdevelopment and Development in Brazil* (Boston: Allen and Unwin, 1982).

[3] Ascher, *Scheming for the Poor*, ch. 3 and 6.

TABLE 8.1. Indicators of the Comparative Positions of
Argentina and Brazil

Gross domestic product per capita in 1970 dollars	1880	1945	1955	1970	1980
Argentina	470	1,280	1,380	1,960	2,184
Brazil	139	470	670	1,100	1,924
Ratio, Argentina/Brazil	3.4	2.7	2.1	1.8	1.1
Employment in manufacturing as percent of labor force		1950	1960	1970	
Argentina		25.3	27.7	24.0	
Brazil		12.9	13.7	14.8	
Illiteracy: percentage of population over 14 years in Argentina and over 15 years in Brazil		1950	1960	1970	1980
Argentina		13.6	8.6	7.4	—
Brazil		50.5	39.7	33.8	26.0

Income distribution: percentage share of the lowest 40 percent in total income	
Argentina, 1970	14.1
Brazil, 1972	7.0

SOURCES: GDP from Carlos Díaz-Alejandro, "No Less Than One Hundred Years," table 1, p. 331; employment and illiteracy from ECLA, *Statistical Yearbook for Latin America, 1983*, pp. 77–79 and 102; income distribution from World Bank, *World Development Report, 1980*, p. 157.

come per capita.[4] The counterpart of increased consumption by urban workers was a combination of lower income in the rural sector and a rising import surplus, leading to a series of foreign exchange crises. Ascher concludes that the redistribution was successful in the sense that, even when the economy began to come to pieces and all incomes fell, the share of income going to labor stayed close to the peak reached in 1949. If one were concerned about the trend of real wages rather than shares of a blocked total, or with the capacity for economic growth, the picture would not appear so successful: the

[4] Díaz Alejandro, *Essays*, table 133, p. 538.

country headed into a long period of stagnation and increasingly bitter social conflict.

Brazilian policy through the 1950s was also adverse to the primary sector, through protection raising costs of manufactured goods, export taxes, and an overvalued currency which reduced earnings of primary exporters.[5] But the balance of costs and gains was not the same as in Argentina. On one side, the degree to which agriculture was penalized was somewhat lower. An estimate for 1966 suggests that real incomes in agriculture were reduced about 21 percent by protection of industry in the late stages of import substitution.[6] On the receiving side, the industrial sector, the gains went much more to the industrialists and much less to labor. Where Argentina in the first three years under Perón carried out real wage increases greatly exceeding the rise in production, Brazil held down the increase of real wages in manufacturing to only 2.4 percent a year from 1949 to 1959, against a rate of increase of 6.6 percent a year in output per worker.[7] The difference permitted transferring to industrial investment a greater share of the income taken away from agriculture in Brazil and held down the diversion of potential agricultural exports into domestic consumption.

Argentine wage policy was particularly adverse for earnings of foreign exchange because of the nature of its exports. The main primary exports—meat and wheat—are wage goods that get pulled into domestic consumption whenever real wages rise. Brazilian ability to keep up primary exports was in this respect doubly helped, first by the slower rate of increase in consumption by urban workers and second by the fact that its leading export at that time, coffee, was not a crucial wage good in the sense of meat in Argentina. The Argentine approach clearly accomplished more for incomes of urban workers and for equality in the first three years of its application, but its consequences for external deficits and blocked growth then went the other way.

Partly because of these policy differences, and partly because of Brazil's structural advantage of underutilized labor and land, it did much better in restoring exports even while industrializing, and in aggregate growth. Comparing export earnings in dollars for 1950–54 to their averages for 1946–49, Brazilian exports increased 14

[5] Nathaniel H. Leff, *Economic Policy Making and Development in Brazil, 1947–1964* (New York: Wiley, 1968).

[6] Little, Scitovsky, and Scott, *Industry and Trade*, table 2.12, p. 73.

[7] Joel Bergsman, *Brazil: Industrialization and Trade Policies* (New York: Oxford University Press for the OECD, 1970), pp. 59, 151–57.

percent while Argentina's decreased 19 percent. On a per capita basis, Argentina's export volume in 1950–54 was only 40 percent of its level in 1930–34.[8] The growth of GDP per capita in Brazil for the 1950s was one of the highest in Latin America, at 3.6 percent a year. Argentina's growth rate for the decade was less than half the Latin American average, at 0.9 percent a year (see table 4.5).

Perón was driven to retreat from the extremes of 1946–49 by growing foreign exchange difficulties, directly related to the destruction of export incentives. Argentina then began a long series of attempts to redress the imbalance. But efforts to restore incentives for primary exports ran into potent resistance from well-organized workers and industrialists. From 1949, inflation took off, as primary producers fought for devaluations to restore their export earnings while industrialists and workers fought back to increase their prices and wages. In the periods in which devaluation lagged behind inflation, real wages and domestic consumption increased, but at the cost of increasing external deficits. When devaluation outpaced inflation, that helped revive exports but reduced real wages, consumption, and total output.[9]

The industrialization drive need not have caused deepening conflicts to anything like this degree. The central economic difficulty was self-strangulation on the side of foreign exchange. Transfers of income from primary producers to the urban sector were not used either to generate industrial exports to replace those lost from the rural sector or to deepen the structure of production by developing capital equipment and supplies for industry. The incentives went instead to investment in ever-changing consumer products for rising domestic consumption.[10] That particular kind of industrialization is understandable in terms of the political balance in Argentina at the time, but it practically guaranteed economic breakdown. The only way to reduce external deficits was to stop growth; as soon as growth resumed, the deficits came right back. As if these economic strains were not enough, an additional conflict was created by at-

[8] Export values from United Nations, *Yearbook of International Trade Statistics, 1960* (New York: UN, 1962), pp. 51 and 81; export volume on a per capita basis from Díaz Alejandro, "One Hundred Years," table 6, p. 347. See also Díaz Alejandro, "The 1940s in Latin America," in Moshe Syrquin, Lance Taylor, and Larry E. Westphal, eds., *Economic Structure and Performance: Essays in Honor of Hollis B. Chenery* (New York: Academic Press, 1984).

[9] Díaz Alejandro, *Exchange Rate Devaluation.*

[10] David Felix, "The Dilemma of Import Substitution," in Gustav F. Papenek, ed., *Development Policy—Theory and Practice* (Cambridge: Harvard University Press, 1968), pp. 55–91; Díaz Alejandro, *Essays*, p. 383.

tacks of some Perónist factions against the Catholic Church.[11] But
the workers—and the majority of the population—stayed loyal.
When the military forced Perón into exile in 1955, that scarcely
changed the basic deadlock. Perónism had created a durable interest group that had to be either incorporated into a new political coalition or repressed by force.[12]

Brazil ran into increasing problems with external deficits too, but
its deficits were consequences of success rather than failure with industrialization: a high rate of industrial growth raised import requirements too rapidly for external balance. The policy response to
the deficits was to try cutting imports more steeply by vertical integration, especially from 1956 under the Kubitschek administration.
This was not an attempt to reduce reliance on foreign technology
but rather the contrary: it was an option in favor of bringing in foreign firms.[13] From the Brazilian side, foreign investment was pulled
in by protection, exerting pressure on former exporters to the
country to invest in local production in order to hold their market
positions. From the outside, multinational firms were especially eager to enter the country because of the size of its domestic market
and the evident dynamism of the economy. That special appeal
helped Brazil carry import substitution through to vertical integration much more successfully than Argentina.[14] But the process
greatly increased foreign participation in Brazilian industry and
fostered a structure of production biased toward capital- and energy-intensive methods, toward labor saving rather than creation of
employment opportunities.

Throughout this period of rapid growth in the 1950s, inflation
and an import surplus were persisting but not overwhelming problems. Government spending was sufficiently restrained to keep
down budget deficits, though moderate excess demand and extensions of protection gradually pulled up prices. As in Argentina, in-

---

[11] Political and economic interactions are emphasized in Guillermo O'Donnell,
"Permanent Crisis and the Failure to Create a Democratic Regime in Argentina,
1955–66," in Juan J. Linz and Alfred Stepan, eds., *The Breakdown of Democratic Regimes: Latin America* (Baltimore: Johns Hopkins University Press, 1978), pp. 138–77.
Thomas E. Skidmore and Peter H. Smith explain the immediate cause of Perón's
overthrow chiefly in terms of the conflict between Perónists and the church: *Modern
Latin America* (New York: Oxford University Press, 1984), pp. 94–95.

[12] Richard Mallon and Juan Sourrouille, *Economic Policy Making in a Conflict Society:
The Argentine Case* (Cambridge: Harvard University Press, 1975), p. 14.

[13] Evans, *Dependent Development*; Gereffi and Evans, "Transnational Corporations."

[14] Bergsman, *Brazil*, ch. 5; Werner Baer, *Industrialization and Economic Development
in Brazil* (Homewood, Ill.: Irwin, 1965).

vestment was directed to the home market rather than exports. Growing need for external credit led in the second half of the 1950s to Brazil's first major conflict with the IMF as the latter, and the United States through its aid program, began to put pressure on the Kubitschek administration to change its policies away from protection and toward greater restraint on inflation. Kubitschek responded by trying a brief stabilization program but backed away quickly when both industry and labor began to protest. That backing away could be cited as evidence of the constraints of a relatively open political system, but the main factor may rather have been that Kubitschek himself gave high priority to industrialization. Perhaps more importantly, he saw that Brazil, in sharp contrast to a floundering Argentina, had achieved an exceptionally broad consensus on an economic strategy that was achieving rapid growth.[15]

Kubitschek passed the unresolved dispute with the IMF on to the administration of Janos Quadros, elected in 1960. The conflict then became part of a dramatic struggle leading to the breakdown of Brazilian democracy in 1964. In his campaign for election Quadros promised change toward more concern for poverty and regional inequality, while also insisting on the need for a stabilization program and continued rapid growth. As a proponent of everything at once, he was elected with broad majority support. In office, he reached temporary agreement with the IMF and the United States on resumption of external credit and proposed major tax and land reforms. In the context of the beginning of the 1960s, on the eve of the Alliance for Progress, these reform proposals were approved and supported by the United States. They were not approved by everyone in Brazil. The Congress accepted a tax reform but dug in to oppose changes in land ownership. Instead of negotiating to pull everyone together, Kubitschek style, Quadros stunned everyone by resigning the presidency, announcing that the Brazilian political system was impossible to operate.

The vice-president who would legally succeed him, João Goulart, was initially blocked by a segment of the military leadership which considered him too radical. A compromise was reached allowing him to take office but only after an amendment to the constitution gave the Congress increased authority to restrain actions of the president. Instead of dealing with the economy, or pursuing any coherent line of reform, Goulart concentrated on working up pres-

[15] Thomas E. Skidmore, *Politics in Brazil, 1930–1964: An Experiment in Democracy* (New York: Oxford University Press, 1967), pp. 174–82.

sure for a plebiscite to reverse the constitutional limit on his powers. Appealing primarily to labor and to peasants, and supporting mass demonstrations, he frightened the conservative side as much as possible. Foreign investors were singled out for attack as an affront to national autonomy; their previously enthusiastic welcome was reversed by a new law limiting repatriation of profits. Budget constraints were relaxed and the public sector deficit grew rapidly. The rate of inflation as measured by the GDP deflator began climbing from 26 percent in 1960 to 72 percent by 1963. The U.S. government, reacting both to evidence of economic deterioration and to overtones of dissent from American policy toward Cuba, began to cut aid.[16] Foreign investment dropped sharply. The rate of growth of GDP fell from a fairly steady average of 7 percent for 1957–1961 to 1.6 percent for 1963.[17]

Celso Furtado, writing in late 1963 just a few months before the military takeover, described this period as prerevolutionary.[18] It was evident to all sides that the crisis was becoming worse and the government was not doing anything to cope with it. Goulart won a plebiscite restoring full powers of the presidency but continued to blame the crisis on institutional limitations, doing little either to check the descent of the economy or to implement specific reforms. "Quadros and Goulart were both pessimistic about the chances of the political system working effectively, and it could be argued that they worked harder at attempting to change the regime than at achieving more limited goals within the existing framework."[19]

Intervention by the military might have been avoided if the government had gone back to the IMF and the United States for additional credit and adopted the kind of stabilization program they required, but this would have meant placing the government in direct conflict with the workers who constituted its main support. A contrary alternative might have been to go toward nationalization of foreign firms and intensified self-sufficiency, cutting loose from external financial and trade relationships.[20] Goulart was not interested in the first option, and the nation's business and financial leaders

[16] Alfred Stepan, "Political Leadership and Regime Breakdown: Brazil," in Linz and Stepan, eds., *Breakdown*, pp. 110–37.

[17] Bergsman, *Brazil*, p. 55

[18] Celso Furtado, *Diagnosis of the Brazilian Crisis* (Berkeley: University of California Press, 1965), p. xiii and ch. 8.

[19] Stepan, "Political Leadership," p. 116.

[20] Michael Wallerstein, "The Collapse of Democracy in Brazil: Its Economic Determinants," *Latin American Research Review* 15, 3 (1980), pp. 3–40.

would not accept the second. A conceivable third alternative might have been to try a nationally designed program of stabilization and reform, along the lines discussed in chapter 5 as an alternative to IMF programs, combining specific structural reforms to aid lower income groups with negotiated restraints on wages and monetary expansion. Such an approach might have gained sufficiently broad support to hold the society together until the next election. Or it might not; it was not tried. With pressures for explosion already high, the United States helped make them worse first by stopping aid and then by making clear the desirability of Goulart's departure from the presidency.[21] The previous centrist coalition of industrialists and workers came apart completely. "The right saw its salvation to lie in the expeditious use of force."[22]

The marvelously elusive nature of historical interpretation is demonstrated by the many opposing interpretations, based on essentially the same facts, of why Brazilian democracy was demolished in 1964. From the dependency perspective, a good case can be made that transnational firms and an internationally oriented business and financial community became determined to get rid of an erratic populism which had lost the confidence of the world financial community, allowed inflation to get out of hand, and encouraged dangerous demonstrations by peasants and workers. From the conservative side, the problem perceived was that impossible demands from the left, fostered by intellectuals obsessed with hostility to foreign influence, had badly hurt a dynamic economy that could otherwise have continued to make strong progress.[23] From this latter point of view, the great need was to replace Goulart and get back to business. A striking feature of the two interpretations, squarely opposed on what ought to be done, is that they agree so closely on the nature of the crisis: the conservative side of the society could not accept the changes insisted on by the left, and the left could not accept the kind of society insisted on by the conservatives.

The military takeover in Brazil created the first of what was to be-

---

[21] Phyllis R. Parker, *Brazil and the Quiet Intervention.*

[22] Wallerstein, "Collapse," p. 34.

[23] Baer, *Industrialization,* pp. 193–202, argues that the claims for major social changes came too early, at too low a level of national income to allow combining redistribution with continued growth. In his view, another fifteen years of priority on economic growth were necessary to bring Brazil to a point that would permit significant moves toward equality without stopping growth. Leff, *Economic Policy,* blames Brazilian intellectuals, especially the group surrounding Goulart in the government, for aggravating hostility to foreign investors and stimulating claims for redistribution beyond any possibility of a satisfactory answer.

come a series of market-authoritarian regimes, not just eliminating civilian government but suppressing labor leaders and organizations, closing down all established channels of political and social dissent, and radically reversing national economic policies. This was a much more decisive and fundamental revolt than the exile of Perón in Argentina. In terms of prior history it was a loss of a better established civilian governmental system, far from representative of the whole nation but beginning to grow toward wider participation.[24] It was not just a displacement of a particular person or group but a rejection of the right of popular preferences to determine the character of national economic policy.

2. Economic Growth and Authoritarianism in Brazil from 1964

The economic strategy of the authoritarian regime in Brazil went through several very different phases, all based on a common foundation. The first stage was deflationary, forcing down real wages and employment, but from 1967 the strategy was reoriented toward expansion and succeeded in promoting an exceptionally high rate of growth. The new orientation included much greater attention to exports and to macroeconomic balance. Up to 1974 it succeeded in the miracle of avoiding rising inflation or external deficits. From 1974, rising oil import prices began to upset this balance and national economic policies failed to respond effectively. The growth rate remained high through 1980 but at the cost of rising inflation and external debt. Brazil was then forced back into macroeconomic contraction, output actually fell, and real wages were driven down once again in the process of difficult negotiations with external creditors. The scene was familiar, but even in the midst of the debt crisis the Brazilian economy was in all basic respects far stronger, in agriculture as well as industry, than it had been twenty years earlier.

The common foundation of economic policy in all these phases might be termed managerial capitalism. It was by no means a rejection of state intervention or an option for the kind of purist monetarism adopted later in Chile. It included extensive controls and protection but also some fundamental changes from preceding policies: a determined effort to promote exports, erratic but significant attempts to increase efficiency, extensive development of indexation to limit distortions due to inflation, more effective taxation, and

[24] Stepan, "Political Leadership."

greater restraint on public sector deficits. The system included much greater concern for use of market forces compared to the 1946–64 period, but always within an overall context of active state intervention to guide the economy.

The managerial character of the Brazilian system after 1964 was highly profit-oriented but not a simple case of domination by business interests. The bureaucratic-professional side of the government, along with the managers of many of the largest private and state firms, formed a coalition based on an active promotional regime.[25] Public firms were used to lead investment in heavy industry and allowed to raise their share of output relative to private. Those private firms not interested in exporting or in vertical integration, not regarded as contributors to the kind of growth desired by the coalition, got little government support. If reductions in protection hurt them, they were allowed to lose out. If firms were instead able to move in directions favored by the government, they could count on a great deal of individually tailored help.

On this interpretation of the Brazilian system, it resembles the Japanese and Korean styles of export-oriented economic management and comes particularly close to the methods used in postwar France to break out of preceding stagnation. In France, a coalition of government and business interests, using public enterprise and negotiated cooperation of individual firms in a system of indicative planning, greatly changed the structure and the operating success of the economy.[26] In both cases the new strategy shifted emphasis from protection to promotion of exports. In both cases this worked to favor high rates of growth but also gave a disproportionate share of the gains to the groups best able to cooperate. Perhaps the most striking difference is that the French were able to use this style of economic growth without recourse to repression, in an open political system with active labor organizations. There is nothing in the strategy of managed capitalism itself that precludes an open political system, though the way it was implemented in Brazil certainly did.

In Brazil, with highly concentrated access to education and skills as well as ownership of property, a strategy directing rewards to those who could respond best to new promotional incentives had far

[25] David R. Dye and Carlos Eduardo de Souza e Silva, "A Perspective on the Brazilian State," *Latin American Research Review* 14, 1 (1979), pp. 81–98; Mendonça de Barros and Graham, "Economic Miracle."

[26] John Sheahan, *Promotion and Control of Industry in Postwar France* (Cambridge: Harvard University Press, 1963).

more inegalitarian consequences than it need have had. Social expenditures and real wages were cut back, and real wages were driven down steadily from 1964 to the low point in 1968. Estimates of exactly how much real wages were cut vary from 17 percent for the minimum wage in Rio de Janeiro to 31 percent for the median wage in Sao Paulo.[27] The wage share in national income went down from approximately 56 percent as of 1959 to 51 percent by 1970.[28] That could hardly have been done without blocking the right to strike. But repression went far beyond restraints on organized labor. Independent political parties and intellectual leaders, student opposition, peasant organizations, and any evident source of potential threat to the military regime were repressed as well.[29] It was a program to destroy possible spokesmen for workers and the poor, or indeed for any opposition at all. But at the same time the regime changed other economic policies in ways that had previously been blocked by the business sector. Protection and subsidies to business were reduced, interest rates were increased, and even the previously entrenched resistance to more effective taxation was overcome.[30] Along with monetary restraint, these changes brought the rate of inflation, as measured by the General Price Index, down from 92 percent for 1964 to an average of 25 percent for 1967–68.[31]

If the government had stayed with the original intent of stopping inflation completely, that could have required keeping the economy down for many years. While the IMF and part of the Brazilian government favored staying with that course, the side of the government more interested in economic growth fortunately overruled them. The deflationary policy was reversed in 1967. A key factor in that decision was the recognition that the remaining inflation was no longer a matter of excess demand, or excess monetary expansion, but rather of the dynamics of inflationary expectations in conditions of weak competition.[32]

[27] The lower estimate is from Alejandro Foxley, "Stabilization Policies and Stagflation: The Cases of Brazil and Chile," *World Development* 8 (November 1980), p. 890. The higher is from Wallerstein, "Collapse," p. 18.

[28] Edmar L. Bacha and Lance Taylor, "Brazilian Income Distribution in the 1960s: 'Facts,' Model Results, and the Controversy," *Journal of Development Studies* 14 (April 1978), pp. 271–97, data from pp. 290–91.

[29] Knight, "Brazilian Socioeconomic Development," esp. pp. 1066–67.

[30] Thomas E. Skidmore, "Politics and Economic Policy Making in Authoritarian Brazil, 1937–71," in Alfred Stepan, ed., *Authoritarian Brazil*.

[31] Foxley, "Stabilization," p. 889.

[32] Albert Fishlow, "Some Reflections on Post-1964 Brazilian Economic Policy," in Stepan, ed., *Authoritarian Brazil*, pp. 69–118.

The remedies adopted for this kind of inflation combined expansion of demand with frequent small devaluations to offset negative effects of inflation on exports, indexing to minimize distortions in contracts expressed in current money values, and partial controls of wages and prices. Wage indexing applied to the minimum wage and did not block discretionary increases above that level, at least not until inflation began to rise again in the mid-1970s. As demand and output began to rise rapidly from 1968 on, the share of wage income stopped falling and real wages began to go up again. The most dramatic evidence of a significant change is that real wages in the agricultural sector began to rise more rapidly than industrial wages and continued to outpace the latter through the whole decade of the 1970s.[33]

In the period of macroeconomic contraction, from 1964 through 1967, the distribution of income became drastically more unequal. Even the shift back to rising wages from 1968 on left a significant net increase in inequality for the decade of the 1960s as a whole.[34] World Bank data indicate that the income of the poorest 60 percent of the population increased 1.2 percent a year in real terms during the 1960s, while that of the whole population was increasing 3.1 percent a year (see table 2.3). The share of the poorest 40 percent fell from 9.8 to 8.4 percent of total income. But then the extraordinary growth of output and employment from 1968 on through the 1970s helped to raise real incomes of the poor at a rate fast enough to keep up with the growth of national income, with rural wages growing even faster than urban. In terms of the Lewis model Brazil seems to have reached a real "turning point" toward a more integrated economy.[35] But even then, under these favorable conditions, inequality did not actually decrease: the rise in rural incomes relative to urban, acting to reduce inequality, was offset by increasing inequality within the agricultural sector.[36]

---

[33] PREALC, *Mercado de trabajo en cifras*, table III-3, p. 150.

[34] Cf. Albert Fishlow, "Brazilian Size Distribution of Income," *American Economic Review* 42 (1972), pp. 391-402, and the subsequent conflicts of interpretation reviewed in Bacha and Taylor, "Income Distribution," Pfefferman and Webb, "The Distribution of Income in Brazil"; Fields, *Poverty*, pp. 210-18. None of the later evidence seriously changes Fishlow's conclusion that inequality increased markedly between 1960 and 1970, though the expansion starting in 1968 stopped the process of deterioration.

[35] Denslow and Tyler, "Perspectives"; Samuel Morley, *Labor Markets and Inequitable Growth: The Case of Authoritarian Capitalism in Brazil* (London: Cambridge University Press, 1983).

[36] Denslow and Tyler, "Perspectives," pp. 18–30.

Expansion combined with export promotion and with concern for overall balance also began to decrease the country's dependence on industrial investment by transnational firms. In the early postwar phase of import substitution, from 1949 to 1962, one-third of the growth of manufacturing output came from foreign-owned firms.[37] As of 1968, transnational firms accounted for 37 percent of total invested capital and 28 percent of the net worth of the one hundred largest nonfinancial firms in Brazil.[38] But the tide then began to recede. The transnationals' share of invested capital of the hundred largest firms fell from 37 percent in 1968 to 27 percent by 1974, and that of net worth fell from 28 to 15 percent. The declines were not results of a rising share for Brazilian private enterprise: it was public enterprise that increased its share, at the expense of both categories of private firms.[39]

The increase in the relative role of national Brazilian firms was a result of their own growing capacities, aided by the government, rather than of limitations on foreign entry. But the welcome to foreign firms has always been a touchy matter. The strongly nationalist strand within the military government and the state administrative system, as well as the suspicions and opposition of the part of the business sector competing with foreign firms, maintained an opposing tension. From 1973, as the government began to allow more open debate and to pay somewhat more attention to public preferences, the unpopularity of foreign ownership became increasingly clear. As of 1980 two strategic fields of expected rapid growth, minicomputers and health care, were closed to foreign investors.[40]

In the third phase of the authoritarian regime, from 1974, inflation and external deficits again began to rise seriously. They were stimulated by the oil price increases of 1974 and aggravated by the energy-intensive character of Brazilian industrialization. The volume of energy imports grew by 11 percent a year from 1965 to 1980, while prices were shooting up. Export growth was formidable in this period too: volume increased 9.5 percent a year. But a country does not eliminate external deficits by fast export growth if imports grow still faster. Total imports increased 10.2 percent a year in volume terms, so the external deficit would have increased steadily even in the absence of any change in the terms of trade.[41]

[37] Gereffi and Evans, "Transnational Corporations."
[38] Mendonça de Barros and Graham, "Economic Miracle," p. 8.
[39] Hewlett, The Cruel Dilemmas of Development, tables 8 and 9. See also Baer, Kerstenetzky, and Villela, "The Changing Role of the State," pp. 23–24.
[40] Gereffi and Evans, "Transnational Corporations," p. 47.
[41] Knight, "Brazilian Development," p. 1065.

Such strong demand for imports might be explained primarily by the high rate of growth of domestic income, but in addition to this macroeconomic relationship structural questions of income distribution and demand patterns made import requirements greater than they need have been. Given the high concentration of income in the upper-income groups, the pattern of consumer expenditure was strongly oriented toward luxury housing and the latest consumer durable goods. The character of final demand helped pull investment toward activities dependent on foreign technology, imported capital equipment, and inputs of imported oil. National economic policies reinforced the pattern, providing such strong incentives for capital investment that they encouraged capital-intensive techniques and thereby made import coefficients higher than they need have been. The character of transportation development had similar effects, with rapid growth in use of private automobiles and little effort to expand public transportation.[42] This was what the market dictated, given the concentration of income and the relative economic and political powerlessness of the poor. Inequalities of income and political voice worked together to make the economy more dependent on foreign technology and on energy inputs.

It is at least conceivable that Brazil could have avoided the debt crisis and contraction of the early 1980s if its export drive had been combined with attempts to restructure domestic production and spending patterns. The main specific change required would have been to use steeply higher prices for oil sales on the domestic market to drive industry and consumers away from energy-intensive spending. The import coefficient might have been held down more generally by increased taxation of higher incomes and of consumer durable goods, decreased subsidies for capital-intensive investment, credit reforms to cut down the transfers of income toward the wealthy through subsidized credit, and increased public expenditure on basic health, education, and transportation services. Such changes would work jointly toward lessened inequality and less import-dependent growth. But they were checked by two opposing kinds of political considerations.

On one side, the property owners and professional-technical groups able to dominate economic policy decisions in the absence of a democratic system were able to prevent changes adverse to their interests. On the other side, the military leadership began from about 1973 to pay somewhat more attention to public preferences and to move haltingly toward restoration of civilian government.

42 Ibid., p. 1066.

That highly desirable political goal was taken to require, or at least to favor, keeping up the growth of real wages and avoiding macroeconomic contraction as long as possible, regardless of inflation and external deficits. The wish to gain popular support led even the authoritarian government to act like a populist regime. Does concern for public preferences, and return to democracy, necessarily mean a return to excess demand and renewed external deficits? Not necessarily, but the conflicts are real. Possible alternatives are discussed after consideration of problems in Argentina; they almost make those of Brazil look easy.

3. IMPASSE AND REACTION IN ARGENTINA

Interlocking economic and political frustrations continued to hurt Argentina long after the exile of Perón. Short bursts of recovery were repeatedly undercut by one common feature: just as in the 1940s, the groups best placed in each positive swing used their advantage to reach beyond the gains made possible by growth and force down the incomes of the other side. That approach constantly intensified pressures for the losers to destroy whatever new set of policies had permitted the upswing.

Each upswing led to excess demand and increasing external deficits, followed by devaluation when the situation became bad enough to discourage foreign lending, then to a period of contraction in which investment and growth were sacrificed to restore external equilibrium. Devaluation forced down real wages and consumption of workers, releasing meat and other foods for export, but it also caused a collapse of domestic demand for industrial products. With industry wholly directed to the home market, dependent on the protective system and unable to export, the devaluations that might otherwise have released growth capacities instead choked them off.[43] After each such period of contraction industrialists rejoined workers to exert pressure for expansion, the economy recovered well enough at first, and then the external deficit dependably reappeared.

Given the persistence of the external constraint, solutions might be sought in either of two directions. One would be to limit the proliferation of new industrial products in periods of expansion and thereby reduce the recourse to imported capital equipment and technology. The other would be to redirect industrial production

[43] Díaz Alejandro, *Exchange Rate Devaluation.*

toward exports so that the industrial sector could pay for some of its own imported inputs. The first would aim at reducing imports relative to national income and the second at increasing exports instead. The first would imply lower efficiency and slower growth of real income for any given rate of investment, but more autonomy. The second would permit higher efficiency and incomes and require closer integration into the world market. With either route, or a combination of them, Argentina could have escaped its trap.

The civilian governments in between Perón and the military takeover of 1966 did not follow either path. Both conservative and *desarrollista* governments clung to protection but without any restraints on diversification of domestic consumption and production. Neither made any strong efforts to promote industrial exports. Absent such actions, even the otherwise promising Frondizi government (1958 to 1962) could not make any real headway. That government directed its efforts toward one of the essentials for any sustained improvement: it aimed at reconciliation of conflicting group interests, with elements of compromise that might have forestalled the disasters of the 1970s.[44] Wage earners were included in the gains of growth, and at the same time the government appealed to many conservatives because of its support for investment and its role as an alternative to Perónism. That required a delicate balancing act. It might have succeeded if the policy set had included industrial export promotion and attention to macroeconomic balance. But aggregate demand was raised much too rapidly and industrial exports were not.

The military government that took power in 1966 came closer to breaking the economic deadlock. This regime, which O'Donnell characterizes as the first Argentine bureaucratic-authoritarian state, adopted economic policies similar to those used in Brazil from 1967. Expansionary macroeconomic policy was combined with export promotion through both exchange rates and direct subsidies, the growth of demand was kept close to that of production, and controls were used for wages and some prices.[45] That combination fused a structuralist incomes-policy approach, rejecting reliance on free markets, with attention to macroeconomic balance and market-

---

[44] Marcelo Cavarozzi, "El 'desarrollismo' y las relaciones entre democracia y capitalismo dependiente en *Dependencia y desarrollo en América Latina*," *Latin American Research Review* 17, 1 (1982), pp. 152–65; Mallon and Sourrouille, *Conflict Society*, pp. 20–22.

[45] Mallon and Sourrouille, *Conflict Society*, pp. 28–30 and 116.

based export incentives: the kind of unholy mixture that has a chance of succeeding.

This economic strategy escaped the stifling polarization between programs that were either against industry or against agriculture. It stimulated growth on both sides. GNP per capita increased 3.1 percent a year from 1965 to 1970, double the rate of the preceding fifteen years. Manufactured goods as a percentage of total exports rose from 5.6 in 1965 to 13.9 by 1970.[46] But one vital component of a sustainable solution was left out: wage restraint was applied so tightly that average real wages in the industrial sector were cut by 7 percent between 1966 and 1969.[47] Labor revolted in 1969, in a bloody battle that touched off such general resistance that the whole approach was abandoned. The method broke down because it included only two of the three groups needed for continuing acceptance: industry and agriculture, but not labor.

Would it have been possible to get the exports and growth without driving down real wages? In the fundamental sense of internal consistency, yes. With output per capita increasing 3.1 percent a year, wages could have been raised along with investment and exports, provided that total claims on output did not rise faster than that rate. A more immediate question was the relationship between wage costs and export prices. To export at all, prices have to match external levels. This is precisely the point at which more popular governments often back away from export promotion. To hold wages down to fit the outside world's prices seems to reject, as Cardoso put it, "what since Prebisch has been fundamental: the incorporation of a decently paid labor force into the price of the export product."[48]

A possible reply to this concern is that decent wages can easily be reconciled with industrial exports if efficiency and labor productivity are high enough. The problem is to raise efficiency rather than impede it by restrictions on trade. But that does not answer the initial conflict if labor costs are too high to permit exports at given levels of productivity. The most conservative approach, the one attempted in Argentina, is to force down real wages. The main alternative is to subsidize labor costs for exporters, which would permit them to sell at external prices without reducing wages. Another possibility is to establish a separate exchange rate for the industrial sector, based on existing productivity and wages, which

[46] UN, ECLA, *Statistical Yearbook for Latin America, 1983*, p. 160.

[47] Tokman, "Mercados de trabajo," p. 20.

[48] Cardoso, "Development Under Fire," Instituto Latinoamericano de Estudios Transnacionales, mimeo, 1979.

would permit those particular industries closest to comparative advantage to become exporters.[49] Subsidies require offsetting increases in taxes, which raises the issue of who is pay the taxes, but that simply makes clear that the question is essentially one of internal income distribution rather than an externally imposed conclusion. The Argentine government used some subsidies and thereby lessened pressure on real wages but chose to force them down to some degree as well. It could be given credit for financial prudence or instead blamed for a bias against labor. The net result was to destroy the acceptability of an otherwise successful approach.

The violence of the 1969 labor uprising, and the continuing evidence of mass support for Perón along with the lack of success of everything else, finally induced the military to allow him to return and to become president again. But the gamble did not work. Conflicts within the Perónist movement aggravated all the preceding destructive forces. After his death in 1974, with his widow as president, the economic situation deteriorated rapidly. The price level nearly tripled between 1974 and 1975. The external deficit on current account rose to 36 percent of total exports of goods and services in 1975. Total output fell in both 1975 and 1976.[50] Behind the scenes, assassinations of Perónists by each other, and in both directions between the left and the military, made the economic confusion almost trivial in comparison. Few people were either surprised or sorry when the military removed Isabel de Perón from office in March 1976. But then, few people foresaw how vicious the military regime was about to be.

The military group that took power in March 1976 represented both many characteristics of the past and something new in Argentine history. The more familiar aspects include repression of labor and the left in general, restraint on wages and to some extent on the money supply, and a general effort to restore internal and external macroeconomic balance. But beyond all that the regime demonstrated a ruthless determination to restructure the economy and the society in radically different ways. This was not stabilization: it was a radical kind of structuralism, moving structures backward.

The character of the new economic policies is caught accurately in an analysis by Adolfo Canitrot: "Discipline as a Central Objective of Economic Policy."[51] The essence might be described as a rejection

[49] Marcelo Diamand, *Doctrinas económicas, desarrollo e independencia* (Buenos Aires: Paidos, 1973).

[50] World Bank, *World Tables*, 3d ed., vol. 1, pp. 8–9.

[51] Canitrot, "Discipline."

of the kind of society shaped by thirty years of conflict over industrialization. Argentina's troubles were identified as the end product
of a dissolution of national life that dated back to 1946. The goal became no longer economic growth, or industrialization, but a complete transformation of Argentine society such that a repetition of
populism and the subversive experiences of the first half of the
1970s would be impossible.[52]

Real wages were forced down over 40 percent between 1975 and
1977. Subsidies for industrial exporters and then for industry in
general were practically eliminated. For the first time since 1946,
protection was drastically reduced. This clearly had elements of a
pro-agriculture strategy, but that was contradicted by policies that
caused the value of the currency to appreciate in real terms. Nominal exchange rates were depreciated at a pace slower than the rate
of inflation, while high nominal interest rates—high enough to attract foreign lending even after adjustment for currency depreciation—brought a capital inflow to finance rising imports. That combination (similar to the economic policies of the Reagan administration in the United States at the start of the 1980s) produced a
"transitory euphoria" of cheap imports and downward pressure on
inflation.[53] The hidden costs, in Argentina as in the United States a
few years later, were severe damage to all exporters, both agricultural and industrial, and a rapid rise in external debt.

The real value of foreign exchange earnings in terms of domestic
purchasing power was steadily reduced each year from 1978
through 1980. Agricultural exporters were penalized by the exchange rate policy at the same time as industry was exposed to
strong negative pressures on both its exports and its ability to compete with imports. What was the purpose? It might have been explained as an obsession with inflation, or perhaps as an elaborate
means to subsidize the financial interests able to take advantage of
the twisted combination of interest rates and exchange rates. But its
essential meaning was more in the nature of a determined drive to
force all producing groups to accept the discipline of market forces.
The military and some significant fraction of the rest of the society
had come to conclude that Argentina's social conflict was intolerable, and they determined to end it by eliminating not only popular

[52] Ibid., pp. 913 and 916. See also Luis Beccaria and Ricardo Carciofi, "Recent Experiences of Stabilization: Argentina's Economic Policy, 1976–81," *Bulletin of the Institute of Development Studies*, University of Sussex, 13-1 (1981), pp. 51–59.

[53] Rudiger Dornbusch, "Argentina since Martínez de Hoz," National Bureau of
Economic Research, Working Paper no. 1466 (September 1984).

political expression but also the power of contending producer interests. The initial architect of the regime's economic policies, Martínez de Hoz, "nurtured within the government the concept of a farsighted and remote authoritarianism, possessed of a morality and discipline higher than that of a surrounding society made sick by mismanagement."[54]

It comes as something of a shock that participants in a regime that sponsored the brutal disappearances of thousands of its citizens could identify its goals with far-sighted morality. The economic policies used were adverse to industry, to agriculture, and to labor. They had to be changed and have been, by getting rid of the military government. That regime gave up after general disgust over its singularly inept economic policies and ruthless tactics against Argentine civilians was compounded by equal ineptitude in war with England over the Islas Malvinas in 1982. But beneath all these perversities a crucial question remains: what can be done to break out of the paralyzing conflicts of the last thirty-five years, to permit a growth process in which all interests share to some degree instead of circles of mutually destructive conflict? Or is there any such possibility?

4. SUSTAINABLE ECONOMIC POLICIES

The return to civilian government in Argentina, and then in Brazil in 1985, should permit broader interests to be expressed in the formulation of economic policy. The crucial question is whether these openings can be used to draw conflicting social groups closer to the kinds of mutual acceptance and negotiation necessary to live together without repression. That question goes far beyond economic issues, but it is inescapably tied up with the quality of economic policy: if strategies are well chosen in the first place and then adapted as new problems arise, that kind of success will help greatly with reduction of social strains. What clues from the past suggest workable future strategies, and what are the real possibilities of such choices?

Brazil may be the easier case because it has such a strongly demonstrated capacity for economic growth and also managed to raise real incomes of the majority of the population after 1967. Its society is less polarized, its business sector more dynamic, and its military and economic leadership relatively free of obsessions with purist monetary methods, or indeed of any hangups about the use of state

[54] Canitrot, "Discipline," p. 916.

support to get economic results. None of that guarantees ability to
deal with the burden of external debt or with the new problems certain to lie ahead, but the country clearly has a resilience favorable
for a more constructive kind of economic growth. The chances for
such success will be much improved if concern *both* for structural
changes and for macroeconomic consistency are used jointly as
guides to policy.

A more open political process would give more weight to the preferences of workers and the poor in the formulation of economic
policy. This would support the kinds of changes in social investment, tax structures, and factor input requirements favorable for a
more sustainable pattern of growth. In turn, such a reorientation
should, by increasing the weight of the mass of the population in the
structure of final demand, reinforce the kinds of economic activity
favorable for employment and reduction of poverty. But such
structural changes would not eliminate the need to limit aggregate
demand to fit productive capacity. Some sense of a maximum feasible rate of growth of final demand, and of real wages, must be accepted by the majority if an open system is to remain viable.

The role of foreign capital is another important consideration for
Brazil. Transnational firms contributed greatly to the growth of the
economy in the 1950s and again from the mid-1960s. They stopped
investing in the period of more popular government at the beginning of the 1960s, and then again when growth stopped at the beginning of the 1980s. With a government more responsive to popular concerns it is possible that foreign investment will remain
cautiously low, at least until the capacity for growth is clearly restored. Would such a reserved attitude by foreign investors hurt
Brazil? Given the strength demonstrated by Brazilian business firms
prior to the slowdown of the early 1980s, both private and public, it
is hard to see why the economy needs a high rate of foreign investment. The country might gain by encouraging specific kinds of foreign investment complementary to domestic capacities, but if the total were to stay down this might be regarded more as a blessing than
a tragedy.

Argentina has seemed at times to be almost hopelessly trapped, but
both the Frondizi government of 1958–62 and the military regime
from 1966 to 1969 managed to come close to sustainable strategies.
The first moved toward the kind of social agreement on participation that is fundamental but failed in terms of economic consistency.
The second did not try for freely established agreement but used a
mixture of structuralist and conventional techniques that gave pos-

itive economic results. It included two significant correctives to pure structuralism: maintenance of export incentives and concern for keeping the rate of growth of demand from outrunning the increase of output. At the same time, the strategy included a significant corrective to conventional economics. Instead of allowing free movements of prices and wages, this regime recognized the weakness of market constraints on protected oligopolies and on powerful labor organizations: it used price and wage control to keep both sides under constraint, while increasing aggregate demand at a rate within the capacity of the system to answer in real terms.

This policy combination permitted industrial growth through exports as well as through domestic sales, which meant for once that the import requirements of rising income did not imply an unmanageable deterioration of the external balance. The weak point that proved to be fatal was that real wages were driven down, until the workers revolted and broke the policy in 1969. This was yet one more example of a repeated pattern in Argentina in which the current losers in the power struggle have been *unnecessarily* forced down in their real income. In economic terms it would have been perfectly possible to allow real wages and consumption to increase within the limits of the increases in output per capita. That would have meant a corresponding limit on the rate of gain of the winners in the power contest. It would also have meant that all sides might have continued to gain from a successful development strategy, instead of falling into the economic disintegration and vicious social conflict of the following decade.

5. Constraints and Possibilities

The conservative forces that have supported authoritarian governments in Argentina and Brazil fear that popular government will mean prolonged economic breakdown, if not the loss of existing institutional protections and property rights. The repression and inequity fostered by the reactionary regimes when they are in power repeatedly validate the conviction of those left out that there is little hope for improvement without complete social overturn. Except for the fact that nothing goes on forever, this costly mutual distrust looks as if it might.

Any sustained consensus permitting open political systems requires more mutual trust than demonstrated in the past, and that requires more restraint on group aggression. To change the underlying reality that has given such deadly results in the past looks hopeless at times but not always. In both countries, people have learned how deeply the damage can go if civilized restraints break down. There may well be at present more resolve to seek cooperative solutions than at any time in their modern histories. It probably is not true that property owners would readily return to acceptance or support for military repression, unless frightened to death. Neither business firms nor landowner-exporters gained much out of the military regime in Argentina. Large firms and landowners in Brazil did better, most of the time, but smaller firms in more traditional activities often lost out, and must often have suffered from the favoritism shown to large domestic and foreign rivals. And even large firms that do well under selective support by an authoritarian government must often consider that arbitrary decisions can go the other way tomorrow. Business interests concerned for their own protection helped promote restoration of public discussion of economic policies in Brazil from 1973 onward, opening the way first to debate over income distribution and then slowly toward restoration of civilian government.[55]

Partly because of the kinds of instability generated by conflicting interests of the private business sector, partly because of the generous doses of inefficiency and gratuitous irritation built into all authoritarian systems, partly because of conflicting interests within the military, and perhaps most of all because Latin American societies as much in touch with the modern world as Argentina and Brazil include many people who give great value to an end of arbitrary government, it would be reasonable to expect that they will keep trying to achieve more open and responsive political systems. But can such systems perform well enough in economic terms to maintain their acceptance?

In many of the ways suggested above, popular preferences would favor structural changes away from excessive dependence on imports, on foreign technology, and on energy-intensive lines of production. The more difficult side is that they would exert pressure for excess aggregate spending, and unselective protection. The potential for costly miscalculation recurs even in such an acute analysis of Argentina as that of Canitrot cited above: "Tariff protection may increase economic freedom and political power in the whole industrial sector."[56] It can, of course, increase the power of the industrial sector as opposed to the rest of the society, but it cannot strengthen

55 Knight, "Brazilian Development," p. 1070.
56 Canitrot, "Discipline," p. 920.

the economy as a whole. If such an approach is pursued to any significant degree the system would go right back into the early postwar trap. With such an approach, the more pessimistic of the dependency predictions would surely be fulfilled.

If a popular government did manage to restrain excess demand and to limit external deficits on current account, would it have to play safe by avoiding all significant measures of redistribution and structural change? That depends on whether or not it sets up conditions of weakness in the first place. The real test would come if a popular government tried to implement major changes in social programs, taxation, and perhaps also in land ownership, in the context of a balanced budget and an exchange rate favorable for exports. The truly unfortunate character of both structuralism and dependency analysis is that they direct attention away from, or positively oppose, the effort to provide an initial context for reforms that would raise the chances of success. The at least equally unfortunate character of neoclassical economics is that it directs attention away from, or positively opposes, any significant reform at all.

At early stages of industrialization, to pay too much respect to allocative efficiency and macroeconomic balance may block the promotional drive needed to get the process of change under way. But at the levels of industrialization and economic integration of Argentina in the early postwar years it was much more urgently necessary to pay attention to opportunity costs, to raise real wages more through increases in productivity than through taxation of export earnings, and to take seriously the fact that an open society requires acceptance of limits on how much the winning side in elections can take away from the losers. The later stages of the industrialization process probably do increase the likelihood of recourse to authoritarian repression, but the odds may be made somewhat less fearsome by redirecting economic policy toward more concern for macroeconomic consistency, and toward inclusion of all social groups in the gains of growth.

NINE

REFORMISM, MARXISM, AND
MILITANT MONETARISM: CHILE

Of the many traumatic experiences of Latin American countries in the last twenty years, those of Chile stand out for extremes of hope and violence. Under three successive governments the country has tried, or been subjected to, three drastically contrary regimes. Eduardo Frei as president from 1964 to 1970 started out with an exceptionally well-conceived program of gradualist reform but ran into so many difficulties and ended so weakly that the experience came to be regarded as a classic demonstration that nonradical reformism simply cannot succeed. Salvador Allende as president from 1970 until the military seized power in September 1973 attempted to change the society fundamentally as the world's first, and so far only, democratically elected Marxist president. The military regime under General Pinochet since 1973 has combined intense political repression with an almost religious dedication to free market economics. The question is, what do all these experiences suggest about the courses that might be open for the society once it regains freedom?

The first three sections of this chapter pick out leading themes of the strategies and problems of the three regimes. The first emphasizes the near-miss character of the reform program under Frei. His approach could serve as a reference base for a new democratic program, though there is plenty of room for disagreement over three key questions: relationships between private and public ownership, international economic policy, and the difficult balance between wages and other income shares. Section 2 reviews some of the main economic difficulties of the Allende government, in the belief that many of them were aggravated by potentially avoidable characteristics of the strategy adopted. The emphasis is on internal Chilean conflicts; intervention by the United States, which made many things go worse than they would otherwise have gone, and played an important role in the seizure of power by the military, is discussed in chapter 13. Section 3 suggests a two-sided interpretation of the economic strategies used under the military government: (a)

many particular aspects of these policies would be worth considering under a democratic system, and (b) this regime's obsession with
private enterprise and free markets has seriously hurt Chile in economic terms, totally apart from the deeper wounds in human terms.

Section 4 considers the disquieting idea that proponents of free
markets in Chile simply do not dare trust democratic choices because they are convinced that the choices will go against them. This
is not to suggest that those in favor of free markets are tied to the
repressive political system in place since 1973: a good many Chilean
conservatives may well prefer to get out from under a kind of authoritarianism which, besides being a disgrace to humanity, has
given poor results even in economic terms. But still the fear remains
that openly contested public choices will pull the economy in directions so nonfunctional that it will again break down. Is there any
combination of economic policies that could gain wide public acceptance in a democratic system and still work well in practice?
Probably yes if the obsession with free markets regardless of their
costs can be discarded and replaced by a strategy oriented more toward employment, growth, and equity. Otherwise, probably not.

1. REFORMISM: THE GOVERNMENT OF EDUARDO FREI

Chile began the postwar years with an exceptionally participatory
society, able to allow political expression of sharply differing social
goals. Democracy had a firmer hold than in most other Latin American countries. The common tensions of industrialization were accentuated by well-organized social groups in direct conflict with
each other, but the conflicts were held within the bounds of a viable
democratic system by an "Estado de compromiso," which allowed
for significant degrees of social change under active state leadership.[1] The structural balance of the economy, with exports provided
mainly by foreign-owned copper companies, with the agricultural
sector a net importer, favored wide agreement on the desirability of
industrialization through protection and state promotion. Private
industrial interests accepted an active government role, and a great
deal of public investment through the state holding company
(CORFO), in return for protection, cheap credit, low taxes, and subsidies. They also accepted an active and well-organized urban labor
force; given protection from import competition they did not need
to fight to the death to hold down wage increases. Landowners went

[1] Oscar Muñoz Gomá, *Chile y su industrialización*, esp. ch. 10.

along fully with industrialization, subject to an implicit understanding that labor organization would not extend to the rural sector, and that property ownership would be left intact. This network of compromise had serious costs on the economic side: it led to an exceptionally high rate of inflation, a great deal of inefficiency, and much slower growth than the average for Latin America (see table 4.5).

In the presidential election of 1964 the Christian Democratic party came to the fore as a newly powerful reform party, promising both greater economic growth and greater equality. It rejected compromise with the traditional conservative forces on the right and equally with Marxism on the left. Partly because of its genuine appeal to the political center, and partly because of widespread dissatisfaction with the preceding government's unsuccessful attempt to stop inflation by economic contraction, Eduardo Frei was elected president with enough support in the legislature to allow a strong reformist program. At the same time, he had the serious disadvantage of determined opposition from much of the side that might be expected to gain from reform: organized labor and the left in general were split about equally between moderate reformists and a further-left movement that both distrusted reform in general and wanted to discredit a rival for influence in the labor force. The context meant that reforms were subject both to the inevitable resistance from conservatives and to hostility from the left, ready to denounce any moderate gain as totally inadequate.

Against these political handicaps, the Frei government carried the promise of an unusual collection of strengths: it had a thorough and consistent plan of action for stimulating economic growth and reducing inequality; it included as members or advisers an extraordinarily strong group of reform-minded and technically able social scientists; it came in under conditions of high inflation and unemployment but with inflationary pressures beginning to fall and with a good deal of room for expansion; it was helped by a period of rising activity in the world economy, providing good markets for copper exports; and it could count on support from the international financial community as well as substantial aid through the Alliance for Progress. Nobody from the outside tried to do it in. It got off to a fairly impressive start. Why did its initial success break down?

The economic program started off with increases in minimum wages for both rural and urban workers, generalized increases for public sector employees, direct aid to private investors, increased public investment, tax reforms aimed both at raising more revenue and at placing more of the burden on higher income groups, proposals for land reform, and detailed measures to improve efficiency and promote exports.[2] Beyond its economic program the government took surprisingly effective actions to mobilize excluded groups, both peasants and urban slum dwellers, to make them more active participants in the political process.[3]

The evident potential of this mobilization effort to radicalize the society might make the Frei government sound almost revolutionary. The stated theme was "a revolution in liberty." It might have sounded revolutionary to the more conservative side of the society, but Frei was strongly attached to the existing political system and emphasized the importance of private investment, both foreign and domestic. He rejected strong popular pressures to nationalize the American-owned copper mines. This last issue was of all structural questions the one of greatest visibility in Chile: copper accounted for approximately two-thirds of the country's exports, and U.S.-owned mines for 90 percent of the copper exported, so more than half of the country's foreign exchange earnings were out of direct domestic control. Frei's formula for dealing with the question was a program of "Chileanization" as opposed to nationalization, buying partial ownership with a view to eventual control, and offering tax advantages in return for agreements on production and export targets. The government bought an ownership share in one of the three major mines but paid such high prices for that and its other agreements that the step could fairly be attacked as a loss for Chile in economic terms.[4] In political terms it could be seen as a way of reassuring investors while gaining greater national voice in the industry, but by the same token it was seen by those opposed to foreign investors as a sell-out.

The first two years of the Frei government were successful on most counts of growth and of improved distribution. Given the initial economic conditions of high unemployment and idle capacity, it was possible through expansionary policies to raise output rapidly and at the same time to work toward lower rates of inflation. Gross

[2] Ricardo Ffrench-Davis, *Políticas económicas en Chile, 1952–1970* (Santiago: Centro de Estudios de Planificación Nacional, Ediciones Nueva Universidad, 1973). William Ascher, *Scheming for the Poor*, p. 125, makes the important point that the coherence of the program was a result of technocratic design, without drawing on input from the labor and business leadership; leaving them out of the design made things easier in the first instance but made it difficult to get their cooperation later.

[3] Karen Remmer, "Political Demobilization in Chile, 1973–78," *Comparative Politics* 12 (April 1980), pp. 275–301; de Wylder, *Allende's Chile*, pp. 174–76.

[4] Griffin, *Underdevelopment in Spanish America*, ch. 4; de Wylder, *Allende's Chile*, pp. 116–25.

national product increased 6 percent in 1965 and 9 in 1966, while
the rate of inflation came down from 49 percent in 1964 to 24 percent for 1966.[5] Inflation was reduced by some use of price controls,
by improved tax collections, and by new techniques of monetary
management that gave the government better control over extensions of credit. Most of the intended tax reforms went through; current tax revenue in real terms increased rapidly. Both the minimum
wage in agriculture and the average wage rate for urban workers increased rapidly too, at first as intended and then a great deal more
than intended.

The macroeconomic strategy provided target rates for desired
wage increases, consistent with expected increases in output, but
once the process got under way it took on more momentum than
expected. Real wages and salaries increased at annual rates between
11 and 14 percent in each of the first three years. These rates greatly
exceeded increases in output per man even with the rapid growth
of the economy in 1965–66. The difference became extreme in
1967 when output growth practically stopped. Payments to labor as
a percent of total income increased from 45 percent in 1964 to 48
percent by 1966, along with the general expansion, and went up to
52 percent by 1970 in much less successful macroeconomic conditions.[6]

On the external side, the Frei government introduced a major
policy innovation, followed soon after in Brazil and Colombia, under which the price of foreign exchange was raised by small
amounts, once or twice a month, at preselected rates intended to
move slightly ahead of domestic inflation. The purpose was both to
restrain imports and to stimulate nontraditional exports. For manufactured exports the effects were fairly impressive: they doubled,
from their initially low base, between 1965 and 1969.[7] The policy
was not pursued aggressively: Jere Behrman suggests that the es-
cudo was greatly overvalued in the first place, and that the new approach did little more than keep the degree of overvaluation from
increasing.[8] Still, in comparison to most other Latin American ex-

---

[5] Ffrench-Davis, *Politicas económicas*, table 34, p. 252, and table 9, p. 57.

[6] Ibid., table 75, p. 345.

[7] Ibid., table 43, p. 273.

[8] Jere Behrman, *Macroeconomic Policy*, pp. 57, 178–79, and 288. He may have
underestimated the degree of devaluation in real terms, when external inflation is
taken into account. Ffrench-Davis calculates that real earnings per dollar for nontraditional exports, taking subsidies into account, increased about 5 percent between
1964 and 1970; *Politicas económicas*, table 41, p. 269.

periences in this period, the result might be regarded more as an incomplete step in the right direction than as a failure. In the event, this approach, combined with good external demand for copper, brought the Chilean current balance of payments into a rare surplus.

Although the external side of the program worked well, internal problems became compounded by the tortured course of land reform and by weak private investment. Frei pushed through the land reform, against determined opposition from landowners, by getting a change in the constitution to allow for appropriation of property. By the end of his administration the program had redistributed land to some twenty-eight thousand families. But it proved to be an example of a positive step that angered almost everyone. It did not get much credit from the rural poor because the scale of the redistribution fell far short of the government's promise to redistribute land to fully half of the rural labor force. Some of those left out responded by illegal seizures of land, which led the government to use police action against the very people the program was intended to help. On the side of landowners, the appropriations and perhaps even more the accompanying efforts to promote organization of rural workers constituted a repudiation of what they had considered to be a basic social pact. The answer must be that any serious reform has to change the prior balance under which the system has functioned—it was necessary to pursue the land reform if the whole program was to have any meaning—but in this case the process caused unnecessary trouble even outside of agriculture. The constitutional change forced through to permit the reform spread distrust among urban private investors as well because it authorized the government to take over property for social purposes generally, not just land necessary for the specific reform.[9]

Whether because of fears over the course of reform, or for more narrowly economic reasons, private investment began to fall well short of the rates expected by the government and needed for continuing growth. The government responded by increasing both public sector investment and direct financial support to private investors. Public financing was raised from 12 percent of total private investment in 1964 to 50 percent by 1969.[10] Despite this two-

[9] William Ascher, *Scheming for the Poor*, ch. 7; Robert Kaufman, *Land Reform in Chile.*

[10] Carlos Fortín, "The State and Capital Accumulation in Chile," pp. 15-48 in Jean Carrière, ed., *Industrialization and the State in Latin America* (Amsterdam: Center for Latin American Research and Documentation, 1979), tables 2 and 4.

sided effort to keep up investment, it fell from 17 percent of GNP in 1963 to 15 percent by 1966, and it stayed between 14 and 15 percent thereafter. Was this a matter of a fundamental lack of dynamism by the private sector, a supercautious holding back in the presence of a reformist government, or a reaction to economic uncertainty? It may well have been a mixture of all three. The balance of social choice was clearly moving toward redistribution of income and limitations of property rights. But that might not have led to any fall in private investment if economic conditions had remained favorable. They became distinctly less favorable as the government proved unable to slow down wage inflation, unwilling to allow controlled prices to move up fully in response, more cautiously conservative in monetary policies and its own spending, and unable to keep up the growth of aggregate demand in real terms.

When the budgetary costs of meeting public sector wage increases outran what was at first an impressive increase in tax revenues, the government cut back on planned public investment to compensate. On the monetary side, the costs of bank credit were sharply raised. Even allowing for special fiscal advantages to business borrowers, the real cost of bank credit shot up from zero in 1965 to 11 percent for 1966–67.[11] The rate came down to the 6 percent range in 1968–69, but this too is fairly high for any economy, especially so when the growth of aggregate demand in real terms has practically stopped. The brakes put on both private and public investment themselves took away the driving force of growth. Output per capita in real terms during the last four years of the Frei period increased no more than one-half of one percent a year.

Why did Frei allow the whole macroeconomic balance of his program to be undermined this way? Looking back at what could be regarded as a particularly striking example of sensible reformism going down to defeat, one could easily argue that reformism never has any real chance when caught between an understandably impatient left and an understandably nervous right, plus the inevitable external constraints. There was not a great deal of room to move. There never is. Carlos Fortín concludes that "The combination of the failure to generate and sustain an adequate rate of capital accumulation and the process of rapid mobilization of popular sectors created contradictions that the model was not capable of withstand-

---

[11] Ffrench-Davis, *Politicas económicas*, table 54, p. 298; see also pp. 59–64, 174–85, and 210–20.

ing."[12] Was it the model or the failure to respect the limits correctly foreseen to be necessary?

It may be that the main problems were that the Christian Democrats were too driven by the hope of replacing Marxist influence in the labor force and placed too much weight on the possible political costs of wage restraint. Given the initially intended rate of increase of real wages, the part of their appeal that took the form of mobilizing rural labor and starting land reform could have done more for the basic goal than still greater wage increases, or at least it might have done so in the absence of the costly mismatch between promises and performance. And it might well have been possible to use other strategic nonwage responses to public preferences, above all by one key move clearly desired by the great majority of the Chilean people: if Frei had nationalized the American copper mines, he would have gained wide support, and perhaps enough strength to enforce the original wage policy. The United States might have countered with restrictions on external credit, but Chile's improved balance of payments, with growing new exports, gave it for once a degree of independent strength in this respect. Restraints on external credit need not have stopped the economy; they would have favored continuing increases in the price of foreign exchange and thus continuing export diversification. The Christian Democrats might have become identified with the search for autonomy, rather than being blamed for subservience.[13]

With a more sustainable rate of wage increase, and therefore less need to be concerned with inflation, demand could have been kept up better, rates of return on investment could have been better maintained, and the chances of continued growth in employment and productive capacity would have been much improved. More of the Chilean people might then have recognized that the basic approach could truly work in their interests. Was such a set of alternatives really feasible? With the country split into three noncompromising and almost equally strong political forces, quite possibly not for Frei. But the essential point is that any future reform pro-

[12] Fortin, "The State," p. 26.

[13] The Christian Democrats had a special handicap in this respect because of the widespread belief in Chile, later confirmed by U.S. Senate hearings, that the CIA had helped finance Frei's campaign in 1966 (without telling him) and had also intervened in several elections for parliament: U.S. Senate, Select Committee to Study Governmental Operations with Respect to Intelligence Activities, *Covert Action in Chile, 1963–1973*, Staff Report (Washington, D.C.: Government Printing Office, 1975), pp. 9, 19, and 54.

gram that included most of the elements of this one, in a society more interested in negotiation to keep political freedom alive, should have a decent chance to succeed.

2. THE GOVERNMENT OF SALVADOR ALLENDE

The period in which Salvador Allende was president of Chile lasted only thirty-four months but left such emotionally charged memories that it remains extraordinarily difficult to sort out questions of motives and the scope for choice open to the government.[14] Had Allende been allowed to live through his term of office; had the military regime that overthrew him not followed up with such a prolonged, vengeful reign of terror; had the government of the United States not intervened covertly to aggravate the disruption of the economy and to promote the violent overturn of a still-functioning democracy, it might be easier to reach agreement on the character and implications of the government's own programs. Absent a fair test, it may still be worthwhile to consider what the government did and might have done, for the sake of understanding what was going on and just possibly for the sake of future attempts by any democratically elected socialist regime to deal with some of the most likely difficulties.

Exactly what the objectives of the government were was a matter of intense dispute within the coalition of parties that made up the Unidad Popular. To judge from what Allende said and did, the goal was a radical change in the structure of the society intended to give greater income and power to workers but not a complete takeover of production or an authoritarian Marxist state. His "Chilean Road to Socialism" was a pluralistic and democratic conception.[15] It in-

---

[14] For detailed economic analysis by a participant in the Allende government, see Sergio Bitar, *Transición, socialismo y democracia: La experiencia chilena* (Mexico: Siglo Veintiuno, 1979). Federico G. Gil, Ricardo Lagos E., and Henry A. Landsberger, eds., *Chile at the Turning Point: Lessons of the Socialist Years, 1970–1973* (Philadelphia: Institute for the Study of Human Issues, 1979), includes particularly helpful political and economic discussions by Chilean participants in this period.

[15] This statement refers to Allende himself, as demonstrated by his actions and explained by his statements; it would not apply to the more extremist wing within the UP. Radomiro Tomić, who was Allende's opponent as the Christian Democrat candidate for president in 1970, is particularly clear on Allende's position: see his discussion in Gil et al., *Chile at the Turning Point*, pp. 209–39 (especially pp. 224–25). See also the discussion by Jorge Tapies Valdés, ibid., pp. 297–315; De Wylder, *Allende's Chile*; and Stephany Griffith-Jones, *The Role of Finance in the Transition to Socialism* (London: Francis Pinter, 1981).

cluded nationalization of all foreign firms and those domestic firms considered to be monopolies, but it envisaged a continuing private sector of small and medium-sized firms and landowners. He hoped to keep a good deal of the middle class on his side, or at least accepting and cooperating within the limits of a different kind of society, while giving more power to workers. That position was backed by the Communist party and by all of the more moderate groups within the Unidad Popular. It was never accepted by the Socialist party and the other more radical groups within the coalition. They saw the conflict as one between workers and all the rest of the society. They did not want anything to do with preservation of small business in a continuing private sector, and they did not consider it to be either desirable or safe to temporize with measures meant to reassure the middle class. "The Revolutionary Left inside and outside the UP never did believe in a 'Chilean Road to Socialism.' "[16]

Both wings of the UP were in full agreement on the goals of raising incomes for workers and giving them decision-making powers in firms, as well as on structural changes in the sense of nationalization of foreign-owned firms and domestic monopolies, redistributing land more completely, and carrying out a host of specific social welfare measures. That general agreement left room for flatly contrary positions on some fundamental questions of both method and ultimate objectives. For the pluralistic side it was important to maintain enough balance in the economy to keep production from being disorganized, and in particular to keep small and medium-sized private firms able to operate. Claims on them by their workers had to be kept in line with their ability to earn profits. More generally, the remaining private business sector had to be given reassurance that they would not be arbitrarily taken over and that the economy would function well enough to allow them to survive in ordinary business terms. For the more radical side of the Unidad Popular such restraints were unnecessary. Since they did not want any private sector to survive, they had no need to worry about reassurance to small and medium-sized firms, and no need to oppose or limit claims against private firms by their workers. They might not have worried at all about a breakdown of ordinary market processes under conditions of overwhelming excess demand; that could be taken as a proof that continuing use of a market system was hopeless. The necessary alternative would then have been a thorough centralized plan to allocate resources and incomes. There was no

[16] De Wylder, *Allende's Chile*, p. 40.

such plan, or any system for implementing one, but disintegration of private markets might push the government to adopt that alternative.

As if these inner conflicts were not enough, the government also had to deal with an opposed majority in the legislature and an implacably hostile judiciary. Allende was elected with only 37 percent of the presidential vote. This was not a rare result in Chile, where the left, center, and right all had strong parties or coalitions; elections were normally three-way splits rather than two. It did not mean that the president was condemned to inaction as might be the case with a hostile Congress in the United States. The Chilean constitution allowed a wide range of powers to the executive, including controls over wages and prices, changes in the composition of public expenditure, and emergency intervention to take over private firms under conditions that proved to be common. But it could also be harassed constantly by delaying tactics and imaginative obstructionism in the legislature and the judiciary, and after the first few months it constantly was.

The first major structural change, nationalization of the copper mines, was so widely popular that it was even approved by the legislature. Since it was possible to initiate changes in controls and in macroeconomic policies without legislative approval, the government wasted no time in promoting major increases in minimum wages and public sector salaries, applying price controls to keep the wage increases from being offset by price increases, and initiating new investment and spending programs in the fields of health and education. In agriculture, a rapid step-up in land reform wiped out the country's remaining latifundia.

Wage-price and foreign trade policies as adopted in 1971 could be characterized as extreme versions of populism, similar to many non-Marxist regimes. Much as at the beginning of the Frei period, the government set up targets for wage increases but then found that the actual pace overshot the targets. Wages and salaries increased 52 percent in nominal terms and 23 percent in real terms in 1971, far above the initial government objective.[17] The increase in real wages might be compared to the increase of total output, in itself exceptionally high, of 9 percent. In an all-out application of structuralist principles, increases of government spending and the money supply were treated as necessary instruments of desired structural change, with no meaningful negative connotations. Infla-

[17] Ibid., pp. 53–54 and 71–72. For real wages see table 9.3.

tion was considered to be mainly a matter of bottlenecks on the supply side to be cured by investment, an indicator of real supply difficulties but in itself of no great importance.[18] Interest rates were reduced, government expenditures increased approximately 80 percent in one year, and the money supply doubled. As that surge of expenditures and liquidity hit the economy output at first increased rapidly. GDP went up by 8.6 percent in 1971. And the initial conditions of excess capacity and unemployment had the same effect as in the first year under Frei: the rate of inflation actually came down, from 35 percent to 22 percent in 1971. From early 1972 on, the trend went into reverse, to rates of inflation beyond any previously known in Chile.

Price controls helped restrain inflation in the first year, before generalized excess demand swamped them, but then may have made things worse by disorganizing production and driving supplies into black markets. They were applied differentially between agriculture and industry, to raise incentives for agricultural producers while holding down prices for industry. For agricultural products price floors and subsidies were used on a large scale to assure incomes for the producers. For industrial products, the conception was instead that the producers were likely to take advantage of rising demand by arbitrary price increases rather than raise output, and that controls to prevent such price increases would force firms to raise production as the only way of getting more profits. That version of prices and supply response is logically coherent for firms with market power, able to set prices above marginal costs, as long as the costs stay down. If they do, firms may treat the fixed price as given by outside forces in much the same sense that competitive firms ordinarily must. They should then respond to increased demand by raising output, more dependably than would be the case in the absence of price control. But the logic works only as long as marginal costs stay below prices. In Chile, the principle worked at first and output rose in response to increased demand. But then rising wages and increasing problems with material inputs pulled marginal costs above controlled prices, and output stopped rising.

---

[18] Bitar, *Transición*, ch. 4. Stephany Griffith-Jones suggests that the disdain for monetary constraints was not so much an expression of structuralism as an ingrained Socialist distrust of money, a failure to take monetary variables seriously, which must be overcome for any successful transition to socialism. "One can even believe in the socialization of the means of production and yet support policies to control the growth of the money supply." *The Role of Finance*, p. 16.

Supply limits showed up first and worst for food. As the incomes of the poor came up they immediately tried to raise their food consumption. Agricultural output went up considerably in the first year, in part because of strong demand plus government subsidies and possibly in part because it was understood that land reform would concentrate first on land not being fully used for production. But even with higher output the increases in demand so far outpaced supply that they had to be met with greatly increased imports. Imports of agricultural products had provided about 20 percent of total supply on average for 1965–1970; that share increased to 26 percent in 1971 and 33 percent in 1972.[19] By 1972, the rising imports of food, and systematic U.S. opposition to extensions of international credit, created tight constraints on the foreign exchange available for imported inputs. With an import-dependent industrial structure, shortages of materials and parts began to choke off production. Domestic supplies of food and materials increasingly disappeared into black markets. Erratic disruptions of production by conflicts between workers and plant owners became commonplace. The transportation system, badly strained by the pressure of excess demand in the first place, began to break down completely as private truck owners used their key position to call repeated strikes. By the end of 1972 the situation had changed from specific areas of supply shortage to something more like economic warfare.

Conflict became particularly intense in food distribution. With nominally controlled prices at the retail end but no effective governmental program to assure supply, the life of the Chilean housewife became ever more preoccupied by the need to stand in line and fight everyone else for food, which became ever harder to find. The government began belatedly to set up public distribution channels, but that worked badly: the black market was usually able to outbid the public system in getting supplies. And the attempt to introduce state-run food distribution aggravated hostility throughout the transportation and distribution sectors, which formed between them a large share of the small-business class Allende had hoped to keep on his side.

Keith Griffin and Jeffrey James, reviewing this experience in the light of similar problems in other newly socialized economies, conclude that the best alternative would have been to establish from the start a state-run distribution system for a few basic food products of central importance for the poor, while allowing the rest of the food

---

[19] De Wylder, *Allende's Chile*, p. 201.

supply and all other consumer products to be bought and sold freely without attempts at control. For the particular food items to be under control, their central point is that claims on supply must be matched to the supply actually available.[20] Since private sellers can increase profits by diverting supply to black markets, they cannot be trusted to take part in a legally controlled distribution process. For the products designated as vital, the government must actually control supply from the point of production to the point of distribution. Excess aggregate demand could then be allowed to work itself out in the form of rising prices for noncontrolled products. The poor would probably be shut out of these markets, but their consumption of basic foods could be protected by a direct method that would avoid any subsidy or income windfall to higher income groups.

Selective use of such direct controls over supply of key foods would have been consistent with the goals of the Allende government and could have lessened the strains of a problem that greatly intensified antagonism to the government. But it is not a sufficient answer in itself. Even if it were possible to reserve key commodities for the poor, the rest of the economy was going to pieces at the same time. Chile needed both specific and overall balance. The policies actually used failed on both counts.

By the latter part of 1972 the government's self-inflicted wounds were becoming compounded by systematic sabotage. The trucking industry, vital to move food to cities and supplies to industry, came to be the spearhead of aggressive attempts to break down the functioning of the economy. Strikes by owners of trucks crippled supplies erratically from October on. The strikers could be considered to be fighting for their private interests, but at least part of their financing came from subsidies provided to anti-Allende groups by the United States.[21]

In addition to questions of excess demand and disrupted supply, the ownership and operation of industrial firms and the copper mines raised a host of conflicts. The government was sharply divided on the degree to which nationalization was to be pursued, and how it was to be related to worker control. Allende opted for a restricted list of large firms to nationalize, but that ran into bitter opposition from two sides: from those totally opposed to any nation-

[20] Keith Griffin and Jeffrey James, *The Transition*, ch. 4 and pp. 82–86.
[21] U. S. Senate, *Covert Action in Chile*, pp. 2, 31.

alization and from those groups within the Unidad Popular who did not want any private firms to remain.

On the left, the opposition was intensified by contrasts between treatment of workers in the nationalized mines and in private industry. The workers in the state-owned mines, historically much higher paid than the rest of the labor force, had exceptionally good working conditions as well, to a degree impossible for private industry to match. In effect, these workers captured the economic rent previously going to the mining corporations. The rest of the labor force saw themselves being left behind and began to press for much wider nationalization in the belief that this would ensure them equal treatment.[22] Since the government did not want such widespread nationalization, the workers began to force the issue by seizing factories. When such seizures happened, or when owners shut down factories to forestall physical occupation, Chilean law authorized the government to "intervene" in the sense of taking control to maintain production. Caught between a wave of shutdowns blocking production and its own split preferences about continuing private ownership, the government found itself swamped with hundreds of unwanted firms for which it became responsible. It was not a process of purposeful expansion of the public sector. It was a collapse of control.

Much the same kind of direct action by individual groups took place in the farm sector. Alongside the systematic program of redistribution under the land reform law, groups of farm workers began to seize private land on their own. The government found itself caught here, too, between an anarchic process implemented by many of its own supporters, strongly desired by part of the governing coalition, and a contrary wish to proceed with an intended program within legal limits. It is hard to see how there was any way out of this box, short of large-scale police action against the rural poor. The government's refusal of this route meant that remnants of middle class support for the regime, sensitive to concern for the breakdown of legal rights to private property, moved even further toward the side of unrelenting opposition.

While the combination of new programs, excess demand, and illegal seizures created increasingly confused conditions in the rural sector, one important point about the regime's policies deserves special attention. In marked contrast to the usual populist style of redistribution in favor of urban labor and against the rural poor, the

[22] De Wylder, *Allende's Chile*, pp. 121–32 and 143–50.

Allende government kept trying to channel income to the rural sector. Generous subsidies to cover input costs in agriculture, plus guaranteed minimum income supports through subsidized product prices, created a significant transfer of income to small landowners and rural workers. The resource flow went in the opposite direction from the Peruvian land reform implemented at the same time: toward the rural poor, rather than away from them. The problem, the same problem as in so many other directions, was that nothing was done to limit claims on output from the other sectors while they were being raised so rapidly in agriculture.

Many of the economic policies of the Allende government made the situation worse than it need have been, both in terms of the capacity to produce and in terms of the bitterness of opposition. There is no way to know whether or not more careful economic management could have lessened support for the military coup, to a degree that would have changed the outcome. It could have made the odds less fearsome, but that may not have been enough. The critical question may have been the government's inability to compromise and form alliances with any forces outside of the original coalition. In the very first months, the balance of forces within the Christian Democratic party was favorable toward the kind of socialism advocated by Allende, and ready to enter a coalition that would have had a majority in the electorate and in the Parliament, but the more revolutionary side of the UP refused to accept the idea.[23] By the time Allende did turn to the Christian Democrats for help in trying to save the democratic system, the weight of the party had moved very much against him, effectively in coalition with the far right and unwilling to compromise on any terms that did not repudiate the goals of the UP.

The idea that a left coalition in favor of socialism was initially possible, and would have had a clear majority behind it, suggests that a democratic kind of socialism was at least conceivable. Sergio Bitar's analysis of the economic and political struggles of the period would support this possibility: in his view, a quantitatively consistent macroeconomic program combined with a more carefully controlled process of nationalization could have avoided most of the economic disorder that turned the middle classes so strongly against Allende, and the army would not have entered to destroy the system

[23] Cf. the essays in Gil et al., *Chile at the Turning Point*, especially the statement by Radomiro Tomić, pp. 209–39.

if the middle classes had not turned against him.[24] Against that view, others argue the classic thesis of Oscar Lange that gradual social revolution cannot work: a capitalist system cannot function if the capitalists expect their property to be taken away from them.[25] In this contrary view, considerations such as the degree of inflation or foreign exchange deficits, breakdowns of production, and similar dimensions of stress are not what mattered: the key to survival was to seize control of the whole productive system quickly. That might have been done by calling a plebiscite to change the constitution, without any necessary violence. De Wylder suggests that a plebiscite might have succeeded at the peak of the government's popularity in early 1972. Perhaps so. Allende did not choose to try it, possibly because of the costs of intensified conflict bound to result, possibly because he did not think it would work, or possibly because he remained too attached to the existing norms of Chile's open political system.[26]

Apart from the question of practical possibilities for Allende, how convincing is the argument that progressive socialization simply cannot succeed? Progressive expansion of public sector investment and ownership of productive facilities had a long and peaceful history in Chile, well before Allende. Frei pushed the process much further than before, and the Christian Democratic party promised to go still further if successful in the 1970 elections. Nationalization of the American copper mines raised general enthusiasm. The society was not one that backed away from progressive socialization in this sense. But the breakdown of control in the form of spreading direct seizures by workers, and government acceptance of this process, greatly weakened any basis for belief that takeovers would be limited to specific cases implemented through legal process. From then on, the Lange argument may well be considered right: capitalist groups could see only the two alternatives of leaving the country or destroying the government.

The preceding may sound as if the issues were purely internal. It does not give a dominant role to the determined efforts of the American government, partly in response to pressures from particular American corporations operating in Chile and partly out of ideological antagonism to the Allende government, to disrupt the economy and pull down the government. That intervention made

[24] Bitar, *Transición*, ch. 11–12.
[25] De Wylder, *Allende's Chile*, pp. 41–42 and ch. 8.
[26] Griffith-Jones, *The Role of Finance*, pp. 125–26.

for increased bitterness within Chile, lessened the chances of any peaceful compromise, and encouraged military action. It may have made the coup come more quickly, and made its vengeful extremes more likely. Intervention by the United States should not be underestimated as a destructive factor in the situation. But to see it as a sufficient explanation of the breakdown would be to miss the vital play of economic and political tensions within the country.

3. MILITANT MONETARISM

The economic policies introduced by the military regime from 1973 constituted a new extreme, the most all-out application of conservative free market principles seen in Latin America since the 1920s.[27] Many aspects were similar to the changes in Brazil from 1964: tighter control of the money supply and government spending, reduced protection, efforts to eliminate currency overvaluation and to promote exports, renewed encouragement of foreign investors, and an initial sharp cut in real wages. In both countries this redirection of economic policies was enforced by authoritarian government, sweeping aside prior legal protections of the individual against violence by the state. But in Chile the economic and political reversals were carried to extremes far beyond those in Brazil. The economic program was far more fully an all-out application of free market principles, the withdrawal of the government from direct intervention in markets more nearly complete, and the government's violence against its own people far greater as well. The freest of free markets was purchased with the most severe repression.

The economic goals emphasized in this period were chiefly to restore a free market system and make it operate efficiently, to eliminate inflation, and to restore external equilibrium in a more open economy. Alejandro Foxley rightly insists that a good deal more than these traditional economic objectives was involved. The government was also determined "to reduce the influence upon the new economic and political system of the supposedly antagonistic

[27] Ricardo Ffrench-Davis, "El experimento monetarista en Chile: Una síntesis crítica," *Colección estudios cieplan* 9 (December 1982), pp. 5–40; Foxley, *Latin American Experiments*; and Oscar Muñoz, "Crecimiento y desequilibrios en una economía abierta: El caso chileno, 1976–81," *Colección estudios cieplan* 8 (July 1982), pp. 19–41. For two interpretations from the monetarist side see Sebastian Edwards, "Stabilization and Liberalization: An Evaluation of Ten Years of Chile's Experiment with Free-Market Policies, 1973–1983," and Arnold Harberger, "Observations on the Chilean Economy," both in *Economic Development and Cultural Change* 33 (1985), pp. 223–54 and 451–61.

workers' groups, this objective being achieved by the modification
or abolition of labour legislation and by holding down real wages,"
and "to redistribute resources toward the private capitalist sector
with the aim that this sector should dynamize growth, based on a
free-market economy."[28]

The new economic model was in a sense the exact opposite of the
earlier import-substitution strategy: it gave priority to the particular
concerns most often neglected or repudiated in that system. Foxley
rightly attributes to the new Chilean model a high degree of intellectual coherence. That quality owed a great deal to the presence
and cooperation of a surprising number of foreign-trained economists with a common background in one of the most message-ori-
ented economics departments of all American universities. The
University of Chicago had for many years been a preferred graduate school for Chilean economists from the Catholic University,
providing good opportunities for graduate fellowships, continuing
contact back in Chile with a like-trained and like-minded group,
and a brand of economics with the special flavor of an integrated
system able to generate mutually consistent answers to all questions.[29] Chicago has many distinctive economists with individual
ideas but it also has, to a degree rare among American universities,
a special theme recognized by everyone: something more like a phi-
losophy of social process, bordering on a conservative religion.
Chile from 1973 became an example of what can happen when a
government implements the message, without being forced by an
open political system to compromise with the people who are hurt
in the process.

Some of the results can be interpreted in relatively objective terms
by measures of what happened to inflation, output, exports and external balance, employment, and indicators of income distribution.
Such measures are worth careful attention: they have supported
both glowing praise of the accomplishments of the system and de-
nunciation of its failures. But perhaps the more interesting ques-

[28] Foxley, "Stabilization Policies and Stagflation," p. 887. On the interactions between economic and political objectives of the regime, see Karen Remmer, "Political
Demobilization," pp. 283–84, and "Public Policy and Regime Consolidation: The
First Five Years of the Chilean Junta," *Journal of Developing Areas* 13 (July 1979), pp.
441–61. See also Jackie Roddick, "Labour Relations and the 'New Authoritarianism'
in the Southern Cone," in Carriere, ed., *The State*, pp. 249–98. Roddick emphasizes
the contrast between extensive new legislation adopted to weaken organized labor
and "the utter lawlessness of the state itself" (p. 254).

[29] Foxley, *Latin American Experiments*, ch. 4, pp. 91–109.

tions lie beyond these indicators, in attempts to assess what efficiency and a order mean in such a context, and what they cost.

Table 9.1 shows two areas of success for the new policies. The rate
of inflation was brought down from the fantastic levels inherited in
1973–74, by an extraordinarily tenacious struggle. It took four
years to get the inflation rate below 100 percent, and three more to
get it down close to 30 percent. Of course the process started from
phenomenally high rates, but it is still striking how long prices kept
on going up rapidly in an economy operating under conditions of
very high unemployment. Brazil did a much faster job of reducing

TABLE 9.1. Chile: Rate of Inflation, Industrial Production, Foreign Trade,
and Exchange Rate in Real Terms, 1970–1984

Year	Inflation (% rise in consumer prices)	Index of industrial output (1970 = 100)	Exports (mill. U.S. dollars)		Imports (million U.S. dollars)	External current account balance	Index of real rate of exchange[a] (1977 = 100)
			Nontra-ditional	Total			
1970	36	100	338	1,249	941	− 91	83
1971	27	115	228	997	980	− 198	76
1972	255	118	179	855	941	− 421	57
1973	606	113	159	1,231	1,098	− 279	70
1974	369	109	756	2,481	1,911	− 292	108
1975	343	78	571	1,552	1,338	− 490	148
1976	198	82	750	2,083	1,643	+ 148	120
1977	84	90	921	2,190	2,259	− 551	100
1978	37	97	1,127	2,478	3,002	− 1,088	111
1979	39	104	1,871	3,894	4,218	− 1,189	109
1980	31	111	2,360	4,671	5,124	− 1,971	95
1981	10	111	2,029	3,906	6,364	− 4,733	81
1982	21	94	1,821	3,710	3,528	− 2,304	94
1983	23	98	1,888	3,836	2,969	− 1,068	112
1984	23	108	1,959	3,657	3,191	− 2,060	116

SOURCES: Colección estudios cieplan no. 16 (June 1985), pp. 125–40, for all except trade data; latter
from IMF, International Financial Statistics, 1984 Yearbook, and May 1985.

[a] Real rate of exchange is nominal rate inflated by index of external prices and deflated by consumer price index of Chile.

extreme inflation from 1964 to 1967, not only because the rate was not so extreme in the first place but also because the government was willing to use direct price restraints on firms with market power, while Chilean ideology ruled this out.

A second area of relative success, up to 1980, was a great increase in nontraditional exports. In terms of dollar value, exports other than copper and iron ore tripled between 1974 and 1980. The possibilities of such effective export diversification had been shown earlier in the Frei period when exchange rates were made more favorable for exports, without the necessity of any apparatus of political repression. The military government returned to this policy and pushed it for a time by aggressive devaluation. By 1975 the cost of a dollar in real terms, adjusted for inflation, was 80 percent higher than in 1970 (table 9.1). That depreciation in real terms was central to the striking success with new exports, but it added its own strong impact to the rate of inflation. It was surely desirable to slow down or stop the depreciation, but Chilean policy then swung over to the opposite extreme, all the way back to the old populist remedy of trying to freeze the exchange rate in nominal terms.

Brief experiments with revaluations in June 1976 and March 1977 proved some help in reducing inflation, without stopping the growth of exports. That encouraged a decision in 1979 to stop devaluing and announce a firmly fixed exchange rate.[30] The explicit rationale was that a fixed rate, with nearly all tariff protection removed, would force domestic firms to match competitive international prices. Inflation would then be driven down to the world level. That approach can work well for competitive markets in standardized commodities, but for prices of industrial products set by discretion of sellers it may take a long time for world market forces to pull domestic prices into line with external levels.[31] It is

[30] Ffrench-Davis, "El experimento moneterista," p. 15; Vittorio Corbo, "Reforms and Macroeconomic Adjustments in Chile During 1976–82," *World Development* 13 (August 1985), pp. 893–916.

[31] The slow and uncertain effects of external competition on domestic prices of industrial products (as distinct from standardized primary commodities) are brought out well in Irving B. Kravis and Robert E. Lipsey, "Export Prices and the Transmission of Inflation," *American Economic Review* 67 (February 1977), pp. 155–62, and Peter Isard, "How Far Can We Push the Law of One Price?" *American Economic Review* 67 (December 1977), pp. 942–48. For Chile, it turned out that prices and earnings of *exporters* were tightly constrained, but sellers on the domestic market remained relatively immune: Vittorio Corbo, Jaime de Melo, and James Tybout, "What Went Wrong with the Recent Reforms in the Southern Cone?" *Economic Development and Cultural Change* 34 (1986).

least likely to work rapidly for countries in which firms have come to learn the hard way that they risk bankruptcy if they do not move prices up fast enough to keep ahead of increases in costs.

Pressure to raise prices to deal with actual and expected increases in costs was especially strong in the Chilean context because existing labor regulations provided for periodic wage adjustments to offset preceding inflation: even if import competition acted to slow the rate of inflation, firms had to cope with the effects of on-going wage adjustments. A possible solution might have been to continue a policy of gradual devaluation along with tapering rates of wage increase. Another alternative, suggested by Arnold Harberger, was to repudiate the system of wage adjustment and force down real wages to fit the fixed exchange rate.[32] For those who do not see the necessity of placing all the burden on real wages, still another alternative might have been to use subsidies to replace the wage indexation and take the pressure off the firms, while using taxes to offset the subsidies, as suggested in chapter 5. The actual choice was to go ahead with both the fixed exchange rate and rising nominal wages, which could not work. As domestic prices continued to rise while import prices stayed fixed, everything began to come apart. Imports more than doubled between 1978 and 1981, and the previously impressive growth of new exports suddenly went into reverse.[33] The external deficit on current account shot up to 14.5 percent of GDP in 1981,[34] with the inevitable result for regimes of both left and right when they try to maintain an overvalued currency for too long: a good old-fashioned foreign exchange crisis.

It may seem disconcerting that a successful drive to increase exports should be followed by a foreign exchange crisis, but this result was built into the situation by the perverse choice of a fixed exchange rate in conditions of continuing inflation, aggravated from 1981 by the impact of world recession. The success of nontraditional exports up to 1980 had added $1.6 billion to export earnings,

[32] Harberger, "Observations on the Chilean Economy." In his view (p. 451), freezing the exchange rate was "not a major policy mistake (though it may have been a minor one)." Given the picture of real wages in Chile shown in table 9.3 below, it makes an interesting commentary on the quality of the monetarist policies in effect since 1973 that defenders of the approach would still, in the 1980s, conclude that balance of payments problems are due to excessively high real wages and can only be answered by cutting them still further.

[33] Corbo, "Reform and Macroeconomic Adjustments," p. 907, calculates the appreciation of the peso "and ensuing loss in competitiveness of the tradable sector" at about 28 percent between the middle of 1979 and the end of 1981.

[34] Edwards, "Stabilization and Liberalization," p. 238.

as compared to 1974. Even when adverse external market conditions hit the economy in 1981, the export total remained $2.4 billion
above 1974. But that achievement was swamped by the rise of imports. By 1981 they were $4.4 billion above the level of 1974. Ex-
ternal debt more than doubled between the end of 1977 and the end
of 1981.[35] The net result looked much like that of a typical populist
government abandoning financial consistency.

If the Chilean government had been a populist or reformist regime, the international financial community might have become
more disturbed, a good deal earlier, about the growing external
deficits and debt. But the IMF, the World Bank, and private international banks were apparently mesmerized by the officially
conservative character of the regime. The external debt was not
governmental but private. Chile was both reducing inflation and
promoting exports, so how could it go astray? The first clear sign
that it was going astray even in financial terms (apart from the growing external deficit on current account) was a sudden rash of failures by domestic credit institutions in 1981. The theology of non-
intervention and minimal regulation had been carried to such an
extreme that speculative abuses had been able to proceed to a degree reminiscent of, though more costly than, those in the United
States in the 1920s.[36] When Chilean financial institutions suddenly
began to look less reliable, the international financial community
began to recognize that the Chilean debt, though private, could conceivably be hard to manage.[37] And it was, as everyone discovered
when the lenders hesitated: the inflow of net new lending was all
that had been keeping the wingless economy up in the air.

How did such a conservative regime manage to get the country in
such a crisis of external borrowing and overspending? The key is
perhaps that the overspending was private, not public. The government certainly was not wasting funds on social programs for the
poor or on any public investment. The budget was kept close to balance. It was the private sector that was overspending, and doing it

[35] Ricardo Ffrench-Davis, "External Debt and Balance of Payments of Latin America: Recent Trends and Outlook," Inter-American Development Bank, *Economic and
Social Progress in Latin America, 1982 Report* (Washington, D.C.: IADB, 1982), p. 167.

[36] Carlos Díaz Alejandro, "Good-Bye Financial Repression, Hello Financial Crash,"
Yale University, Economic Growth Center, Discussion Paper no. 441 (May 1983).

[37] From the dependency perspective, it is particularly interesting that the collapse
of 1981–82 was directly related to the way that monetary deflation in the United
States and England was beginning to strangle banks all over the world. Monetarism
in the industrial countries helped to pull the rug out from under the brand of
monetarism being practiced in Chile.

much more for consumption than for investment. Chicago training
in economics provided infinite warnings about the dangers of government borrowing and overspending, but private external borrowing was seen as a healthy manifestation of market preferences.
Private firms do not borrow for wasteful purposes. And private consumption spending could not be excessive if government deficits
and credit creation were held tightly in check. What went wrong?

In financial terms, a basic problem was that the monetarist recipe
of strict restraint on domestic monetary expansion resulted in such
high real interest rates that domestic borrowers turned ever more
to foreign sources of finance. They did it to keep alive in conditions
of a persisting squeeze on liquidity, in some spectacular cases to buy
up land and existing firms, and apparently also to finance increased
consumption. International lenders happily provided the loans because interest rates were kept high and the government's conservative image made earnings seem safe and sound. The process depended on a perception by both borrowers and lenders that the rate
of devaluation of the currency would not be so rapid that it would
make repayments impossible by exceeding the interest rate differentials between Chile and the rest of the world. The likely relationship between interest rates and exchange rates had been something
of a restraining question until the government announced its decision in 1979 to hold to a fixed exchange rate. That decision was the
answer to a maiden's prayer for lenders and borrowers: if adhered
to, in the context of continuing high real interest rates in Chile, it
assured high returns to financial intermediaries. That is when the
money really poured in, and set the stage for the crisis of 1982.[38]

Meanwhile, back at the farm and factory, things were never really
going well. Gross domestic product per capita measured at constant
prices increased at an annual rate of only 1.8 percent a year from
1974 to 1981, then dived in 1982. The 1.8 percent growth rate prior
to the 1982 collapse was itself very much on the weak side compared
to the rest of Latin America in this period. But perhaps the more
revealing fact is that what growth there was in Chile consisted almost entirely of commercial and financial activities, as distinct from
either agricultural or industrial production. The index of industrial
production was only 2 percent higher in the boom years of 1980 and

[38] Corbo, "Reform and Macroeconomic Adjustments"; Díaz Alejandro, "Goodbye
Financial Repression"; Juan Pablo Arellano, "De la liberalización a la intervención:
El mercado de capitales en Chile 1974–83," *Colección estudios cieplan* 11 (December
1983), pp. 5–49, and "La difícil salida al problema del endeudamiento interno," ibid.
13 (June 1984), pp. 5–25.

1981 than it had been in 1974. But the growth rate for value added in import trade was 14.2 percent a year, and that in financial services 11.8 percent a year.[39] A pair of triumphs for Chicago. The per capita growth rate for all other components of GDP combined was 0.2 percent a year.

The near-absence of industrial growth in this period contrasts with a striking increase of consumption. A study intended to demonstrate that the military regime's open market policies had not destroyed the business sector, or the middle class in general, brought out convincing evidence of a remarkable rise in purchases of consumer durable goods.[40] The point of the study was that removing protection and regulation had not so much hurt the middle class as transformed its character, or function: many people lost professional-level employment with public agencies, and many lost ownership or employment in previously protected business firms, but that did not wipe them off the map. They shifted into new lines of activity, particularly in commerce, finance, and exporting. Of course, unemployment went up greatly too. But those with continuing or new employment raised their consumption greatly. How could they do so in the absence of corresponding increases of production? In the aggregate, by borrowing foreign exchange and using most of it to import consumer goods.

While consumption increased for the middle class as for the rich, it did not do so for those at the bottom of the income scale. Comparing 1978 to 1969, consumption in real terms by the poorest 20 percent of families fell 31 percent.[41] This decrease for the the poorest quintile was a direct result of greatly increased unemployment. As measured by the University of Chile for the Greater Santiago region, open unemployment, which had been slightly above 7 percent in both 1960 and 1970, and then 4 percent in 1973, climbed to a temporary peak of 17 percent by 1976 (table 9.2). A recovery was allowed to begin in 1977, bringing open unemployment down to 11 percent by 1981. At least, that was the measure excluding those people without regular employment who were given temporary makework jobs by the government, at rates of pay below the minimum wage, in an "emergency" program expected to end quickly. If these people were counted as unemployed, the national rate for the rel-

---

[39] Ffrench-Davis, "El experimento monetarista," table 3, p. 29.

[40] David E. Hojman, "Income Distribution and Market Policies: Survival and Renewal of Middle Income Groups in Chile," *Inter-American Economic Affairs* 26 (Autumn 1982), pp. 43–64.

[41] René Cortázar, "Distribución del ingreso," table 3, p. 11.

TABLE 9.2. Chile: Investment, Unemployment, and
Real Interest Rates, 1970–1984

Year	Fixed investment as percent of geographical product	Unemployment percentages (greater Santiago)		Real interest rates (short-term)
		Open	Open + PEM[a]	
1970	20.4	6.9		
1971	18.3	5.8		
1972	14.8	3.7		
1973	14.7	4.3		
1974	17.4	9.4		
1975	15.4	15.4	16.8	
1976	12.7	17.2	20.1	51.2
1977	13.3	13.3	16.2	39.2
1978	14.5	13.8	16.1	35.1
1979	15.6	13.7	15.3	16.6
1980	17.6	11.9	13.9	12.2
1981	19.1	10.8	12.5	38.8
1982	14.0	21.4	23.8	35.1
1983		22.3	27.6	16.0
1984		19.6	20.4	11.4

SOURCES: Investment shares from José Pablo Arellano, "De la liberalización a la in-tervención: El mercade de capitales in Chile, 1974–83," *Colección estudios cieplan* no. 11 (December 1983), table 10, p. 28; real interest rates and unemployment data from statistical appendix to *Colección estudios cieplan* no. 16 (June 1985), pp. 128 and 136.

[a] Workers without regular employment, given temporary jobs by the government with payments below the minimum wage, are excluded from the national data for open unemployment; this column adds the workers under this program to the offi-cially reported unemployment percentage in the preceding column.

atively prosperous year of 1980 was 14 percent, double the level of 1970 when conditions were considered (rightly) to be a recession. The unemployment rate including those still without regular em-ployment, still working under the special emergency program started years earlier, reached a low of 12 percent in 1981, and then shot up to 28 percent in 1983. For the whole decade 1973–1983, the average share of the labor force without regular employment must have been about two and a half times as high as in the 1960s.

Real wages were pulled down sharply from 1973 to 1975 but then started up again as production began to recover. Exactly how much they were driven down and how much they came back up is a matter of dispute. Table 9.3 gives two measures, one based on deflation of nominal wages by the official index of consumer prices and one based on a corrected price index. By both measures, real wages as

TABLE 9.3. Two Estimates of Real Wages in
Chile, 1970–1984 (1970 = 100)

Year	Average real wage in industry, using official price index as deflator	Real wage based on corrected estimate of consumer prices
1970	100	100
1971	118	123
1972	98	96
1973	60	78
1974	69	65
1975	62	63
1976	70	65
1977	80	71
1978	90	76
1979	99	82
1980	111	89
1981		97
1982		98
1983		87
1984		87

SOURCES: Average real wage in industry using official price index from PREALC, Oficina Internacional del Trabajo, *Mercado de Trabajo en Cifras, 1950–1980* (Santiago, 1982), cuadro III-3, p. 149; estimates based on corrected consumer price index from René Cortazar y Jorge Marshall, "Indice de precios al consumidor en Chile: 1970–78," *Colección estudios cieplan* no. 4 (November 1980), table 2, p. 162, partially revised and extended in no. 16 (June 1985), cuadro 8, p. 132.

of the low point in 1975 were about 40 percent below the pre-Allende level of 1970. From then, both measures show increases, though at very different rates. The corrected index (corrected to remove understatement of the consumer price index) shows real wages as of 1981–82 back almost exactly at the 1970 level, then a plunge once again under macroeconomic contraction in 1983.

Production, like employment, has proven to be extraordinarily variable in Chile's monetarist model. In the intense deflation of 1975, industrial production fell 28 percent below the previous year.[42] Again in 1981–82, industrial production was cut 27 percent between the third quarter of 1981 and that of 1982. These sharp downswings were much more extreme than in the rest of Latin America, or the rest of the world. The worldwide recession of 1981–83 brought GDP for Latin America down by 4 percent between these two years; for Chile the drop was 15 percent.[43] The free market regime has been extraordinarily unstable. Even the most basic Keynesian prescriptions for macroeconomic stabilization have been resolutely ignored.[44] Chile moved back to the style of Herbert Hoover, responding to decreases in demand and threatened budget deficits by tightening up on spending and increasing taxes, reinforcing downswings with merciless consistency.

Underneath the oscillations of current production, a persistent structural characteristic of the whole period has been a low level of domestic saving and investment. Gross fixed investment was between 20 and 21 percent of GDP in both 1960 and 1970. It then fell to an average of 14 percent for 1976–78, increased to a peak of 19 in 1981, and then immediately fell back to 14 percent in 1982 (table 9.2). Free market policies and regressive income distribution gave Chile a decade of exceptionally low investment.

Comparison of the course of events to that in Brazil after the military took over in 1964 demonstrates many parallels but also important differences.[45] Both military regimes enforced initial periods of

[42] IDB, *Economic and Social Progress, 1984 Report*, table 3, p. 420.

[43] If the comparison were made between 1980 and 1983 the difference would be less pronounced: GDP for Latin America fell 3 percent between these years, while for Chile it fell 10 percent.

[44] Ricardo Ffrench-Davis calculates that the internal deflationary response to the adverse change in terms of trade in 1975 multiplied by three the cost of that initial negative impact: "El experimento monetarista," p. 14, note 3. See also Muñoz, "Crecimiento y desequilibrios," p. 33, and "Economía mixta de pleno empleo," *Colección estudios cieplan* 9 (December 1982), pp. 107–38; Alejandro Foxley, "Cinco lecciones de la crisis actual," ibid., 8 (July 1982), pp. 161–71.

[45] Foxley, "Stabilization," and "Stabilization Policies."

sharp contraction and then achieved following expansions widely
regarded as demonstrating the success of the new strategies. But
while Brazil's growth was centered on investment and kept on for
more than a decade, Chile's recovery featured consumption rather
than investment and was soon aborted. The differences may be due
to the fact that the Brazilian government, in contrast to that of
Chile, never bought the idea of withdrawal from direct intervention
to promote industrialization and growth. In Brazil, the government
kept up export promotion and at least some concern for efficiency
but also continued to use selective protection and subsidies to promote investment, as well as price controls for specific problem areas.
That strategy kept alive a sense of public responsibility to foster
growth. The Chilean government followed more conservative advice, and the country paid dearly.

The goal of both regimes can be interpreted as a systematic reversal of preceding efforts toward redistribution of income: Alejandro Foxley concludes that both were determined "to redistribute resources toward the private capitalist sector."[46] That was certainly
true at the start, but then both allowed real wages to start coming
back up again: Brazil from 1967 and Chile after 1975 (table 9.3).
The model could accept rising real wages provided that they were
part of overall growth permitting higher property income at the
same time. What both of these regimes rejected and tried to take
back was any increase of wages *at the expense of* property income. In
this view, Foxley's point might be restated: a fundamental target was
to reverse the immediately preceding shifts of income toward workers, and then to maintain the growth of property income while allowing wage increases as long as aggregate income was increasing.
That approach allowed for gains in employment and in wages for a
long period in Brazil, because macroeconomic management was
more successfully expansionary.

In Chile the government stuck grimly with the job of driving out
inflation, instead of settling for the stable mid-20s rate which Brazil
accepted from 1967 on. That meant repeated recourse to macroeconomic contraction, and much higher unemployment. These differences might be explained by a more stubborn streak on the side
of the Chilean military and economists, or perhaps more by their acceptance of monetarist conceptions of how a private enterprise
economy should work. They seem to have believed that sound public finance and the absence of regulatory intervention (except for

[46] "Stabilization," p. 887.

suppression of labor!) would bring private enterprise vigorously to life. It did not. The failure was not because of any eternal inability of Chilean private enterprise, but because the strategy was crippled, and the economy therefore crippled, by obsession with constraint and a conservative ideology fully as extreme as the opposite ideology to the left of Allende.

To all or most of such criticism, the reply might be that neoclassical economics never promised growth, or stability, or equity, just efficiency. The Chilean economic strategy under the military regime probably did improve efficiency in some respects. Particularly inappropriate high-cost lines of production were weeded out and new mistakes of this kind discouraged. The structure of production shifted from dominance by producers needing protection to a greater role for those producers able to compete in external markets. Many obstacles to efficiency that had been weighing down the economy ever since the depression of the 1930s were cut away. These changes could have contributed significantly to the welfare of the Chilean people if they had been achieved in the context of policies also appropriate for economic growth and reduction of poverty. But they were not.

4. Economic Policies, Political Repression, and Future Possibilities

Contrasting economic strategies have constituted only one strand, probably not the most important, in a truly tragic sequence. One of the most civilized countries in the world has been dragged through more than a decade of violent repression as if this were the only possible response by those who believe in social order. Economic principles thought by many to be associated with political freedom have become closely identified with a police state.

To support market-oriented economic policies surely does not imply a preference for repressive government, but is it possible that the specific context of Latin American countries, or at least of some of these countries in some periods, turns the pursuit of such policies into systematic opposition to popular government? Or should the economic policies be regarded as totally separate issues to be considered apart from political connotations? Arnold Harberger argues that there is nothing intrinsically authoritarian about the economic policies themselves: "no single component of policy in the Southern Cone countries is without its precedents in a democratic setting.

Economic policies should be judged on their merits."[47] In a way, that
is a readily defensible position: an economic policy does not become
antidemocratic just because it is used by an authoritarian government. But in another way this position begs the question. Does it
mean that evaluation of their merits properly includes explicit consideration of necessary conditions for their adoption? Does it include evaluation of their full social consequences or only their effects on economic efficiency? Does it mean that any policy that is
accepted by a democratic process in a country with a well-functioning economy should always be equally acceptable to the majority in
any other country and context? The stated outlook does not exclude
regretful acceptance of a need to curb erratic choices by democratic
majorities.

Alejandro Foxley suggests that advocates of an unregulated price
system based on private ownership, who do in the abstract prefer a
democratic society, sometimes come to the conclusion that the combination is at present unworkable in Latin America because leftist
ideologies have misled too many people into thinking that capitalism is unfair. From this point of view it remains correct that capitalism will benefit the majority if allowed to function properly, and
so could become consistent with democracy, but to make that clear
a free market system must be held in place long enough to prove
how well it works.[48] Ten years may not be enough, especially when
the demonstration has not as yet been totally convincing.

Perhaps the main economic problem in Chile has not been the recourse to free markets so much as the particular monetarist model
imposed on the country. This approach is not a helpful guide to
economic policy in any country, whether Chile, England, or the
United States. In democratic countries monetarist policies are
either modified in practice or drag down the economy concerned
until the voters get rid of the government unwise enough to rely on
them. The monetarist approach as applied in Chile is inconsistent
with democracy because an *informed* majority would reject it.[49] The
main reasons it cannot win popular support are that it neither as-
sures employment opportunities nor provides any other way to ensure that lower income groups can participate in economic growth.

[47] Harberger, "Comments," on Foxley, "Stabilization," in Cline and Weintraub,
eds., *Economic Stabilization*, p. 229.

[48] Foxley, *Latin American Experiments*, pp. 101–102.

[49] Muñoz, "Crecimiento y desequilibrios," and "Hacia una nueva industrialización:
Elementos de una estrategia de desarrollo para la democracia," *Apuntes cieplan* 33
(May 1982).

The search for efficiency could be helpful: the problems are that some forms of efficiency cost too much, and others, although helpful, are not sufficient. Efficiency as an objective needs to be placed in perspective as a relevant but secondary consideration, in a participatory growth strategy that includes direct social investment, promotion of high levels of employment, and generally more active macroeconomic leadership by the government.

When this military government is gone, would Chile be well advised to keep some of its economic policies? Yes, it would. The concern for avoidance of high-cost lines of investment, for avoidance of high levels of protection, for keeping down particular kinds of regulation that inhibit flexibility of production without any compensating social gain, for the use of policies to stimulate diversified exports, for effective taxation, and for limitation of public sector deficits could all be positive components of a set of policies aimed more toward equity and growth. A better set of policies would include vastly greater concern for the level of unemployment and the incomes of those at the lower end of the income distribution. Such concern could be made effective by more expansionary monetary and fiscal policy in periods of recession, steadier use of promotional exchange rates, and direct social investment. That sounds a good deal like the original Frei program, with its target of rising real wages but with an intended upper limit on the rate of increase consistent with macroeconomic balance. It is silent on another costly aspect of the Frei period: his favorable policy toward foreign investment. It would seem now, after all the revelations of complicity by foreign firms in destroying Chilean democracy, that a newly democratic society would be well advised to reverse that position and severely restrain foreign investment.

A particularly promising sign is the energy and depth of thought that Chilean economists outside the government have used to examine the details of policy alternatives and constraints a new civilian government would be likely to face. Their central theme is the need to select those particular kinds of economic policies that, while meeting the critical test of consistency in economic terms, also meet the tougher test of jointly negotiated acceptance by both labor and capital.[50] That second requirement might turn out to be an impossibility, though they suggest that a great many people on both sides have come to value more highly the avoidance of all-out confron-

[50] Foxley et al., eds., *Reconstrucción económica para la democracia* (Santiago: CIE-PLAN, 1983).

tation. In any case, it is possible to see that the economic alternatives envisaged in these studies would be more consistent with equality and more favorable for growth than the system of the last decade. Chile can do far better than it has done under its obsessively market-oriented system since 1973, without the violence of this particular regime against the Chilean people.

TEN

TWO KINDS OF REVOLUTIONARY
ALTERNATIVE: CUBA, AND PERU
UNDER VELASCO

Both the Cuban Revolution and the Peruvian experience under Velasco accomplished sharp breaks with the past, in very different
ways. Cuba remains the only long-term test of what a Marxist government can mean in a Latin American country, while Peru attempted an emphatically non-Marxist "third way." This particular
kind of third way succeeded in changing Peru but not in surviving;
it was cut off in the midst of a deepening economic crisis after seven
years. Although it broke down badly, the experience reveals an in-
triguing mixture of unexpected possibilities and a familiar theme:
what can be done in terms of social change depends to a high degree
on the quality of the policies used to manage the economy in the
process.

    In terms of the three main themes of this book—poverty and in-
equality, interactions between domestic and external economic factors, and the relationships of economic development strategies to
the political system—Cuba has been extraordinarily successful in
dealing with the first but not with economic growth, dependency, or
political freedom. Have the problems with growth and trade been
caused by conflicts between social goals and production, by the pressures of the cold war, or by internal confusions? How has the society
responded to conflicts and where is it headed? Compared to the rest
of Latin America, has it been better or worse for the people who live
in it?

    The Velasco period in Peru, from 1968 to 1975, started with an
emphasis on national autonomy, elimination of social control by the
traditional landowner-exporter families, greater participation by
workers in ownership and control of industry, and greater capacity
for organization and self-help by the poor. One of the main themes
was close to the Cuban vision: to promote a new society based on
"solidarity not individualism; . . . cooperation, not competition; so-

cial conscience, not selfishness."[1] Critics on the left have come to reject the idea that the experience was ever anything more than another case of industrialization through protection, covered up by a
radical vocabulary, while those on the right mostly denounce it as an
extreme of irresponsible populism. It was something of all these
things. Still, the regime demolished the profoundly rooted resistance to change of the traditionally dominant landowners and initiated a striking variety of social experiments. Its economic policies
went wrong, and they left a costly heritage, but it carried Peru into
a necessary and long-delayed transition.

1. Background Similarities and Differences

Cuba and Peru are linked in this chapter mainly because they both
experienced radical changes breaking out of prior institutional
structures. They had both been among the most conservative Latin
American countries, hardly participating at all in the regional import substitution drive of the 1930s and early postwar years. When
they implemented radical changes they had an additional factor in
common that differentiated them from most reformist governments in Latin America: they did not have hostile domestic military
forces waiting in the wings. The Cuban Revolution was accomplished by force, allowing the government to replace the previous
military establishment, and the Peruvian semirevolution was carried out by the military itself. Of course, Cuba had active United
States opposition and armed emigrant groups to worry about, and
the leftist Peruvian military leaders had a divided military at home,
but neither one was under the gun in the direct sense of the civilian
governments in Argentina, Brazil, and Chile in the Allende period.
That made a big difference. Economic mistakes could be corrected
(or not corrected), without bloodshed.

Further back in history the two countries were very different.
Peru was the proud and rich center of Spanish rule in the colonial
period. The landowning oligarchy maintained a dominant position
and with few interruptions managed to block significant changes in
economic policy, all the way up to the Velasco break in 1968. Peru

[1] Cynthia McClintock and Abraham Lowenthal, eds., *The Peruvian Experiment Reconsidered* (Princeton: Princeton University Press, 1983), pp. xi–xii. This post-Velasco
review complements a valuable earlier volume written when the regime appeared to
be more successful: Lowenthal, ed., *The Peruvian Experiment: Continuity and Change
under Military Rule* (Princeton: Princeton University Press, 1975). See also Alfred
Stepan, *State and Society*.

also had a strong cultural and literary tradition and was far enough away from the United States to escape being drowned by direct American influence. Cuba was left out of the independence movement of the early nineteenth century, gaining nominal independence only when the control of Spain was broken in the Spanish American War. Once free of Spain, it immediately came under more effective influence by the United States. From the end of the war up to the Cuban Revolution the United States government considered Cuba to be a dependent special relationship, not quite in the same sense as Puerto Rico, but almost.[2] Cuba was always regarded as particularly critical for American security, to a degree that led to two military interventions prior to the 1930s and to continued direct influence on domestic policy thereafter.

Cuba and Peru both depended heavily on primary exports. Cuba's economic growth was tied closely to earnings from sugar exports to the United States. In the 1930s the country was required to agree to strict limits on its own trade control practices in exchange for quota rights to sell in the United States market. Cuba had little scope for choice of an import substitution strategy. On the eve of the revolution half its supplies of fruit and vegetables were imported from the United States.[3] Another strong attachment to the American economy came through tourism, including that of upper-income Cubans going north but mostly Americans seeking the wide-open night life of Havana. Tourism to Macchu Picchu may convey something of the austere grandeur of the Andes and of the Inca civilization; tourism to Havana had more the effect of strengthening the city's reputation for vice. A good part of the impetus for the revolution came from Cuban disgust with the country's notorious corruption at all levels of government and society. That may help account for something of a puritanical strain in the revolutionary regime. Castro's government has been dramatically different in its unswerving and successful efforts to prevent significant corruption, particularly among higher government officials.[4]

Peru had more varied primary exports than Cuba and kept find-

[2] Hugh Thomas, *Cuba: The Pursuit of Freedom, 1762–1969* (New York: Harper and Row, 1971); Jorge Domíngue, *Cuba*, ch. 2.

[3] René Dumont, *Cuba: Socialism and Development* (New York: Grove Press, 1970), ch. 1.

[4] Domínguez, *Cuba*, pp. 36, 45–46, 93–95, 103–104, 110–14, and 229–33. Domínguez gives credit to the revolutionary government for ending the pervasive kinds of corruption related to money but blames it for another form: "the corruption of power to gain more power" (p. 5).

ing new ones to make the variety grow.[5] To its existing major exports of copper, cotton, and sugar it added in the 1950s a spectacular growth of fishmeal exports from the *anchoveta*. Most of the exports based on agriculture and fishing generated income for landowners and subsequently for the fishmeal industry of the coastal region, but not for the isolated and extremely poor Andean peasants. Copper mining provided some jobs in the Andean region, but foreign ownership of the largest mines meant that much of the income went abroad. The share captured by Peru in taxation helped finance imports, but most of them consisted of consumer goods for upper income groups on the coast.

Rural labor remained poor in both Cuba and Peru, though in different ways. The Cuban rural labor force was something of a proletariat, working seasonally in the sugar plantations and refineries as hired labor, and held in poverty mainly by long periods of unemployment.[6] Peru had somewhat similar conditions in its coastal sugar areas, but most of the rural labor force consisted rather of peasants outside both the Spanish culture and the earnings of the export economy. Their poverty was more identified with small holdings of very poor land. In the Sierra, the average of cultivated land per worker was only 2.1 hectares in 1972, much below the average for other Latin American countries in quantity and probably in quality as well.[7] The low ratio of land to labor at the start of the postwar period was bad enough, and it has gone in the wrong direction since: the total number of workers in agriculture increased by 20 percent between 1960 and 1984 (see table 3.1).

When Cuba and Peru were hit by falling exports in the depression of the 1930s, their reactions contrasted greatly to those in Argentina and Brazil. Where the latter two used active promotional policies behind strong protection to revive domestic income and production, Cuba and Peru remained relatively passive. They handled their monetary and fiscal policies in conservative style, allowing the

---

[5] Rosemary Thorp and Geoffrey Bertram, *Peru 1890–1977: Growth and Policy in an Open Economy* (London: Macmillan, 1978).

[6] Arthur MacEwan, *Revolution and Economic Development in Cuba: Moving Towards Socialism* (New York: St. Martin's, 1981), pp. 11–12.

[7] José Marie Caballero, *Economía argraria de la Sierra Peruana* (Lima: Instituto de Estudios Peruanos, 1981), pp. 67–91. See also Giorgio Alberti, *Basic Needs in the Context of Social Change: The Case of Peru* (Paris: OECD, 1981), and F. LaMond Tullis, *Lord and Peasant*.

external depression to be transmitted fully to the internal market.[8]
They continued to follow this approach right on through the early
postwar years of vigorous import substitution in many other Latin
American countries. At the end of the 1950s Peru had the lowest
level of effective protection of all the countries compared in table
4.5. This clearly reflected policy dominance by primary exporters:
free trade was much more in their interest than any policy of protection for industrialization. With low protection, the economics of
successful primary exports in the early postwar years acted to discourage industrialization because these exports provided good foreign exchange earnings, kept up the value of the Peruvian sol, and
thus kept down the cost of imported consumer goods.[9]

Cuba's passive economic policies in the depression and early postwar years might be explained in much the same terms, with the additional factor of direct influence from the United States. Still, with
a higher income level than Peru and with more of the population
able to participate in consumer goods markets, Cuba was able to
move somewhat more toward light industry even in the absence of
active import substitution policies. Cuba's higher income level, and
superior standards of education and health, owed a great deal to
American investment and influence. That influence had its positive
side as well as its negative effects. René Dumont expressed squarely
the main drawback: the United States "deprived Cuba of the initiative for her own economic development."[10]

The extremes of domestic corruption and governmental brutality
so visible in Cuba from the time of the Machado dictatorship (1924–
1933) created considerable sympathy in the United States for the
struggle of opposition groups. The sympathy extended to Castro's
group in the 1950s in its fight against the dictatorship of Batista. As
that group proved to have enough tenacity and popular support to
survive against greatly superior armed force, opposition in the
United States to arms shipments to the government led President
Eisenhower to stop such assistance in 1958. That decision constituted a declaration of nonsupport for a corrupt regime unwanted
by anyone. Batista's government suddenly dissolved on New Year's
Day of 1959, as if it had no real substance at all. Castro was able to

[8] Carlos Díaz Alejandro, "Latin America in the 1930s."
[9] John Sheahan, "The Economics of the Peruvian Experiment," p. 389.
[10] Dumont, Socialism, p. 10.

take power as a self-made success against great odds and was given wide acclaim in the United States as in Cuba.

At the time of Castro's success, Peru remained stubbornly conservative, perhaps the most conservative of all the major Latin American countries. The indigenous Alianza Popular Revolucionaria Americana (APRA) founded by Victor Haya de la Torre gained wide support, initially radical and later from both industrial and urban labor interests, but the traditional landowner-exporter groups were usually able either to control elections or to call in the army when they could not. A more circumspect reformist party led by Fernando Belaúnde Terry won election in 1964 with a program calling for land reform, major public works, and increased protection for industrialization. But then Belaúnde failed to follow through against conservative opposition: the land reform was aborted from the start, economic growth slowed down, and the country's profound problems of inequity and poverty remained unchanged.[11] Outbreaks of guerrilla action by Andean peasants were put down by strong military repression but left a heightened sense that drastic changes were necessary to make it possible for the country to move. The military leadership gradually came to that position too, whether because of a conviction that they could accomplish something to change the society for the better or, as more critical interpretations argue, to head off truly radical change.[12]

Belaúnde's administration of the 1960s could be seen as a parallel to that of Frei in Chile at the same time: yet one more example of a reformist government blocked by domestic opposition. In both cases their ability to deal with opposition was weakened by failure to handle decisively the most politically charged conflicts with foreign companies in their countries. For Frei, the problem was his unwillingness to take strong action to assert national control of the American-owned copper mines. For Belaúnde the key issue was the role

[11] Julio Cotler, *Clases, estado y nación en el Perú* (Lima: Instituto de Estudios Peruanos, 1978), pp. 353–83, and "Democracy and National Integration in Peru," in McClintock and Lowenthal, eds., *Experiment Reconsidered*, pp. 3–38; Alberti, *Basic Needs*, pp. 36–38; Pedro-Pablo Kuczynski, *Peruvian Democracy under Economic Stress: An Account of the Belaúnde Administration, 1963–68* (Princeton: Princeton University Press, 1977).

[12] Javier Iguíñiz combines the two views: the military acted because they realized "the need for truly radical reform to solve some of the country's crucial problems and to impede further radicalization of the social and political process." From "Basic Needs and Capitalist Production in Peru," in Claes Brundenius and Mats Lundahl, eds., *Development Strategies and Basic Needs in Latin America* (Boulder: Westview Press, 1982), p. 115.

of the International Petroleum Company, a subsidiary of Exxon and the country's major oil producer. If all else had been going well the case might not have been crucial, but much of the public and of the military leadership had become impatient with the government's lack of positive action: signs of weakness in defending national interests against foreign firms were suicidal. In 1968, seizing the occasion of a particularly frustrating turn in the legal dispute between the government and the International Petroleum Company, the military leadership under General Juan Velasco Alvarado took power and attempted a dramatic break with the past.[13]

2. ASPECTS OF CUBA SINCE ITS REVOLUTION

Both the Cuban and the Peruvian revolutionary governments showed real concern for poverty, but the Cubans did more about it. In that respect the Cuban record since the revolution is hard to beat. In terms of economic growth, external dependence, and centralization of authority it is not so great. But the country's policies keep changing, and some of the changes at least open up the possibility of doing better on the weaker sides of the experience.

Some of the main facts about Cuba's high performance in social terms are summarized in chapter 2 above, particularly its success in reducing infant and child mortality, providing mass education, and raising life expectancy. Cuba stood out relative to the rest of Latin America in these respects even before the revolution, but it did not just stay at earlier high levels: further progress between 1960 and 1984 kept up its superior record (cf. table 2.1). Estimates by Claes Brundenius for the distribution of personal income suggest that the poorest 40 percent of the population received 6 percent of the total in 1953, 17 percent in 1962, and 20 percent in 1973.[14] Carmelo Mesa-Lago has pointed out uncertainties about these estimates but concludes that "Cuba's distribution is probably the most egalitarian in Latin America."[15]

---

[13] The negotiations with the IPC are described and placed in context by Cotler, *Clases*, and Jane Jaquette, "Belaúnde and Velasco: On the Limits of Ideological Politics," in Lowenthal, ed., *Peruvian Experiment*, pp. 414-16.

[14] Brundenius, "Development Strategies and Basic Needs in Revolutionary Cuba," in Brundenius and Lundahl, eds., *Development Strategies*, pp. 143–64, data from table 8.7, p. 156, and Brundenius, *Economic Growth, Basic Needs, and Income Distribution in Revolutionary Cuba* (Lund: Research Policy Institute, University of Lund, 1981), ch. 5. Comparable estimates of family incomes by Arthur MacEwan are discussed in MacEwan, *Revolution and Development*, pp. 82–91 and appendix 1, pp. 229–31.

[15] Carmelo Mesa-Lago, *The Economy of Socialist Cuba*, p. 144.

Four major factors helped to increase equality after the revolution. The first was the government's fundamental rural orientation at the start, directly contrary to that of most Latin American populist regimes. The rural sector got the dominant share of social investment in education and health and of productive investment as well.[16] The second factor was the elimination of large private landholdings (leaving only about one-third of the land in smaller private units), and of private ownership and profit incomes in practically all other productive activities. This both wiped out the highest prior incomes and released many small farmers, and urban residents, from rent payments. The third factor was the creation of full employment, going at times to generalized labor shortage, by giving both state industry and state farms encouragement to hire as many workers as they could use regardless of effects on costs. This had great drawbacks for efficiency, but during the 1960s it also wiped out that part of poverty due to unemployment. From the early 1970s, with changes in economic policies intended to allow more choices on the employing side and to increase incentives for work effort, some unemployment reappeared (though on a much smaller scale than in other Latin American countries). The fourth was another line of policy adverse for efficiency but favorable for equality: the use of a thorough system of rationing which took away most of the meaning of money incomes in excess of the amounts required to buy basic necessities.

All of these equalizing measures helped to increase demand for basic consumer goods and services, but some of them also acted against incentives or ability to produce. Cuba was transformed quickly from the most common imbalance of capitalist societies—insufficient demand to activate productive capacity fully—to the standard imbalance of socialist societies, a persisting inability to produce the goods that people are eager to buy.

Exactly what has happened to production is a matter of differing estimates based on incomplete information. Among other problems, national accounts are unavailable for some years and are not systematically corrected for price changes when available, agricultural output on farms that remain under private ownership is not counted except to the extent that it is sold to state agencies, and services included as part of the national product in capitalist accounting systems are excluded in Cuban accounts. But many researchers, of whom Carmelo Mesa-Lago has long been recognized as a leading

[16] MacEwan, *Revolution and Development*, pp. 83–84 and 224–26.

authority, have done a good deal to provide estimates that narrow the range of uncertainty.[17] Table 10.1 gives estimates by Mesa-Lago for agricultural and industrial production and by Brundenius for supplies of some categories of consumer goods.

According to the estimates for agricultural and industrial production, output per capita fell in both sectors in the period 1960–66. Agricultural output per capita moved erratically thereafter, with no real growth. Industrial production continued weak up to 1969 but then did much better: its growth rate in the 1970s was similar to that of Latin America as a whole. Looked at from the side of supplies available for domestic consumers, excluding exports and adding imports, the Brundenius estimates give a somewhat different picture. Food supplies per capita show no growth in the 1960s but then an increase of about 2 percent a year between 1968 and 1978. The data for clothing show a decrease in the 1960s and then a recovery bringing the 1978 level back up to equal that twenty years earlier. The lack of growth shown by this index might be considered contradictory to the estimates of production, which suggest a significant increase for total industrial output. The explanation could be that the composition of industrial output was not oriented to consumer goods. The estimates for availability of housing, like those for clothing, show almost no improvement for the twenty-year period, consistent with a general picture of policy emphasis on social service and on investment.

World Bank estimates of Cuban economic growth were uniformly dismal until the late 1970s, but as the figures became a subject of dispute the Bank stopped even guessing and commissioned a major study to try to establish some solid estimates of what has been happening. That new study considerably revises the prior picture. The growth of GDP per capita between benchmark years seems very much on a par with the rest of Latin America; the level of GDP per capita estimated for 1977, the most recent year studied, appears to be slightly higher than in Mexico, well above the average for the region.[18] Previous interpretations of poor results in the second half of the 1960s stressed the negative effects of reliance on psychological mobilization rather than individual incentives, and of distortion of resource allocation in the great drive for record levels of sugar pro-

[17] In addition to the work of Mesa-Lago and Brundenius, see Archibald Ritter, *The Economic Development of Revolutionary Cuba: Strategy and Performance* (New York: Praeger, 1974).

[18] Carmelo Mesa-Lago and Jorge Perez-Lopez, "Cuba's Material Product System."

TABLE 10.1. Indexes of Cuban Agricultural and Industrial Production and of Domestic Supplies of Food, Clothing, and Housing, 1958–1978

Year	Agricultural output (1959 = 100)		Industrial output (1967 = 100)		Per capita availability of consumer supplies (1958 = 100)		
	Total	Per capita	Total	Per capita	Food and beverages	Clothing	Housing
1958					100	100	100
1959	100.0	100.0					
1960	101.8	100.0					
1961	109.0	105.0					
1962	89.3	84.2	86.2	96.8	99	52	107
1963	76.8	71.3	84.7	92.7			
1964	83.9	74.3	88.3	94.1			
1965	100.0	88.1	91.4	95.0			
1966	83.9	71.3	89.7	91.4			
1967	102.7	87.1	100.0	100.0			
1968	94.6	78.2	98.2	96.6	102	86	104
1969	88.4	72.3	99.8	96.5			
1970	126.8	101.1	125.6	119.8			
1971	99.5	77.8	131.1	122.9			
1972	85.4	65.8	139.9	128.5	110	90	103
1973	96.9	73.0	156.6	141.1			
1974	106.5	77.8	169.3	150.1	120	95	103
1975	111.0	80.2	188.6	164.8			
1976	105.7	73.8	194.8	167.9	123	100	103
1977	—	—	197.1	167.9			
1978					125	100	104

SOURCES: Production indexes from Carmelo Mesa-Lago, *The Economy of Socialist Cuba: A Two-Decade Appraisal* (Albuquerque: University of New Mexico Press, 1981), table 5, p. 39; domestic supply availabilities from Claes Brundenius, "Development Strategies and Basic Needs in Revolutionary Cuba," in Brundenius and Mats Lundahl, eds., *Development Strategies and Basic Needs in Latin America* (Boulder: Westview, 1982), table 8.3, p. 149.

duction.[19] The problems were surely real, but their costs may not have been so high after all: these new estimates of the course of production suggest that it was not particularly weak.

It has always been clear that Cuban strategy has, after the two initial years, emphasized high rates of investment rather than rapidly increasing consumption. The ratio of gross investment to gross material product was probably low during the first three years after the revolution, but from 1962 to 1967 it climbed steadily, from 16 to 25 percent. Statistical information for the next few years is so scarce that little can be said about the ratio until 1974, when it was 22 percent. In the 1975 sugar export boom the gain in income was used mainly to raise investment to the extraordinary ratio of 33 percent; then it apparently fell back again in the more difficult following years.[20]

Cubans as consumers have not been spoiled. The per capita ration of meat was 3 pounds per month in 1962 and 2.5 pounds in 1978–79; that of coffee 1 pound in 1962 and 2 ounces in 1978–79; that of beans 1.5 pounds in 1962 and 1.25 in 1978–79.[21] So what do people eat? Through the 1960s and 1970s, while alternative supplies outside of the rationing system were generally scarce and illegal, consumption was held down for most goods but apparently rose for some items, particularly fish. Fish supplies went from a ration of one pound a month in 1962 to four pounds by 1971–72, then to completely free access by 1978–79. Butter and eggs also were released from tight rations to free access. Household consumer good often went the other way. Toilet paper was freely available in 1962 but held to a ration of one roll per month by 1978–79. Soap and toothpaste have also become more tightly rationed, but beer, held to one bottle a month as of 1969 in the era of moral incentives, became again freely available in the 1970s. In the early 1980s off-ration supplies, sold legally at the prices far above those for rationed goods, became much more abundant. Nelson Valdés reports being struck in 1984 by rapid improvements in dress and consumption, as well as in the availability of consumer durables, but also notes that for the off-ration goods "prices are so high that Cubans refer to the stores where they are sold as *las tiendas de los ricos*."[22]

[19] MacEwan, *Revolution and Development*, pp. 132–40; Mesa-Lago, *The Economy of Socialist Cuba*, pp. 35 and 57–61; Leo Huberman and Paul Sweezy, *Socialism in Cuba* (New York: Monthly Review Press, 1969), pp. 173–80.

[20] Mesa-Lago, *The Economy of Socialist Cuba*, table 7 and pp. 43–47.

[21] Ibid., p. 158.

[22] Nelson Valdés, "Cuba Today: Thoughts After a Recent Visit," *LASA Forum* (Fall 1984), p. 23.

At least for the first two decades of the revolutionary government
Cuba sounds exactly contrary to the standard Latin American
model of populist governments, carried away so often by consumption leaping past the limits of productive capacity. An absolutely
fundamental difference in Cuba is that consumption has not been
allowed to spill over freely into imports or to squeeze out investment. It was raised greatly in the first two years, by putting productive capacity fully to work, but then the government made the key
change that so many others have failed to make: resources were al-
located with priority to investment, the external deficit was held
down to the level of external aid, and private consumption was cut
back to fit what was left.[23] There is nothing inherent in socialism as
a system that makes this inevitable, or in capitalism that makes it impossible, but it takes a sense of priorities and political will. Cuba has
had many problems about competing priorities but has had plenty
of political will.

The tight rationing system used for so long, with almost no scope
for private transactions at market-clearing prices, kept the level of
consumer prices so low relative to wages that a normal monthly income was enough to pay for a great deal more than the supply of
consumer goods actually available.[24] The objective was to prevent
inequalities of money income from driving anyone below the minimum level of consumption set by the rations. The system thus
served a double purpose: as a macroeconomic constraint to fit total
consumption to available supplies and as an egalitarian protection
of a minimum level of consumption for all. Against these advantages, the costs have been considerable. In terms of the use of human time, standing in line for scarce supplies can use up a substantial part of the day. It may be that Cubans do not mind this as much
as would the harried middle classes of the northern countries, but
one of the consequences of the need for each family to have people
standing in line is to hold down the participation of women in the
labor force.[25] That many people dislike it, or have more valuable
things to do, is suggested by the practice of hiring people to hold

[23] James Malloy, "Generations of Political Support and Allocations of Costs," in
Carmelo Mesa-Lago, ed., *Revolutionary Change in Cuba* (Pittsburgh: University of
Pittsburgh Press, 1971), pp. 23–42.

[24] Mesa-Lago, *The Economy of Socialist Cuba*, pp. 47–50, calculates the "monetary
surplus," or excess of incomes over the value of consumer goods available, as an indicator of suppressed inflation. The ratio reached a peak of 86 percent in 1970 and
then was brought down to 38 percent by 1978 (table 9, p. 48).

[25] MacEwan, *Revolution and Development*, p. 80.

places in line, converting the delays of the system into opportunities for employment.

Another important cost of the system was that it decreased incentives to work. Since a fraction of the normal wage could buy all the goods permitted by rationing, and there was no possibility for weekend trips to Miami or any scope for private investment, the point of working hard became open to doubt. Absenteeism became a plague.[26] People may enjoy life more when they do not have to work full time, but it is difficult to raise consumption and achieve economic growth if a high fraction of the potential labor force does not do much work.

Responses to the conflicts inherent in these objectives have varied a great deal. Inspired particularly by the ideas of Che Guevara, the government leadership tried hard during the 1960s to encourage everyone to break away from selfish material incentives. The ideal was to promote and rely on a community sense of participation in the creation of a new society.[27] The theme is often stated as an emphasis on moral rather than material incentives, but this could be misleading: the revolutionary government emphatically wished to raise everyone's material standard of living but wanted to lead people toward concern for collective material gain by the society rather than individually differentiated success.[28]

Degrees of achievement in such a fundamental dimension are not easily measured. In the 1960s, the record of absenteeism suggests that it was not working very well. Still, the emphasis on community goals might have moderated concern with individual material interests. Although self-interest in some sense is both desirable and inescapable, the degree to which it excludes interest in others certainly varies among individuals and among periods within every society. Two sets of interview tests suggest some impact in Cuba: (1) students in 1965 gave less weight to personal salary in deciding on employment goals than the counterpart students in 1960, and far fewer believed in 1965 that external obstacles would block their choices; (2) for students from six nations compared in 1962, the Cu-

[26] Ibid., pp. 144–48; Huberman and Sweezy, *Socialism in Cuba*, ch 8; Lowry Nelson, *Cuba: The Measure of a Revolution* (Minneapolis: University of Minnesota Press, 1972), ch. 7.

[27] Bertram Silverman, ed., *Man and Socialism in Cuba: The Great Debate* (New York: Atheneum, 1971), especially the introduction by Silverman; Robert M. Bernardo, *The Theory of Moral Incentives in Cuba* (University, Ala.: University of Alabama Press, 1971).

[28] MacEwan, *Revolution and Development*, pp. 104–106.

ban students were the only ones who placed "justice" at the top of their list of cherished values. More Cuban students than any others said that they believed humanity was improving.[29] Jorge Domín-guez, reporting and commenting on these surveys, points out that they were made in the early years of the revolution, and that the downgrading of concern for differences in earnings may be less of a change in ideals than a realistic response to the limits of consump-tion actually possible. He does not cast doubt on the conclusion that the Cuban students express less preoccupation with individual ma-terial superiority than the students in the other societies compared.

Increased concern with collective performance, and reliance on group rather than individual goals, has a negative side. In Cuba, the system fostered group pressure on individuals to conform with a kind of compulsory cooperation. When people did not choose to volunteer for Sunday work in the country, or when they did not show up regularly for their own jobs, neighbors and factory work groups were encouraged to use considerable collective pressure to shame or otherwise push them into action.[30] That might have en-couraged a sense of community action for some people but it must have generated profound antagonisms for many others.

Whatever particular Cubans felt about the matter, Castro clung faithfully to this side of the revolutionary objective for a long time, very much against the preferences of Soviet economic advisers. But after the poor economic results of the late 1960s the government turned more toward the use of differential earnings as an encour-agement to work. Differentials would not have had much effect if there continued to be nothing beyond the basic rations to buy, but the change was made more significant by taking some items off ra-tioning and beginning to provide small quantities of consumer du-rable goods at high prices. That process of relaxation speeded up at the end of the 1970s, leading to the partial free markets for con-sumer goods noted above, and to a gradual diffusion of consumer durable goods in the process. For better or worse, the economic sys-

[29] Domínguez, *Cuba*, pp. 474–78. Domínguez also notes that Cuban student re-sponses to these surveys show enthusiasm about enjoying "a great many pleasures." He considers this to be "in clear contradiction to socialist values" (p. 477). Is it? That seems to be an unnecessarily dreary view of what socialism means.

[30] Malloy, "Political Support," pp. 39–42. MacEwan, *Revolution and Development*, pp. 41–42, notes that "The direct role of the military and the reliance on campaign rhet-oric were increased as part of the attempt to make moral incentives more effective. Regulations were established to curb 'loafing' and more thoroughly regulate the movement of the labour force."

tem took some steps toward greater use of prices and greater scope for differential individual choice.

The production problems of the 1960s also led to fundamental changes in the balance of emphasis between agriculture and industry, and between centralized control and public participation. These questions are closely involved with issues of trade policy and Cuban-Soviet relations. The economic considerations get submerged in questions of survival in a dangerous world. But they are still there, acting to shape the political options too.

In terms of natural conditions for production, Cuba has a strong comparative advantage in sugar. But sugar has always been synonymous with external dependence. Of all primary products it has one of the worst records for volatility of world prices. The first instinct of the revolutionary government was to turn away from it and promote industrialization. For about three years they tried to promote everything except sugar, all at once. Production began to disintegrate rapidly in all directions and forced a new set of decisions. The reaction was to go back to agriculture and then, in the great campaign to break all prior production records, to a nearly exclusive concentration on sugar. That reorientation was favored by trade agreements with the Soviet Union, which provided an assured market for a significant share of Cuban sugar and an assured supply of oil in exchange. At one point in the 1970s when world oil prices were rising steeply, the Soviet Union was paying Cuba more than double the world price for sugar while charging less than half the world price for oil.[31]

Looking back at the record of output performance in table 10.1 it can be seen that the concentration of attention on agriculture during the 1960s did not pay off in terms of growth. Output and productivity were poor for the whole economy but especially so for agriculture. This was certainly not for lack of investment, either in terms of equipment for production or in terms of education and health. A lot of resources were poured into the sector for very little return. One side of the problem was the success of the revolution in ensuring jobs by hiring people on the state farms without concern for costs or contribution to output. At the individual level, incentives to work were weak. But perhaps the other side of the problem

[31] Mesa-Lago, *The Economy of Socialist Cuba*, pp. 88–89. The year in question (1976) was exceptional, but in general the agreements served both to raise the price of sugar exported to the Soviet Union and to make its prices less unstable than those in world markets. For analysis of the terms of trade between Cuba and the Soviet Union see Domínguez, *Cuba*, pp. 155–59.

was what hurt most. The organization of most agricultural production in state farms, run by centralized administrative decisions, neither encouraged individual concern with results nor provided any constructive direction.

René Dumont, the French agronomist and socialist who was an adviser to Castro in the early 1960s, concluded that the Cuban approach to agriculture was hopeless. He located the problems on two levels.[32] One was Castro's personal penchant for enthusiasm about new methods or crops or strains of cattle found to work wonders in other countries, often launched on a large scale in Cuba before it was discovered that natural conditions or Cuban work habits made them totally inappropriate. Sometimes the projects were truly promising and sometimes not, sometimes they ran at cross purposes to each other and sometimes not; what was missing was a system of restraints to stop the mistakes and sort things out. The other level of difficulty was with the institution of the state farm. Dumont's striking descriptions of wasteful methods and lost opportunities— tomatoes intended for export rotting on the trucks, a wholehearted campaign to plant orange trees leading to the death of all the trees because nobody watered them, wrecked machinery, destructive misuse of land, and wholesale waste of human time—apply in most cases to the state farms. They offered employment at equalized wages, often much more employment than on the same land prior to the revolution, but with no corresponding increase in production.

Dumont's work in Cuba was in the early 1960s, before the wastes in agriculture became clear enough to the government to induce changes in incentives and in institutional mechanisms in order to lessen centralized control of production. Greater decentralization and participation encouraged in the 1970s should have helped overcome some of the worst problems, but Mesa-Lago's estimates of productivity in agriculture indicate that output per man was still one-third lower in 1976 than it was in 1962.[33] As long as Cuban agriculture is dominated by the state farms, comparative advantage must lie elsewhere. The policy changes of the 1970s recognized that by revising emphasis back toward industrialization. That was appropriate in view of the superior growth of industry even in the 1960s, and it should favor better overall growth in the future. From

[32] Dumont, *Socialism and Development*, and *Cuba, est-il socialiste?* (Paris: Editions du Deuil, 1970).

[33] Mesa-Lago, *The Economy of Socialist Cuba*, table 34, p. 134.

1970 to 1976, with somewhat more differentiated individual incentives and also more effort to develop participation in decision making, industrial production increased 55 percent. In the same period, agricultural output fell.

To change emphasis toward industry implies a possible decrease in the degree of dependence on trade agreements with the Soviet Union. Diversification should permit new export possibilities, to new countries, with somewhat less drastic consequences hanging on negotiations over sugar. But such possibilities depend to a considerable degree on the future of efforts by the United States to block trade with Cuba. Cuba's trade pattern is not just a question of comparative advantage or domestic preference for sector development; it is tied up with the cold war.

The peculiar tragedy of relationships between Cuba and the United States is of course an expression of contrary ideologies, but ideologies don't explain everything: the United States finds it readily possible to trade with the People's Republic of China and the Soviet Union, and Cuba on its side has been able to maintain trade and financial relationships with many capitalist countries. Geography is an important complication. The two countries might be able to get along better if the United States were moved to the vicinity of Norway. In any case, the brief period of mutual enthusiasm at the overturn of Batista turned very sour, very fast. The land reform of 1959 included nationalization of estates belonging to Americans and incited congressional moves to strike back by cancelling the Cuban sugar quota. Cuba countered by a trade agreement with the Soviet Union, in February 1960, giving the country a favorable market for sugar plus an assured supply of Soviet oil. Sugar suddenly became the less important side of the question. The oil companies, which had previously supplied the island with crude and owned the local refineries, refused to refine the Soviet oil. The Cuban government answered swiftly: the refineries were taken over. By that time there was little room for friendly discussion. President Eisenhower authorized the preparation of an invasion by Cuban emigrants in March 1960, the month following the trade agreement with the Soviet Union.[34]

Dumont argues that the United States gratuitously destroyed the

---

[34] Michael Tanzer, *The Political Economy of International Oil and the Underdeveloped Countries* (Boston: Beacon Press, 1969), pp. 327–44. The refusal of the U.S. oil companies to refine Soviet oil was not an independent commercial decision; they were requested to do so by the U.S. Department of State: Philip W. Bonsal, "Cuba, Castro, and the United States," *Foreign Affairs* 45 (January 1967), p. 232.

chances of an independent Cuban socialism. After the cold rejection of Castro on his visit to Washington in 1959, "the chances of establishing a humanist socialism, reasonably independent of the USSR, fell apart."[35] Jorge Domínguez suggests rather that it was less a matter of specific rejection by the United States than a conviction on the part of the Cuban leadership from the start that any truly revolutionary changes would provoke attack unless Cuba were supported by the Soviet Union. The Cubans were very much aware of the operation by which the United States overturned the government of Jacobo Arbenz in Guatemala in 1954. Eisenhower clearly regarded that result as a positive achievement. Cuba was more important, more of a potential threat, and closer to hand for a similar operation. To the Cuban leadership, if they were to curtail their policies to the degree necessary to satisfy the United States it would mean disavowing the revolution itself.[36] That interpretation puts more of the decision making on the Cuban side and at the same time puts the issues in a dependency framework: the United States had created a situation in which only the most limited national change was possible without recourse to support from the opposing external power.

The embargo on trade with Cuba applied by the United States may or may not have made a great deal of difference to Cuban production and income. It probably hurt the economy for the first few years, since nearly all industrial equipment had been imported from the United States and there was often no alternative source for spare parts. As the years went on, this problem was lessened by the growing availability of machinery and current inputs from both Eastern and Western Europe. New American technology that could be helpful is still blocked, but by now the policy may not greatly matter in terms of its effects on Cuban economic performance. It remains a potent symbol of unrelenting hostility.

Offsetting the embargo, Cuba has received a great deal of direct aid and credit from the Soviet Union. The aid comes in many forms, and information about some of them is not public, but there seems little doubt that on a per capita basis the level of support has been one of the highest in the developing world.[37] It has certainly permitted investment to be a good deal higher than it otherwise would have been. That economic assistance could of course be regarded as distinctly secondary in importance to the backing provide for Cu-

[35] Dumont, *Socialism and Development*, p. 31.

[36] Domínguez, *Cuba*, pp. 144–48.

[37] Mesa-Lago, The Economy of Socialist Cuba, ch. 5.

ban security. This is a dependent relationship, in the sense that Cuba would immediately be in deep trouble if it stopped. While it clearly would stop if Cuba turned against the Soviet Union, it does not imply any insistence on ownership rights by Soviet or any other foreign investors. It has not blocked Cuba from following economic strategies that would never have been allowed in the Soviet Union itself.

Jorge Domínguez suggests that hegemony as exercised by the Soviet Union implies pressure for centralized social control, whereas that of the United States implies instead pressures for pluralism.[38] That is an interesting distinction, and clearly valid to some degree, though to the extent that pluralism is taken to mean the right to diversified control of productive assets through private ownership it is more a matter of what the Cubans decided to do in the first place than a matter of Soviet influence. Domínguez means more than that: influence of the Soviet Union favors centralization of power in all its forms, whereas that of the United States has often been identified with support for both diversified nongovernmental institutions and for open political systems. That identification may be open to question: as suggested in chapter 13 below, opposition by the United States to pluralistic societies considered to be dangerous in one way or another, and support for authoritarian regimes, make the record in Latin America look more like that attributed by Domínguez to the Soviet Union.

Cuban society has clearly been run in a highly centralized way, and this has had a great deal to do with its economic difficulties. Centralized decisions that made little sense were not checked by active public debate. Although the country has many mass organizations, their main function has not been to bring public preferences to bear on leadership decisions as much as to mobilize people to implement the government's preferences. Labor unions do not so much represent workers as provide the government a mechanism through which to apply pressure on workers. That may be changing. Arthur MacEwan suggests that redirections introduced in the 1970s have made the mass organizations more nearly vehicles for the expression of public preferences.[39] As he explains, the changes

---

[38] Domínguez, Cuba, pp. 137–39.

[39] MacEwan, Revolution and Development, ch. 23–28. To judge the reality of public influence on government in Cuba is no easy matter. Jorge Domínguez gives a considerably different picture, agreeing on an increase in debate through legislative channels but presenting the final conclusions as set forth above: Domínguez, "Rev-

open up more participation in operating choices of economic policy but not on the basic questions of the economic and political structure. The system itself and the leadership of the government are not matters of public choice.

Cuba does not make a strong case for belief in efficiency through centralized rule. Policy contradictions and costly misdirections seem to have been at least as common as in countries with more open political systems. But no representative government in Latin America has done nearly as much to alleviate poverty and equalized income. Would the Cuban people voluntarily undo this system if they were allowed to vote freely for new leadership? Who knows? The rich and many of the nonrich who would have done their best to change it have left the country. Those who grew up under the present regime and have not chosen to leave may be staying because they like the way the society operates or because they like Cuba and think they may eventually be able to change the way the society operates. That need not mean a reversion to prerevolution corruption and inequity. If the government's themes of participation in a new society have had real effect, one might guess that a common preference might be to change priorities in the direction of more decentralized decision making and more freedom of expression but keep a society still concerned with equality.

Is Cuba a good place to live, compared to the other countries in Latin America? The answer surely depends on where one is born in the society. If one is born into a relatively poor family in Latin America, the odds in favor of survival, education, and dependable employment are distinctly higher in Cuba than almost anywhere else. Costa Rica may be a close match in these respects, and certainly offers more varied individual opportunities. But it is somewhat unfair to pick the best case on the non-Cuban side: for the poor, anything much below the best would be likely to be worse than Cuba. On the other hand, if one has the good sense to be born into a wealthy family, the Cuban style would be a real comedown. It must be confining both to those who would have superior power to move as individuals and to those who give high value to contrary individualism. Economic and personal constraints are probably both important in the recurring evidence that many Cubans, when given the chance to leave the country, leave it. That does not prove Cuba to be an extraordinarily poor place to live: probably 90 percent of

olutionary Politics: The New Demands for Orderliness," in Domínguez, ed., *Cuba: Internal and International Affairs* (Beverly Hills: Sage, 1981).

Haiti would emigrate quickly to the United States if welcomed in. Cuba does not leave out the poor, the economy functions in a mediocre but slowly improving way, and the government is not violently repressive. Those are not values to be disdained. Still, Cuba places severe constraints on individual freedom and life styles while not doing very much, so far, to improve standards of living. It is not so far the ideal of a productive and free socialist society.

3. PERU UNDER VELASCO

The Velasco regime had just enough of a boldly revolutionary strand, and just enough duplicity and fear of public preferences mixed up with it, to incite both admiration and profound distrust. At the beginning it looked like little more than a military coup in response to disillusionment with the weakness of the Belúnde reformist government, mainly intended to assert national interests as opposed to foreign firms while not really changing much else. After all, Peru was an exceptionally conservative country, and the military had always helped keep it that way. Still, in one of the surprises that keep Latin America in motion, the military leaders declared their determination to change the country's basic structure of ownership and economic organization, and began to act as if they meant it.

Was there ever any real chance for a successful "third way" by this route? Did the government really mean all the pronouncements about a cooperative society with effective participation by workers and the poor? Or was it simply a tool of the industrialists aiming to assert their own control in place of the traditional oligarchy?[40] Did the regime break down because of bad luck and external pressures, poor management on its own part, or simply because the industrialists decided that it was not dependably serving their interests?[41]

[40] E. V. K. FitzGerald, who worked with the military government as an economic adviser interprets its objectives in *The Political Economy of Peru, 1956–77* (Cambridge: Cambridge University Press, 1980), and "State and Its Limitations," McClintock and Lowenthal, eds., *Experiment Reconsidered*, pp. 65–93. Cotler, "Democracy and National Integration"; Elizabeth Dore and John Weeks, "Class Alliances and Class Struggle in Peru," *Latin American Perspectives* 14 (Summer 1977), pp. 4–17; and Dennis Gilbert, "The End of the Peruvian Revolution: A Class Analysis," *Studies in Comparative International Development* 15 (Spring 1980), pp. 15–38, interpret the regime as an instrument of the urban upper classes. For Dore and Weeks (p. 6), the "national bourgeoisie . . . enlisted the armed forces to be both its front man and its force."

[41] On the regime's economic policies, Rosemary Thorp is especially generous in her interpretation of the government's objectives and achievements, in "The Post-Import-Substitution Era: The Case of Peru," *World Development* 5 (January-February

The first major actions of the military leadership had a great deal of public support. They quickly nationalized the International Petroleum Company and initiated a land reform that converted practically all the country's large private estates into worker's cooperatives. They destroyed the basis of economic and political power of the traditional oligarchy, forcibly shifting the interests of the former landowners to the urban sector. As compared to industrialization based on changing the internal terms of trade against landowners, while leaving concentrated ownership intact, the Peruvian reform had the great advantage of creating a situation in which measures favorable for rural incomes would be more likely to help the poor without adding to the income and power of a conservative minority. That could have been part of a true third way. But id did not turn out to be the Velasco government's actual path.

Land reform was accompanied by a policy of almost total protection for domestic industry, and by greatly increased tax incentives for private industrial investment, both of which fit the interpretation of a strategy aimed at fortifying the private business sector. So do the regime's otherwise contradictory policies toward income distribution and poverty. The land reform was presented as a means to help rural workers by giving them collective ownership of both the traditional haciendas and the commercially oriented plantations. Large holdings were turned over to the permanent workers on the estates, but the other four-fifths of the rural labor force got few gains or none at all. Some of the highland peasant communities were given small additional land, and they gained by being relieved of feudal obligations to nearby haciendas. Families with very small landholdings were not included in the distribution and may have lost income because the new collectives cut back on employment of outside seasonal labor. The great majority of the rural poor were simply left out.[42] To make things worse, allocations of public investment and of rural credit turned even more against the individual peasants than they had been before the reform, and both price controls on food and subsidized food imports were used to favor urban

---

1977), pp. 125–36, and "The Evolution of Peru's Economy," in McClintock and Lowenthal, eds., *Experiment Reconsidered*, pp. 65–93. Daniel Schydlowsky and Juan Wicht, "The Anatomy of an Economic Failure," in the same volume, pp. 94–143, are strongly critical. Sheahan, "The Economics of the Peruvian Experiment," criticizes the government's macroeconomic policies and protectionism but defends the potential of the structural reforms.

[42] José María Caballero, "Sobre el carácter de la reforma agraria"; Tom Alberts, *Agrarian Reform*.

consumers at the expense of domestic producers. The Peruvian strategy went exactly contrary to the Cuban method of equalization by directing resources to the rural sector first.

Although the agrarian side of the regime's actions fits the view that the new measures were psuedo-reforms intended mainly to support the urban middle class, policies adopted on ownership and authority structures in the industrial sector do not. The government created many new state corporations, took over some Peruvian-owned companies, and struck against traditional private ownership by its program of "Industrial Communities" requiring firms to distribute part of their profits to workers in the form of equity rights. The goal was to bring the workers' share of ownership up to 50 percent of the total so that they would have an equal voice in company management. Further, labor laws and regulations were changed to support union organization and to limit employers' rights in dealing with workers. Firms could no longer fire workers without going through a legal process structured to make it nearly impossible. These attempts to change the structure of authority within private companies contradict any picture of the regime as a servant of the industrialists.

Some of the other aspects of the institutional measures also give weight to the interpretations of a genuine effort to change the balance among social classes. These include efforts to extend and restructure the educational system and programs to help the poor living in urban squatter settlements (rebaptized as "pueblos jóvenes"). One of the most appealing objectives was to help the squatters get legal title to the land on which they constructed homes.[43] That could be seen as a way to build up new property interests to foreclose radical antiproperty pressures; it could also be seen as a way to lessen one of the worst insecurities of the poor. A later measure directly contrary to conservative interests was to expropriate the country's leading newspapers and assign them to diverse socioeconomic groups to present a wider range of interests than those of the previous private owners.

Although the government's programs cannot be explained adequately in terms of serving private industrialists, they were certainly meant to promote industrialization. A more accurate way to view the matter may be that the government was so determined to promote industrialization that it provided great advantages for investment in this sector even though that helped industrialists. The in-

[43] Stepan, *State and Society*, ch. 5.

dustrialists were given better profit opportunities and lower taxes, but accompanying measures included improvement of conditions for workers and for urban fringe groups as well. Industry was helped and was placed under more constraints at the same time. The same was true of urban labor and members of the agricultural cooperatives. All this suggests an underlying intent to moderate class conflict in a rather special sense: to construct a social order made peaceful under supervision of military leaders who alone knew best.

Industrialization led by state investment, with a great deal of public ownership alongside private industry, is a theme with wide appeal in Latin America. The concept is close to the Brazilian post-1964 model, and to Mexico's style of development as well. But in Brazil since 1964 and in Mexico from the same period it has been associated with an effort to break out of the import substitution trap and promote growth more through industrial exports; in contrast, the Peruvian version went back to the old style of industrialization based almost wholly on protection. Rosemary Thorp suggests that the strategy was better than the earlier versions of import substitution because it included a real effort to develop greater capacity for primary exports.[44] That was an improvement, but there does not seem to have been any conception of the need for limits and selectivity on the side of industrial protection. The government created no coherent plan to guide investment according to any criteria of efficiency, employment creation, or escape from reliance on foreign technology. It repeated most of the old mistakes.

On the side of macroeconomic management, the regime started out with a good balance. Increased public sector spending and tax incentives for private investment were both appropriate in the initial conditions of a recession with a great deal of underutilized capacity, and with a net export surplus. Output grew at 6 percent a year from 1968 to 1971 and inflation was brought down from 19 percent to 7 percent. Real wages in the industrial sector increased slowly, at 2 percent a year, while the minimum wage in agriculture was raised 6 percent a year in real terms.[45] The net export surplus was allowed to fall but not to disappear.

That promising start then led to the inevitable testing stage in which populist governments steadily destroy themselves: as capacity limits show up in sectors with inelastic supply, the external balance

[44] Thorp, "The Post-Import-Substitution Era."
[45] PREALC, *Mercado de trabajo*, p. 150.

begins to turn adverse, and inflation starts to speed up, the question is whether the government is able to recognize the new constraints and respond to them. The Velasco government followed the stand-ard script by failing to respond. The growth of demand was main-tained and that of real wages suddenly increased, while inflation be-gan to rise and the export surplus turned into a deficit. That was the time to restrict government spending, raise taxes to restrain private spending, raise interest rates and the price of foreign exchange to reduce buying of imported equipment, and initiate more active measures to promote industrial exports. The choices actually made were to borrow abroad, keep interest rates down and foreign ex-change cheap, impose domestic price controls, and keep up the growth of spending. By 1975 the public sector deficit and the net import surplus were both close to 10 percent of gross domestic product.[46]

This government had a strangely ambivalent attitude toward for-eign capital. It was outspoken on the need to restrain direct invest-ment by multinationals, and it became a leader in the efforts of the Andean Group to define new rules to control them.[47] But obsession with multinationals seems to have blinded everyone to the ways in which external borrowing can increase dependence. Borrowing was used to finance current government deficits, to pay for the imports of capital goods stimulated by tax exemptions for investment, and to import food for subsidized consumption. Still another factor that added to external borrowing was the breakdown of efforts to get foreign-owned copper companies to carry out major investment projects needed for expansion. The government resolved the im-passe by taking over the mines, but then it was stuck with getting the finance for expansion.[48] The combination was too much. With greatly rising imports and little action to promote new exports, the external debt rose swiftly. Private international banks were eager to lend at first, because of their own high liquidity in this period and the regime's initial evidence of good macroeconomic management,

[46] Sheahan, "Peru: Economic Policies and Structural Change, 1968–1978," *Journal of Development Studies* 7, 1 (1980). Schydlowsky and Wicht, "Economic Failure," em-phasize the failure to activate industrial capacity for exports and disagree with ex-planation of the breakdown in terms of excess demand.

[47] Shane Hunt, "Direct Foreign Investment in Peru: New Rules for an Old Game," in Lowenthal, ed., *Peruvian Experiment*, pp. 302–49.

[48] Laura Guasti, "The Peruvian Military Government and the International Cor-porations," in McClintock and Lowenthal, eds., *Experiment Reconsidered*, pp. 181–205.

but they began to hold back as the debt mounted and the government failed to take any corrective action. That forced the government to turn to the International Monetary Fund. "Having sought to end external dependence, Peru found itself so deeply in debt in the late 1970s that the International Monetary Fund became the country's principal economic policy maker."[49]

The deterioration of the economy owed a great deal more to macroeconomic mismanagement than to problems of specific structural reforms, but some of them did raise a lot of difficulties. Apart from those connected with the agrarian reform, two of particular interest were the changes in laws governing labor relations and ownership in the industrial sector, and the creation of new organizations for popular expression. The complex measures affecting ownership and labor relations in the industrial sector, including extensive use of state-owned firms and the attempt to create shared management rights for workers in private industry, were not very successful. The state firms failed to break away from prior patterns of relatively capital-intensive, import-dependent technology. In the private firms, the attempt to require owners to distribute equity rights to workers, with the eventual objective of bringing worker ownership up to 50 percent of equity, never got very far. Between real difficulties of production in an increasingly disorganized economy and elaborate measures to channel reported profits away from companies to which the regulations applied, only a small minority of industrial workers got such benefits. They became more a new source of inequality than any generalized improvement in the position of workers.

Both the idea of shared ownership and the regulations intended to give workers permanent job tenure were rejected soon after Velasco lost power. Employers detested restriction of the right to fire workers because it weakened their authority to enforce work discipline. It may in fact have reduced productive effort. It also encouraged firms to keep hiring new workers on a rotating basis and firing them within the trial period so that they could never become permanent employees. But at the same time it had at least some of the intended effect of protecting established workers from arbitrary discharge. That means a great deal more in personal terms in a society without a National Labor Relations Board, and with persistent excess labor, than it might in a Northern industrialized economy. That benefit might have been considered of enough significance to

---

[49] McClintock and Lowenthal, preface to *Experiment Reconsidered*, p. xiii.

justify trying to amend the defects in these regulations rather than scraping them at the first opportunity.

The rapidity with which most of the Velasco-period reforms were discarded after 1975 can be explained as a reaction to the deterioration of the economy, to the return to greater power of private business interests, or to pressures from the International Monetary Fund. But it was still surprising how little public support remained for anything except the agrarian reform. That may have been due to the Velasco government's inability to maintain an acceptable balance between its ideas of how the society should be managed and its willingness to take account of the preferences of the Peruvians being managed. The regime came to be distrusted by practically everyone, perhaps particularly by labor, for arbitrary action and duplicity.[50]

Luis Pásara's illuminating review of SINAMOS, the agency created to promote organization and self-help for the urban poor, and of the series of related steps to create new labor and agricultural organizations along with a new judicial system less biased against the poor, makes clear a constant tension between promotion of participation and suppression of opposition. It is often possible to identify shifting positions with particular people in the government, some truly trying to make underprivileged groups more aware of what they could do to improve their position and others trying rather to make sure that they did what the government wanted. But Pásara rightly insists that personal difference within the government were secondary to the basic problem. An authoritarian state may be more or less willing to allow open public debate of its policies, but it is rarely inclined to give much weight to positions adverse to its own major premises. The Peruvian military always kept control of the organizations established to promote popular action; whenever the chips were down it treated the people involved as "receivers of information and transmitters of applause."[51]

All this has a clear parallel with Cuban mass organizations in the 1960s. The Cuban government created an even greater variety of

[50] See especially Cotler, "Democracy and National Integration," McClintock, "Velasco," and Pásara, "When the Military Dreams," in McClintock and Lowenthal, eds., *Experiment Reconsidered.*

[51] Pásara, "When the Military Dreams," p. 317. Cf. the similar interpretation by David Booth in his study of the government's press controls: "The Reform of the Press in Peru: Myths and Realities," in David Booth and Bernardo Sorj, eds., *Military Reformism and Social Classes: Aspects of the Peruvian Experience* (London: Macmillan, 1982).

institutions for groups of many different economic and civic interests and then used them mainly to make people aware of what the
government wanted them to do. Popular organizations were instruments of mobilization. Non-Marxist authoritarianism, when it tries
to establish a popular base "from above," follows much the same
pattern. The reformed judicial system in Peru worked out similarly:
the military created a judiciary that "ended up attempting to see the
will of the government as the source of law."[52]

Is the theoretical model of state-led economic development im-
plicitly a call for an authoritarian government? E.V.K. FitzGerald
concludes from the Peruvian experience that "it is difficult to see
how a democratic government, constrained electorally and institu-
tionally from moving too far to the right or to the left, can make the
economy work, reestablish a balanced rate of growth, and construct
a stable accumulation model (involving a high rate of productive investment and a reasonable income distribution) any better than the
military."[53] Such downgrading of democratic government can be
defended by many examples of weak results in Latin America, but
the specific Peruvian experience with military government would
seem to cast a great deal of doubt on any implication that authoritarian rule makes for better results. Schydlowsky and Wicht turn
FitzGerald's suggestion on its head: many other Latin American
governments ran into similar difficulties by using the same kinds of
economic policies but "because the Velasco government pursued
this strategy in a most vigorous, extreme and steadfast manner—as
only an autocratic government could—the crisis was more severe
and more rapid." Peru might never have gotten into such deep
problems if the government had been "less convinced of its own
righteousness and/or more diffuse in its power structure."[54]

Was a non-Marxist and noncapitalist third way really possible in
Peru? In economic terms, sure. Many of the reforms were at least
potentially positive for the underprivileged without being fatal for
economic growth or autonomy. The program was a failure for two
avoidable reasons: too little attention to internal and external
macroeconomic balance, and too little attention to rural poverty and
food production. It would have been readily possible to do better on
both counts, while pursuing reforms in many needed directions. In
the end, the breakdown and replacement of the regime was more a

[52] Pásara, "When the Military Dreams," p. 338.
[53] FitzGerald, "State Capitalism," p. 93.
[54] Schydlowsky and Wicht, "Economic Failure," p. 111.

blessing than a tragedy. The government's authoritarian character, exercised with considerable restraint in the first place, veered more and more toward manipulation and repression, undercutting the autonomy of Peruvians within their own society. Decentralized groups were just fine as long as they did not conflict with centralized control. Compared to the military regimes in Brazil, Chile, and Argentina after 1976, Velasco's government was much more interested in a just society, and was much less an engine of drastic repression, but it too succumbed to disdain for those popular preferences opposed to its own.

4. Peru since Velasco: Inflationary Stabilization and Deepening Poverty

In the decade following Velasco, from 1975 to 1985, the performance of the Peruvian economy disheartened everyone. Two of the many weak aspects were a persistently worsening inflation and deepening rural poverty. The transitional military government in power until 1980 was moderately successful in correcting the imbalances of the Velasco period, but then a conservative civilian government under Belaúnde made practically everything worse.[55] Still, Peru held on to its newly recovered democracy, and that permitted a markedly different political choice in 1985. Alan García Pérez, the first president coming from the APRA party, switched to an unorthodox economic strategy which could easily go astray if mishandled, but which started off by checking inflation, stimulating an upturn in the economy, and introducing at last some steps in favor of the rural poor.[56]

On the side of macroeconomic management, the military group under General Morales Bermúdez, which replaced Velasco in 1975, started a necessary process of correction with a relatively mild ver-

[55] Daniel Schydlowsky, "The Tragedy of Lost Opportunity in Peru," ch. 10 in Hartlyn and Morley, eds., *Latin American Political Economy*, pp. 217–42. On problems and policies in agriculture see Adolfo Figueroa, *Capitalist Development and the Peasant Economy in Peru* (Cambridge: Cambridge University Press, 1984); Cynthia McClintock, "After Agrarian Reform"; and Daniel Martínez, "El agro en el Perú: 1980–1984 y perspectivas," in Germán Alarco, ed., *Desafíos para la economia peruana* (Lima: Centro de Investigación de la Universidad del Pacífico, 1985), pp. 143–85.

[56] Cynthia McClintock, "Why Peru's Alan García Is a Man on the Move," and Alfred H. Saulniers, "The Peruvian President's Economic Dilemmas," *LASA Forum* 16 (Winter 1986); Jürgen Schuldt, "Política económica y restructuración social en el Perú, 1985–86: un modelo para armar," paper presented at the meetings of the Latin American Studies Association, Boston, October 1986.

sion of monetarist remedies, including some but not intense fiscal
and monetary restraint, rapid devaluation, and reduction of real
wages. The contraction also forced down incomes for the rural producers who had gained little or nothing in the Velasco period.
Adolfo Figueroa estimates that the real incomes of peasants were
probably cut by 13 to 15 percent between 1975 and 1980.[57]

The Bermúdez government did not slam on the brakes in the
Chilean post-Allende style. It put them on most gently as far as domestic demand was concerned. And it used both selective promotion and overall devaluation to stimulate industrial exports. The results in terms of export growth were fairly good. Measures of the
growth of manufacturing exports by a group of nine leading Latin
American countries show that Peru's share was a miserable 2.0 percent for the period 1970–74, but for 1975–79 its share picked up to
10.9 percent.[58] Still, the mixture was clearly not optimal: real incomes of the poor were cut back more than necessary to restore
overall balance, and the devaluations began to accelerate in a process that made the rate of inflation grow steadily worse.

Devaluation was imperative in 1975, after appreciation of the exchange rate in real terms for eight years had steadily eroded returns
to exporters. It worked well at first by helping to restore external
balance through promotion of exports, not just through contraction
of demand. By 1978 the initial import surplus had been cleared up
and replaced by an export surplus (measured in terms of national
accounts, excluding net factor payments abroad) equal to 3 percent
of GDP. That surplus rose to 13 percent in 1979. That was the time,
with exports rising and GDP once more increasing, to cut down
greatly on rates of devaluation and exercise special caution on monetary expansion in order to break the inflation. But the rate of
growth of the money supply was allowed to rise from 21 percent in
1977 to 71 percent in 1978, overshooting the rate of inflation. The
rate of devaluation was reduced but still ran at 50 percent for 1978.
Persistently rising inflation is not a necessary consequence of a strategy of progressive devaluation but can become the result when the
rate of depreciation is kept too high.

Worsening inflation under the more free-market approach of the
following civilian government, along with its generally disappoint-
ing response to the deepening sense of national despair, favored a
political swing to the left in 1985. The new government of Alan Gar-

[57] Figueroa, *Capitalist Development*, pp. 105–13.
[58] IDB, *Economic and Social Progress in Latin America, 1982 Report*, p. 119.

cía quickly reintroduced controls on prices, imports, interest rates, and wages. The controls were used in more imaginative ways than those of the typical populist governments, and no immediate macroeconomic imbalance was created because the government did not step up its own spending. Wages were increased in a series of steps, at rates that could cause considerable trouble if not soon slowed down, but the immediate consequences for costs in the modern sector were offset by sharply reducing nominal interest rates: for some firms, the saving on the side of financial costs possibly more than offset added wage bills, making it at least conceivable to keep on price controls without choking off production.[59] Given higher real wages, urban consumption rose rapidly and led an upswing in production. Naturally, demand for food rose rapidly too, leading to shortages and emerging black markets in the classic pattern. But at that point the government demonstrated reassuring flexibility: prices of perishable food were allowed to rise, which meant that peasant producers could share in the gains of the new policy, and that incentives were improved for increasing food production. This choice made the rate of inflation in 1986 higher than it would otherwise have been, but still left the rate less than half that of the preceding year.

The new measures included a return to import controls, increased tariffs, and a new set of exchange rate policies that greatly slowed devaluation. They also included a vigorously publicized rejection of debt service payments in excess of 10 percent of export earnings, leading to an early break in relations with the IMF. The government ruled out the previous practice of continuing devaluation at high rates, but as in many other respects the officially clear policy of stopping devaluation was moderated in practice. The government implemented one general devaluation at the start of its program and started a new dual-rate system that has permitted gradual shifts to the higher rate for particular product groups. Avoiding the Chilean trap of a determined effort to stick to an indefinitely fixed set of rates, the government stated its intention to review the rates periodically. As with the decision to force down interest rates, the unorthodox set of methods had immediate advantages and a large element of future danger. They greatly helped to slow down what had seemed to be an inexorable inflation, to stimulate internal demand and production in initial conditions of excess capacity, and to restrain the spillover of rising demand into rising

[59] Saulniers, "Economic Dilemmas," and Schuldt, "Política económica."

imports. They were well designed for the immediate set of problems. But they still imply incentives adverse to exports, to the use of labor relative to use of capital in production methods, and to investment in the modern sector. They add up to a striking example of unorthodox policies that help greatly in the short run but must be changed soon or the whole program will come apart.

The most appealing side of the García government's strategy is its reiterated intent to direct more resources to the rural sector in an attempt to raise productivity and reduce poverty, rather than concentrate on renewal of industrialization. If followed through persistently, the approach could do something at last about a problem that has seemed almost intractable, and surely contributed to growing violence throughout the country. Analysts of the origins and the strength of the Sendero Luminoso movement do not by any means agree, but some of them emphasize the deterioration of conditions of subsistence in exactly the areas in which the movement had its greatest initial effect.[60] This is not a communist movement in the urban-intellectual sense at all: it is a violent Maoist-style destructive force, supported by peasants who have had little objective reason to expect the Peruvian society to provide more positive alternatives to worsening poverty.

The García government's intent to do something to reduce rural poverty has been given reality by policies on relative prices, credit, and interest rates, and multiple programs of direct support for the rural sector. The question is, can all this be kept up when the initial margins of excess capacity and available exchange begin to be used up, making urban pressures for higher wages and for investment financing much more difficult to answer? Jürgen Schuldt, reviewing the trend of decisions in late 1986, concluded that attention and resources are being pulled back toward the urban sector: it would take a striking uphill fight by the García government to stick to its original intentions because the weight of political pressures goes the other way.[61] As he emphasizes, it is almost impossible to raise real income through increasing output in the rural sector at all rapidly, because the problems involved require profound structural changes in conditions of production; urban revival is both easier and more visible.

A complementary argument that not much can be done about ru-

[60] McClintock, "Why Peasants Rebel," and David Scott Palmer, "Rebellion in Rural Peru: The Origins and Evolution of Sendero Luminoso," *Comparative Politics* 18 (January 1986), pp. 127–46.

[61] Schuldt, "Política económica," section 6.

ral poverty, at least under a capitalist system, is that the scale of the problem is too great relative to the income of the society.[62] It surely is too great to allow any adequate answer through income transfers from the urban sector, or to achieve any really adequate solution in a few years under capitalism or any other form of social organization, but that does not mean that nothing can be done. One fundamental requirement is to change the allocation of investment resources in ways that could gradually raise rural incomes through increased production. A second requirement is to stimulate opportunities for productive employment in nonagricultural activities, at rates faster than the growth of the labor force, in something like the styles of Brazil and Colombia. That implies a greater need for labor-intensive methods of production in industry than now being encouraged, and a faster growth of investment and productive capacity than Peru has managed at any time in the last two decades. All this may be asking too much, but it would seem to come fairly close to the most recently expressed choices of strategy favored by the majority of Peruvian people, and it is certainly not impossible in economic terms.

5. Concluding Suggestions

Revolutions mean hope to some and fear to others. They more often justify the fears than the hopes. The Cuban and Peruvian experiences both fell far short of the highest hopes held for them but both accomplished real changes without failing into extremes of repression. For the rural poor, the Cuban system has worked out much the better. The Cuban economic strategy has not been brilliant, just vastly more equitable. Agricultural production has been extraordinarily weak but industrial production somewhat better, and social achievements far better. On the negative side, the country's dependence on the Soviet Union remains extreme. It would probably be a good deal less if it were not for the continued threat posed by the hostility of the United States, but that hostility might itself be less if it were not for the Soviet alliance with Cuba. This is one of those depressingly persistent circles that have so much mutual fear built into them that no resolution may be possible. But since both sides would be safer if the circle could be broken, it may

[62] Iguíñiz, "Basic Needs," gives a suggestive measure of the scale involved, showing that resource transfers sufficient to answer the problem of absolute poverty in the rural sector would exceed total profits of the modern sectors.

be just possible that statesmanship could find a way to negotiate a solution, if any statesmanship is ever forthcoming.

Whether one chooses to consider the Peruvian experience under Velasco a revolution, an experiment, or a washout, it should not be taken as evidence that a more independent "third way" is impossible. While the complications of all the imaginative but aborted reforms lend themselves to many different interpretations, the two major causes of the regime's ignoble ending were its abrasively authoritarian character and a fairly straightforward failure to respect the necessity of internal and external macroeconomic balance. A more open political system, less ruled by secrecy and duplicity, might have brought out the economic problems for public debate and possible correction.

The Alan García government brought back a new sense of possibilities in 1985, with greater attention to rural poverty and an imaginative economic program. That program stimulated renewed growth after years of stagnation, but it will need changes to hold back excess demand, to get away from the incentives toward capital-intensive techniques of production implicit in its increase in wage costs relative to interest rates, and to encourage growth of new exports before the recovery is stopped by lack of foreign exchange. Such changes need not mean repudiation of social reform; they could mean instead that any genuine reform will have a better chance to survive.

ELEVEN

MIDDLE-ROAD MARKET ECONOMIES:
COLOMBIA, COSTA RICA, AND MEXICO

Economic strategies of individual Latin American countries took three distinct paths in the 1930s and early postwar years: Argentina, Brazil, and Chile were leaders in promotion of industrialization for the internal market, using aggressive protection and state action; Cuba, Peru, and most of Central America stayed close to the free-trade model with reliance on primary exports; Colombia, Mexico, and more gradually Costa Rica went between these two styles by using considerably more state intervention and protection than the second group, while staying well short of the pressures applied by the first. Insofar as the main objectives were industrialization and economic growth, they did not do as well as Brazil but outperformed Argentina, Chile, and the more passive second group. Their in-between path of negotiation and compromise proved to have another advantage of possibly greater importance: it enabled these countries to proceed with industrialization and to reduce absolute poverty while avoiding, at least so far, the unmanageable degrees of polarization and reaction that proved so costly in human and political terms in Argentina, Brazil, and Chile.

While these countries proved able to go a long way toward industrialization and modernization without falling into the market-authoritarian kind of repression of the Southern Cone, they have certainly not been free of intense economic and social strains. They have for long periods shown unusual ability to compromise among conflicting interests, but that may actually be the counterpart of violent periods that left strong memories of the high costs of conflict. Few revolutions have been as bloody and prolonged as Mexico's, and few countries in the modern world have gone through anything like the slaughter of *La Violencia* in Colombia. Costa Rica's near-breakdown of democracy and Revolution of 1948 were mild in comparison but also left their mark as a warning of the costs of extreme positions.

This chapter considers some of the distinctive characteristics of these countries, focusing on a common set of questions. Has their

relative stability, and avoidance of relapse into market-authoritari-
anism, depended on keeping down full political participation and
suppressing independent labor movements? Is this general style of
development something to be deplored as hopelessly inegalitarian,
something that might provide helpful clues for other countries, or
simply something built into these societies by their own histories, for
better or for worse?

1. INCOME DISTRIBUTION AND GROWTH

Although the three countries share important characteristics they
differ in levels of income, rates of growth, breadth of political participation, and degrees of inequality (table 11.1). Mexico's income
per capita is much higher than those of Colombia and Costa Rica,
with Colombia slightly above and Costa Rica slightly below the median for Latin America. All three are close to the region's average
share of manufacturing in GDP. From 1960 to 1984 both Colombia
and Mexico maintained rates of growth well above the Latin American average, with Colombia coming up from a below-average level
and Mexico moving from the middle to one of the higher income
countries. Costa Rica also did well up to 1979 but then ran into serious problems with exports and external debt, even before the
whole region was hit by world recession.

Costa Rica has the most fully democratic political system in Latin
America, one of the least unequal distributions of income, and the
most thorough system of social services. Mexico's dominant political
party has controlled the government since the 1920s; other parties
can compete for local offices and Congress but there has so far been
no hint that the PRI, the Partido Revolucionario Institucionalizado,
intends to risk losing the all-powerful presidency. The system rests
(if that peaceful word is still appropriate) more on mechanisms of
inclusion and moderate reform than on repression. Presidential
styles have varied from highly conservative to reformist, with real
land reform in the 1930s and new efforts to reduce poverty in the
1970s, prior to reversal in the severe economic contraction starting
in 1982.

Colombia is between the other two in terms of political openness.
The political process allows participation from all sides, but the two
traditional center parties have dominated the scene since the mid-
nineteenth century. While reaching out to include wide cross sections of the country they stay close to conservative orientations at
the top. With one cliff-hanging exception in the election of 1970,

TABLE 11.1. Colombia, Costa Rica, and Mexico: Indicators of Per Capita Product and Growth, Manufacturing Production and Exports, Poverty and Inequality, and Child Mortality

	Colombia	Costa Rica	Mexico	Latin America
Per capita product				
As percent U.S., 1974, Kravis-adjusted data	19	24	27	22
GNP 1984, U.S. dollars	1,390	1,190	2,040	1,240[b]
Growth rate, GDP per capita, 1960–1984	2.6	2.1	2.7	2.3
Manufacturing sector				
As percent GDP, 1981	21	20	22	21
Industrial exports as percent total, 1980	20	34	40	22
Social indicators				
Percent families below CEPAL poverty line, around 1970	45	24	34	40
Share of lowest 60 percent in income, around 1970	21	28	20	n.a.
Increase in income of lowest 60 percent, relative to nation[a]	1.4	1.6	0.75	n.a.
Child mortality, per 1,000, 1981	3.5	0.8	3.5	5.5

SOURCES: World Bank, *World Tables*, 3d ed., 1983, for manufacturing sector and for child mortality; IDB, *Economic and Social Progress in Latin America, 1985 Report*, for GDP growth rates. All other information is from tables 2.1, 2.3, and 2.4 above.

[a] Periods for which relative income changes were estimated are 1964–74 for Colombia, 1961–71 for Costa Rica, and 1963–75 for Mexico (shares and source given in table 2.3).

[b] Estimate for Latin American GNP per capita is median value in column 5 of table 2.1.

they have usually managed either to absorb or to freeze out any real challenge from left or populist parties. To keep this up has required the two dominant parties to compromise frequently. That approach has favored moderate reform programs while protecting the core of the traditional social structure. When reformist measures threaten to involve profound changes, as with the land reform program at the end of the 1960s, the cautious side always comes to the fore and quietly shelves whatever is seen to be a danger.[1]

Although Costa Rica's income per capita is the lowest of the three countries, it has had a much lower proportion of families living in poverty. The ECLA measures of poverty in the years around 1970, shown in table 2.4, report 45 percent of Colombian families below the poverty line, 34 percent in Mexico, and 24 percent in Costa Rica. The estimates of families in deep poverty, or "destitution," include 6 percent of Costa Rican families, 12 percent in Mexico, and 18 percent in Colombia. The counterpart of these differences, shown in table 2.3, is that the share of total income going to the lowest 60 percent of income receivers was 28 percent in Costa Rica, versus 22 percent in Mexico and 19 percent in Colombia.

Another difference shown by this ECLA study is that rural poverty, although higher than urban in all countries, is not as disproportionately high in costa Rica as in the other two. The measures of destitution show a near balance between sectors in Costa Rica: 7 percent rural versus 5 percent urban. In Colombia the difference was between 23 percent rural and 14 percent urban, and in Mexico between 18 percent rural and 6 percent urban. The rural sector has not been subject to such great disadvantage in Costa Rica as in the other two countries.

Any reasonably complete explanation of these differences would require exploration of many different variables, some of which are considered in the separate country sections of this chapter, but two structural conditions are surely near the center of the story. One of them is that Costa Rica has been among the leaders of Latin America in extending education to the rural areas, as to the whole population. Colombia had a fairly miserable record of rural education until the 1970s, and Mexico not much better, which meant a continuing handicap to productivity and to mobility for people in the rural sector. The second major structural difference is that Costa Rica has for most of its history had relatively abundant land relative to labor. Although the ownership of land has become highly concentrated, it was not difficult until very recent years for rural families to get farms either by colonizing new areas or by government grants and

[1] Merilee Grindle, *State and Countryside*, pp. 134–59; Bruce Bagley and Mathew Edel, "Popular Mobilization Programs of the National Front: Cooption and Radicalization," pp. 257–84 in R. Albert Berry, Ronald G. Hellman, and Mauricio Solaún, *Politics of Compromise: Coalition Government in Colombia* (New Brunswick: Transactions Books, 1980).

assistance through land reform programs.[2] Access to land made for equality of income and opportunity, and access to education helped people participate more fully in both economic growth and the political system.

These pronounced prior differences in land and labor relationships have been changing for the worse in Costa Rica and for the better in Colombia. In Costa Rica, high rates of population growth combined with gradual exhaustion of further land availability have created more adverse conditions for rural incomes, and may undercut the country's unusual degree of equality. In Colombia the balance has instead been improving. Between 1960 and 1970 the absolute number of workers in agriculture began at last to decrease, slightly in this decade and then more rapidly in the next (see table 3.1). That decrease helped initiate a gradual improvement in the relative income of rural labor, at least up to the interruption of aggregate growth in the world recession of the early 1980s.[3] The change was not revolutionary, but if it is sustained it will amount to a quiet revolution. To raise the real income of the poorest 60 percent of the population at a rate of 4 percent a year for any length of time is more than just trickling down: it was raising up, or beginning to do so. When aggregate growth can be resumed, the new structural balance offers a good chance to make the trend of income distribution less unequal than it was prior to the 1960s.

2. ECONOMIC POLICY AND POLITICAL BALANCE IN COLOMBIA

Colombian development since the 1930s has involved an uneasy balance between democracy and restrictive elite control in the political sphere, and between structuralist and efficiency-oriented management in the economic. For those of us who would like to believe that fully responsive democracy and coherent economic management can coexist in Latin America, the experience has been a mixture of frustration and achievement. At times the society seems heading toward disaster, and at others effective economic policies and a relatively open political system interact in ways that strengthen each other.

[2] Mitchell A. Seligson, *Peasants of Costa Rica and the Rise of Agrarian Capitalism* (Madison: University of Wisconsin Press, 1980).

[3] Urrutia, *Winners and Losers*, gives details of gains through 1979. Berry and Thoumi give measures of the following setback in the recession of 1980–84 in "Colombian Economic Growth."

If one comes to Colombia from Europe or even the United States
it is bound to seem a highly conservative country. Presidential candidates of both of the major parties almost always come from the
same small set of families, churches on Sundays are full of men as
well as women, land ownership is highly concentrated, and the distribution of income has long been among the most unequal in the
region.[4] It must be one of the few countries left in which highly educated members of leading families explain earnestly to the confused foreigner that the rest of the society—the masses, the poor,
the Indios—simply do not have the capacity to understand a modern society; they must be kept firmly in their places if Colombia is to
be a civilized country. Of course, other members of the same families are ready to reply with great conviction to the contrary, and
sometimes to take roles in public life that help to open up the society. Political leadership is still seen as a high calling, not to be left to
hired hands. But it is a tough fight between those who would like to
make the country move and those who would much prefer that it
did not move, except possibly backward.

If one comes to Colombia instead from Ecuador or Peru, the
impression of extreme conservatism is less likely. Not many Latin
American countries have such active entrepreneurial groups or so
many different cities and areas starting to generate their own poles
of growth. Colombia's industrial sector does not consist of one overwhelming capital absorbing most of the country's income but of
multiple center of initiative. It is not a closed society: people from
small towns without family connections can make it up the ladder of
professional opportunities fairly well, either through government
or through business. The long-standing handicap to the poor of restricted access to education has been greatly reduced by the rapid
expansion of primary and secondary education in the 1960s and
1970s. Although the church is very influential and is conservative at
the top, many priests have been social activists. Beginning in the
1960s, ahead of most of the rest of Latin America, the church qui-

[4] On the character of Colombia's economy and society see Berry et al., eds., *Politics
of Compromise*; Lauchlin Currie, *Accelerating Development*, part 2; Robert H. Dix, *Co-
lombia: The Political Dimension of Change* (New Haven: Yale University Press, 1967);
Orlando Fals Borda, *La subversión en Colombia, el cambio social en la historia* (Bogotá:
Ediciones Tercer Mundo, 1967); Pat M. Holt, *Colombia Today—and Tomorrow* (New
York: Praeger, 1964); World Bank, *Colombia: Economic Development and Policy under
Changing Conditions* (Washington, D.C.: World Bank, 1984); and Jonathan Hartlyn,
"Producers Associations, the Political Regime, and Policy Processes in Contemporary
Colombia," *Latin American Research Review* 20, 3 (1985), pp. 111–38.

etly allowed the spread of family planning.[5] On the other hand, forceful efforts to remake the society are consistently stopped. Father Camilo Torres, an outstanding example in the 1960s of a priest from a well-placed family who devoted himself to promoting social change, became too much of a challenge and was firmly blocked, driving him into the guerrilla movement and early death.[6]

The world depression of the 1930s pushed Colombia into rapid economic transformation and then to political crisis. The Liberal president elected in 1934, Alfonso López, made a major break from the country's long tradition of a low-profile, nonpromotional state. He adopted social welfare programs on the lines of the New Deal in the United States and began to promote industrialization with a moderate version of the import substitution package being used in Argentina and Brazil.[7] The industrial sector began to grow more rapidly and the balance of national power to shift toward urban-industrial interests. For a time, this seemed to be a peaceful transition to a more modern society. But then reaction hit hard and the country's political system broke down.

Most interpretations of the breakdown of the 1940s emphasize long-standing conflict between the country's two traditional parties as the central factor.[8] That conflict was clearly crucial, but to consider it as the whole story would unduly minimize the economic tensions of this period. Rivalries between Conservatives and Liberals had included a century of intermittent violence at the local level over land, control of the police, and patronage. With the new economic activism of the Liberals at the national level in the 1930s, and the growth of urban interests dependent on governmental decisions, the stakes at issue in winning national elections were greatly

[5] Alexander Wilde, "The Contemporary Church: The Political and the Pastoral," and William Paul McGreevy, "Population Policy Under the National Front," chapters 7 and 14 in Berry et al., Politics of Compromise.

[6] Fals Borda, La subversión, ch. 8, summarizes the ideas of Father Torres prior to his joining the guerrillas. See also W. Broderick, Camilo Torres: A Biography of the Priest-Guerrillero (Garden City, N.Y.: Doubleday, 1975); Dawn Fogel Deaton, "The Failure of Utopia: Camilo Torres Restrepo and the United Front," paper presented at meeting of the Latin American Studies Association, Albuquerque, New Mexico (April 1985); and Wilde, "The Contemporary Church," pp. 215–20.

[7] Carlos Díaz Alejandro, "Latin America in the 1930s."

[8] Monseñor German Guzmán, Orlando Fals Borda, and Eduardo Umana Luna, La violencia en Colombia, vol. 1 (Bogotá: Ediciones Tercer Mundo, 1962); Mauricio Solaún, "Colombian Politics: Historical Characteristics and Problems," in Berry et al., Politics of Compromise; Paul Oquist, Violence, Conflict, and Politics in Colombia (New York: Academic Press, 1980); James D. Henderson, When Colombia Bled: A History of the Violence in Tolima (University, Ala.: Alabama University Press, 1985).

raised. The conflicts were not the same as the urban versus rural confrontation in Argentina at the time; they were more like those in the United States over the New Deal. The Conservatives were not opposed to industrialization and urbanization but wanted the changes to be on their terms. That included trying to check labor activism, to fight what they considered to be a socialistic bent in the Liberals, to protect the special relationships between the government and the church, to regain control of local political machinery, and to make sure that regions and interest groups traditionally associated with their party got most of the breaks.

The tensions of the period split the Liberal party in two, between its safe-and-sane established leadership and an antisystem reformer, Jorge Eliécer Gaitán. Gaitán brought into the center of the stage a previously irrelevant force: the mass of the people. Their votes had always counted but only through the choices offered to them by the restricted circle of traditional leaders. Gaitán allied with them against that kind of elite control through the two parties: "hunger is neither Liberal nor Conservative."[9] His economic and social ideas were on the non-Marxist left, defined more clearly by opposition to the existing form of social control than by explicit programs. That is practically a definition of populism, and it often means futility when power can be achieved. In his case, the imaginative intelligence and sympathy with the poor that show through his public statements make one wonder if somehow, in this early stage of postwar populism, generous objectives might have been effectively implemented. But no one will ever know. He became so enormously popular that he was recognized by all sides as the likely winner of the presidential election scheduled for 1950, but he was assassinated before he could get the chance to try.[10]

[9] Gaitán's appeal to the mass of the people across party lines is vividly recalled in the interviews with both followers and enemies collected by Arturo Alape, *El Bogotazo: Memorias del Olvido* (Havana: Casa de las Américas, 1983), quotation from p. 49. Their views about his fundamental ideas and likely social-economic policies often conflict: see especially pp. 63–64, 87–92, and 129–38. Herbert Braun, *The Assassination of Gaitán: Public Life and Urban Violence in Colombia* (Madison: University of Wisconsin Press, 1985), gives a more analytical, and equally fascinating, interpretation of of Gaitán's ideas and impact on Colombia.

[10] No organized plot behind Gaitán's murder has ever been established. Since the government and the leaders of the society considered him a dangerous threat, and he had also been fiercely opposed by the Colombian Communist party in the election of 1946, no one lacked for plausible themes about guilty parties. Given the intensity of the emotions he awakened, it is possible that the killing was another example of the individual violence that has struck political leaders in so many countries in the

Gaitán's murder touched off one of the most dramatic explosions of mass fury in Latin American history, the *Bogotazo* of 1948. The center of Bogotá was to a great extent destroyed, with government offices and churches, and the main Conservative newspaper, particular points of attack. In the countryside, supporters of Gaitán attacked Conservatives and villages linked to the party, and then the wave of vengeance swung right back at the Liberals. Rioting in the cities was soon stopped, but violence in the countryside intensified as displaced and vengeful groups turned into guerrilla bands: some of them Liberals trying to protect themselves, some pure bandits thriving on the collapse of public order, and some radical groups committed to fighting the whole existing social system.

As the massacres in the countryside continued into the 1950s, often carried out by politicized police, many Conservatives joined the opposition in the conviction that the extraordinarily vindictive president should be forced to resign. The army came to agree too: it was more of a response to common despair than a simple military coup when General Gustavo Rojas Pinilla took power in 1953. He succeeded quickly in negotiating an end to the violence in those areas where it involved straight party conflict. But with the radical guerrilla groups Rojas's method was to step up military attack rather than negotiate. No lasting peace was achieved then or has been since. Relative quiet in the second half of the 1960s might be attributed in part to a fairly active program of land reform in this period. But the land reform was cut off in the early 1970s, and that coincided with a disputed election which stimulated an important new guerrilla group. The violence worsened again and was not resolved by intensified military repression under the administration of 1978–1982. The next president, Belisario Betancur, made the most serious effort so far to achieve peace through a more conciliatory approach but that promising attempt was only partially successful.[11]

In his four years as a military ruler, Rojas made considerable ef-

---

modern period. Both Alape, *El Bogotazo*, and Braun, *The Assassination*, bring out the ambiguities well.

[11] President Betancur demonstrated a strong personal committment to stopping the violence and the intensified repression of 1978–82. He managed to negotiate a truce and general amnesty, still holding in 1986 for the largest guerrilla group (the FARC), but rejected by other groups and frequently violated by the army as well. Bruce Bagley brings out the close connections between Betancur's efforts to negotiate peace in Central American through the Contadora process and his peace initiatives inside Colombia: "Colombian Foreign Policy in the 1980s: The Search for Leverage," *Journal of InterAmerican Studies and World Affairs* 27 (Fall 1985).

fort to develop social institutions favorable for the urban poor, and he had for a time the good luck of rising coffee export prices to stimulate the economy. Both of these factors helped him to develop considerable popular support. At the same time, his arbitrary and sometimes ruthless repression of opposition, including allowing the shooting of student demonstrators in Bogotá and closing opposition newspapers, united most of the middle and upper classes against him. Their opposition drove the two parties into a contract—rare for Latin America but consistent with prior Colombian experiences—to limit their own efforts at mutual destruction. Their leaders agreed to form a National Front intended to depose Rojas and to share the government for sixteen years, with alternating presidents and equal division of congressional seats, administrative offices, and the judiciary.[12] With the two parties in agreement it proved to be easy to displace Rojas and to install the National Front government in 1958. The political compact meant a restricted kind of democracy, with limited scope for choices independent of the traditional party leaderships, but also a rejection of recourse to force. For economic development, it meant that programs had to be negotiated in ways acceptable to all the main interests involved: extreme steps in any direction were fairly well ruled out.[13]

Economic policy through all this turmoil alternated between periods of coherence and the contrary, with intervals of just plain drifting. Even in the worst days of the violence of the late 1940s the Conservative government tried to pursue industrialization. When it turned to the World Bank as a new source of possible financing the Bank sent down its very first comprehensive country mission, organized by Lauchlin Currie. The mission recommended a broad program of economic and social projects, in a style adopted by the Bank much later but not acceptable in 1949: the social proposals were given short shrift. But the economic projects got under way on a large scale and "Colombia became a favorite country of the Bank

[12] Alexander Wilde, "Conversations among Gentlemen: Oligarchic Democracy in Colombia," ch. 2 in Juan J. Linz and Alfred Stepan, eds., *The Breakdown of Democratic Regimes: Latin America* (Baltimore: Johns Hopkins University Press, 1978); Jonathan Hartlyn, "Military Governments and the Transition to Civilian Rule: The Colombian Experience of 1957–1958," *Journal of InterAmerican Studies and World Affairs* 26 (May 1984), pp. 245–81.

[13] Edgar Reveíz and María José Pérez, "Colombia: Moderate Economic Growth, Political Stability, and Social Welfare," in Hartlyn and Morley, eds., *Latin American Political Economy*, ch. 10, pp. 265–91.

throughout the following decades."[14] Beyond these particular projects, Currie had a special impact of his own. Invited to return to Colombia as a personal adviser to the president for development issues, he encouraged choices going in a different direction from the kind of import substitution being practiced in Argentina and Brazil. His advice and Colombian policy leaned toward negotiation among private interest groups and the use of price incentives rather than extensive government controls. Protection was kept far below the levels in Argentina, Brazil, and Chile (see table 4.3). To cope with continuing foreign exchange constraints, Colombia used devaluation to stimulate exports rather than intensify import controls.[15] With more attention to the dangers of excessive monetary expansion, as well as restraint on degrees of protection, the rate of inflation was held much below those in Brazil and the Southern Cone.

This character of Colombia's economic strategy at the end of the 1940s served as something of a forerunner of the style adopted more definitively from 1967. It is significant in two key respects. One is that it provided a way to stimulate industrialization and modernization, to break away from the prior structure of production and from reliance on export agriculture, without disdain for efficiency considerations. The second is that it relied on the private sector and lacked social objectives. Although it was an activist approach it was not in any sense egalitarian. That socially conservative character was a natural result of the goals of the Colombian government and of the World Bank at the time, but not an inherent characteristic of the efficiency-oriented approach to industrialization. When Colombia returned to an effective strategy of economic growth from 1967, it had many of the efficiency characteristics of the earlier version but they proved to be consistent with greater attempts to promote employment, with more progressive taxation and government expenditure patterns, and with at least modest steps toward more direct social programs.

The National Front government adopted a land reform program at the beginning of the 1960s, but as discussed in chapter 6 this proved to be an example of aborted reformism, brought to an end in 1973 after it threatened to get out of hand. A reform effort with more sustained effect began in 1965, with gradual movement to-

[14] Lauchlin B. Currie, *The Role of Economic Advisers in Developing Countries* (Westport, Ct.: Greenwood Press, 1981), pp. 59–60.

[15] Sheahan, "Imports, Investment, and Growth—Colombia," in Gustav F. Papanek, ed., *Development Policy—Theory and Practice* (Cambridge: Harvard University Press, 1968), pp. 93–114.

ward a more progressive tax system. The first step was a multiple-rate sales tax, with a high rate for commodities thought to be more important for wealthier groups. This was introduced as a means to reduce inequality and to restrain luxury consumption, though Richard Bird's analysis makes clear that it was not well designed for either purpose.[16] That could be seen as deliberate, to keep down any real impact, but it proved to be only the first in a series of tax changes, repeatedly undermined and then tightened up again.[17] Comparison with Mexico as of the mid-1970s brings out the differences possible by such reform: taxes then took 17 percent of the income of low-income groups in Colombia but 40 percent in Mexico; for high-income groups they took 30 percent in Colombia but only 15 percent in Mexico.[18] Mexico too, after tougher resistance discussed in section 4 below, managed to adopt a significant tax reform at the end of the 1970s. It is not that particular countries deserve praise or blame but rather that this highly important variable of economic policy can be redirected, within a given economic system, from an instrument fortifying inequality into one promoting equality.

Changes toward more progressive taxation were accompanied by a pattern of public expenditure for education and health that was also relatively favorable for lower income groups. Public subsidies for education and health per household as of 1974 were equal to nearly 25 percent of private family income for the poorest quintile, compared to less than 3 percent for the highest quintile.[19] The distribution of educational enrollments remained very unequal at the university level—even more unequal than the distribution of income—but as compared to a decade earlier, enrollments had become much more equal among income groups for both primary and secondary education.

The administration of Carlos Lleras Restrepo adopted in 1967 a key change in economic strategy, the use of continuing small devaluations to keep up incentives for exports without aggravating infla-

[16] Bird, *Taxation and Development: Lessons from Colombian Experience* (Cambridge: Harvard University Press, 1970).

[17] Malcolm Gillis and Charles E. McLure, Jr., "The 1974 Colombian Tax Reform and Income Distribution," pp. 47–68 in R. Albert Berry and Ronald Soligo, eds., *Economic Policy and Income Distribution in Colombia* (Boulder: Westview Press, 1980); World Bank, *Colombia*, pp. 87–101.

[18] Jimenez, "Public Subsidization of Education," table 5, p. 116.

[19] Marcelo Selowsky, *Who Benefits From Government Expenditures? A Case Study of Colombia* (New York: Oxford University Press for the World Bank, 1979), table 1.6, p. 23.

tion. Exports other than coffee and oil responded well, as they systematically do when incentives improve.[20] For exports of manufactures considered separately, the growth rate in the period 1971–78 was double that of Latin America as a whole if expressed in terms of a volume indicator (10.6 percent a year compared to 5.0 for Latin America), and about 60 percent higher if measured in terms of foreign exchange earnings. Manufacturing exports as a share of value added in manufacturing increased from practically nothing in 1960 to 22.4 percent by 1977.[21]

The change in emphasis from protected industry selling in the home market toward export industry was directly helpful for employment: per unit of value added at international prices, the industries from which the exports came in this period generated approximately 63 percent more employment than the set of import substitution industries.[22] The rate of growth of factory employment increased from slightly below 3 percent a year in the preceding five years to more than 6 percent a year from 1967 to 1978.[23]

Stimulus to industrial employment from increasing exports of manufactured goods, and the broader effect of the country's general shift toward a more labor-intensive structure of production, were further supported in 1971–74 by financial innovation promoting greater employment in construction. A new method of financing for housing construction, pioneered by Lauchlin Currie, released a striking burst of construction activity.[24] The whole pat-

[20] Díaz Alejandro, *Foreign Trade Regimes*, pp. 63–71; Miguel Urrutia, "Experience with the Crawling Peg in Colombia," pp. 207–20 in John Williamson, ed., *Exchange Rate Rules* (New York: St. Martin's, 1981); Sebastian Edwards, "The Exchange Rate and Noncoffee Exports," appendix B in Vinod Thomas et al., *Linking Macroeconomic and Agricultural Policies for Adjustment With Growth: The Colombian Experience* (Baltimore: Johns Hopkins University Press for the World Bank, 1985).

[21] Inter-American Development Bank, *Economic and Social Progress in Latin America, 1982 Report* (Washington, D.C.: IDB, 1982), pp. 112 and 122.

[22] Francisco E. Thoumi, "International Trade Strategies, Employment, and Income Distribution in Colombia," in Anne C. Krueger, ed., *Trade and Employment in Developing Countries* (Chicago: Chicago University Press for the National Bureau of Economic Research, 1981), table 4.7, p. 154.

[23] Berry, ed., *Industrialization in Colombia*, table 2.20, p. 68. Berry doubts that the change toward export promotion was the main factor in improvement of employment conditions: he gives more credit to a concurrent, independent, "resurgent growth of small and medium industry with greater labor intensity than large industry" (pp. 51–59 and 67–68, quotation from p. 68).

[24] Colombia, National Planning Department, *Guidelines for a New Strategy* (Bogotá: Departamento Nacional de Planeación, 1972); Corporación para el Fomento de Investigaciones Económicas, *Controversias sobre el plan de desarrollo* (Bogotá: CORP,

tern of wages began to change in this period, in ways favorable to the lowest income workers. The new employment openings helped to speed up movement out of agriculture and to pull up real wages in that sector, while also increasing relative wages for unorganized groups at the bottom of the urban distribution.[25]

In economic development, no battle is ever over. Successful promotion of industrial exports after 1967 by keeping the value of foreign exchange from falling behind domestic inflation began to weaken after 1976 as devaluations failed to keep up with the excess of Colombian over external inflation. This change of a crucial ingredient in the country's growth strategy might have been due in part to a change of policy emphasis, toward more concern with inflation, or to the effect of a singularly perverse market factor: illegal earnings of dollars from drug exports to the United States helped swell the supply of foreign exchange and gave the government a difficult problem trying to keep the peso from rising in real terms. Drugs began to undercut development.[26]

The improvement in real income for lower-income groups in the 1970s, achieved by combining employment-creating policies with a fairly rapid rate of growth, came into serious question at the end of the decade. GDP per capita had increased 39 percent between 1970 and 1980, but it fell one percent in the next four years as the world recession hit export earnings.[27] Colombia's relative restraint in borrowing during the 1970s allowed it to escape the debt crisis that forced more drastic reductions in so many Latin American countries: the 1980–84 decrease in GNP per capita was one of the lowest in the region. Still, the interruption of growth almost surely reversed much of the progress made in reducing poverty.

The persisting Colombian mixture of cautious reform with promotional economic strategy suggests a likelihood of renewed success in reducing poverty when aggregate growth can be resumed, though the basic approach could of course be changed either for the better or for the worse. It very nearly took a turn for the worse in the disputed election of 1970: an antisystem candidate favoring a

1972); Currie, *Economic Advisers*, ch. 4; Sheahan, "Aspects of Planning and Development in Colombia," University of Texas, Institute of Latin American Studies, Technical Papers series no. 10 (1977).

[25] Urrutia, *Winners and Losers*, especially table 2, p. 15.

[26] Francisco Thoumi, "Some Implications of the Growth of the Underground Economy in Colombia," paper presented at the meetings of the Latin American Studies Association, Boston, October 1986.

[27] IDB, *1985 Report*, p. 388.

costly kind of populism came close to winning the presidency. That testing point deserves careful consideration both by anyone who believes in the value of an open political system and by those who believe that almost anything would be preferable to Colombia's version of technical management under elite control.

The challenge to the country's narrow circle of political leadership in 1970 came from a new coalition, the Alianza Nacional Popular (ANAPO). Its leader was none other than Rojas Pinilla, back after temporary exile. With his political rights restored in 1967 he proved able to bring together a good deal of the support from lower income groups he had established when in power. Echoes of Perón are striking in many ways, though Rojas never gained much support from organized urban labor: his backing came from small business, sales and clerical workers, part of the military, and the slum areas of the cities.[28] He represented the have-nots against the haves. And Colombia has a great many have-nots. The National Front agreement did not stop him from running, but ANAPO was treated to nearly complete silence by the leading newspapers and all the established communications media, and was scorned for lack of a program by those who did not just laugh at it. It is true that the coalition ran on dissatisfaction rather than an economic program. A leading campaign theme was that Rojas would return food prices to the level of the 1950s, reversing all the inflationary consequences of industrialization. He appealed to tradition, for closer ties between the state and the Catholic Church, against technical-managerial economic policies, and against the modern world in general. He was not *for* any particular producer interest, though he expressed "lesser hostility to the landed than to the industrial elite."[29]

With little financing and none of the political machinery of the established parties, Rojas came so close to winning the election that many Colombians thought a fully honest count of the vote would have made him president. Instead, the Conservative candidate, supported in principle by both traditional parties, was declared elected. One of the main present guerrilla groups, the M-19, began as a protest against this outcome. But by the next election four years later, the tide had turned and ANAPO ran far behind. That decrease in the appeal of the coalition has many possible explanations: the period of alternating candidates under the National Front had ex-

[28] Robert H. Dix, "Political Oppositions under the National Front," in Berry et al., *Politics of Compromise*, pp. 131–79.
[29] Ibid., p. 160.

pired so both of the traditional parties could again run their own candidates; replacement of Rojas Pinilla by his daughter as the ANAPO candidate may have weakened support even though she was herself a dramatically powerful candidate; and at least some of the earlier participants in the coalition may well have given up on the electoral process.[30] Although these political considerations may have been dominant, an economic factor was important too: the continuing high rate of growth of employment from 1967 on through the 1971–74 development plan must have built support for the existing path.

The ANAPO experience left a troublesome question about the relationships between popular preferences and economic strategy. If Rojas's campaign themes had been followed through in practice they would have included social reform projects, price controls on food, a turn away from promotion of industrial exports, and more government spending without taxes to finance it. They could have been helpful to the poor if they did not lead to economic break-down, but the signs of a consistently unsuccessful approach were clear. The poor could have lost badly if national policies had turned incoherent. Colombian peasants probably would have sunk into deeper poverty, much as the peasants of Peru did in the 1970s, in-stead of gaining real income through this decade. An open political process can certainly lead to costly choices.

Popular reforms need not mean chaos: if they are coherently re-lated to objective possibilities they can improve the operation of the economy as well as meet specific social objectives. Gaitán might have been able to work out a successful kind of populism, but Rojas's vi-sion was too negative to promise any real help. When the particular kind of populism in question seems so likely to have high costs, and also likely to win elections, the dilemma is real. The best defense against becoming caught between economic disintegration and repression may be the actual course in Colombia after 1967: stim-ulate employment and growth of incomes of the poor. If the system brings benefits to more people it will lead more of them to support it. If the majority still votes for a regime likely to pursue hopeless economic policies the cost is bound to be high but not nearly as high as resort to repression.

Some of the social scientists who know Colombia best insist that it should not be considered a democracy because a relatively stable group of national leaders retains control and manages to prevent

[30] Ibid., p. 167.

kinds of change they consider dangerous.[31] That certainly is a possible interpretation, though continued domination of the political scene by the two traditional parties has been a far cry from rule through repression in the Southern Cone sense. The means of control do not seem greatly different from those common in the Northern industrialized countries. Traditional leaders maintain their positions within the two parties through patronage and personal style, and the two parties occupy most of the political space through well-organized local machinery, by allowing limited but real options for changes in response to public preferences, and through compromises where necessary to keep conflicting interests within the party. The main ingredients of the system on the economic side have been gains in employment opportunities and access to education, reduction of the number of people in poverty in the rural sector, and a background context of fair success in economic growth. If all that were to deteriorate it is possible that outsiders could challenge the system through the electoral process, and also possible that the conservative side would harden and block such a development by repression. For better or worse, reasonably good economic policies over nearly two decades have done a lot to avoid sharpening the tensions.

The degree of inequality in Colombia is still exceptionally high, as is the strength of resistance to radical social reform. Another side is important to see as well: the reality of gains in education, structural change favorable for reduction of rural poverty, lessened dependence on primary exports, creation of a more progressive tax system, and ability to pull back from signs of deepening repression. Satisfaction with the positive side can be dangerous: it can verge toward acceptance of increased political repression if necessary to keep the system intact, quiet approval of abandoning reforms when they threaten real change, and the millions of other compromises that could turn an imperfect society into a truly reactionary one. But a strongly negative view can go wrong too: it can obscure the promising fact that, despite powerful resistance to deliberate social change, fairly good economic management combined with moderate reforms has done a good deal in the last quarter century to improve living conditions for the majority of the Colombian people. No one who cares about inequality should be in any sense satisfied

[31] Bruce Bagley, "Colombia: National Front and Economic Development," in Robert Wesson, ed., *Politics, Policies, and Economic Development in Latin America* (Stanford: Hoover Institution Press, 1984), pp. 124–60; Bagley, Thoumi, and Tokatlian, eds., *State and Society in Contemporary Colombia.*

with the results so far; no one who cares about reducing poverty and avoiding mass repression should fail to see that by careful economic management a lot can be done, has been done, and is worth working on to improve.

3. Costa Rica: Two Great Assets and Many Problems

The two great assets of Costa Rica are its open political system and its relatively inclusive society, with much less inequality than Colombia, Mexico, or most of Latin America. Shared economic growth has favored what is for the region a nearly unmatchable climate of confidence that the society is worth holding together. But the country's very real problems underline the fact that it is after all part of Central America, still considerably dependent on exports of bananas and coffee, weighed down by heavy foreign debt, and caught under intense pressures by the conflict between the United States and its immediate neighbor to the north, Nicaragua. Costa Rica's economy is in serious trouble and its democracy under strain. But it has so far been a hopeful contrast to the rest of the region, something of a promise of possible escape from the nightmares more common to the rest of Central America.

The particular problems of most direct concern here center on the effort to reconcile a social welfare state in a very small country with an economic system sufficiently productive to keep improving the standard of living. Costa Rican economic management and performance were exceptionally successful for a long time, but strains of transition to industrialization culminated at the end of the 1970s in a breakdown of ability to respond to current problems. For a full four years a combination of inaction with seriously damaging policies fed into accelerating inflation and external deficits, falling production and employment, and increasing social conflict. Participatory democracy can make it difficult to cope with specific problems, when conflicting interests block almost any action at all. That loss of control demonstrated the need to find a new consensus on the economic role of the state, welfare programs, and relationships to the world economy.

Costa Rica's relatively open egalitarian characteristics trace back in part to the early colonial period. Absence of significant gold or silver deposits dampened the area's attraction for Spanish settlers, and the effects of European-brought diseases so decimated the Indian population that labor was exceptionally difficult to find for work on large estates; the colonists who did come had to do their own farming in order to survive.[32] The country was thinly populated for a long time, with land readily available. It was not until well into the nineteenth century that any large-scale plantation agriculture began to develop. Coffee production for export then began to concentrate ownership of land in the main settled area, the central highlands, and to pull people into hired labor. That common process had more positive implications in Costa Rica than in the rest of the region. Wages were driven up by the need to draw scarce labor into the plantations, and more land remained available outside the settled area. "Peasants found that because of a scarcity of manpower they could sell their labor for a high price to coffee plantation owners. Those who chose to reject this alternative could do so only because they had another, farming the virgin farmlands off the meseta."[33]

Coffee production and exports were for the most part run by Costa Ricans, in contrast to the subsequent enclave-style development of banana exports by the United Fruit Company. Both kinds of export activities raised wage earnings as well as national income, and both raised problems of political control. Relationships with the United Fruit Company were never easy, though they never degenerated to the character of those in Guatemala, where for many years the company and the dictator jointly exploited the country. The more important political influence in Costa Rica came from the "coffee barons," who dominated choices of presidents and policies most of the time until the 1930s. Their dominance was exercised in classic nineteenth-century liberal style: they emphasized private property with protection of individuals from arbitrary government, nationwide education, and an orientation toward free trade. That kind of liberalism helped nourish an open society, but the economic side of it also acted to discourage industrialization.[34]

Plantation agriculture gradually built up concentrated land ownership, and the basic balance in Costa Rican agriculture changed greatly as rapid population growth in the modern period kept the rural labor force increasing without adequate access to new land. Costa Rica's rural labor force is now predominantly landless, though a significant fraction has become squatters growing crops il-

[32] Seligson, *Peasants of Costa Rica*, ch. 1; Charles D. Ameringer, *Democracy in Costa Rica* (New York and Stanford: Praeger and Hoover Institution Press, 1982), ch. 2.
[33] Seligson, *Peasants of Costa Rica*, p. 154.
[34] Rodolfo Cerdas Cruz, *La crisis de la democracia liberal en Costa Rica* (San José: Editorial Universitaria Centroamericana, 1972), pp. 37–85.

legally on others' land.[35] Still, the rural sector keeps getting active government attention through public education and other social services, as well as technical assistance and modest land reform programs. The contrast to Guatemala or El Salvador is extreme, and even compared to Colombia and Mexico the differences are striking. What keeps this process of rural-urban sharing so strong?

The answer might be that a democratic government favors such sharing, and would anywhere else where the rural population becomes educated and aware, because any party that pays attention to rural welfare will gain political support. On that view, the nearly universal "urban bias" in developing countries might be mainly a matter of the common absence of democracy in these countries.[36] But in Latin America even those countries that have had fairly open political systems, such as Colombia and Peru, have failed to do much to promote social investment in the rural areas and have had until very recently weak records of providing education for the rural poor. That points toward an alternative explanation of the relative absence of urban bias in Costa Rica: beyond the role of a democratic political system, it may rest on willingness of the urban society to accept the rural population as full-fledged fellow citizens because the great majority are of European descent and not Indian.[37] Costa Rican society has been less inequitable than those of the Andean countries and Mexico, and it functions better, partly because it has been much less affected by racial bias.

Although Costa Rican democracy was subject for a long time to disproportionate influence from coffee landowner-exporters, they kept the political system open and did not block a shift toward more urban and popular political strength in the 1930s. The reformist government elected in 1940 liberalized labor legislation, introduced a progressive income tax, and initiated a modern system of social welfare programs. But that move toward a welfare state was followed by strains somewhat similar to those in Colombia at the same stage and time. Opposition from the conservative side became vir-

[35] Seligson, *Peasants of Costa Rica*, pp. 167–69.

[36] Michael Lipton brought everyone's attention to the pervasive bias in developing countries toward urban interests at the expense of rural in *Why People Stay Poor: Urban Bias in World Development* (Cambridge: Harvard University Press, 1978). Dudley Seers, "Urban Bias—Seers versus Lipton," Institute of Development Studies at the University of Sussex, Discussion Paper 116 (1977), brings out with reference to South Africa a point relevant to explaining weak rural education in Latin America outside of Costa Rica and the Southern Cone: what looks like generalized bias against rural interests may in some cases be essentially bias against the race in the rural areas.

[37] Seligson, *Peasants of Costa Rica*, ch. 7, esp. p. 165.

ulent, fiercely so after the government accepted cooperation from the Costa Rican Communist Party, renamed the Vanguardia Popular. The elections of 1944 were marked by a great deal of violence and claims of fraud; the governing coalition apparently won, but the election process itself became seriously suspect. One of the opposition leaders, José Figueras, concluded that the governing group would never give up office peacefully, and he began shortly after that election to organize a movement to turn it out by force.[38]

The next four years were marked by increasing tension, and the election of 1948 by violent disputes over alleged fraud. The Electoral Commission ruled that the opposition candidate had won, after giving rise to considerable doubt about their own objectivity. The governing coalition then validated Figueras's suspicions: they refused to accept the decision and annulled the election. Figueras immediately put his military force into action. They proved able to defeat the poorly organized Costa Rican army in a series of small-scale but bloody battles. As the communists organized a militia to defend San José, and a Nicaraguan force entered the country to add menace on that side, the president decided to stop the fighting and signed a peace treaty allowing Figueras's group to take power. In power, they proved vengeful toward the communists, exiling or imprisoning many of them, but they did not try to reverse the preceding government's social policies. They truncated political participation by outlawing the Vanguardia Popular (and in principle any other party considered to be antidemocratic), but at the same time they fortified the election process by creating what is perhaps still one of the world's strongest systems of protection for open elections. They also solidified the social reform measures of the preceding government, nationalized the banks, and abolished the army. The next elected government was more conservative but confirmed these changes and set Costa Rica more firmly than ever on the track of a modern welfare state.[39]

Welfare states work well if production can be increased steadily but not if it cannot. Especially in a small country, rising production requires rising imports and exports to pay for them. Costa Rica has had trouble on this latter side. Its long dependence on primary ex-

[38] John Patrick Bell, *Crisis in Costa Rica: The 1948 Revolution* (Austin: University of Texas, 1971).

[39] Ibid.; Robert Rinehart, ch. 1, "Historical Setting," pp. 3-70, in Harold D. Nelson, ed., *Costa Rica: A Country Study* (Washington: Foreign Areas Studies, American University, 1984), pp. 38–52; Ralph Lee Woodward, Jr., *Central America: A Nation Divided* (New York: Oxford University Press, 2d ed., 1985), pp. 224–29.

ports remained practically unchanged as of 1960, when they were
still 95 percent of total exports. Starting in the 1950s, the country
attempted much the same kind of import-substituting industrialization as everyone else, though the continued influence of the agricultural exporters kept the degree of protection and subsidies to
industry well below the heights then effective in Argentina and Brazil. Restraint on the degree of protection might also be attributed in
part to a realization on all sides that such a small country cannot go
very far toward a diversified industrial structure limited to the domestic market. With Costa Rica's size and income level as of the
1950s, few industries limited to that market could achieve reasonable economies of scale; those new industries that did try required
high protection to cover high costs, which means that they could not
contribute much of anything to real income of the country.

A partial solution to the handicap of small size was opened up by
creation of the Central American Common Market in 1960, allowing much greater regional trade behind common external tariffs.
Regional trade favored Costa Rican industrial exports because its
industrial base was slightly more developed than those of the other
members and especially because its better educated labor force and
deserved reputation for greater social peace drew in new foreign investment.[40] For many Costa Ricans, that foreign role—consisting for
the most part of investments by U.S.-owned multinations—was not
so much a solution to the needs of industrialization as a new problem in itself. Costa Rican industrialists scarcely participated in the
new export trade at all; the country's industrial sector rapidly
changed to one divided between local small-scale industry and export-oriented, large-scale, foreign-owned corporations.[41]

Criticism of this foreign-led kind of industrialization involved all
the issues discussed in chapter 5 above, and a certain amount of
wishful thinking. Costa Rica would have been better off if its own
industrialists had shown or quickly learned the capacities needed to
occupy the terrain effectively before the U.S. firms moved in. That
is certainly an understandable wish, but they did not do so. The next
best position preferred by some, both economists and local firms,
was to refuse participation in the Common Market: to stay with an
individually protected domestic market, with little or no foreign in-

[40] William R. Cline and Enrique Delgado, eds., *Economic Integration in Central America* (Washington, D.C.: Brookings, 1978); Victor Bulmer-Thomas, "Trade Structure
and Linkages in Costa Rica: An Input-Output Approach," *Journal of Development Economics* 5 (March 1978).
[41] Cerdas Cruz, *La Crisis*, pp. 87–131.

vestment. The problem with this approach, though perfectly feasible if the nation were willing to forgo growth of income, is the near-certainty that it would preclude rising living standards.

The alternative of participation in the Common Market helped considerably in the 1960s by widening the market area for Costa Rican industry. But it could not provide a longer-run solution because all the member countries combined still did not constitute a market large enough for efficient diversification of industry, none had any significant capital goods production, and all continued to depend on primary exports in trade with the outside world. Regional trade was severely disrupted after 1968 by internal conflicts, but even if they had not arisen the whole group remained dependent on external demand for a few dominant primary exports. In any world recession they were bound to be forced into collective contraction, as they were at the end of the 1970s.

What is the solution, if any? It surely must be based on development of capacity to export outside the region both industrial products and newer primary products with better long-term market prospects. In a small country, industrial exports require a relatively high degree of concentration on the most efficient industries, as opposed to broad diversification behind protection. With Costa Rica's well-educated and skilled labor force, that should mean modern technologically oriented industries rather than old-style heavy industry. It could well include some lines of capital equipment. The process need not, and should not, squeeze out additions to employment and to foreign exchange earnings from pursuing new primary exports as well. The target cannot be self-sufficiency, or growth of income may be next to impossible.

If any small developing country ever united the basic conditions necessary for effective industrial competition, in terms of an educated labor force and a relatively flexible society, Costa Rica does. But it certainly did not look that way at the end of the 1970s. The Central American Common Market was greatly weakened by political conflicts after 1968, and industrial exports within the region slowed down. The next blow was the rise of oil import prices in 1973–74. Like Brazil, Costa Rica tried to ride out the problem without slowing down the growth of domestic demand. External deficits began to mount. So did domestic budget deficits as the country pushed ahead with social welfare programs and then added a new drive for public investment in the industrial sector. With rising deficits, the government tried to avoid either domestic restraint or devaluation by increased external borrowing, which was easy at first because of the country's prior record of stability. This unbalanced system was pushed over the brink by a steep fall in coffee prices in 1978. That blow uncovered a deep division within the country blocking any adequate answer.

Domestic conflicts over economic strategy centered on the division between those interests favoring continued government promotion and management of the economy, behind considerable protection, and those export and financial interests in favor of moving back toward a more open economy with less active government. This second side gained strength in the course of the 1970s because growing government deficits, and the expansion of state investment, were undermining stability and were threatening to the private sector. Costa Rica thus ran into a relatively mild version of much the same kind of conflict that threw so many other Latin American countries into reaction and repression at similar stages. It did not look like a mild version at the time.

Proponents of a more open economy, with less active government, won the election of 1978. The new administration, faced with the foreign exchange crisis provoked by falling prices of coffee exports, turned to a friendly IMF for emergency credit. The IMF agreed to help in return for much the kinds of policy changes the government wanted to introduce anyway: elimination of subsidized credit for favored sectors, ending control of interest rates to allow them to be determined by market forces, reduction of public sector spending, and reductions in tariff protection.[42] The government and the IMF agreed, but it proved to be nearly impossible to get the country itself to agree. The attempt to eliminate subsidized credit brought both agricultural producers and industrialists into battle, a token reduction of tariffs on consumer goods frightened the industrial sector to the core, and public sector employees—who constituted fully a fifth of the whole labor force—dug in against retrenchment of government programs. The president backed off from confrontation, and within a short period Costa Rica had defaulted on all its commitments to the IMF.[43]

For the next four years, economic policy vacillated between contradictory alternatives. The government first refused to consider devaluation, despite rapidly widening external deficits, then sud-

[42] Eugenio Rivera Urrutia, *El Fondo Monetario Internaciónal y Costa Rica*.

[43] Ibid.; Juan Manuel Villasuso, "Foreign Debt and Economic Development"; Juan Diego Trejos, "Costa Rica: Crisis económica y política estatal 1978–1984," Florida International University, Latin American and Caribbean Center, Occasional Paper no. 11 (May 1985).

denly allowed the exchange rate to float. In conditions of near-total uncertainty about what would happen next, the value of the currency plunged. From the end of 1980 to the end of 1982 the price of foreign exchange rose 4.5 times. Inflation broke loose to a degree never before seen in modern Costa Rica. External credit was almost completely shut off. GNP per capita fell 16 percent between 1980 and 1982.[44] By the time the next government came into office, in April 1982, conditions were so bad that its program met little resistance. That program went in exactly the right direction: it was a promotional rather than a contractionary package.

Protection was maintained, and so were differential interest rates, as well as a system of multiple exchange rates. But taxes were increased and monetary restraint tightened. Government spending was cut back by negotiated reduction of real wages for public sector employees, rather than by eliminating programs or firing workers.[45] The government gave priority to imports of inputs for production, refusing to use foreign exchange to resume debt repayments. With these policies, helped by an upturn in world demand, the deterioration of the economy stopped in 1983 and a fairly promising recovery started the next year. Industrial exports increased along with rising real wages, a combination that should permit sustained recovery provided they are kept in balance, with neither the external nor the internal side rising so fast that it crowds out the other.

This turn for the better in economic policy offers new hope for successful transition to a more competitive industrial economy, but at the same time the country has become subject to intensifying pressures from the U.S. conflict with Nicaragua. These have included efforts by the United States to get Costa Rica to step up spending on its civil guard and police forces, and to crack down on groups supporting Nicaragua, as well as violence from those supporters. At least so far, the country has not become a military base for insurgent operations against Nicaragua, financed by the United States, in the manner of Honduras. But its heavy external debt puts it in a weakened condition to resist.[46] One might guess that if the

[44] Inter-American Development Bank, *1984 Report*, p. 184.

[45] Rivera, *El Fondo Monetario*, pp. 158–68.

[46] "In one form or another, Costa Rica will have to seek financial assistance from the United States and is therefore not going to steer too far away from the latter's Central American policy." Juan M. del Aguila, "The Limits of Reform Development in Contemporary Costa Rica," *Journal of Inter-American Studies and World Affairs* 24 (August 1982), pp. 353–74, quotation, p. 369. In 1985, Costa Rica accepted a group of U.S. military advisers.

country had any substantial military forces of its own, and if they had been trained by U.S. advisers, it might no longer be a democracy. But it has been blessed by the absence of a strong anticommunist military, and so it has a fighting chance to come out intact.

4. MEXICO: STABILIZING CONSTRAINTS VERSUS NEED FOR CHANGE

Mexico started the twentieth century with the most concentrated land ownership and probably the highest proportion of foreign investment in Latin America, under an authoritarian government convinced that foreign investment was the key to modernization. The revolution of 1910 changed those conditions drastically: by the 1930s the country had become the most independent in the region, with a government able to carry out thorough land reform, to nationalize the previously foreign-owned oil industry, and to incorporate peasants and workers in an extraordinarily inclusive political system. From that point, the side of national preferences favoring economic growth and modernization came back strongly. The country adopted an import substitution strategy, though a better-balanced version than that in Argentina at the time, and achieved strikingly successful economic growth between 1940 and 1970. But in terms of equality and national autonomy, and of restriction of democracy, the system went directly against the achievements of the revolution and the 1930s: it began to look a good deal like the prerevolutionary Porfiriato.[47]

Acceptance of the post-1940 strategy began to disintegrate as its inegalitarian consequences became clearer. Concern for social issues came back strongly in the 1970s, not enough so as to regain dominance but enough to pull both of the administrations of this decade in two nonreconciled directions at once. Both administrations ended up with costly macroeconomic failures, partly for extraneous reasons but mainly because they did not want to impose a one-sided solution to the conflict of objectives and did not succeed in finding a new balance. The Mexican people have been paying a high price for inability so far to find a viable new course.

Two of the key themes at issue go right back to the main problems

[47] Lorenzo Meyer, "Historical Roots of the Authoritarian State in Mexico," pp. 3–22 in José Luis Reyna and Richard S. Weinert, eds., *Authoritarianism in Mexico* (Philadelphia: Institute of Human Issues, 1977). Susan Eckstein also emphasizes the authoritarian character of the present system in *The Poverty of Revolution: The State and the Urban Poor in Mexico* (Princeton: Princeton University Press, 1977).

of the prerevolutionary period: foreign influence and extreme inequality. During the thirty-five year rule of Porfirio Díaz the preeminently stable climate favoring investors achieved a fairly good rate of economic growth, but independent domestic investment came to be distinctly secondary and poverty may well have increased. Foreign investment was on the order of two-thirds of the total for the decade 1900–1910; foreign ownership by 1910 has been estimated at half of national wealth.[48] Although data for this period do not permit any great confidence about measures of poverty, it seems to have risen both because of greatly intensified concentration of land ownership displacing peasant agriculture and because new industries drove out a great deal of prior small-scale production.[49] The revolution blew all this apart, at enormous cost in terms of lives and destruction as leaders competing for control fought on endlessly with each other. That long and bloody process, from 1910 to 1920, built up strong counter-pressures to restore a more stable society. The institutional embodiment of that thirst for stability, the party organization that became the PRI, was founded in the 1920s and has dominated the country politically ever since.

The external side of the party is a massive national organization that incorporates representation for labor, peasants, and the middle class and serves to mobilize their support in elections. Other parties can campaign for local and state offices but in practice so far they cannot threaten to elect presidents. The internal side of the PRI, so secretive it makes the Colombian system look transparent, consists of a small group of leaders who choose each succeeding nominee for president in a behind-the-scenes process of negotiation with the outgoing president. Once elected, the new head of government is left with practically unlimited authority for a single six-year term. Memories of Porfirio Díaz have helped keep alive respect for the basic rule that no president can stay in office for a second term.

Early postrevolution leaders sympathetic to and supported by peasant and worker groups gave them a real voice in decisions. Ruth Berins Collier terms the period of the 1920s and 1930s one of "radical populism," in the sense that the government's strategy included genuine advantages for popular groups, going against the prefer-

[48] Dale Story, "Sources of Investment Capital in Twentieth Century Mexico," in James W. Wilkie and Adam Perkal, eds., *Statistical Abstract of Latin America, 1984* (Los Angeles: UCLA, Latin American Center, 1984), pp. 837–56.

[49] Leopoldo Solís, *La realidad económica mexicana : Retrovisión y perspectivas* (Mexico: Siglo Veintiuno, 1970), pp. 47–85; Clark Reynolds, *The Mexican Economy* (New Haven: Yale University Press, 1970), pp. 15–26.

ences of the business community, in order to bring them into a stable system.[50] This included support for labor organization, for wage increases, and in the 1930s a far-reaching land reform to answer the main demand of peasants. That reform, under President Cárdenas, greatly cut down the largest estates and went a long way toward providing all of the rural population with access to land.[51] In the same period, when labor conflict with foreign-owned oil companies led to demands for intervention, Cárdenas responded by nationalizing the companies. These measures answered deeply held popular preferences and helped enormously to solidify support for the political-economic system. The Mexican government can still in the 1980s get away with what looks like murder, in the sense of running against popular preferences, without drastic protest.

The period of postrevolutionary incorporation created an unusually stable social base but also fostered conflict with the private business sector. Party leaders divided in the late 1930s between the side that wished to stay close to popular preferences and those who wanted instead to reassure investors in order to emphasize economic growth. The latter side won, both in the choice of more conservative presidents and in an economic strategy bending advantages toward private industry and export agriculture. Labor and peasants were still included in the sense of remaining within the party, but they were given much less weight in basic decisions.

The labor force was simultaneously integrated and defused.[52] Some unions remain relatively independent, but none is allowed to rock the boat seriously. Particularly outspoken labor activists are unlikely to rise to high offices within unions, and if too insistent they may be in genuine personal danger. But the system does not keep control mainly by such methods: the government has provided extensive social services for urban workers, subsidies for basic foods, and public health care, while supporting wage increases whenever

[50] Ruth Berins Collier, "Popular Sector Incorporation and Political Supremacy: Regime Evolution in Brazil and Mexico," pp. 57–109 in Sylvia Ann Hewlett and Richard Weinert, eds., *Brazil and Mexico: Patterns in Late Development* (Philadelphia: Institute for the Study of Human Issues, 1982).

[51] Cf. discussion in chapter 6.

[52] Nora Hamilton, *The Limits of State Autonomy: Post-Revolutionary Mexico* (Princeton: Princeton University Press, 1982), pp. 241–86; Kenneth Paul Erickson and Kevin J. Middlebrook, "The State and Organized Labor in Brazil and Mexico," pp. 213–63 in Hewlett and Weinert, *Brazil and Mexico*; Robert R. Kaufman, "Mexico and Latin American Authoritarianism," pp. 193–232 in Reyna and Weinert, eds., *Authoritarianism in Mexico*; Evelyn P. Stevens, *Protest and Response in Mexico* (Cambridge: MIT Press, 1974).

the economy is functioning well. Conversely, when the country is hit by an economic crisis, as in 1982–84, real wages can be cut without explosion. So far, Mexico has been able to get away with the kinds of tight stabilization policies that Argentina has not.

Compromise and inclusion made for a relatively moderate form of import substitution, keeping down the degree to which commercial, export-oriented agriculture was penalized.[53] This relative balance helped sustain growth of agricultural production and exports, and for many years kept external borrowing down to a low ratio to GNP. Industrialization moved ahead rapidly under a kind of bureaucratic management oriented toward economic growth, ready to keep going indefinitely on the same track but lacking flexibility to meet new problems or to change the society in any fundamental way.[54] New problems were not long in building up, from three directions. The first adverse change was the gradual slowdown of agricultural growth in the 1960s, and increase of landless rural labor, discussed in chapter 6. A second was that the system of low taxation on private business and in general on high-income groups restricted government revenues and fostered increasing recourse to foreign borrowing. The third force for change came from increasing opposition toward a style of growth that favored a minority with high incomes while doing little about poverty.

The problems in agriculture stemmed in part from reduction of public investment in that sector, which itself resulted from conflict between growing state spending in urban areas and inability to generate sufficient tax revenue. Growth dependent on subsidized credit and low taxation forced the public sector into increasing deficits, financed by a combination of foreign borrowing and domestic monetary expansion, while the private sector fought off any change. An international comparison of "tax effort," measured by tax revenue relative to national income and to structural characteristics of the particular economy, ranked forty-seven developing countries for the period 1969–1971: Mexico's tax effort ranked

---

[53] Solís, *Economic Policy Reform in Mexico: A Case Study for Developing Countries* (New York: Pergamon, 1981), ch. 1, pp. 1–38; René Villarreal, *El desequilibrio interno en la industrialización de México (1929–1975): Un enfoque estructuralista* (Mexico: Fondo de Cultura Económica, 1976), and "The Policy of Import-substituting Industrialization, 1929–75," pp. 67–107 in Reyna and Weinert, eds., *Authoritarianism in Mexico*; Douglas H. Graham, "Mexican and Brazilian Economic Development: Legacies, Patterns, and Performance," pp. 13–56 in Hewlett and Weinert, eds., *Brazil and Mexico*.

[54] Raymond Vernon, *The Dilemma of Mexico's Development* (Cambridge: Harvard University Press, 1963).

forty-fifth, avoiding last place by edging out Guatemala and Nepal.[55]

Resistance to changes in taxation was simply one aspect of a political structure built around the existing political and social pattern as the revolution faded into the past. When a moderately conservative administration was succeeded in 1964 by one dedicated even more to reassuring private investors, criticism from the side favoring social change began to mount. The tensions came out in the open in 1968, in student demonstrations expressing generalized demand for change, for a break away from the country's rigid post-1940 system. Protest itself was not new: criticism by intellectuals is constant, and is allowed as long as it does not come across too clearly in newspapers or broadcasting, but the whole fabric of governmental influence over mass media is used to keep in minor key any basic questioning of the system. The students broke the implicit rule by demonstrating violently in the center of the city, where protest could be seen by everyone, not merely in the schools. Their demonstrations were not as massive and persistent as the French student uprising earlier that year, but the Mexican government is not used to dealing with such problems: where the French police held back aggressive mass demonstrators for weeks on end without killing anyone, the Mexican government reacted with a devastating slaughter. Hundreds of students were killed and many imprisoned for years. It was as if the government and the safety-first side of society were frightened to death, unable to answer public opposition with even minimal flexibility.[56]

The official most directly responsible for repression of the students, Luis Echeverría Alvarez, was selected the following year by the PRI as the country's next president. Whether by his own decision or by agreement within the party, he turned away from the conservative version of "stabilizing growth" which had linked the government so closely to private business. One attempted reform, bitterly contested and finally blocked, was to change the tax system

[55] Alan A. Tait, Wilfrid Gratz, and Barry J. Eichengreen, "International Comparison of Taxation for Selected Developing Countries, 1972–76," IMF *Staff Papers* 26 (1979), pp. 123–56. Some details of tax advantages for business in Mexico, and for the personal incomes of business owners, are given in Solís, *Policy Reform*, pp. 19–25.

[56] Octavia Paz, *Posdata* (Mexico: Siglo Veintiuno, 1970), esp. pp. 31–42; Stevens, *Protest and Response*, ch. 6, pp. 185–240. The timing of the outbreak and the intensity of the Mexican government's reaction may have been related to the impending start of the Olympic Games in Mexico City; if violent demonstrations were going on during the games they would have received extraordinary world attention.

both to increase revenue and to place more of the burden on business and on wealth. Changes actually carried out included tighter restrictions on foreign investment; greatly increased public investment to speed up growth of the economy and of employment; direct social programs aimed at reduction of poverty; and modest redistributions of land. None of this was revolutionary, but it was enough to arouse great consternation in the private business sector. A climate of hostility between the government and many business leaders, and within the business community between those who sided with the government and those who attacked it, set the stage for a slowdown of investment by both domestic and foreign firms, touched off instances of violence, and led to large-scale capital flight.[57]

The sudden drop of foreign investment and accompanying capital flight could be seen as an example of the way in which multinational firms can exert pressure on a government to change policies adverse to their interests.[58] But that interpretation may obscure the fundamental conflicts of national purpose at work in Mexico itself. The threat of serious change in the balance of power, and of reduced advantages for private business as the counterpart of greater concern for social measures, thoroughly frightened the business community. In the face of their fears and resistance Echeverría dropped the main aspects of the tax reform.[59] But then, unwilling to give up on the attempt to redirect national economic strategy, he pushed ahead aggressively with public sector spending, both for social purposes and for investment by state firms. Government deficits and foreign borrowing went up fast, restraint of inflation began to break down, and the current account deficit in the balance of payments widened rapidly.[60] The government clung grimly to a fixed exchange rate in the face of rising inflation, undermining the competitive position of domestic production and keeping up incentives to take capital out as fast as possible. The whole set of inconsistencies finally fell apart in 1976. The surface-level problem was

[57] Carlos Tello, *La política económica en México, 1970–1976* (Mexico: Siglo Veintiuno, 1979); Miguel Basáñez, *La lucha para la hegemonía en México, 1968–1980* (Mexico: Siglo Veintiuno, 1981).

[58] Gereffi and Evans, "Transnational Corporations."

[59] Solís, *Economic Policy Reform*, ch. 3, pp. 67–77.

[60] Tello, *La política económica*, gives a well-informed account of the increasing strains on government policy but a misleading version of the causes of rising inflation and external deficits: they are explained by practically everything going on *except* excess demand. His proposed remedies were to stop the central bank from trying to apply monetary restraint, and to nationalize the private banks.

that the economic policies followed had been radically destabilizing; the underlying reason was that Mexico was beginning to change but had no consensus on how to do it, for what ends.

In the 1976 crisis, complying with both IMF requirements and the preferences of the private sector, the government backed away from expansion of state industry and public sector spending, applied tight credit constraint, and forced the economy into recession. The next administration, that of López Portillo, started off as a model of financial prudence. Then a new economic factor entered the scene and changed the balance of forces. Mexico's known oil reserves suddenly shot up with discoveries that seemed to promise release from financial constraints. The contribution to GDP of the state oil firm, PEMEX, evaluated at international prices, increased from 2.4 percent in 1977 to 18.5 percent by 1980; its tax payments increased from 8 percent of federal government current income in 1977 to 25 percent by 1980.[61] Investment went right back up again and the country went rapidly "from bust to boom."[62]

The dramatic increase in foreign exchange earnings and government revenue stimulated both a revived effort to reshape Mexico's development and a near-total collapse of any kind of restraint. After the frustrating breakdown of attempted reforms under Echeverría, the many people in the Mexican government who wanted to promote significant structural change seized the new context as a chance to break through at last, to a stronger and more independent industrial structure and toward greater employment and equality. Goals on the industrial side were spelled out in the industrial plan of 1979. The objectives included very high rates of investment and growth, with investment aimed especially at deepening the structure of production in capital goods and fields of more advanced technology.[63] The plan called for reserving a high fraction of the newly discovered oil for domestic development rather than

[61] Socrates C. Rizzo, "Generation and Allocation of Oil Economic Surpluses," ch. 5 in Pedro Aspe and Paul E. Sigmund, eds., *The Political Economy of Income Distribution in Mexico* (New York: Holmes and Meier, 1984), tables 5.17 and 5.5.

[62] Laurence Whitehead, "Mexico from Bust to Boom."

[63] Mexico, Secretaria de Patrimonio y Fomento Industrial, *Plan Nacional de Desarrollo Industrial, 1979-1982* (Mexico: SEPAFIN, 1979); Terry Barker and Vladimiro Brailovsky, "Economic Policy Making in Mexico Between 1976 and 1982 and the National Industrial Development Plan," paper presented at the Seminar on the Mexican Economy: Current Situation and Macroeconomic Perspectives, El Colegio de Mexico, August 1982. José Ayala and Clemente Ruiz Durán, "Development and Crisis in Mexico: A Structuralist Approach," in Hartlyn and Morley, *Latin American Political Economy*, ch. 10, pp. 243–64.

exports and for restriction of imports in the interest of a more self-sufficient kind of development. The image suggested was that of Japan, with government leadership to stimulate new industries, with foreign investment strictly limited, and with a high rate of growth for the sake of both creating a new industrial structure and generating employment opportunities. Correspondingly, the plan projected rapid growth of nonoil exports. The problem, exactly as before, was that neither the plan nor the policies actually adopted provided for the kinds of constraints and incentives that might have made the project feasible.

On the side of social reform and lessened inequality, one of the most important programs adopted was the Sistema Alimentario Mexicano, which introduced support for the small agricultural producers of foods for the domestic market, along with subsidies for consumption of traditional foods particularly important for the poor. Among many other direct social programs, public-supported health services which had previously been confined to urban areas were extended to the rural poor as well. In the eternal battle over taxation this administration was successful where Echeverría had failed. Major revisions shifted the balance of taxation from labor income to capital and from lower wage ranges to higher: between 1978 and 1981 taxes on capital were raised from 57 to 69 percent of the total collected from capital plus labor, while income taxes on workers were changed to raise the share collected from those earning more than ten times the average minimum wage from 24 to 46 percent of such taxes.[64] Such changes could have made this administration one of the most constructive in postwar Mexico, if they had been accompanied by effective concern for macroeconomic balance.

The joint impact of rising revenue and spending from oil exports, of all the new social welfare programs, and of greatly increased investment, was to drive up demand very rapidly. Output rose fast too, but it could not keep up with the growth of demand: the difference was made up by a surge of imports. The growth of imports would have been very rapid in any case but was made more so by a departure from the specifications of the industrial plan. Instead of keeping on restrictions, the government gave way in this respect to the preferences of those concerned more with free markets, and liberalized imports by taking away quantitative restraints with very lit-

[64] Francisco Gíl Díaz, "The Incidence of Taxes in Mexico: A Before and After Comparison," ch. 4 in Aspe and Sigmund, eds., *Income Distribution in Mexico*, tables 4.2 and 4.1.

tle offsetting increases in tariffs. Policy similarly departed from the industrial plan with respect to a critical issue of pricing: instead of raising the domestic price of oil up toward world levels as a form of taxation to restrain consumer demand, the government kept the internal price far below that being received for exports. Roughly half of the export value of oil production was turned into a subsidy for domestic consumption.[65] Government spending rose so fast that it overwhelmed increases in revenue from oil; the deficit shot up to 15 percent of GDP by 1981. Imports tripled between 1978 and 1981; the external deficit on current account went up from $3 billion to $14 billion.[66]

Internally, the pressures of rapidly increasing spending and output began to drive up prices despite the flood of imports adding to supply; domestic capacity to raise output without inflationary consequences proved lower than expected.[67] Perhaps because of fears of further aggravating inflation, and perhaps for the same set of ideological preferences that had led the preceding administration to reject arguments for devaluation, the government again held on to a fixed exchange rate despite the squeeze on exporters of rising domestic costs. In consequence, the growth of exports other than oil was choked off just as imports were rising swiftly. With foreign banks eager to keep on lending, it was possible to keep borrowing to finance rising external deficits longer than usual on this round: by the time the inevitable crisis hit, in August 1982, the country was far deeper in debt than ever before and was forced to apply far more drastic devaluation and contraction. Four years later, no clear solution is yet in sight.

Apart from a natural tendency to overstate future possibilities when things are going well, on the part of foreign bankers as on the part of the Mexican government, much of the trouble in this period probably should be assigned to narrow perceptions on the real al-

[65] Rizzo, "Oil Economic Surpluses," estimates the subsidies to consumption at close to half of the total resources provided by oil (table 5.28). He emphasizes the distortions implied by keeping domestic oil prices far below world levels and by differentially high wages in PEMEX. Another aspect that played a major role in public revulsion when the facts began to come out was that individuals in favored positions were able to sidetrack phenomenal amounts of oil revenue, and to take much of it out of the country.

[66] International Monetary Fund, *International Financial Statistics, 1984 Yearbook* (Washington, D.C.: IMF, 1984).

[67] Peter Gregory, *The Myth of Market Failure*, suggests that the government had an inaccurate picture of employment conditions and believed that there was more room to expand than was actually the case: misreading the state of the economy encouraged overshooting (see discussion in chapter 3).

ternatives. An influential statement of the need for structural change, by Rolando Cordera and Carlos Tello, posed the issues in terms of a narrow kind of dualism: as a conflict between "neoliberal" and "national" strategies of development, presented as if these were mutually exclusive choices.[68] The neoliberal side, identified with all the defects of Mexico's own prior version of stabilizing growth, is presented as if it stood for any and all kinds of strategy that pay attention to macroeconomic stabilization and potential gains from trade. The wide range of possibilities—state-led growth using market forces and emphasizing export promotion as in Brazil, Chicago-style economic strategy as in Chile, the mildly reformist and cautious Colombian approach, the welfare state version of Costa Rica, and the many conceivable variations of such strategies—all merge into one gray mass of inequity. Concern with costs is seen as a hangover of outdated conceptions of comparative advantage, to be answered by restricting imports and redirecting production to the internal market, as if exclusion of international competition would somehow eliminate any significance to costs in terms of foregone opportunities. The "national" side similarly suffers from an intellectual short-circuit: the many possible versions of a more autonomous style of development seem to be tied down to a particular vision that downgrades attention to possible excess demand and to the connections between relative prices and behavior of firms.

Although the rejection of conventional economic considerations in this period was overdone in ways that have cost Mexico dearly, it had some good reasons. One was a well-founded distrust of a key feature in the country's earlier economic strategy: freedom for international movement of financial capital. Such freedom was a striking feature of postwar Mexican policy up to 1982, contrasting to the use of exchange controls in nearly all developing countries. It can encourage investment by reassuring both domestic and foreign investors that they can move funds freely in response to changes in economic conditions. But such freedom also means that the private sector can move funds out of the country on a large scale, using up foreign exchange reserves and frightening off new lenders, when they believe that changes in government policy are adverse to their interests. Capital flight, or the threat of it, can become a political weapon.

The breakdown of attempted reforms under Echeverría, and the beginning of deep trouble for the López Portillo administration,

---

[68] Rolando Cordera and Carlos Tello, *México: La disputa por la nación: perspectivas y opciones del desarrollo* (Mexico: Siglo Veintiuno, 1981).

were both associated with capital flight. After the stabilization program of 1976 private capital started to come back in, but then in 1982 it headed back out fast and became a major part of the foreign exchange crisis.[69] From the point of view of economic incentives the outflow was readily understandable: the country's external deficit on current account was increasing rapidly, the fixed exchange rate was becoming untenable in the context of domestic inflation, and anyone who could convert pesos to dollars while the price was low could be sure to gain. But from the point of view of many of the people concerned with domestic reform, the capital flight itself is what made it impossible to stave off devaluation and retrenchment. Those holding the latter view were able to act on it in the desperate last months of the López Portillo administration. The government nationalized all the Mexican private banks, in the belief that this would stop capital flight.[70] The belief proved to be wrong but that does not settle the question of whether allowing completely open capital movement is or is not a desirable strategy.

It is difficult to take seriously any belief that Mexico would have been free of trouble in 1981–82 if exchange controls had been in effect, but there is little doubt that capital flight can inflict high costs of its own. No conceivable system of controls on capital movements could have staved off trouble in conditions of a rapidly growing current account deficit fed by excess demand plus currency overvaluation. But it is also true that open conditions for capital flight may severely constrain the government's ability to carry out reforms which the business community distrusts; it may provoke a foreign exchange crisis even in the absence of prior economic imbalance. It became a special plague in Mexico after 1982, despite all the efforts made by the next administration to correct the causes by deflation and devaluation. A significant share of the new external credit negotiated with great difficulty by the government after 1982 has gone right back out again in the form of private capital movement.[71]

[69] Barker and Brailovsky, "Economic Policy Making"; Lance Taylor, "The Crisis and Thereafter: Macroeconomic Policy Problems in Mexico," in Peggy B. Musgrave, ed., *Mexico and the United States: Studies in Economic Integration* (Boulder: Westview Press, 1985), table 2, p. 150.

[70] Carlos Tello, who was brought in as the head of the central bank near the end of the López Portillo administration, explains the position in *La nacionalización de la banca en México* (Mexico: Siglo Veintiuno, 1984). In an analytical review of this book, Carlos Bazdresch Parada makes a convincing counterargument that nationalization of the banks could not possibly have stopped capital flight in this period, and was in no sense an answer to the financial crisis under this administration: *El Trimestre Económico* 206 (April–June 1985), pp. 616–29.

[71] Rudiger Dornbusch, "Special Exchange Rates for Capital Account Transac-

Under a stabilization program aimed at restoring macroeconomic equilibrium with a competitive exchange rate, through devaluation and deflation, continuing capital flight has forced greater devaluation, caused higher inflation, and forced greater restraint on domestic production and employment than would otherwise have been necessary. Reduction of real wages in pursuit of stabilization can stimulate exports, but if a significant share of export earnings disappears into private assets held abroad the system amounts to a tax on workers to finance the acquisition of foreign assets by others. The conservative answer—"restore confidence"—does not come to grips with the costs involved. Further, in its common meaning that domestic demand should be held down and real interest rates raised to high levels to attract capital back in, it may point in the wrong direction. Renewed economic expansion and the prospect of profitable new investment openings would seem to offer greater promise of reassuring investors as well as everyone else. But to restore expansion while capital flight remains a problem may be nearly impossible unless controls can be used to hold down the loss of foreign exchange due to capital movement. Controls are bound to be evaded to some degree, but if not made futile by adverse basic economic conditions they could be an important temporary help. An exchange rate determined by open-market forces would be ideal if those forces were mainly related to current export and import transactions, but when they are dominated by one-way capital flows (either outward or inward), a market-determined exchange rate can be seriously detrimental.

Economic reform had a good chance up to 1982, but the next administration had little room to move. The PRI chose as the next president a technically oriented person well aware of problems of economic management, Miguel de la Madrid. His administration faced the combination of external debt crisis and internal inflation in a very businesslike way—businesslike in the double sense that the corrective program was carefully designed to meet the immediate problems, and that it placed the main burdens of adjustment on the public sector and on workers.[72] Government spending was scaled back greatly, reducing investment and social programs and raising unemployment, while bringing down the excess of spending over

tions," National Bureau of Economic Research, Working Paper Series no. 1659 (July 1985). Table 1 shows that the liabilities of U.S. banks to Mexican residents increased by $4.7 billion from the end of 1982 to the end of 1984.

[72] Taylor, "The Crisis;" Wayne A. Cornelius, "The Political Economy of Mexico under de la Madrid: Austerity, Routinized Crisis, and Nascent Recovery," *Mexican Studies* 1 (Winter 1985), pp. 83–124.

domestic production. Real wages in manufacturing were cut approximately 25 percent in 1983 and a further 5 percent in 1984; by
the latter year they were about one-fifth below their level a decade
earlier.[73]

Drastic devaluation of the currency to catch up with the effects of
the preceding inflation naturally pushed the current rate of inflation even higher at first, but it also served to revive industrial exports and to lessen negative pressures on agricultural production.
Imports were cut by two-thirds, from $24 billion in 1981 to $8 billion by 1983. The trade balance swung from a deficit of $5 billion in
1981 to a surplus of $14 billion by 1984 but even then the surplus
barely exceeded current interest on the external debt.[74] Unless the
debt burden can be reduced either by negotiation, by unilateral decision, or by world inflation that cuts down the value of the debt in
real terms, it is hard to see how Mexico can both keep up payments
and begin to restore living conditions to their former level. Perhaps
the fundamental question is whether the resilience of postrevolutionary Mexican society can remain intact under this kind of stress.
The PRI, the government, the capacity of national leadership in
general, have all suffered badly in terms of public acceptance.
Would a more honest and open political system have helped restrain the excesses of the 1978–82 period, and help now to keep the
society together?

President de la Madrid started out by insisting on the need for
more honest elections, but as opposition parties began to win more
and more local elections, the repressive elements of the system went
into action again: all elections from mid-1983 through 1984 were
declared victories for the PRI.[75] That has given rise to rioting and at
least one case of military intervention to put down outraged local
opposition. On this path increasing repression would seem inevitable. The alternative, to allow a fully open and honest political system, might well mean defeat for the PRI, at least temporarily. It
might also mean that competing parties could check each other's excesses, giving Mexico a better-functioning system deserving renewed public confidence.[76]

---

[73] International Labour Office, *Bulletin of Labour Statitistics* 1985 no. 2, and *Yearbook of Labour Statistics, 1983* (Geneva: ILO, 1983).

[74] Inter-American Development Bank, *1985 Report*, table 1-3, p. 99.

[75] Cornelius, "Political Economy," p. 103.

[76] Esperanza Durán effectively links the economic and political possibilities in "Mexico: Economic Realism and Political Efficiency," *The World Today* (May 1985), pp. 96–99.

5. THREE MIXED RECORDS, WITH ROOM
TO DO BETTER OR WORSE

These three countries are all walking tightropes between successive problems. They can scarcely be considered to have achieved the kind of egalitarian, participatory, self-determined styles of development most of us would like to see. But they are examples of something that for a time seemed almost impossible in Latin America: they have gone a long way through the strains of transition from old-style societies dependent for their growth on primary exports, and dependent internally on the preferences on a relatively small group of landowners opposed to change, toward urban-industrial economies able to reduce poverty and to respond to more diverse interests without falling into the reaction and repression that hit Brazil and the Southern Cone. That is not everything but it is a lot.

As contrasted to the Southern Cone these societies have all been marked by greater efforts at inclusion through negotiation among conflicting groups as opposed to aggressive attempts at class domination, expressed on the economic side by avoiding the extremes of early postwar import substitution and, much but not all of the time, both Chicago-style economic repression and structuralist excess demand. Mexico in the early 1970s and again at the end of the decade, and Costa Rica from 1978 to 1982, lost macroeconomic balance and have been under unusual strain since. Neither has as yet been able to find the new balance they need, but both have so far avoided polarizing confrontation.

In response to the question raised in the introduction to this chapter, this general style of development certainly can be inegalitarian but the extent to which it is so can be changed greatly by choices of national economic strategy. Inequality has been relatively low in Costa Rica because of favorable historical conditions, and very high in the others because of different structural factors, but it has moved in either better or worse directions according to their economic policies in particular periods. The main favorable conditions in Costa Rica were widely diffused educational opportunities, a better integrated labor market, and relative equality of bargaining power among all social groups. In Colombia and Mexico, more concentrated ownership of land and capital, restricted access to education, high rates of labor force growth, and narrow circles of political control have made their market systems work much more inequitably. Still, choices of national policy have made highly significant differences. Mexico's move to the conservative side after

Cárdenas added a severely regressive tax system and systematic bias of government policy in favor of upper income groups on top of structural conditions themselves adverse for equity. Those in Mexico more concerned with equity and autonomy have been able to come back in ways that change the course of events, and particularly to gain influence in the two administrations of the 1970s. The familiar problem is that both fell into structuralist extremes that set the country back badly: their intentions were better but their methods were not. Methods matter greatly.

In comparison, Colombia has done fairly well. The chief ingredients have been avoidance of extremes of protection and excess demand, design of economic policies after 1967 to favor employment opportunities, the use of exchange rate policy to promote industrialization in greater degree through competitive industrial exports, more progressive and more effective taxation, and real progress in extension of access to education. This fairly conservative strategy could have been totally inadequate in conditions of great excess labor and continuing high rates of population growth. But the absolute decline of the rural labor force starting in the 1960s, the reduction of birth rates beginning in the same decade, and the significant rise in real wages in rural areas in the 1970s all suggest that the approach can work: not in the sense that inequality has been adequately answered but in the sense that it should be feasible to combine growth with decreasing inequality in the future.

These three societies are all conservative. They have many characteristics that deserve to be conserved. But if overt repression can be avoided they are bound to be, and should be, pushed toward more egalitarian choices. There is no objective reason in terms of either fundamental economic incapacity or external dependence that precludes any of them from practically eliminating absolute poverty and greatly reducing inequality in the course of the next generation. Nor is there anything in the use of a market system that either ensures reasonable success or rules it out: that depends on exactly how they use it.

PART III

POSSIBILITIES AND QUESTIONS

TWELVE

ECONOMIC STRATEGIES, SOCIAL STRAINS, AND POLITICAL REPRESSION

Choices of economic strategy can never guarantee safe arrival across disaster-strewn seas but they can lessen many common kinds of danger or, even more easily, ensure shipwreck. This chapter is focused on the particular danger that the semi-industrialized countries which have put behind them the "old patriarch" kind of dictatorship, which have been able to develop fairly wide political participation, may be prone to radical reaction and worse kinds of authoritarian repression than anything ever dreamed up by the old-style tyrants. It would be a mistake to conclude that the chilling new kind of repression that hit four leading Latin American countries in the 1960s and 1970s is inescapable but an even worse mistake to consider these cases as accidents unlikely to be repeated. They are avoidable disasters, possible almost everywhere because they grow out of the kinds of tensions intrinsic to industrialization in the modern world, but not necessarily bound to win.

This more modern kind of repression has very special characteristics: it combines free-market economics with destruction of democratic institutions and systematic use of terror to paralyze opposition.[1] At the very least, the combination suggests that democracy and capitalism do not easily go together in contemporary Latin America. To put it more strongly, the fundamental issue may be that informed majorities given the chance to express their preferences can usually be expected to vote for promises to control markets, shut off international competition and foreign investment, and use government rather than private enterprise as the main force shaping economic development. For firm believers in private enterprise, the costs of allowing majority choices in such matters come to seem too high to accept.

Why do such conflicts become so intense in the later stages of in-

---

[1] Guillermo O'Donnell, *Modernization and Bureaucratic-Authoritarianism*; David Collier, ed., *The New Authoritarianism in Latin America* (Princeton: Princeton University Press, 1979); Carlos Díaz Alejandro, "Open Economy, Closed Polity?"; John Sheahan, "Economic Policies and Political Repression."

dustrialization in Latin America? The pioneer explanation in general terms, by Guillermo O'Donnell, helped greatly to raise awareness of the issues but misdirected attention in some ways. His idea that the key cause could be found in problems of capital deepening in the late stage of import substitution, in the sense that these problems created pressures for a technically trained bureaucracy to override public preferences, did not stand up well to careful criticism.[2] While he clarified many of the characteristics of the repressive regimes, it turned out that only the first two "bureaucratic-authoritarian" cases, Argentine and Brazil in the 1960s, were really bureaucratic. The three Southern Cone cases in the 1970s were instead antibureaucratic, trying to get away from detailed economic management. The common theme that binds all five cases together is not bureaucracy but their emphasis on use of market forces, on criteria of economic efficiency and reliance on private enterprise. That is why the alternative term "market-authoritarian" was introduced in chapter 1 and is used throughout this book.

The intensity of conflict over such issues in the late stages of industrialization comes from the basic contradiction between popular preferences and market criteria. On one side, increasing political participation gives greater weight to those who identify market forces and private enterprise with enduring inequality and special privilege: if the societies remain open politically, their economic strategies systematically go against any conventional free market orientation. On the other side, any generalized rejection of orthodox economic criteria in the common populist style almost inexorably leads to breakdown. If democratic choices consistently lead to economic breakdown, opposition to democracy itself is bound to strengthen.

Is it possible to avoid or resolve this conflict? The first section of this chapter answers yes. If populist-style governments can bring themselves to modify their economic strategies in some key respects, to use some traditional criteria even if they reject many others, it should be possible to combine social reform with a well-functioning economy. Section 2 is concerned with the other side of the picture: the dangers built into conventional economic principles and the costs of insisting on them without regard to the damage they may be causing. Section 3 makes more explicit a question running through

[2] José Serra, "Three Mistaken Theses Regarding the Connections Between Industrialization and Authoritarian Regimes," and Robert R. Kaufman, "Industrial Change and Authoritarian Rule in Latin America: A Concrete Review of the Bureaucratic-Authoritarian Model," in David Collier, ed., *The New Authoritarianism.*

all the discussion, the role of transitional strains of the last half century as distinct from persisting conditions likely to plague Latin America in the decades ahead. Political strains come from many directions, outside the region as well as inside it, but perhaps the most persistent difficulty is the need to keep changing strategies as the underlying problems change.[3]

1. THE USEFUL SIDE OF ECONOMICS: AVOIDING BREAKDOWN

The four countries taken over by market-authoritarian regimes were outstanding examples of persisting high inflation and unbalanced structures of production, more prone than the rest of the region to foreign exchange crises even in periods of favorable world economic conditions. Sympathetic observers could always point out that problems of this nature are to be expected in the course of industrialization and social change, as governments attempt to transfer resources to the industrial sector, to encourage industrial investment, to incorporate a growing urban labor force, and to deal with counterpressures from landowners and other traditional interests. It would be impossible to get through all this without intense strains. But strains come in very different degrees: industrialization per se was not a sufficient explanation of the more profound problems. They were more matters of the particular methods used. The methods were nonfunctional in ways that could conceivably have been avoided without selling out the goals of industrialization and social change.

In the table of regime types presented in chapter 1, examples of "middle road" market systems are distinguished from those termed "populist or radical reformist." The point intended is that the former group has generally paid more attention to conventional economic criteria while pursuing industrialization and, at least so far, has not run into such traumatic political outcomes as the latter. It is not that group 3 in that table avoided all social reform while group 4 accomplished a great deal: Costa Rica has probably done more to carry through measures favorable for social participation than any of the populist systems, Colombia has managed some modest reform measures within a conservative framework, and Mexico introduced many valuable changes before blowing things up in its

[3] Albert Hirshman, *A Bias For Hope* (New Haven: Yale University Press, 1971), Introduction, and Hirschman, "The Turn to Authoritarianism in Latin America and the Search for Its Economic Determinants," in *Essays in Trespassing*.

burst of excess demand from 1979 to 1982. The reforms accomplished by the kinds of populism associated with Perón or the Velasco period in Peru do not look especially brilliant in comparison with group 3. The difference between the groups is not the presence or absence of attempts at reform but the presence or absence of some minimal coherence in overall economic strategy.

Conservative economists, and many radicals too, can hardly find a term more scathing than "populist" to denote confusion, inconsistency, and inevitable failure. From the conservative side it is a name for would-be reformism that will not work because it fails to respect criteria of efficiency, macroeconomic restraint, or general consistency between goals and methods. From the more radical side, populism will not work because it is an eclectic multiclass coalition bound to break down in internal conflict over the inescapably contradictory interests of its supporters. It is a coalition of those dissatisfied with the existing order but unwilling to accept any truly revolutionary change. From both sides, populism is a hopeless wish for a third way that does not exist.

When one turns to the work of the historians and political scientists who have studied Latin American populism, perhaps the greatest surprise for an economist is the discovery that many of them view such movements in positive terms. Although everyone notes multiple problems, they are often presented as appropriate for a particular period or stage of development or even—as in the statement quoted in chapter 1—the only hope for social reform.[4] Populism is not merely a name for disorder, but instead a fairly systematic manifestation of widely shared popular objectives. Exactly what systematic features are involved has to be interpreted broadly; even the favorable views admit a lack of clarity in programs of populist governments. But some features are certainly common: dislike of traditional elite dominance, of foreign investment and influence, of erratic and unfair market-determined prices for necessities, and of any appeal to the need for overall restraints on spending or social programs. In the Latin American versions they have all favored activist governments committed, at least verbally, to protection of workers and of wages, to industrialization, to nationalism, to policies of cheap food for urban consumers, and to favors for worthy groups as the norm and goal of good government. Rejection of efficiency criteria and of concern for macroeconomic balance became *principles*, not accidental byproducts.

[4] Torcuato di Tella, "Populism"; Michael L. Conniff, ed., *Latin American Populism in Comparative Perspective* (Albuquerque: University of New Mexico Press, 1982).

To list such shared conceptions of desirable economic orientation should call to mind a particular school of economic thought: ECLA and the early postwar structuralists. Structuralism expressed, and Perón embodied, the kind of incorporating economic style that appealed initially to coalitions of urban workers and domestic business interests, modernizing professionals, much of the military, and perhaps most of the society other than the rural sector and interests involved in international trade. Structuralism presented what the more modernizing side of these societies wanted to hear.

Much of this book is concerned with clarifying reasons why this kind of economic strategy always maximizes trouble. The more aggressively it is pursued the more inexorably it leads to economic crises, to strangulation of the growth of opportunities for productive employment. Besides generating macroeconomic imbalance it usually left out the interests of the rural poor: those who need help the most were among the most consistent victims. All this had political costs as well as economic. On top of the inevitable resistances to reform from conservatives unwilling to yield any shred of privilege, and the all too frequent cases of outside pressure, the actual economic results of populist-style strategies themselves can contribute greatly to the forces making for authoritarian reaction.

Many cases of authoritarian reaction have involved widely shared convictions that the welfare of the country was seriously threatened. The landowners in Argentina have not been the only ones who turn toward military intervention to defend their interests: in some periods a substantial share of the country probably agreed with them that the existing situation was intolerable. In Brazil in the early 1960s, multinationals and national investors in combination helped push the country toward an authoritarian response to the government of Goulart, but they were not the only ones convinced that the country as a whole was being hurt badly. From the conservative side, it can come to seem evident that representative government, however ultimately desirable, is too expensive a luxury for a developing country. If the indignant activists who are always complaining about inequity would keep quiet for another generation or so, allowing consumption to be held down and capital accumulation to continue, then a gradually more productive society could become able to reconcile reasonable demands for social change with sustained investment and growth.[5]

[5] For particularly clear arguments in this sense applied to the breakdown of civilian government in Brazil in the 1960s, see Werner Baer, *Industrialization and Economic Development*, and Nathaniel Leff, *Economic Policy Making*. Edward Mason gives a careful

Any belief in a necessary incompatibility between participatory societies and economic development in Latin America is on very doubtful ground.[6] Apart from the evidence that several countries have been able to continue industrialization without drastic authoritarian reaction, the logic of growth itself clearly allows for a combination of rising investment with rising use of resources for social purposes. If economic growth means anything at all, it means an increasing total capacity to respond to diverse objectives, as long as the quantities involved match the actual capacity to respond. The problem with populism, and structuralism as an economic strategy, has been its rejection of that requirement for consistency, not its drive for wider participation.

Populism as a major factor in Latin America may well have had its day, partly shot down by repressive governments and partly perhaps just outgrown by more stable institutions in the semi-industrialized countries.[7] But the issues are still there. Market forces cannot be counted on to accomplish the structural transformations desired by most of the people in these societies. The populists were right that these countries need a "third way" of some kind. What kind of third way could work? That question has been discussed so many times in specific contexts it would serve little purpose to repeat in any detail but the main need is to balance opposing sets of considerations. On one side, success requires an economic strategy that tries to keep the growth of spending in fairly close relationship to the growth of productive capacity, to promote those industries and technologies that favor employment and learning while discouraging those that have exceptionally high requirements for capital or for imports, to encourage more diversified exports, to raise real wages at about the rate at which output per workers increases instead of either holding them down or letting them outrun real product: in general, to make the parts of the economy add up to a sustainable total system. On the opposite side, participatory development is unlikely to be favored by monetarist extremes, free trade, elimination of all controls and subsidies, and complete reliance on private markets. For reasons reconsidered briefly in the following

---

explanation of reasons for authoritarian responses to the strains of development, or at least for strong governments able to override unrealistic popular demands, in "Authoritarian Development," *World Issues* (October–November 1977), pp. 3–11.

[6] Serra, "Three Mistaken Theses"; Jack Donnelly, "Human Rights and Development: Complementary or Competing Concerns?" *World Politics* (January 1984), pp. 255–83; Oscar Muñoz, "Hacia una nueva industrialización."

[7] Paul W. Drake, "Requiem for Populism?" in Conniff, ed., *Latin American Populism*.

section, this conservative path is promising only for favored minorities. In Latin America it is most unlikely to be consistent with democracy.

2. THE TROUBLESOME SIDE OF ECONOMICS

Any wholehearted drive to create free-market economic systems relying on private enterprise, with emphasis on efficiency criteria and monetary restraint, is in the conditions of most of Latin America almost certain to require a repressive political system. Such a program would always win some votes in an open election, but to use it to campaign for president would be about equivalent to running for president in the United States as an avowed Marxist. The low popularity of free-market economics in Latin America is not evidence that radicals have misled the people: the majority of the public is probably no more confused about what they want and why than the rest of us are. It is rather that the conviction goes deep that market-oriented economic strategies are likely to maintain special privilege, work adversely for the poor, impede industrialization, and strengthen foreign influence. These are not widely popular goals. Emphasis on private enterprise and free markets is identified in Latin American experience with only two kinds of regimes: the old-style landowner-dominated systems which were the norm up to the 1930s, and the modern Southern Cone at its most repressive.

Two of the specific ways in which conventional economic principles conflict with social goals concern reduction of poverty and inequality, and efforts to achieve greater self-determination through industrialization. In some interpretations of what economics as a discipline means, the conflict is mainly a misunderstanding. If the goal is to use resources efficiently to raise national income—if the fundamental question is indeed the wealth of nations—then the problem is not that economics gets in the way but that subsidiary concerns conflict with the basic objective. Attempts to reduce poverty too early, by methods that undermine efficiency, delay the gains in national income that would otherwise resolve it. Similarly, the degree to which rising income is achieved by industrialization or by alternative structures of production should be decided by their respective contributions to national income, not by arbitrary preferences for industrialists as opposed to landowners. The problem is, such attempts at generalized objectivity, appealing to supposedly nonpolitical principles, can come to serve as political weapons themselves. It is not easy to distinguish concern with efficiency as an ever-relevant consideration from an authoritarian strain within the discipline of economics itself. If public preferences expressed through democratic processes ask for the impossible, for more income than the society can produce, then (eventually) economic factors will demonstrate that this democratically chosen objective cannot be reached. But that is not the same thing as an argument that the choice of industrialization when comparative advantage goes the other way is necessarily a wrong choice, nor that subsidies or direct social reform programs to reduce poverty are somehow uneconomic. They may be well or poorly run, but they are the choices economic strategy should serve, not the other way around.

Considering first the problems of poverty and inequality, there certainly are good grounds for expecting free markets to work adversely under conditions common in Latin America. Such negative effects are not a universal characteristic either of markets forces per se or of their role in all developing countries. Both Northern capitalist countries and some Asian developing countries have been able to achieve long periods of growth in which market forces are actually equalizing. The conditions required are that ownership and education be broadly spread in the first place, and that openings for productive employment rise fast enough relative to the labor force to exert generalized pressure for rising real wages. The Asian developing countries that have done particularly well at combining high growth with rising real wages and relative equality have made active use of market forces, but that is not the whole story. The most potent performers—South Korea, Singapore, and Taiwan—also have excellent records for wide access to education, and in the cases of South Korea and Taiwan have used land reform to redistribute property ownership as well.

For most countries in Latin America—those other than Costa Rica and the Southern Cone—the most fundamental negative consequences of reliance on market forces have been caused by long-continued imbalance between growth of opportunities for productive employment and growth of the labor force, holding the growth of incomes of both the rural poor and unorganized urban workers down either close to zero or, at best, to rates of gain below property owners and those who have special skills. That is not a fixed, eternal condition of existence in Latin America: it can be changed, and has been changing in Brazil, Colombia, and possibly other countries as well. But it was very much the general condition as of the beginning of the postwar period, and it remains so in the poorest countries now. In such conditions, market forces persistently press downward on living standards of workers. Some of the poor move upward as employment opportunities increase, but the rate of increase may not be fast enough to keep the total number of people in poverty from rising at the same time. The natural response of reform governments, or of the labor force when it can achieve independent organization, is to push wages upward in opposition to market forces. That helps the minority of workers with regular employment but reduces new employment opportunities of the poor who do not have either adequate land or regular jobs. It is not that these conflicts are unmanageable; it is just that concern for poverty, for incorporating urban labor, and for economic efficiency and growth all run into conflict with each other to degrees that have not been characteristic of twentieth-century capitalism in the North.

High ratios of labor to land and capital make everything difficult, but the difficulties could be much less if ownership of land and capital were itself widely dispersed. "Land is scarce only for the poor."[8] That pungent way to put the matter may be misleading. In the Peruvian Sierra and possibly also in El Salvador (the specific reference of the quotation), even a perfectly equal distribution of land would leave everyone at very low income levels, until enough people can get out of reliance on agricultural production. But the main point is certainly right: in most of Latin America ownership is so highly concentrated it makes market forces operate as negatively as possible. The degree of concentration is not a result of economic performance in open competitive markets. It is much more commonly a result of arbitrary, nonfunctional, historical factors creating special advantages. Concentration of ownership has been reinforced over long periods by effective exclusion of much of the population from opportunities to raise their earnings and acquire capital and skills. The reluctance of the people who have controlled these societies to invest in education and creation of opportunities for the poor has been a powerful factor helping to keep market forces acting in favor of the few.

Restrictions on international trade become a natural public preference in such a context, even apart from the specific interests of industrialists trying to promote protection. When a main component of income growth is the export of primary products from land or mines owned by a wealthy few, efficient patterns of trade imply sharply unequal consequences for income and power. Industrialists

[8] Walter LaFeber, *Inevitable Revolutions: The United States in Central America*, enl. ed. (New York: Norton, 1984).

and those concerned with inequity made a perhaps odd but still understandable pair of interests in favor of at least partial withdrawal
from trade. The East Asian scope for rapid and relatively egalitarian growth by aggressive export promotion was greatly aided by
comparative advantage balanced on the side of industrial exports.
The fact that comparative advantage in Latin America was strongly
on the side of primary products, in conditions of concentrated ownership, greatly weakened the case for growth primarily through
trade. That does not mean that the style of import substitution actually practiced was a constructive response: the societies would
have been much better off if protection had been much more selective, more restrained, and quickly accompanied by measures to promote development of more diversified exports once new economic
activities were established. But to insist on going all the way back to
free trade would have meant rejecting a goal with understandably
wide public support; the only countries that have come close to
going back have been those in the Southern Cone in their most thoroughly totalitarian periods.

Other dimensions of such conflict between public preferences
and criteria of economic efficiency and consistency have been discussed in preceding chapters, including such pervasive issues as
wage policies, exchange rates, the role of foreign investment, and
attempts to eliminate inflation. While each has its own complications, the common pattern is that response to public preferences in
these matters normally requires departure from pure free-market
principles. In almost all such conflicts, it is possible to suggest compromises with market pressures and efficiency criteria that would
go some way toward answering public preferences without blocking
fairly successful economic performance. Sometimes such compromises can be worked out, but the chances of success go down when
international agencies or U.S. loan programs insist on full respect
for free-market solutions as a necessary condition of getting external credit. Similarly, an impatient style of rejection for all this populist nonsense, conveyed systematically to the young Latin American professionals studying in this field, may have done something to
change the odds adversely for the kinds of compromises necessary
to any democratic society. These arguments were not confined to
academic analysis: strong economic interests and well-armed non-
academics were among the most attentive listeners.

Discussions of possible postauthoritarian systems in Brazil and
the Southern Cone have brought out consideration of a variety of
ways to negotiate social contracts, or agreed limits on changes by

both reformist and conservative sides.[9] Such contracts imply limits on representative governments. The winning side cannot, if it accepts the limits in exchange for the protections, try to take all. That may mean that special privileges, or welfare programs costly for growth, may be protected from democratic decisions against them. In general, when such limits involve economic policies they are likely to protect the rich; when they involve protection of human rights they are more likely to protect the poor. Examples of such limits in the United States might be the semi-independent Federal Reserve system, the powers of the Supreme Court to set aside legislation violating constitutional protections, and most vitally the Bill of Rights. A major example in postwar Latin America was the National Front agreement between Conservatives and Liberals in Colombia in 1958, putting a brake on participation by nonelite parties but at the same time putting an end to two decades of extreme violence.[10] That put limits on possible change, but at the same time it helped restore acceptance of a political system able to allow public pressures on government, and transfers of authority without violence. Political pacts do not endure forever but can help societies get past periods of exceptional strain.

Alejandro Foxley, writing from Chilean experience, expresses particularly well the need for agreement to reject "totalizing economic ideologies," meaning those obsessed with free markets and private enterprise just as much as those that want to wipe them out.[11] On one side, competitive markets have great value in keeping a society flexible, by eroding special privileges based on protection against market forces. On the other side, if markets consistently damage the weaker side of the society, democracy cannot thrive without limiting such negative impacts. To insist on the first side and rule out the second requires an authoritarian society: economic efficiency can have excessively high human costs.

3. TRANSITIONAL STRAINS AS OPPOSED TO IMPLACABLE FAILURES

To interpret the strains in Latin American development as the results of transitional processes is more likely to come close to the

---

[9] Guillermo O'Donnell, Philippe C. Schmitter, and Laurence Whitehead, eds., *Transitions from Authoritarian Rule: Comparative Perspectives* (Baltimore: Johns Hopkins University Press, 1986).

[10] R. Albert Berry et al., *Politics of Compromise.*

[11] Foxley, "Cinco lecciones," p. 169.

heart of the matter than any vision of necessary deadlocks. Both the optimistic hypotheses of gradual modernization widely accepted in the early postwar period, and the more pessimistic family of dependency hypotheses popular later on, have a valuable emphasis on conflict between forces making for change acting against counterforces that are unlikely to last. They both exaggerated their respective positions but rightly reject any view that permanent characteristics of Latin American societies make them incapable of successful self-government.[12]

Modernization hypotheses envisaged growth out of underdevelopment and social injustice by a mutually reinforcing process of industrialization, widening educational opportunities, broadening political participation, and increasing recognition that rising incomes can help all groups together. It turned out in practice that industrialization did little to help the poor, reformist governments often set back economic development, conservative forces were either too fearful or too selfish to encourage the kinds of structural changes needed for participatory societies, and authoritarian reaction became a frequent outcome. What was wrong with the modernization thesis was the idea that patience was bound to yield improvement. The path of patience is strewn with victims. What was right about it is that change is possible; that nothing inherent in Latin American conditions rules out either democracy or development or reduction of inequity, *provided that* each society manages to combine requirements for a well-functioning economy with specific measures designed to broaden participation. Modernization in the sense expected is not guaranteed by industrialization or economic growth; it has to be actively promoted by measures that sometimes run counter to requirements for efficient patterns of growth.

The best versions of dependency analysis also emphasize a process of change. For Cardoso and Peter Evans and many others, the older kind of dependency on primary exports was just a difficult phase to pass through on the way to a more complex kind of dependent development. Dependent development in the sense of excessive foreign investment and influence, reinforcing the repressive strands in domestic societies, is in turn another difficult phase to pass through but not an indefinite conclusion. It generates its own new forces for movement past this phase. "Postdependency" may become a name for the current context in the semi-industrialized countries, with decreasing roles of multinational firms, more inde-

[12] Valenzuela and Valenzuela, "Modernisation and Dependence."

pendent domestic entrepreneurship, and possibly a movement away from threats of market-authoritarian political outcomes.[13] Choice of terminology is a matter of taste, but it probably would help to recognize that the possibilities keep changing. It may be that some of the most dangerous tensions were partly matters of historical transition: at least some Latin American societies may have better chances for peaceful modernization in the next twenty years than they had in the past.

Some of the most intense social strains came from the effort to speed industrialization at the cost of direct and serious harm to primary producers. Landowners fought back hard, inevitably, whenever they could. Sometimes that fight led directly to military intervention and repression. More often, it led governments to try to escape this conflict either by shifting the costs of industrialization abroad through external borrowing and foreign investment, or by repressing wages, by accepting inflation, or all of them together. External borrowing and foreign investment took some of the heat out of domestic conflict for a time but badly aggravated dependency and external debt. Accelerating inflation weakened middle class acceptance of representative governments. Putting the burden on workers and peasants helped hold down consumption and imports but it ensured heightened pressures for radical social reform and for authoritarian measures to prevent it. What is somewhat more hopeful now is that further industrialization does not require going back to such a violent initial wrench: conflicts among groups are certain to continue, but at least one major aggravating factor should be less of a problem.

Labor market conditions were particularly adverse in the early postwar years for any successful combination of reliance on private markets with democracy, as discussed in many contexts above. But development is not eternally characterized by surplus labor. The question is the balance between rates of growth of opportunities for productive employment and rates of growth of the labor force. While the balance has been changing for the worse in the poorest countries of the region, it improved considerably in the course of the 1970s, especially in Brazil and Colombia, and possibly also in Mexico. This kind of transition creates conditions under which the

[13] David G. Becker, *The New Bourgeoisie and the Limits of Dependency: Mining, Class, and Power in "Revolutionary" Peru* (Princeton: Princeton University Press, 1983). Peter Evans, "After Dependency," suggests that the real issues have not changed to the fundamental degrees suggested by the concept of postdependency but agrees that it probably would help to get away from the old dependency terminology.

normal operation of market forces in conditions of renewed growth is more likely to pull up real earnings in the rural sector as well as the urban, making reliance on such forces more nearly consistent with an egalitarian set of economic policies. Because market systems can then work in favor of more of the population, they may come to strengthen rather than undermine acceptance of a participatory political system.

The more nearly integrated societies of the Southern cone, with wide public participation and more organized labor forces, could not place the costs of industrialization on workers as long as their political systems remained open. That made for less inequality but at the cost of making it nearly impossible to achieve industrial exports and external balance. To get out of that constraint required some process of raising productivity relative to wages. The potentially peaceful way might have been to use economic policies favorable for growth while negotiating restraints on the rate of increase of wages, until gains in efficiency could permit effective export competition without reducing wages. Once in balance, industrial export promotion is not only consistent with rising wages but highly favorable for them, as demonstrated so clearly in East Asia. The alternative Brazilian and Southern Cone methods, forcing down real wages drastically in a short period through political repression, is not a peaceful way and never could be. But earlier imbalances between wages and productivity have been corrected, at enormous cost. There is no objective necessity to march over this cliff again.

Albert Hirschman's interpretation of the strand of economic causation making authoritarian outcomes so frequent in the last twenty years is especially clear on the importance of transitional processes. Although sympathetic to the goals embodied in the early postwar industrialization drives, and to the temporary need to go against efficiency criteria in the interest of promoting structural change, he suggests that the key problem was the need to redirect economic strategy toward more attention to conventional economic constraints as industrialization went on. Attention to constraints that might have blocked change in the first place became essential in order to keep the process of change going successfully.[14] That way of putting the matter is central to understanding the emergence of the market-authoritarian states. It was not a matter of necessary negative outcomes built into the process of development, but of op-

[14] Hirschman, "The Turn to Authoritarianism."

tions that could have been different, and can be handled better by the countries newly coming up to this crucially difficult phase.

4. SEMI-OPTIMISTIC CONCLUSIONS

Interactions between economic strategies and political pressures take on infinitely varied patterns, providing ammunition both for those who are convinced that the *failures* to follow safe and sane orthodox economic principles are responsible for the breakdowns of representative political systems and for those who are convinced that it is mainly the *efforts* to apply such principles that have favored authoritarian regimes. If either side were completely wrong that would by now have become a generally accepted conclusion. There is no consensus on the matter because they are both right in the sense that either disregard of conventional economic principles or rigid adherence to them is likely to be fatal for representative government in Latin America. The costs of failure to maintain internal and external macroeconomic balance, and of strategies adverse for efficiency, have been detailed in many specific contexts throughout this book. The reasons for repeated choices against criteria of economic efficiency by those governments that try to respond to popular preferences also seem clear: orthodox economic policies would have gone against strong public preferences in terms of conflict with protected industrialists and urban labor, and conflicted with national objectives to industrialize and modernize.

To maintain representative government in these countries requires a treacherous balancing act between response to popular preferences and insistence on enough economic coherence to make continued growth possible. Intense social conflict has left such deep wounds, and so much mistrust on all sides, that some countries may be simply unable to find any solution within a representative system. But such a somber conclusion would not seem to be inescapable: people on all sides can learn from what does not work, and can conceivably adjust their sights if all sides do so jointly. Such an adjustment process requires as a minimum that the kinds of economic strategies used do not allow any side to be pushed down in order to support growth for the rest. Democracies can work only if the economic strategies they use actually benefit most of the people, poor and nonpoor, most of the time.

THIRTEEN

IS IT POSSIBLE FOR THE UNITED STATES
TO PLAY A CONSTRUCTIVE ROLE?

If I knew for a certainty that a man was coming to my house with
the conscious design of doing me good, I should run for my life.
—Thoreau, *Walden*

To explain the persistence of poverty and extreme inequality in
Latin America, and the closely related political tensions so ready to
turn into either explosion or repression, requires taking into account both what individual countries try to do and the ways in which
external factors act on them. Of the many outside influences that
matter, those coming from the United States count most. Some of
the connections are discussed in chapter 7 as questions of dependency, as given conditions that shape behavior in Latin America. The
present chapter considers the other side of the coin: the external
context as itself a variable that can be altered by the United States.

When a state-owned electric power firm in Brazil reverses its decision to buy domestically produced turbines and imports them under AID financing instead, when a conservative Colombian government decides to introduce a long-resisted land reform, when the
president of Ecuador reinstates after a trip to Washington the pro-
vincial elections he had suspended three months earlier, when Chilean truck owners carry out a prolonged strike disrupting production and aggravating problems of a leftist government, or when
Dominican military officers block a reformist president considered
likely to be influenced by communist support, the actions may not
be fully explicable without taking into account inducements
brought to bear by the United States.[1] Latin American governments

---

[1] The significance of the battle over electrical equipment in Brazil during the AID
program is analyzed in Judith Tendler, *Inside Foreign Aid* (Baltimore: Johns Hopkins
University Press, 1975). On U.S. influence and land reform in Colombia see Merilee
S. Grindle, *State and Countryside*, pp. 142–44, and note 23 to chapter 7. Gyrations of
elections in Ecuador under the current president are noted in Latin American News-
letter, *Weekly Report*, WR-85-43 (1 November 1985), and WR-86-10 (7 March 1986).
Sources on the episodes in Chile and the Dominican Republic referred to in this sen-
tence are given in the discussion following in this chapter.

and private groups are not helpless. They may in the great majority of cases be able to resist U.S. pressures that they do not consider to be in their interests. But such pressures—including positive offers of help as well as threats of adverse response—can change both what they consider to be in their interest and the internal balance of power among the groups that make domestic decisions. To leave this side out of the picture would be to leave out a great deal of what determines the character of development in Latin America.

The central question is how the national interests of the United States relate to poverty, repression, and dependence in Latin America. It is unreasonable to expect that the United States will act against its own interests, but there are many different ways to understand what they are and how to implement them. The disagreements cannot be resolved by mere facts and logic: they are matters of both conflicting economic interests and conflicting values. The U.S. administrations dealing with Guatemala in 1954 or Chile in 1970–73 may or may not have realized that their actions were going to result in long periods of intensely repressive governments and increased inequality; even if they had foreseen these consequences and would have preferred less negative outcomes, it is possible that they would have gone right ahead because these were not their main concerns. The pervasive threads in these cases and many others have been strong antipathy toward Marxist influence in any form and a conception of national security that sees any such influence as a genuine danger. These positions are so thoroughly mixed up with economic concerns, with the safety and profitability of private enterprise, that analysis of what can be done requires at least an attempt to deal with these tangled relationships. Section 1 discusses the elusive character of the goals involved, section 2 concentrates on selected aspects of U.S. economic policies, and section 3 on interactions with differing conceptions of national security.

1. Changing Policies within a Common Framework

Three facets of policy toward Latin America persist through thick and thin but keep changing in relative importance. On the economic side, the United States consistently tries to keep open the possibilities of direct investment and access to raw materials, to protect property claims of investors, and more generally to favor private enterprise and reliance on market forces. On the side of national security, the United States consistently tries to limit Soviet and Cuban

influence, to favor survival of governments that have the same orientation and to oppose those that do not. The third facet is a fairly
consistent preference, at least in the absence of concerns about security or threats to private ownership in the particular case, for rising incomes and more representative governments in Latin America. This concern for improving economic and political conditions
can be viewed as a selfish interest because rising Latin American incomes stimulate markets and investment opportunities, and because more broadly accepted governments decrease the likelihood
of explosions. It can also be viewed as including a genuine wish that
life could become safer and less miserable for the majority of the
people in Latin America.

These three persisting lines of policy often collide with each
other. To put most of the emphasis on national security, when this
means supporting repressive governments as long as they are anticommunist, or opposing popular movements of all kinds whenever
there is the least hint of any radical element involved, runs directly
contrary to any goal of reducing poverty and promoting broad political participation. The same policy orientation can weaken pop-
ularly based governments by blocking specific actions that are
wanted by the great majority of the country but run counter to particular U.S. interests. As discussed in chapters 9 and 10, the pro-
U.S. reformist governments of Belaúnde in Peru and Frei in Chile
in the 1960s were both badly damaged by parallel cases of inability
to respond to nearly unanimous popular pressure to assert control
over specific U.S. corporations that had become highly charged examples of subservience.

Conflicts between public preferences and particular U.S. interests
are not always that sharp. The more generous line of policy sometimes has a chance. Few U.S. administrations would oppose, and
some have positively aided, reformist governments that have gone
against the interests of particular corporations, and carried out significant social reforms, provided that they stay clear of Marxist influence. If such governments can implement domestic reforms
without economic breakdown they can be seen as vindications of the
possibilities of a better life in Latin America *outside* communism.
They could enhance U.S. long-run security interests at the same
time as they improve conditions of life in Latin America.

The crucial borderline cases are those in which reformist or revolutionary movements, or governments, promise real change from
inequitable and corrupt regimes but include communists or accept
their support. The United States may not attack even fairly radical

reform governments that are strongly anticommunist, as in Peru under Velasco, but the more usual case is that those governments and those opposition movements that care about reform accept support or even participation by Marxist groups. Both Latin American ideological traditions and the reality of gross inequality ensure the presence of active communist groups in these countries. They are natural supporters of almost any drive for social change. If their support is enough to condemn any reformist government that does not strenuously disavow it, the United States is almost automatically placed in opposition.

Opposition to any kind of "instability" that could conceivably lead to communist influence, in the belief that preserving stability is equivalent to support for freedom as well as for U.S. national security, can take many different forms. It can lead to seriously pursued programs of economic or technical aid intended to help the poor, or to pressure on national military leaders to overturn civilian governments trying themselves to help the poor. It can lead to concern for protection of human rights, or to supplying weapons with which to repress them. Differences among U.S. administrations have often been of great importance in such respects but even in those of Presidents Kennedy and Carter the pressure to put anticommunism at or close to the top of priorities whenever conflicts arise, to be on the safe side of the cold war realists, seems to take effective hold of many of the very people who would otherwise be among the most concerned for social welfare. The sequence seems to be first to bomb the villages to get rid of the guerrillas, then to help those who survive, if any, with a generous aid program.

The early postwar period in which the relative wealth and power of the United States were at their peaks in the world as a whole was not a constructive period for relationships with Latin America. That could be blamed on the cold war but an additional factor was that U.S. economic interests in Latin America became much greater than ever before. From being primarily a source of raw materials and a zone to be kept free of enemy powers, many Latin American countries became for the first time major fields for investments by U.S. industrial firms and also much more important markets for exports. That new set of economic ties fostered a new set of interests in the avoidance of left-wing governments adverse to trade and foreign investment.

If economic dominance made things worse in terms of adding to the pressures to support conservative regimes in Latin America, the gradual postwar decrease in relative economic weight and power of the United States might possibly lead to some lessening of such pressures. The possibility is real, but decreasing dominance of the world economy could lead in either of two very different directions. One might be to retreat into increasing protectionism, to reject aid and turn against the international financial institutions (as well as the United Nations and the World Court) and rely on unilateral answers to what are perceived to be external threats. The main alternative, also conceivable because it would also fit many interpretations of the national interest, would be to support more collective responses to problems, to fortify international institutions and accept more nearly equal participation in their decision making, and perhaps to accept some versions of the repeated attempts by developing countries to promote more collective management of world trade and finance.

In Latin America, the counterpart of lessening U.S. economic dominance has been an increase in scope for independent action. Brazil's drive for worldwide trade and financial connections in the 1970s, Panama's pressure to gain sovereignty in the Canal Zone, Argentina's flat rejection of U.S. efforts to stop war over the Malvinas, the formation of the Contadora Group, and Peru's suddenly more independent stance under Alan García, could all be seen as examples of increased room to move. For the United States, alternative responses are clearly possible: to negotiate and share power for agreed goals, as in the Carter administration response to Panama, or to opt for more militaristic efforts to demolish opposition, as in the Reagan administration response to Nicaragua.

Declining relative power both heightens pressures for unilateral response and increases the costs of mistakes. When the country is put in a severely frustrating position as it was in 1979–80 by danger to the American hostages in Iran, the context favors aggressive actions and political success for belligerent candidates. The latter then magnify public fears and drum up militancy because that is what they believe in and thrive on. Every issue gets interpreted in one-track terms of Soviet moves aimed at domination, most insistently those in relation to leftist movements in Latin America, as if there were no independent reasons for Latin Americans themselves to want fundamental changes.[2] In such a context, U.S. policy almost

[2] See the particularly illuminating discussions of such narrowing of perspective in John P. Lewis, "Can We Escape the Path of Mutual Injury?" and Abraham Lowenthal, "Latin America and the Caribbean: Toward a New U.S. Policy," in John P. Lewis and Valeriana Kallab, eds., *U.S. Foreign Policy and the Third World, Agenda 1983* (New York: Praeger for the Overseas Development Council, 1983), pp. 7–65.

automatically runs against social change. It also leads closer to war, both in Latin America and worldwide. Since those risks are visible too, opposition to the warlike path has increased in response to the dangers. The second side gives grounds for hope, though hardly for confidence, that the very real national interests pulling in more cooperative directions will be able to have a significant influence on U.S. strategy.

2. ECONOMIC OPPORTUNITIES AND CONFLICTS

If a reasonably farsighted and well-intentioned U.S. administration wanted to help lessen poverty and promote more participatory growth in Latin America, it could conceivably do a great deal of good. But even with such a favorable context there would be plenty of room for disagreement about what is desirable and what is possible. The traditional U.S. orientation toward open economies, freedom for private investment, and reliance on the price system has some implications favorable for Latin American development and others more likely to be adverse. Governmental aid and credit, also with potential to be helpful, can similarly have adverse effects. And even the rare attempts to go beyond conventional conceptions of cooperation, as with the Alliance for Progress, the Inter-American Foundation, or the Carter administration's use of aid programs to exert pressure in support of human rights, have been seen as sources of trouble. In these treacherous areas, what room is there to do anything clearly helpful?

Troublesome questions of economic policy include U.S. positions in response to the proposals of developing countries for stabilization of prices of basic commodities, unilateral decisions on protection aid programs, and conditions related to external credit. The United States has consistently rejected proposals for general worldwide commodity agreements, while participating in the coffee agreements that have transferred significant foreign exchange earnings to Latin America.[3] Wider agreements have usually been rejected on principle, as distortions of efficiency by interference with market forces; the inconsistent decision to participate in the coffee agreements is constantly brought back in question, and may well

[3] On Latin American interests in commodity price stabilization see Roberto Junguito and Diego Pisano, "Primary Products in Latin America," and Ernesto Tironi, "National Policies Towards Commodity Exports," in Ricardo Ffrench-Davis and Ernesto Tironi, eds., *Latin America and the New International Economic Order* (London: Macmillan in association with St. Antony's College, Oxford, 1982).

be broken off. If it is, that will lower foreign exchange earnings and real income for many Latin countries, but will probably reduce U.S. trade deficits and the average domestic price of coffee. It is easy to see direct U.S. interests in withdrawing, and in resisting most other such agreements, but then why was this one accepted in the first place?

The main complicating factor, running contrary to immediate U.S. economic interests as far as national income and the balance of payments are concerned, is precisely the U.S. longer term interest in stability and economic growth in Latin America. That is both an economic interest—to favor improving export markets, investment conditions, and the possibilities of payment on existing debts to U.S. banks—and a political concern. If Costa Rican or Haitian earnings from coffee exports turn seriously worse, countries that might well be stable allies in an area of intense conflict are less likely to be either allies or stable. Why is it easier to agree on coffee than on other commodities? Possibly because the impact is so direct in Latin America and the political interest so strong, and possibly because coffee prices, unlike those for industrial raw materials, do not constitute costs for particular U.S. industries. But these are questions of degree within a general set of conflicts among U.S. interests. Would it be preferable to change the balance toward more such agreements, or instead to back away from this one?

The side of U.S. objectives concerned with cooperation, with political stability, and with Latin American economic growth would probably be better served by finding an alternative method of meeting Latin American goals than either insisting on free-market forces or adopting general commodity controls. There is an excellent case for allowing commodity prices to move in response to changes in demand and supply: it could be a costly mistake to try to fix commodity prices in order to keep them high and thereby encourage increased production of goods that are in excess supply, or to hold them down and discourage production of those in short supply. But the Latin American objective of reduced instability, of preventing exactly the kind of perverse plunge that hit the region when interest rates increased and the terms of trade turned drastically adverse at the end of the 1970s, could be answered by agreements to provide generalized support financing in conditions of weak world demand. Such support financing exists on a limited scale through the IMF; it could be made much more effective without fixing any prices, introducing perverse incentives, or creating producer controls over supply. If the United States wished to cooperate with the goal, rather than merely cast deserved doubt on the particular method, it would be possible to do a lot to lessen these sharply negative pressures.

Trade restrictions provide another important area for continuing choices that can change conditions for the better or the worse. U.S. restrictions on imports are biased toward above-average degrees of restraint on more labor-intensive lines of industrial production. To reduce such protection would selectively favor expansion of those lines of output most favorable for employment and reduction of poverty in Latin America. The restrictions are there for a purpose: to take them away would hurt the particular firms and workers competing with imports. They are part of public concern too; the appropriate compromises in specific cases are not matters that can be decided in general terms. This classic conflict of interests will always swing decisions back and forth as one side or another gains political weight, but the balance has been moving toward more restriction as the competitive position of the United States in the world economy has weakened. A possible response would be to do more to foster new industries able to export, rather than retreat behind increasing protection. If it proved to be possible to reduce barriers against labor-intensive imports, this would surely help to improve employment conditions and to reduce poverty in Latin America.

From a dependency perspective, options by the United States to keep trade relatively open might be seen as adverse: reduced protection by the United States pulls Latin American producers away from internal demand patterns toward export markets and, by providing more foreign exchange earnings to pay for more imports, reduces pressures toward self-sufficiency. The same argument applies to aid and provision of external credit. Greater availability of external financing links Latin American economies more firmly to the outside world economy. The issues raised by this perspective are discussed in chapter 7, with mixed conclusions. On the side of trade, growth of exports of labor-intensive manufactures does indeed affect the structure of production, but in a way systematically favorable for employment: to follow the dependency argument would be adverse for the poor. But on issues of governmental aid and external finance in general, the case for greater insulation is distinctly stronger.

Economic aid and general external credit have two-sided effects. They provide additional resources that can permit greater production, investment, and consumption than would otherwise be possible. They can lessen social strains and support democratic governments, when such governments exist in the first place. On the

negative side, they can reduce pressures to promote savings, tax reform, exports, and vertical integration of production. They can
prop up corrupt and repressive governments as well as democracies. They are not intrinsically good or bad; they are shot through
with contradictory possibilities.

Support for increased aid and commercial credit can be seen as a
case for generosity as opposed to tight-fisted conservatism. That
would be an accurate way to look at it if the societies receiving finance were relatively democratic and egalitarian, with governments
actively interested in using additional resources for majority welfare. It would be a drastically misconceived kind of generosity if the
initial situation were just the opposite, or if the conditions under
which financing is made available are directed against social reform.
The preceding chapters are meant to underline the diversity and
changing character of actual conditions in Latin American societies,
arguing against any blanket conclusion that external support systematically works against desirable change or is consistently helpful
for welfare. It could go either way in particular cases. The main
problems are that decisions on aid and credit are dominated so
much of the time by insistence on U.S. conceptions of desirable economic systems and by fears of radical change.

The positive and the negative possibilities are both visible in the
marked change of U.S. policy toward external finance between
1981–82, the first years of the Reagan administration, and its reorientation from late 1982. The original insistence on tight monetary restraint, with strong resistance to increased support for international financial institutions, helped bring on the debt crisis and
stop growth in Latin America. Subsequent reversal toward promotion of external credit helped lessen those downward pressures and
favored resumption of growth in Latin America. Then, as private
banks continued to hold back on new lending because of doubts
about service of their prior loans, the administration proposed a
more active financing effort (the "Baker Plan"), to combine large-
scale public and private loans to those particular debtor countries
able to put together promising recovery programs. The proposal is
a striking example of a repeated pattern: a welcome turn toward
generosity that could be helpful but comes with conditions all too
likely to work against social change. The conditions are specified in
the definition of what constitutes a promising recovery program: it
is not just a matter of macroeconomic balance but a committment to
adopt free-market policies, favor private enterprise, encourage foreign investment, get away from any use of subsidies, and either close

down state-owned firms or sell them to the private sector. Countries in which private property and income are extraordinarily concentrated, in which market forces very often work systematically against the poor, were to be required to stack the cards even more strongly against any attempts at corrective action.

Official aid programs can in principle favor more equitable societies as well as economic growth. In practice, it is doubtful that they do more good than harm. The largest-scale effort to promote both social reform and economic growth, the Alliance for Progress created in the Kennedy administration, had a great many positive components. It provided financing and technical advice for better public health programs, education, agricultural research and extension, more effective tax systems, and land reform programs which—though woefully limited in scale—helped thousands of rural families. It helped many young people gain more education than would otherwise have been possible, and it helped build up governmental administrative capacities as well as productive capacity in the private sector. The accompanying Peace Corps program got out into small rural activities otherwise almost entirely neglected. And yet, despite all such positive elements, it is a real possibility that the program did a great deal of damage.

Why consider the effects of the Alliance so doubtful? Partly for disappointment in its limits: the land reforms slowed down or stopped, improvements in agricultural productivity had very mixed effects on the landless rural poor, the educational opportunities more often helped upper income groups than the poor, tax systems did not actually become more progressive, and in general the institutional structures of these societies showed little change. How could they, when a central premise of the whole effort was that private enterprise, most especially including foreign investors, was the key to national progress? The program lacked any definition of what to do about the many possible conflicts between the concerns of private investors and the goal of structural reform.[4] Private enterprise *can* be an important key to progress, but if intended reforms are checked whenever they run contrary to the interests of the people responsible for the society's existing institutions, the reforms cannot be expected to change the institutions. The program

[4] Albert Fishlow, *The Mature Neighbor Policy: A New United States Economic Policy for Latin America* (Berkeley: Institute of International Studies, University of California, 1977).

took for granted the desirability of supporting the very interests making the societies what they were in the first place.

This way of summarizing the impasse suggests only that the gains of such a program are inescapably limited, not that it need cause deeper trouble. Many of the microlevel activities, such as helping to increase rural education or improving water supplies to lessen disease, were almost surely favorable for the poor. But increased loan financing for imports lessened pressures to switch toward the kinds of export promotion favorable for more independent growth. The use of aid funds to pull country spending toward U.S. exports, as in the Brazilian case of diversion away from potential domestic suppliers of capital goods, may well have acted to slow up desirable diversification. Beyond that, when the government of Brazil in the first two years of the Alliance did try to initiate land reform and tax reform, but stirred up social protests and weakened fiscal restraint at the same time, the United States cut off aid. That action seemed a clear declaration that reforms had to stay carefully clear of arousing populist expectations. It must have served to encourage in some degree the military coup that soon followed.

Dealing with moderately reformist governments, reasonably coherent in their objectives and very careful about any conflicts with U.S. investors (as in Chile and Colombia in the 1960s), the Alliance supported them and favored reforms. Dealing with ruthlessly repressive governments, as in Guatemala and Nicaragua, it equally supported them and thereby lessened the likelihood of any real reforms. Dealing with everyone, the Alliance was accompanied by a sharp increase in U.S. military aid, advisers, and training programs devoted to handling domestic subversion. There is little room for doubt that all this contributed to the frequency of military coups in the 1960s and 1970s, and to the chilling efficiency of repression.

In the 1970s, congressional leaders promoted a more modest and differently oriented program, creating the Inter-American Foundation to support small firms and local cooperatives. The foundation has provided both technical aid and support financing, usually for small rural producers, especially for cooperative projects that create employment, initiate new lines of production, and raise the capacity of local groups to organize and defend their interests.[5] This kind of program can and has helped the poor while increasing productive capacity. At least it did until the Reagan administration decided in 1983 that this focus did not fit its sense of desirable goals.

[5] Albert O. Hirschman, *Getting Ahead Collectively*.

The timing and objectives of the Inter-American Foundation closely paralleled President Carter's attempt to use U.S. pressure to protect human rights. That was of course a worldwide concern but particularly relevant for Latin America where governments closely allied to the United States were stepping on human rights to extreme degrees. Two notable characteristics of the Inter-American Foundation and the drive for human rights were that they were not designed to serve the interests of U.S. corporations and did not take their directions from the people running national governments. They were correctly seen as working in long-run U.S. interests by improving conditions of life in Latin America, but they were outside of, and to some degree opposed by, the concerns of U.S. corporations. Where the Alliance for Progress worked through and gave way to the preferences of existing governments, the Inter-American Foundation worked directly with small local groups and tried to build up their power to defend themselves, even against higher levels of government. And the human rights program ran head-on against the preferences of some of the worst governments of the time. The problem with the Alliance for Progress was that it sided most easily with the wrong people.

It is possible to do a great deal of good on the local level, and that may be where the chances are best, but there are of course many other issues of possible cooperation or harm in macroeconomic terms. One of them might be to support rather than oppose the efforts of Latin American governments to move IMF conditionality more toward solutions through growth than through contraction, as discussed in chapter 5. In practice, the United States did side with this move and helped increase flexibility in IMF programs in the late 1970s, but then went into reverse and pushed the IMF back to more contractionary methods in the early 1980s. The United States could also side with the desire of Latin American governments to gain greater voice in the international economic institutions. These were aspects of the fierce debates in the 1970s over proposals for a New International Economic Order; debates in which the United States often had the better side in terms of economic analysis but distinguished itself by refusing to look for alternative ways to accomplish desired changes.

The essence of the preceding is that many of the lines of economic policy that fit naturally with U.S. interests and appeal to people with generous intentions are likely to do more harm than good. One-tenth as much economic aid, directed toward improved social conditions in countries where there is a real effort to develop participatory societies, could be vastly more helpful. When U.S. administrations call for large-scale new aid programs, such as the Caribbean Basin Initiative in 1982 or the aid recommendations of the Kissinger Commission report on Central America, anyone who cares about autonomy and participatory societies in Latin America has good cause to expect trouble.[6] It is possible to design constructive actions that would be in the long-run interests of the United States, but that is neither easy nor the normal result.

3. POLITICAL ECONOMY AND NATIONAL SECURITY

Economic analysis may be more precise if it is kept clear of debate about security interests, and for many purposes that detached precision is exactly what is needed. But if one wants to examine the main variables acting to change the life chances of the people of Latin America, it should be recognized that a modest gain by improvement of economic strategy may be swamped by the human and institutional damage when external forces strengthen a repressive system or undermine more open societies. The United States may within a few years give warm support to land reform in general and destroy a government promoting a sorely needed reform in Guatemala. The deciding factor is not the effect of the reforms on production or poverty: it is the security assessment by the United States of the government involved. Colombia and Peru may be actively encouraged to carry out land reforms as long as their governments are firmly anticommunist; if the government of Guatemala is perceived as being influenced by communists, then positive effects for the poor of its intended land reform become irrelevant.

Both of two common beliefs—that the United States only intervenes to support or to change governments in rare cases of clear-cut danger, or that it is constantly intervening to block any significant reforms—are inconsistent with the actual record of oscillation and uncertainty. Specific instances during the postwar period include overturning the government of Guatemala in 1954; the change from initial acceptance of the Castro regime in Cuba to condemnation and then unsuccessful attack; initiation of the Alliance for Progress in 1961; pressure against the populist government in Brazil and unreserved approval of the military takeover there in 1964;

[6] Richard E. Feinberg and Richard Newfarmer, "The Caribbean Basin Initiative: Bold Plan or Empty Promise?" in Newfarmer, ed., *From Gunboats to Diplomacy: New U.S. Policies for Latin America* (Baltimore: Johns Hopkins University Press, 1984), pp. 210–17.

direct military intervention in the Dominican Republic in 1965; attacks on the Allende government in Chile and encouragement of its overthrow by a particularly reactionary military in 1973; a reversal to negotiation and to an eminently sensible resolution of the Panama Canal dispute in 1978; briefly promising efforts under President Carter to restore more civilized relationships with Cuba and to promote concern for human rights, reversed quickly as short-term security considerations were again allowed to become dominant; determined opposition to the Sandinistas in Nicaragua prior to the overturn of Somoza, followed by temporary acceptance of the Sandinista government and even economic aid, and then by obsessive efforts to destroy it; and the ghastly interplay of calls for reform in El Salvador accompanied by military and economic support for governments fighting against any serious change, either unable to control or actually fostering right-wing death squads. There is more than a little room for doubt that all this has actually strengthened U.S. security. It has certainly included actions adverse to a better life for many people of Latin America.

What patterns are visible in such choices? They might be divided into a relatively clear-cut set of cases that suggest that the United States is irretrievably opposed to any forces favoring radical economic change, and more mixed cases suggesting that this interpretation misses important angles. Examples of the first set include the interventions in Guatemala, Brazil, the Dominican Republic, and Chile. The second group concerns divisions within the United States in relation to Cuba, the Panama Canal, the human rights program, El Salvador, and the Sandinista government in Nicaragua.

The first postwar intervention, in Guatemala, was small scale and had low immediate cost for the United States, though not for the people of Guatemala. In 1944, in part responding to the U.S. wartime theme of defending freedom, middle class and professional groups in Guatemala overturned their old-style dictatorship and replaced it with "the first government approaching political democracy and the welfare state in the nation's history."[7] The first elected

---

[7] John Gillin and K. H. Silvert, "Ambiguities in Guatemala," *Foreign Affairs* 34 (April 1956), pp. 469–82. For more detailed discussion of the situation in Guatemala and changes following overturn of the government, see Richard Newbold Adams, *Crucifixion by Power: Essays on Guatemalan National Social Structure* (Austin: University of Texas Press, 1970); Thomas and Marjorie Melville, *Guatemala: The Politics of Land Ownership* (New York: Free Press, 1971); and Lars Schoultz, "Guatemala: Social Change and Political Conflict," in Martin Diskin, ed., *Trouble in Our Backyard: Central America and the United States in the Eighties* (New York: Pantheon, 1983), pp. 173–202.

president, Juan José Arévalo, concentrated on replacing the centralized personal controls of the deposed dictator with multiple channels of political expression, including organizations of local government, peasant groups, and labor unions. New legislation significantly altered relationships between property owners and workers and abolished the "vagrancy" laws that had tied rural workers to particular landowners in a form very close to serfdom. These changes brought the government into direct conflict with the United Fruit Company, the largest landowner and employer in the country. The government also supported the company's workers in disputes over wages and working conditions, and adopted a project to build a highway to the coast in competition with the railway line owned by the company. The United States criticized many of Arévalo's actions, but it took no militaristic steps as long as he remained in office.

Jacobo Arbenz succeeded Arévalo in 1952 with an overwhelming two-thirds of the popular vote as the candidate most closely associated with the same set of economic and social policies. He took them an important step further by introducing a major land reform. He also took the risk of bringing communists into the administration of the land reform.[8] But his government was not in any sense militaristic or involved in any alliance with the Soviet Union. When the chips came down he was not able even to count on the country's armed forces for defense against invasion. But for President Eisenhower the participation of communists in government offices, in flagrant disregard of U.S. preferences, and the likely damage to property interests of a U.S. corporation were too much: he authorized an invasion by U.S.-armed rightist exiles, with the support of planes provided by the United States.[9]

[8] Gillin and Silvert, "Ambiguities," noted evidence that there were very few identifiable communists in the whole country but still agreed with the official U.S. position that several had important positions in the Arbenz government. Other social scientists go further toward the view that the government was "dominated" by communists. Cf. Theodore Geiger, *Communism versus Progress in Guatemala* (New York: National Planning Association, 1953), and Fredrick B. Pike, "Guatemala, the United States, and Communism in the Americas," *Review of Politics* 17 (April 1955), pp. 232–61. The open question is not "Were there communists in the government?" but rather "When there are, is that in itself a sufficient reason for the United States to overthrow a democratic government?"

[9] Eisenhower's explanation of his decision is given in his book, *Mandate for Change, 1953–56: The White House Years* (Garden City, N.Y.: Doubleday, 1963), pp. 421–27. Detailed accounts of the character of U.S. intervention include Adams, *Crucifixion by Power*, ch. 3; Melville and Melville, *Guatemala*, pp. 73–86; Richard H. Immerman,

With Guatemala's own military forces divided and uncertain, with constant public confusion fostered by false news broadcasts from CIA stations on the country's radios frightening everyone with imaginary battles, and with no way to protect the capital from air attacks by the planes provided by the United States, Arbenz resigned. The invading exile group took over the government and stopped the land reform program. The laws enacted over the previous nine years to build up protection for workers and peasants were replaced by new legislation prohibiting any political activity by labor groups, and the stage was set for thirty years of spasmodically ferocious repression and terrorism, alternating with brief periods of aborted hopes for improvement. Eisenhower considered the result to be a blow for freedom.

Intervention in Brazil was more indirect, but no less costly for the balance between repression and open societies in Latin America. As discussed in chapter 8, an inept populist government, with some intentions of reform but with fairly dismal economic management, brought on deepening trouble for itself prior to any U.S. involvement. Brazilian conservatives, bitter about the weakening economy and prone to see unlimited danger in the new phenomenon of a government supporting radical demonstrations, began to express fears of a leftist coup. The United States emphasized its rejection of the government by stopping aid. Brazilian generals seemed to hear a call. On the eve of the military revolt, U.S. naval forces were being moved into place in case they encountered trouble.[10] In the event, the generals had no difficulty: the fearsome radical forces cited as a reason for military action turned out to be nonoperative. The United States immediately resumed economic aid and stated its confidence that order would now be restored. Order was restored in the form of a reign of terror by the military lasting three years (and revived in 1969). It was also restored in the sense that the Brazilian economic policies were changed greatly, toward control of inflation (by monetary-fiscal restraint plus a dramatic cut in real wages), greater emphasis on exports and efficiency, and firm elimination of labor activism.

Following so quickly after the hopeful introduction of the Alliance for Progress, the Brazilian overturn was a potent demonstra-

---

The CIA in Guatemala: The Foreign Policy of Intervention (Austin: University of Texas Press, 1982); Stephen C. Schlesinger and Stephen Kinzer, Bitter Fruit: The Untold Story of the American Coup in Guatemala (Garden City, N.Y.: Doubleday, 1982).

[10] Alfred Stepan, "Political Leadership and Regime Breakdown," p. 132 and note 70; Phyllis R. Parker, Brazil and the Quiet Intervention.

tion that the United States would welcome the end of any democratic government so thoughtless as to distort economic policies and worry private investors. It was as if three years of bad economic management were enough to warrant throwing out representative government. And when the military opted for some of the most bitter repression seen up to that time in the modern world, the U.S. government did not recant initial expressions of warm approval. That could be seen as a welcoming sign for what was to follow in Chile, Uruguay, and Argentina.

Military intervention in the Dominican Republic in 1965, just one year later, brought out with unusual clarity a fundamental conflict of U.S. policy. When Juan Bosch was elected as a reform president in 1962 he was treated as a promising exponent of just the kinds of changes intended by the Alliance for Progress. The Dominican military drove him out of the country after seven months in office, acting on their own: the Kennedy administration was bitterly critical and suspended aid. The United States seemed to be clearly on the side of democracy and reform. But then both the Dominican Republic and the U.S. administration changed. Widespread dissatisfaction with the conservative government led to a division in the Dominican military: one faction, quickly supported by much of the civilian population, demanded the return of Bosch. That immediately brought out the other side of U.S. policy: the embassy reported that local communists were among the groups favoring Bosch, and the Johnson administration replied by encouraging the more reactionary side of the military to put down the forces demanding his return.[11] The new position seemed to say that any noticeable element of communist support makes an elected government unacceptable. That comes close to total reversal of the idea of reform: in the deeply unequal conditions of Latin America there are always *some* communist groups on the scene, and they are likely to be on the side of reform. A suspicious embassy can always identify and report communists among those supporting a reformist political leader even if he had never paid any attention to them and is unlikely ever to do so.

From the possibly distorted perspective of economic analysis, the

[11] Theodore Draper, "The Dominican Crisis: A Case Study in American Policy," *Commentary* 40, 6 (December 1965), pp. 33–68; Abraham F. Lowenthal, *The Dominican Intervention* (Cambridge: Harvard University Press, 1972); Jerome Slater, *Intervention and Negotiation: The United States and the Dominican Republic* (New York: Harper and Row, 1970); Howard J. Wiarda, *The Dominican Republic* (New York: Praeger, 1969).

relevant question about a major policy decision would seem to be the balance between gains and losses. What were the intended gains in the Dominican case, and what were the costs? For the Johnson administration, the main intended gain was to prevent any form of communist takeover. But then one might ask how likely such a takeover actually was: if the probability in the circumstances was nearly zero, intervention would suggest almost unlimited opposition to potential reformist government. In this case, the elected president was not in any sense a Marxist and had not while in office demonstrated any tendency in that direction. The communists of the country were not a powerful unified movement but a fringe group divided into three warring factions. But the eventual possibility that a reformist president might become influenced by Marxists was taken to be enough of a reason for military action against his supporters.

The costs in this case seem much clearer than the gains, if any. One cost was that Kennedy's prior position against military action to block reform was reversed. The far right was renotified that it could count on the United States to back them up when they moved to block reform governments. Another cost was in terms of Dominican lives and then, apparently without any prior expectation in Washington, direct involvement in the fighting by U.S. military forces.

The supporters of Bosch were in the capital city: they constituted most of its population. The embassy and Washington decided to ignore a series of opportunities to negotiate a settlement without violence and encouraged the anti-Bosch military to use air power to bomb and strafe the city, and then to attack it with armored forces.[12] The attack led to many deaths, and at first to apparent success. The United States conveyed its wish to the conquering general, Wessin, that mopping up operations should not be excessively vicious. The embassy cast about for a new junta to take over the government. But then the roof fell in: the combined civilian and military groups defending the capital pushed Wessin's forces back out of the city. "Unused to opposition or even to action, and learning that their tanks were not a very effective means to subdue a civilian population by now well-armed and aroused, Wessin's frightened troops were

---

[12] Draper, "Dominican Crisis," pp. 39–41; Lowenthal, *The Dominican Intervention*, pp. 63–112. The embassy approved the Dominican military's plan to strafe the capital and to attack on the ground, and rejected a series of opportunities to promote a cease-fire, because it was "skeptical about the feasibility of negotiations without a prior demonstration of force by anti-Bosch forces." (Lowenthal, p. 90). Slater, *Intervention*, p. 29, concludes that the embassy rejected appeals to stop the attack on the city because it was from the outset "determined that the revolution must fail."

stopped."[13] The United States was suddenly in the position of holding the hand of the losing general. Never at a loss for imaginative solutions, Johnson sent the marines into the fighting. The official rationale was that lives of U.S. citizens were in danger. They might have been in danger in the capital, but the actual deployment of troops was intended to, and did, save the forces of General Wessin by preventing the civilian and military groups that had defeated him from getting *out* of the city. The ultimate reason for the intervention was abundantly clear in communications between the embassy and Washington: Johnson would go to any length required to prevent "another Cuba."[14]

The interventions in Chile are well known, though by now selective memories have been at work for some of us. In this case, the United States provided covert financing for opposition to the Marxist party in the elections of 1964 and 1970; reacted to its actual election in 1970 by telling Chilean military leaders that military aid would be stopped if they let Allende take office and then, when the chief of staff proved to be committed to supporting constitutional democracy, provided weapons to a militant rightist group to kidnap him; supported the opposition press with financing and planted reports designed to undermine possibilities of negotiation between the center and the left, and to convince everyone that the society was disintegrating; supported street gangs and transportation strikes intended to cripple the economy and spread a sense of hopelessness; encouraged the Chilean military to step in, applauded when they did, and kept on applauding through one of the most vicious cases of repression by terror that Latin America has ever known.[15] No document made public so far demonstrates anything resembling a military alliance between the Allende government and Cuba or the Soviet Union; the Chilean military remained conservative, and Allende turned down proposals to arm any popular militia.

---

[13] Lowenthal, *The Dominican Intervention*, p. 96.

[14] Ibid., especially p. 86 and ch. 5; Draper, "Dominican Crisis," pp. 49–50; Slater, *Intervention*, pp. 45–70.

[15] United States Senate, Select Committee to Study Governmental Operations with Respect to Intelligence Activities, Staff Report, *Covert Action in Chile* (Washington, D.C.: Government Printing Office, 1975), and *Alleged Assasination Plots Involving Foreign Leaders* (Washington, D.C.: Government Printing Office, 1975); Paul E. Sigmund, *The Overthrow of Allende and the Politics of Chile, 1964–1976* (Pittsburgh: University of Pittsburgh Press, 1977), pp. 112–23 and 283–87; Arturo Valenzuela, *The Breakdown of Democratic Regimes: Chile* (Baltimore: Johns Hopkins University Press, 1978), pp. 48–49 and 56–57; Seymour Hersh, *The Price of Power: Henry Kissinger in the Nixon White House* (New York: Summit Books, 1983), pp. 258–96.

What was the security threat? There wasn't any, *unless* the existence of an elected Marxist government is by definition such a threat.

It is all too possible to read these cases as demonstrating that, for reasons of its own history, the United States constitutes an implacable opponent of radical social change in Latin America. But some of the other examples and programs cited make the picture more complex. Particular presidents with strong views respond differently to similar situations, partly for personal reasons and partly because they represent different balances of contradictory public preferences. All administrations in the postwar period have feared and fought communist influence, but the ways in which they have done so have varied enough to allow for real differences in costs and outcomes.

In the Dominican Republic Kennedy supported Bosch initially against the military, advancing the side of reform; it was only after Johnson became president that the U.S. position reversed. It might also be noted that the intervention in Brazil came after Johnson succeeded Kennedy, though it is impossible to be sure that the latter would have acted differently. The Kennedy administration was more interested in reform, but it was also responsible for acceleration of military aid and a military training program that was to be mainly a force to put down internal threats to conservative governments.[16]

The initial approach of the Carter administration in 1977–78 marked a real change toward a less militaristic position, toward negotiation and concern for human rights. Toward the end of his administration Carter turned so far away from this initial position that it is possible to consider the first two years as a nonrepeatable aberration. Without trying to minimize that retreat, or the depressing possibility that he lost reelection precisely because he was not belligerent enough, it is still worth noting that the more constructive side proved to be real long enough to make some difference.

The most successful example of the difference was the way the administration handled growing pressure from Panama to allow that country sovereignty over the Canal Zone. The treaty of 1903 with Panama, negotiated immediately after U.S. support for Panamanian attempts to break away from Colombia, had granted the United States control of the Canal Zone "in perpetuity."[17] Panama's

---

[16] Walter LaFeber, *Inevitable Revolutions.*

[17] LaFeber, *The Panama Canal: The Crisis in Historical Perspective* (New York: Oxford University Press, 1978); Richard F. Nyrop, ed., *Panama: A Country Study* (Washington, D.C.: American University Foreign Area Studies, 1981), pp. 46–49 and 160–70.

subsequent insistence that the agreement was made under duress was mostly ignored until violent demonstrations in 1964 led to armed conflict between U.S. military and Panamanian civilians. The Johnson administration then made an effort to work out new proposals to reconcile U.S. and Panamanian concerns but gave up both because of reluctance to lose control of the canal and fears of domestic political criticism. The essential problem was that for many in the United States the canal and the zone "symbolized America's will to maintain global predominance," while "almost all Panamanians regarded exclusive U.S. control over the canal and zone as an affront to their national dignity and sovereignty."[18]

One of Carter's first foreign policy decisions was to seek a new treaty with Panama as a cornerstone of efforts to build a more cooperative Latin American policy.[19] Two new treaties were negotiated in 1977. The issues were separated to deal with (1) Panama's claim to sovereignty and control of the canal, and (2) U.S. concerns over the right to intervene in the event of threats to security. The first side was easier. The agreements provided for a transition period of joint responsibility for the canal, with U.S. chairmanship of the administrative commission until 1989, Panamanian chairmanship for the next ten years, and full Panamanian sovereignty from 1999. The United States thus gave up the claim to control the canal forever, and gained in return the security advantage of greatly lessened danger that the Panamanians themselves would destroy or disrupt the canal.

The second treaty declared that Panama and the United States, jointly and exclusively, would be responsible for answering any *external* threat to the canal. Taken together, the treaties removed a short-run danger to security while maintaining longer-run protection. In Latin America, they cleared the air of conflict over a long-standing example of U.S. insistence on domination. The administration compromised with domestic opposition on one important issue, by accepting Senate reservations that reassert a unilateral right to intervene, but held on to a key distinction: U.S. intervention would be limited to cases of external threat and not apply in cases of internal conflict. At least officially, the United States repudiated the kind of intervention made in Guatemala in 1954 and the Dominican Republic in 1965.

[18] Cyrus Vance, *Hard Choices: Four Critical Years in Managing America's Foreign Policy* (New York: Simon and Schuster, 1983), p. 41.

[19] Ibid., pp. 33 and 140–57.

The more peace-seeking style at the start of Carter's administration extended even to Cuba, but not for long. Restrictions on travel to Cuba were eased, fishing rights were negotiated, and limited diplomatic contacts were established after a fifteen-year gap. For a time it looked as if the administration might take the United States out of its sullen refusal to accept the existence of the Castro government. But then renewed Cuban involvement in Africa and a worsening international climate proved too much of a test. The United States tried to trade a continuation of modest cooperation for Cuban agreement to stay out of conflicts in Africa, but Castro refused to accept the constraint and in 1978 sent troops into the war in Ethiopia.[20] Then in the course of 1979 the United States was taken by surprise by the intense anti-Americanism of the revolution in Iran, hit economically by the oil price increases that followed, and put in an impossible box by the seizure of U.S. hostages. On top of all that, the Soviet Union made one of its contributions to world peace and sanity by invading Afghanistan. Within the Carter administration, the previous balance changed decisively in favor of more militant options.

The other distinctive side of Carter's initial policy toward Latin America was an attempt to use aid and direct pressure to favor protection of human rights. Both the United States and the United Nations had firmly asserted concern for human rights immediately after the end of World War II, but that position disappeared from view as the cold war intensified and the Eisenhower administration repudiated it by intervention on the opposite side in Guatemala. It is a strand of policy that repeatedly seems to lose all force, and then just as repeatedly resurfaces when its many advocates find any sympathy at all within the government.[21]

The human rights program changed the basic guidelines of U.S. aid to direct it more toward help for the poor and to deny aid to particularly repressive governments. As with the Panama Canal negotiations, the administration helped build up wider awareness that cooperation and concern for human rights could be in the interest of the United States. Did that amount to much in practice? Less than it could have, but still the United States did play a role it rarely has,

[20] William M. LeoGrande, "Cuba: Going to the Sources," pp. 135–46 in Newfarmer, ed., *Gunboats*; Jorge Domínguez, "U.S.–Cuban Relations in the Mid-1980s: Issues and Policies," *Journal of International Studies and World Affairs* 27, 1 (February 1985), pp. 17–34.

[21] Lars Schoultz, *Human Rights and United States Policy Toward Latin America* (Princeton: Princeton University Press, 1981).

actively negotiating freedom for particular political prisoners and supporting people within Latin America trying to stop repression.[22] It is impossible to judge how much all this did to create hope for people in particularly repressive countries, but at least it put the weight of U.S. emphasis on the side of human rights rather than, by implication and sometimes by practice, against them.

Taking actions to promote respect for human rights was certainly in line with a distinctive U.S. tradition in domestic matters. But when applied as a standard expected from other countries it can also be seen as yet another kind of intervention. If the military in Chile chooses to execute prisoners without trial, and the government accepts such behavior as perfectly normal, what right has the United States to criticize? One possible answer is that it is not "Chile" that is choosing to violate human rights but instead a particular military group using tactics of terror to *prevent* the majority of Chileans from choosing the kind of society they want. Another way of looking at the question, suggested by Stanley Hoffmann, is to distinguish between intervention in the sense of pressure on governments to take actions favorable for U.S. economic or political interests, and pressure on them to live up to widely accepted norms of respect for human health and life. There is a vast difference between "recognizing cultural differences" and accepting without comment violations "clearly destructive of human dignity, wherever they occur."[23]

The administration's concern for human rights became an important element in reactions to the Nicaraguan revolution against Somoza. Practically everybody in Nicaragua had joined in the effort to force out Somoza after the family's long career of running the country mainly in their personal interest. In prior and subsequent U.S. administrations, the fact that he was pro-U.S and anticommunist would have been enough to balance the options in favor of continued military support no matter what the majority of Nicaraguans wanted. Under Carter, the United States tried to promote an alternative centrist regime, to remove Somoza but at the same time to prevent the Sandinista forces from taking over.[24] That failed to

---

[22] Ibid., especially pp. 109–34 and 344–79.

[23] Stanley Hoffmann, *Duties Beyond Frontiers: On the Limits and Possibilities of Ethical International Politics* (Syracuse: Syracuse University Press, 1981), pp. 95–140, quotation from p. 105. The second quoted phrase was taken by Hoffmann from Herbert C. Kelman, "The Conditions, Criteria and Dialectics of Human Dignity," *International Studies Quarterly* 21 (September 1977), p. 543.

[24] Richard E. Feinberg, "The Recent Rapid Redefinitions of U.S. Interests and Diplomacy in Central America," in Feinberg, ed., *Central America: International Dimen-*

work because Somoza decided that the United States would never be able to accept a Sandinista victory so there was no need for him to step down. Even dictators can be wrong.

Given the impasse, Carter gave up on trying to force Somoza out and accepted the Sandinista victory that soon followed. That gave the United States, very briefly, the rare chance to start on relatively peaceful terms with a government in favor of radical social change. But then the next explosion in Central America, the sudden and widespread revolution in El Salvador, came too close to Nicaragua and too much under the tensions heightened by Iran and Afghanistan. In El Salvador, Carter committed the United States to military aid against domestic revolutionary forces, despite the government's inability to offer positive alternatives or to control the rightist death squads trying to wipe out all possible leadership in favor of compromise and reform. The Reagan administration then followed with greater military support to help the El Salvadorean government stay in power, and with its determined efforts to use mercenary forces to overturn the government of Nicaragua.[25]

The attacks on Nicaragua come out of the same fears and unyielding opposition to Marxism, with much the same disregard of costs, as those on Chile under Allende. In this case the attacks have been rationalized by an added argument, that Nicaragua has built up the largest military force in Central America, with heavy dependence on Cuban and Soviet support. That charge is true enough, but might be seen as a nearly inevitable cost of the line of U.S. policy that has been predominant so far. Considering the record of postwar interventions, starting with the overturn of the government of Guatemala, it would seem an inescapable lesson to any left-oriented government that it *must* seek quick military support from communist countries, or anywhere else for that matter, because if it fails to strengthen its military capacity for resistance it will

---

sions of the Crisis (New York: Holmes and Meier, 1982), pp. 58–84; John A. Booth, "The Revolution in Nicaragua: Through a Frontier of History," in Donald E. Schulz and Douglas H. Graham, Revolution and Counter-Revolution in Central America and the Caribbean (Boulder: Westview, 1984), pp. 301–30. Walter LaFeber, Inevitable Revolutions, gives a bitterly critical version of the Carter administration's approach, emphasizing its persistent opposition to the Sandinistas and willingness to provide arms to Somoza while trying to find an alternative government to forestall the Sandinista victory.

[25] LaFeber, Inevitable Revolutions, chapters 4–6; Lars Schoultz, "Nicaragua: The United States Confronts a Revolution," pp. 116–24 in Newfarmer, Gunboats; Richard Fagen, "Revolution and Crisis in Nicaragua," in Diskin, ed., Trouble in Our Backyard, pp. 125–54.

be destroyed by the United States. Of the many costs of intervention, one of the highest is the evidence so far that any radical reformist government that gets into power, whether by election or by
revolution, must rapidly prepare for U.S. attack. That incentive to
mobilize, and seek Soviet help, could conceivably be changed by
genuine change in the balance of U.S. policy choices.

4. PERCEPTIONS AND POSSIBILITIES

To the main question asked in this chapter, whether or not the
United States can play a constructive role in lessening poverty, aid-
ing economic growth, and strengthening representative institutions
in Latin America, the answer has to be double-edged: (1) yes, it can
and sometimes does, but (2) it is not easy and is not the usual result.
Actions taken by the United States often do a penny's worth of good
on the level of particular projects or macroeconomic problems but
a pound's worth of damage changing the balance of national preferences by strengthening groups opposed to more participatory societies, or in the extreme by overturning governments considered
by the United States to be too far to the left.

Is there any hope of improving this balance? Possibly so: conflicts
among U.S. interests, and perhaps above all among conceptions of
what those interests really are, mean that the actual course of strategy is bound to be erratic but also that redirection is conceivable. In
the domain of economic policy, the main divisions are over the desirability of open markets, promotion of direct investment, and extension of aid and credit. Private investment, aid, and credit can be
helpful in particular conditions, but a general policy of promoting
them at all times is bound to work against changes desirable for
many of the people of Latin America. The issues are not simple
matters of good and bad. The real complexity of these questions argues for respecting contrary strategies chosen in other societies
(criticizing actively when they seem misdirected but not trying to
buy their elections or their generals), when the decisions are themselves responsive to public preferences. That would seem a simple
and familiar recommendation: why has it so often been violated in
practice?

The drive to intervene has many roots, but much of its power
comes from the ways in which economic interests, security concerns,
and ideology reinforce each other. The direct economic interests of
U.S. corporations are clearly an important aspect: they have a lot to
gain, at least in the short run, from policies protecting private in-

vestment and opposing governmental controls, and from reassurance that more drastic reform governments will not be able to take actions against them. But that is only one strand of the matter. Concern for national security, which can find solid ground for anxiety over the kinds of Soviet military equipment in Cuba, all too easily extends to preoccupation with leaders of strikes, peasant organizations, or public protests against repressive governments. The connection between threatening missiles and peasants who try to defend their interests against landowners would seem distant and doubtful to some of us, but to the National Security Council they apparently come across as closely interwoven aspects of one common menace.

That near-identification between security concerns and immediate U.S. economic interests gains its greatest strength from an ideological presumption which in the present generation goes very deep: communists are, if not at the moment in every single case, intrinsically agents of a hostile military power. It's bad enough that France or Italy give them respectability by allowing them in government, but in Latin America it becomes plainly unacceptable. Why the difference? Precisely because the grossly unequal results and repressive characteristics of the kinds of capitalism Latin Americans have known so far mean that mass public preferences provide real support for drastic change. One side of U.S. policy has aimed at improving objective conditions of life, partly for its own sake and partly to change the identification of capitalism with extreme inequality; the other side short-circuits that approach by trying to silence political opposition. The first approach makes the United States an ally of constructive change, and the second a powerful opponent.

It is unlikely that the more positive side will in any consistent sense dominate U.S. strategy, but it would gain relative strength if clearer distinctions could be made among governments that are Marxist and militaristic, Marxist and not militaristic, not Marxist at all but willing to allow communists to have public roles, or even unwilling to allow them any governmental role but also unwilling to step on them. If governments with Marxist influence or leadership but without any militaristic character achieve power peacefully—as in Guatemala in the early postwar years or Chile during the Allende government—does this constitute a security threat? The United States is bound to be a destructive force for the majority of the people of Latin America if it treats every such case as being so dangerous that it merits intervention. The United States can become a more positive influence if policy distinguishes between (a) the right of other countries to have their own kind of economic system, even if it is not a free enterprise system, and (b) clear-cut threats to security.

Perhaps the most difficult problem at present is that any radical regime in Latin America, however much it may wish to concentrate peacefully on internal reform, must see the United States as a serious danger. History says that if they do not get outside military support they will not be allowed to survive. Whatever they may have intended to do in the first place, it becomes likely that they will be forced toward more militaristic positions. The United States could change that likelihood by abstaining from intervention unless there is a clearly present threat. Increasing pressures from groups of Latin American countries, going beyond the circumspect advice of the Contadora Group, may help force such a change. Or the balance of conflicting interpretations of what is truly in the national interest could change internally. The United States is neither a consistent force for progress in Latin America nor a monolith bent on domination: it is divided and uncertain. If that uncertainty leads to a greater willingness to listen to and respect the interests of the people of Latin America, the world will be a safer place for all of us.

FOURTEEN

FROM CONCLUSIONS TO
ONGOING QUESTIONS

Poverty, political repression, and external dependence can be seen
as manifestations of a deformed kind of economic development that
cannot be corrected except by total overturn, as transitory consequences of a process of economic growth that is slowly succeeding
and will eventually resolve the difficulties if Latin American countries just follow sensible economic policies, or as profound problems
that should and can be better answered without waiting for either
radical or conservative millennia to arrive. They may never arrive.
The odds against successful development in Latin America today
following the paths of Europe or Japan are higher than they were
in those countries. Correspondingly, both the pressures to find radically different alternatives and the counter forces favoring drastic
political repression are much greater. But there are many ways to
make things move in more constructive directions, as well as many
ways of going wrong while trying to do so.

At least four sets of problems need to be kept in view to clarify the
central issues of economic strategy considered in this study: (1) too
rapid growth of population and the labor force relative to land, capital, and employment opportunities, holding people in low-productivity employment and keeping wages down relative to gains from
property ownership; (2) highly concentrated ownership of land and
other assets, long-restricted access to education, regressive tax systems, and weak or nonexistent corrective social programs; (3) conflicts between popular preferences and the kinds of economic strategies that might actually work well, leading to nonfunctional choices
of economic strategy by those governments that have tried to respond to popular preferences, to heightened social conflict in some
countries, and to disdain or fear of democracy on the conservative
side; (4) pressures from the operation of the world economy or
more directly from the United States, sometimes positive but often
not, acting in many respects to narrow down the range of what can
be done.

Straightforward economics can help especially with the first and fourth of these sets of problems but deflects attention from the second and can intensify difficulties with the third. Structuralism helps direct attention to the second, questions of ownership and their connections to trade policy, but it has favored policy choices that systematically make many problems worse than they would otherwise have been. Dependency analysis gives useful insights in all four areas but badly confuses questions of what might be done and would be helpful.

Although these four sets of interacting problems must be in the picture, differences among countries are too important to fit any one pattern. These considerations fit best the conditions of the Andean countries, Brazil, and in most respects Mexico; they require major amendments for Argentina, Chile, Costa Rica, and Cuba. Of these last four, none except Cuba has been subject to structural conditions of excess labor. Correspondingly, they have historically had lower degrees of inequality than most of the region. For Argentina and Chile, as noted below, attention needs to be directed more to the roles of strongly organized labor movements and overt class conflict. Postrevolution Cuba is of course different in fundamental ways. Revolution corrected the second set of conflicts above but not the others: the experience demonstrated that inequality can be very nearly eliminated in short order, but it has so far left open serious doubts about ability to raise standards of living in any sustained way, or to achieve either internal political freedom or national autonomy.

The first of these relationships, between growth of the labor force and opportunities for productive employment, offers both a partial explanation of past difficulties and some grounds for greater hope about the future. On the side of population growth, the striking reduction of birthrates beginning in the 1960s should in the decades ahead lessen the growth of landless rural labor and allow people better chances to move out of low-productivity occupations. It should to some degree shift the balance of bargaining strength away from landowners and industrialists toward workers. On the side of employment opportunities, early postwar policies had systematically negative effects by encouraging use of imported capital equipment and foreign technology, partly because of pressure from both domestic and foreign industrial investors to maintain low-cost access to foreign technology and partly also because proponents of industrialization through import substitution either did not see or did not take seriously the perverse consequences of the methods used. Persistent negative results with this approach, and better results through better policies in a few cases, might make for better choices in the future. Changes in economic policies in Brazil and Colombia from 1967 on provide useful lessons to examine and debate, if not in all respects to imitate.

Against these positive signs and examples of relatively successful economic policies, basic structural conditions have been worsening in many of the poorest countries of the region. By one of the measures used in chapter 3, changes in the number of workers in agriculture, conditions deteriorated between 1960 and 1984 in Bolivia, Central America, the Dominican Republic, Ecuador, Paraguay, and Peru. That is only one possible indicator, conceivably answerable in some cases by investment in agriculture, development of additional arable land, and policies designed to favor nonagricultural employment conditions. But the chances of getting anywhere with such methods alone are pitiful in some of the worst cases. In El Salvador and Guatemala political repression and worsening ownership conditions, on top of rapid growth of the labor force, have made it difficult to imagine any solution that does not include fundamental land reform, and even more fundamental changes in the character of these societies. Still, it is important to recognize that even a thorough land reform and major social changes may be of little help if not followed by policies favorable for growth of economywide employment opportunities. Peru is a particularly sobering case, where a left-oriented military regime was able to implement a long-needed land reform and to experiment with an imaginative variety of other social policies, but fostered macroeconomic imbalances that stopped growth and worsened employment conditions. Ownership is highly important, but consistent economic management is crucial too.

Concentration of ownership, often accompanied by regressive tax systems and refusal to accept the most minimal of social welfare programs, has both sector-specific and systemwide implications. The structuralists were surely right that concentrated land ownership with a rapidly growing labor force drives far more people than necessary into low-productivity occupations, reduces the productivity of agriculture, and keeps the structure of production too narrowly directed toward traditional primary exports. Concentrated land ownership makes poverty worse. More generally, high concentrations of property ownership in industry and finance as well as land, especially if accompanied by restricted access to education, make the consequences of reliance on market forces and private enterprise exceptionally inequitable. Some kinds of inequity may have a positive counterpart in stimulus to productive activity, but the kinds that dominate results in Latin America stimulate chiefly efforts to control political structures in order to protect these advantages.

Market forces can work in favor of equality when labor is scarce, land relatively abundant, ownership dispersed, capital accessible on nearly equal terms even to those without any special political connections, and education widespread. The basic conditions of many Latin American countries were for long close to the exact opposite. Governments determined to do something to respond to majority preferences have been placed in almost automatic opposition to criteria of economic efficiency and consistency, while those that emphasize economic efficiency have by the same token learned to distrust democracy. In such conditions, appeals for reliance on market forces are appeals to accept increasing inequality, and come close to support for repression of majority preferences.

The deep-rooted conflict between democratic forces and functional economic strategies may be changing because some of the basic structural conditions responsible for it have been changing. The clear prospects for slowing growth of labor forces, some examples of policies better designed to favor employment, and widespread improvements in access to education in the last two decades should lessen the contradictions between concern for equality and concern for efficiency. Nothing intrinsic in the nature of Latin America makes it impossible to combine popular choice and workable economic policies within a market system: it is mainly that the past concentrations of ownership and privilege created conditions that make the people with all the advantages better able to hang on against change, and the people on the other side less interested in any step-by-step solutions. High concentrations of wealth are adverse for democracies anywhere.

Given the narrow range of safe movement, it would seem exceptionally desirable to bend economic policies in ways likely to improve the chances of consensus, by designing them to keep within limits avoiding severe losses to any one group in order to favor others. That would sometimes run counter to considerations of economic efficiency, and sometimes allow special privileges to continue. Both such defects argue for trying to undercut harmful positions by gradually reorienting incentives and taking away any artificial protection underlying them. They should not be accepted as eternal. The point is only that shock treatments in the name of restoring efficiency, or the satisfaction of striking back at past injustice, need to be weighed against their costs in terms of the possibilities for social cohesion.

Why have Argentina and Chile, which have *not* been subject to structural conditions of excess labor, which had from long back less inequality and superior records with respect to education and social services, had so many troubles reconciling functional economic strategies with democracy? Does this demonstrate that there is something deeper in the character of Latin American development, or of the world economy, that overrides considerations of labor markets and the other factors suggested above? That may be the more useful way to look at the matter: some of the considerations of dependency theory are clearly relevant for Chile, if less for Argentina, and more nearly adequate kinds of generalization in the future are bound to bring out aspects of causation that none of us sees today. Still, it should be noted that the third case considered of a country with similar structural conditions and record of wide social participation, Costa Rica, has done best of all the region in combining democracy with avoidance of repeated economic breakdown. It is certainly Latin American, small, capitalist, highly exposed to international trade and finance, and yet as far as this imperfect world goes reasonably successful. Proposition: Argentina and Chile would have been much closer to this kind of performance, or quite possibly have done better because they have advantages of their own, if seriously self-damaging economic strategies and a style of class confrontation seeking domination had not reinforced each other in destroying possibilities of social consensus.

In Argentina, it is tempting to place most of the blame on inappropriate economic strategies, but then the reason that these strategies kept swinging back and forth between different unworkable extremes was that noncompromising groups blocked any resolution short of their own total control. With the grim results of the military regime of the late 1970s now behind, and a civilian government apparently able to find a new kind of economic strategy and be given a chance to try it, the fundamental impasse of the past may at last be giving way. If it is, Argentina will move ahead fast. In Chile, democracy and economic reformism nearly succeeded together under Frei at first but then broke down for identifiable reasons described in chapter 9. Under Allende, all that promise and specific initial achievements were undercut by a hopelessly contradictory set of economic policies, aggravated and then turned to tragedy by the vindictive actions of the U.S. government and Chilean conservatives. None of that would have been excusable even if the Chilean economy had thereafter performed brilliantly, which it has not. Still, once the present military regime has been swept away to the dust heap the structural conditions in favor of a combination of democracy with successful economic performance will be there, perhaps backed by greater willingness to search for shared solutions.

Dependency analysis is perfectly correct in many of its arguments that locate trouble in external pressures, or in coalitions between domestic and external conservative forces. Not *all* of its arguments: it can be a costly mistake, if one cares about poverty, to foster an unselective turning away from the world economy. Exporting labor-intensive products can directly improve employment conditions while providing foreign exchange earnings to help build autonomy. But wholly open economic systems are unlikely to work well. Open trade under conditions in which comparative advantage is on the side of a few primary exports, where ownership of the resources necessary for them is highly concentrated, can increase inequality while discouraging diversification of production. The answer is not to reject trade but to use it selectively to favor export diversification and to discourage particularly high-cost lines of domestic investment.

Foreign investment has more often than not tilted the structure of production away from labor-intensive lines of production, reduced the chances of independent domestic technological change, and increased the seeming need to import and to borrow abroad. Not as systematically, but in crucial cases in Guatemala in the 1950s and Chile in the 1970s, some U.S. corporations have actively promoted intervention against egalitarian democratic governments. Latin American democracy could have been healthier in the last generation if foreign investment had been ruled out. But then the eternal other side is also true: those foreign firms that operate in more labor-intensive fields, those that bring in new learning opportunities and kinds of technology relatively close to the capacities of domestic firms, and those that, by exporting, provide foreign exchange earnings, thus reducing the need for external borrowing, can help reduce poverty by improving employment opportunities and help the economy as a whole.

The multifaceted character of international economic relationships means that either wholesale rejection of trade and international finance or the contrary of a fully open system is likely to be damaging. When generalized external financial crisis hits the region as in the early 1980s, or particular countries get into tight corners as a result of their own strategies, external finance can help keep the productive system going and lessen contraction of employment and mass consumption, to the benefit of lower income groups as well as higher. When the credit comes with conditions requiring the adoption of more effective tax systems, or an exchange rate more favorable for export diversification, or more coherent fiscal controls, or many other details on which national policies often go astray, the pressures can push countries toward actions with wide internal benefits. The IMF, the World Bank, and AID often use their resources and influence in constructive ways. But the IMF comes down too hard on subsidies and spending for social programs as if they were necessarily wasteful, all of them interpret foreign investment too broadly as beneficial when it often is not, and they push indiscriminately for free-market policies even in conditions in which such policies imply sharply increasing inequality. Latin American development would be less unequal if aid, external credit, and foreign investment could be held to low levels by national economic strategies geared toward less use of foreign technology and toward development of more diversified exports.

The worst side of external pressure is not the operation of the world economy in general but the quite specific intervention of the United States. At the same time as the United States provides real help in many contexts it has constituted a persistent force on the side of repression whenever any signs of communist influence can be detected. Although the United States stands to gain in terms of safety and of economic opportunities through achievement of less unequal societies and stronger economies in Latin America, past strategies have repeatedly fallen into two costly traps. Because those reformist movements with any serious prospect of achieving change are often supported by local communists, they are almost always opposed out of fear of eventual Soviet influence. That position intensifies political and economic deadlocks by consistently reinforcing those on the conservative side who would prefer not to give an inch. The second kind of trap is that repeated intervention against governments that include any Marxists means that no such government can safely rely on any nonmilitaristic, neutral strategy. The United States has driven home repeatedly the lesson that if they do not reach out rapidly for support from Cuba or the Soviet Union they will not be allowed to survive.

Is it possible for the United States to change toward accepting those radical governments that have broad support in their own countries, to wait for new elections rather than call for overturn when one is foundering, and to accept an active role for radical opposition groups when they are not themselves relying on force? Fear, pride in prior dominance, and selective economic interests combine to strengthen those political leaders who prefer confrontation. And it is true that more radical governments in Latin America are likely to be friendly to Cuba as well as more hostile to U.S. investors. But degrees of hostility may depend on what the other side, in this case the United States, actually does. If the United States could come to accept the right of nonmilitaristic radical governments to exist, that should allow negotiation of agreed limits on mutual damage: such governments would be much less likely to seek active involvement in the cold war if they could consider themselves safe.

It is not surprising that tensions are always high in these societies and often ready to explode. But the capacity for nonexplosive answers is growing too. In countries where employment creation has been pursued with appropriate policies and moderate good fortune, backed by widening access to education, poverty has been lessening. To pursue industrialization along at least moderately efficient lines, with promotion of more diversified exports and restraint on excess demand, can speed up this process and raise the capacity for independent national choices. Examples of relative success do not prove that it can be generalized, or will continue, but at least they point to methods that often help. Frequent defeats underline the depth of resistances but also illuminate the costs of alternatives that need not be repeated. The future is likely to go in very different directions among these countries, sometimes because of strengths built or weaknesses aggravated up to now, but perhaps more often because of the ways they respond to new problems ahead. Our theories provide many useful clues, though none of them has any valid claim to certainty. Montaigne's conclusion about the nature of learning from experience is still valid: neither fixed laws nor multiplying interpretations can ever fully capture "the infinite diversity of human actions."[1]

[1] *Les essais de Montaigne*, ed. Pierre Villey, re-ed. V.-L. Saulnier. 3d ed. (Paris: Presses Universitaires de France, 1978), book 3, ch. 13, p. 1066.

REFERENCES

Abbreviations for journals and series of working papers:

AER   *American Economic Review*
BPEA   *Brookings Papers on Economic Activity*
CEC   *Colección estudios CIEPLAN* (Santiago)
EDCC   *Economic Development and Cultural Change*
JIW   *Journal of Inter-American Studies and World Affairs*
LAP   *Latin American Perspectives*
LARR   *Latin American Research Review*
WBS   World Bank Staff Working Papers
WD   *World Development*

Adams, Richard Newbold. *Crucifixion by Power: Essays on Guatemalan National Social Structure*. Austin: University of Texas Press, 1970.

del Aguila, Juan M. "The Limits of Reform Development in Contemporary Costa Rica." JIW 24 (August 1982).

Ahluwalia, Montek S. "Income Inequality: Some Dimensions of the Problem." In Hollis B. Chenery et al., *Re-distribution with Growth: An Approach to Policy*. Oxford: Oxford University Press for the World Bank and the Institute of Development Studies, 1974.

Ahluwalia, Montek S., Nicholas G. Carter, and Hollis B. Chenery. "Growth and Poverty in Developing Countries." *Journal of Development Economics* 6 (September 1979).

Ahmad, Muzaffer. "The Political Economy of Public Enterprise." In Leroy P. Jones, ed., *Public Enterprise in Less Developed Countries*. New York: Cambridge University Press, 1982.

Alape, Arturo. *El Bogotazo: Memorias del Olvido*. Havana: Casa de las Américas, 1983.

Alarco, Germán, ed. *Desafíos para la economía peruana*. Lima: Centro de Investigación de la Universidad del Pacífico, 1985.

Alberti, Giorgio. *Basic Needs in the Context of Social Change: The Case of Peru*. Paris: OECD, 1981.

Alberts, Tom. *Agrarian Reform and Rural Poverty: A Case Study of Peru*. Boulder: Westview Press, 1983.

Altimir, Oscar. "The Extent of Poverty in Latin America." WBS no. 522, 1982.

Ameringer, Charles D. *Democracy in Costa Rica*. New York and Stanford: Praeger and Hoover Institution Press, 1982.

Arellano, Juan Pablo. "De la liberalización a la intervención: El mercado de capitales en Chile 1974–83." CEC 11 (December 1983).

———. "La difícil salida al problema del endeudamiento interno." CEC 13 (June 1984).

Ascher, William. *Scheming for the Poor: The Politics of Redistribution in Latin America*. Cambridge: Harvard University Press, 1984.

Ayala, José, and Clemente Ruiz Durán. "Development and Crisis in Mexico: A Structuralist Approach." In Jonathan Hartlyn and Samuel A. Morley, eds., *Latin American Political Economy: Financial Crisis and Political Change*. Boulder: Westview Press, 1986.

Bacha, Edmar L., and Lance Taylor. "Brazilian Income Distribution in the 1960s: 'Facts,' Model Results, and the Controversy." *Journal of Development Studies* 14 (April 1978).

Baer, Werner. *Industrialization and Economic Development in Brazil*. Homewood, Ill.: Irwin, 1965.

———. "Import Substitution and Industrialization in Latin America: Experiences and Interpretations." LARR 7, 1 (1972).

Baer, Werner, and Isaac Kerstenetzky, eds. *Inflation and Growth in Latin America*. Homewood, Ill.: Irwin, 1964.

Baer, Werner, Isaac Kerstenetzky, and Annibal V. Villela. "The Changing Role of the State in the Brazilian Economy." WD 1 (November 1973).

Bagley, Bruce. "Colombia: National Front and Economic Development." In Robert Wesson, ed., *Politics, Policies, and Economic Development in Latin America*. Stanford: Hoover Institution Press, 1984.

———. "Colombian Foreign Policy in the 1980s: The Search for Leverage." JIW 27 (Fall 1985).

Bagley, Bruce, and Mathew Edel. "Popular Mobilization Programs of the National Front: Cooption and Radicalization." In R. Albert Berry, Ronald G. Hellman, and Mauricio Solaún, eds., *Politics of Compromise: Coalition Government in Colombia*. New Brunswick: Transactions Books, 1980.

Bagley, Bruce, Francisco Thoumi, and Juan Tokatlian, eds. *State and Society in Contemporary Colombia*. Boulder: Westview Press, forthcoming.

Balassa, Bela. "Export Incentives and Export Performance in Developing Countries: A Comparative Analysis." *Weltwirtschaft-liches Archiv* 114 (1978).

———. *The Newly Industrialized Countries in the World Economy.* New York: Pergamon, 1981.

Barker, Terry, and Vladimiro Brailovsky. "Economic Policy Making in Mexico between 1976 and 1982 and the National Industrial Development Plan." Paper presented at the seminar, "The Mexican Economy: Current Situation and Macroeconomic Perspectives," El Colegio de México, August 1982.

Barkin, David. "La educación: Una barrera al desarrollo económico?" *El Trimestre Económico* 38 (1971).

Barraclough, Solon, ed. *Agrarian Structure in Latin America.* Lexington, Mass.: Lexington Books, 1973.

Basáñez, Miguel. *La lucha para la hegemonía en México, 1960–1980.* Mexico: Siglo Veintiuno, 1981.

Bazdresch Parada, Carlos. Review of Carlos Tello, *La nacionalización de la banca en México. El Trimestre Económico,* no. 206 (April–June 1985).

Beccaria, Luis, and Ricardo Carciofi. "Recent Experiences of Stabilization: Argentina's Economic Policy, 1976–81." *Bulletin of the Institute of Development Studies,* University of Sussex, 13-1 (1982).

Becker, David G. *The New Bourgeoisie and the Limits of Dependency: Mining, Class, and Power in "Revolutionary" Peru.* Princeton: Princeton University Press, 1983.

Behrman, Jere R. *Macroeconomic Policy in a Developing Country: The Chilean Experience.* New York: Elsevier North-Holland, 1977.

Behrman, Jere R., and Nancy Birdsall. "The Quality of Schooling: Quantity Alone Is Misleading." AER 73 (December 1983).

Bell, John Patrick. *Crisis in Costa Rica: The 1948 Revolution.* Austin: University of Texas, 1971.

Bergsman, Joel. *Brazil: Industrialization and Trade Policies.* New York: Oxford University Press for the OECD, 1970.

Bernardo, Robert M. *The Theory of Moral Incentives in Cuba.* University: University of Alabama Press, 1971.

Berry, R. Albert. "Farm Size Distribution, Income Distribution, and the Efficiency of Agricultural Production: Colombia," AER 62 (May 1972).

———. "Predicting Income Distribution in Latin America During the 1980s." In Archibald Ritter and David Pollock, eds., *Latin American Prospects for the 1980s: Equity, Democratization, and Development.* New York: Praeger, 1983.

Berry, R. Albert, ed. *Essays on Industrialization in Colombia*. Tempe: Arizona State University, Center of Latin American Studies, 1983.

Berry, R. Albert, and William R. Cline. *Agrarian Structures and Productivity in Developing Countries*. Baltimore: Johns Hopkins University Press, 1979.

Berry, R. Albert, Ronald Hellman, and Mauricio Solaún, eds. *Politics of Compromise: Coalition Government in Colombia*. New Brunswick: Transactions Books, 1980.

Berry, R. Albert, and Richard Sabot. "Labour Market Performance in Developing Countries: A Survey." WD 6 (1978).

Berry, R. Albert, and Francisco Thoumi. "Colombian Economic Growth and Policies (1970–1984)." In Bruce Bagley, Francisco Thoumi, and Juan Tokatlian, eds., *State and Society in Contemporary Colombia*. Boulder: Westview Press, forthcoming.

Berry, R. Albert, and Miguel Urrutia. *Income Distribution in Colombia*. New Haven: Yale University Press, 1976.

Bird, Richard. *Taxation and Development: Lessons from Colombian Experience*. Cambridge: Harvard University Press, 1970.

Birdsall, Nancy. "Analytical Approaches to the Relationship of Population Growth and Development." *Population and Development Review* 3 (March and June 1977).

Bitar, Sergio. *Transición, socialismo y democracia: La experiencia chilena*. Mexico: Siglo Veintiuno, 1979.

Boissiere, M., J. B. Knight, and R. H. Sabot. "Earnings, Schooling, Ability, and Cognitive Skills." AER 75 (December 1985).

Bonsal, Philip W. "Cuba, Castro, and the United States." *Foreign Affairs* 45 (January 1967).

Booth, David. "The Reform of the Press in Peru: Myths and Realities." In David Booth and Bernardo Sorj, eds., *Military Reformism and Social Classes: Aspects of the Peruvian Experience*. London, Macmillan, 1982.

———. "Marxism and Development Sociology: Interpreting the Impasse." WD 13 (July 1985).

Booth, John A. "The Revolution in Nicaragua: Through a Frontier of History." In Donald E. Schultz and Douglas H. Graham, eds., *Revolution and Counter-Revolution in Central America and the Caribbean*. Boulder: Westview Press, 1984.

Braun, Herbert. *The Assassination of Gaitán: Public Life and Urban Violence in Colombia*. Madison: University of Wisconsin Press, 1985.

Broderick, W. *Camilo Torres: A Biography of the Priest-Guerrillero*. Garden City, N.Y.: Doubleday, 1975.

Brundenius, Claes. *Economic Growth, Basic Needs and Income Distribution in Revolutionary Cuba.* Lund: Research Policy Institute, University of Lund, 1981.

———. "Development Strategies and Basic Needs in Revolutionary Cuba." In Claes Brundenius and Mats Lundahl, eds., *Development Strategies and Basic Needs in Latin America.* Boulder, Colorado: Westview Press, 1982.

Bruton, Henry J. "Productivity Growth in Latin America." AER 57 (December 1967).

———. "The Import-Substitution Strategy of Economic Development: A Survey." *Pakistan Development Review* 10 (Summer 1970).

———. "Economic Development and Labor Use: A Review." In Edgar O. Edwards, ed., *Employment in Developing Countries.* New York: Columbia University Press, 1974.

Bulmer-Thomas, Victor. "Trade Structure and Linkages in Costa Rica: An Input-Output Approach." *Journal of Development Economics* 5 (March 1978).

Burns, E. Bradford. *The Poverty of Progress: Latin America in the Nineteenth Century.* Berkeley: University of California Press, 1980.

Caballero, José María. "Sobre el carácter de la reforma agraria." LAP 4 (Summer 1977).

———. *Economía agraria de la sierra peruana: Antes de la reforma agraria de 1969.* Lima: Instituto de Estudios Peruanos, 1981.

Canitrot, Adolfo. "La experiencia populista de redistribución de ingresos." *Desarrollo Económico* 15 (October-December 1959).

———. "Discipline as a Central Objective of Economic Policy: An Essay on the Economic Programme of the Argentine Government since 1976." WD 8 (November 1980).

Cardoso, Eliana A., and Rudiger Dornbusch, "Brazil's Tropical Plan," National Bureau of Economic Research, Working Paper no. 2142 (February 1987).

Cardoso, Fernando Henrique. "Associated-Dependent Development: Theoretical and Practical Implications." In Alfred Stepan, ed., *Authoritarian Brazil.* New Haven: Yale University Press, 1973.

———. "The Originality of the Copy: The Economic Commission for Latin America and the Idea of Development." In Rothko Chapel Colloquium, *Toward a New Strategy for Development.* New York: Pergamon, 1979.

———. "Development Under Fire." Instituto Latinoamericano de Estudios Transnacionales. Mimeo, 1979.

Cardoso, Fernando Henrique, and Enzo Faletto. *Dependencia y de-*

sarrollo en América Latina. Mexico: Siglo Veintiuno, 1969. Revised English version, *Dependency and Development in Latin America.* Berkeley: University of California Press, 1979.

Carnoy, Martin. "Can Educational Policy Equalize Income Distribution in Latin America?" International Labour Office. World Employment Programme. Research Working Paper on Education and Employment no. 6 (August 1975).

Carroll, Thomas F. "The Land Reform Issue in Latin America." In Albert Hirschman, ed., *Latin American Issues: Essays and Comments.* New York: Twentieth Century Fund, 1961.

Cavarozzi, Marcelo. "El 'desarrollismo' y las relaciones entre democracia y capitalismo dependiente en *Dependencia y desarrollo en América Latina.*" LARR 17, 1 (1982).

Cerdas Cruz, Rodolfo. *La crisis de la democracia liberal en Costa Rica.* San José, Costa Rica: Editorial Universitaria Centroamericana, 1972.

Clark, Ronald. "Agrarian Reform: Bolivia." In Peter Dorner, ed., *Land Reform in Latin America: Issues and Cases.* Madison: University of Wisconsin, Land Tenure Center, 1971.

Cline, William R., and Enrique Delgado, eds. *Economic Integration in Central America.* Washington, D.C.: Brookings, 1978.

Cline, William R., and Sidney Weintraub, eds. *Economic Stabilization in Developing Countries.* Washington, D.C.: Brookings, 1981.

Cole, William E., and Richard D. Sanders. "Internal Migration and Urbanization in the Third World." AER 75 (June 1985).

Collier, David, ed. *The New Authoritarianism in Latin America.* Princeton: Princeton University Press, 1979.

Collier, Paul, and Richard Sabot. "Measuring the Difference Between Urban and Rural Incomes: Some Conceptual Issues." In Richard Sabot, ed., *Migration and the Labor Market in Developing Countries.* Boulder: Westview Press, 1982.

Collier, Ruth Berins. "Popular Sector Incorporation and Political Supremacy: Regime Evolution in Brazil and Mexico." In Sylvia Ann Hewlett and Richard S. Weinert, eds., *Brazil and Mexico, Patterns in Late Development.* Philadelphia: Institute for the Study of Human Issues, 1982.

Collins, Joseph, et al. *What Difference Could a Revolution Make? Food and Family in the New Nicaragua.* San Francisco: Institute for Food and Development Policy, 1982.

Colombia, Department of National Planning. *Guidelines for a New Strategy.* Bogotá: Departamento Nacional de Planeación, 1972.

Conniff, Michael L., ed. *Latin American Populism in Comparative Perspective*. Albuquerque: University of New Mexico Press, 1982.

Cooper, Richard. "Currency Devaluation in Developing Countries." *Princeton Essays in International Finance* 86 (June 1971).

Corbo, Vittorio. "Reform and Macroeconomic Adjustments in Chile During 1976–82." WD 13 (August 1985).

Corbo, Vittorio, Jaime de Melo, and James Tybout. "What Went Wrong with the Recent Reforms in the Southern Cone?" EDCC 34 (April 1986).

Cordera, Rolando, and Carlos Tello. *México: La disputa por la nación: Perspectivas y opciones del desarrollo*. Mexico: Siglo Veintiuno, 1981.

Cornelius, Wayne A. "The Political Economy of Mexico under de la Madrid: Austerity, Routinized Crisis, and Nascent Recovery." *Mexican Studies* 1 (Winter 1985).

Corporación para el Fomento de Investigaciones Económicas. *Controversias sobre el plan de desarrollo*. Bogotá: CORP, 1972.

Cortázar, René. "Distribución del ingreso, empleo y remuneraciones reales en Chile, 1970–78." CEC 3 (June 1980).

Cotler, Julio. *Clases, estado y nación en el Perú*. Lima: Instituto de Estudios Peruanos, 1978.

―――. "Democracy and National Integration in Peru." In Cynthia McClintock and Abraham Lowenthal, eds., *The Peruvian Experiment Reconsidered*. Princeton: Princeton University Press, 1983.

Currie, Lauchlin B. *Accelerating Development: The Necessity and the Means*. New York: McGraw-Hill, 1966.

―――. *The Role of Economic Advisers in Developing Countries*. Westport, Ct.: Greenwood Press, 1981.

Dealy, Glenn Caudill. *The Public Man: An Interpretation of Latin American and Other Catholic Countries*. Amherst: University of Massachusetts, 1977.

Deere, Carmen Diana, Peter Marchetti, and Nola Reinhardt. "The Peasantry and the Development of Sandinista Agrarian Policy, 1979–1984." LARR 20, 3 (1985).

Denslow, David, Jr., and William G. Tyler. "Perspectives on Poverty and Income Inequality in Brazil: An Analysis of Changes during the 1970s." World Bank Staff Working Paper no. 601 (1983).

Diamand, Marcelo. *Doctrinas económicas, desarrollo e independencia*. Buenos Aires: Paidos, 1973.

―――. "Overcoming Argentina's Stop-and-Go Economic Cycles." In Jonathan Hartlyn and Samuel A. Morley, eds., *Latin Ameri-*

can Political Economy: Financial Crisis and Political Change. Boulder: Westview Press, 1986.

Díaz Alejandro, Carlos F. *Exchange Rate Devaluation in a Semi-Industrialized Country: The Experience of Argentina.* Cambridge: MIT Press, 1965.

―――. "On the Import Intensity of Import Substitution." *Kyklos* 18 (1965).

―――. *Essays on the Economic History of the Argentine Republic.* New Haven: Yale University press, 1970.

―――. *Foreign Trade Regimes and Economic Development: Colombia.* New York: Columbia University Press for the National Bureau of Economic Research, 1976.

―――. "Southern Cone Stabilization Plans." In William R. Cline and Sidney Weintraub, eds., *Economic Stabilization in Developing Countries,* Washington, D.C.: Brookings, 1981.

―――. "Open Economy, Closed Polity?" In Diana Tussie, ed., *Latin America in the World Economy.* New York: St. Martin's, 1983.

―――. "Some Aspects of the 1982–83 Brazilian Payments Crisis." BPEA 2 (1983).

―――. "Good-Bye Financial Repression, Hello Financial Crash." Yale University, Economic Growth Center Discussion Paper no. 441 (May 1983).

―――. "No Less than One Hundred Years of Argentine Economic History Plus Some Comparisons." In Gustav Ranis and Robert L. West, eds., *Comparative Development Perspectives: Essays in Honor of Lloyd Reynolds.* Boulder: Westview Press, 1984.

―――. "Latin America in the 1930s." In Rosemary Thorp, ed., *Latin America in the 1930s: The Role of the Periphery in World Crisis.* New York: St. Martin's, 1984.

―――. "The 1940s in Latin America." In Moshe Syrquin, Lance Taylor, and Larry E. Westphal, eds., *Economic Structure and Performance: Essays in Honor of Hollis B. Chenery.* New York: Academic Press, 1984.

Dix, Robert H. *Colombia: The Political Dimensions of Change.* New Haven: Yale University Press, 1967.

―――. "Political Oppositions under the National Front." In R. Albert Berry, Ronald Hellman, and Mauricio Solaún, eds., *Politics of Compromise.* New Brunswick: Transactions Books, 1980.

Domínguez, Jorge L. *Cuba: Order and Revolution.* Cambridge: Harvard University Press, 1978.

―――. "Revolutionary Politics: The New Demands for Orderliness." In Jorge L. Domínguez, ed., *Cuba: Internal and International Affairs*. Beverly Hills: Sage, 1981.

———. "U.S.-Cuban Relations in the Mid-1980s: Issues and Policies." JIW 27 (February 1985).

Donnelly, Jack. "Human Rights and Development: Complementary or Competing Concerns?" *World Politics* (January 1984).

Dore, Elizabeth, and John Weeks. "Class Alliances and Class Struggle in Peru." LAP 14 (Summer 1977).

Dornbusch, Rudiger. "Argentina since Martínez de Hoz." National Bureau of Economic Research Working Paper no. 1466 (September 1984).

———. "Policy and Performance Links Between LDC Debtors and Industrial Nations." BPEA 2 (1985).

———. "Special Exchange Rates for Capital Account Transactions." National Bureau of Economic Research Working Paper no. 1659 (September 1985).

Dornbusch, Rudiger, and Stanley Fischer. "Stopping Hyperinflations Past and Present." National Bureau of Economic Research Working Paper no. 1810 (January 1986).

Dorner, Peter, ed. *Land Reform in Latin America: Issues and Cases*. Madison: University of Wisconsin, Land Tenure Center, 1971.

Drake, Paul W. "Requiem for Populism?" In Michael Conniff, ed., *Latin American Populism in Comparative Perspective*. Albuquerque: University of New Mexico Press, 1982.

Draper, Theodore. "The Dominican Crisis: A Case Study in American Policy." *Commentary* 40, 6 (December 1965).

Dumont, René. *Cuba, est-il socialiste?* Paris: Editions de Seuil, 1970.

———. *Cuba: Socialism and Development*. New York: Grove Press, 1970.

Durán, Esperanza. "Mexico: Economic Realism and Political Efficiency." *The World Today* (May 1985).

Durán, Esperanza, ed. *Latin America and the World Recession*. Cambridge: Royal Institute of International Affairs and Cambridge University Press, 1985.

Dye, David R., and Carlos Eduardo de Souza e Silva. "A Perspective on the Brazilian State." LARR 14, 1 (1979).

Eckstein, Shlomo, et al. "Land Reform in Latin America: Bolivia, Chile, Mexico, Peru, and Venezuela." WBS no. 275 (1978).

Eckstein, Susan. *The Poverty of Revolution: The State and the Urban Poor in Mexico*. Princeton: Princeton University Press, 1977.

Edwards, Sebastian. "Stabilization and Liberalization: An Evaluation of Ten Years of Chile's Experiment with Free-Market Policies, 1973–1983." EDCC 33 (1985).

———. "The Exchange Rate and Non-Coffee Exports." Appendix B in Vinod Thomas et al., *Linking Macroeconomic and Agricultural Policies with Growth: The Colombian Experience*. Baltimore: Johns Hopkins University Press, 1985.

Eisenhower, Dwight D. *Mandate for Change, 1953–56: The White House Years*. Garden City: N.Y.: Doubleday, 1963.

Elliot, J. H. *Imperial Spain, 1469–1716*. London: Edward Arnold, 1963.

Ericksen, Kenneth Paul, and Kevin J. Middlebrook. "The State and Organized Labor in Brazil and Mexico." In Sylvia Ann Hewlett and Richard Weinert, eds., *Brazil and Mexico*. Philadelphia: Institute for the Study of Human Issues, 1982.

Evans, Peter. *Dependent Development: The Alliance of Multinational, State, and Local Capital in Brazil*. Princeton: Princeton University Press, 1979.

———. "After Dependency: Recent Studies of Class, State, and Industrialization." LARR 20, 2 (1985).

Fagen, Richard A. "Equity in the South in the Context of North-South Relations." In Albert Fishlow et al., eds., *Rich and Poor Nations in the World Economy*. New York: McGraw-Hill, 1978.

———. "Revolution and Crisis in Nicaragua." In Martin Diskin, ed., *Trouble in Our Backyard*. New York: Pantheon, 1983.

Fals Borda, Orlando. *La subversión en Colombia: El cambio social en la historia*. Bogotá: Ediciones Tercer Mundo, 1967.

Feinberg, Richard E. "The Recent Rapid Redefinitions of U.S. Interests and Diplomacy in Central America." In Richard E. Feinberg, ed., *Central America: International Dimensions of the Crisis*. New York: Holmes and Meier, 1982.

Feinberg, Richard E., and Valeriana Kallab, eds. *Adjustment Crisis in the Third World*. New Brunswick: Transactions Books, 1984.

Felix, David. "The Dilemma of Import Substitution." In Gustav F. Papenek, ed., *Development Policy—Theory and Practice*. Cambridge: Harvard University Press, 1968.

———. "Interrelations Between Consumption, Economic Growth, and Income Distribution in Latin America since 1800: A Comparative Perspective." In Henri Baudet and Hen Van der Meulen, eds., *Consumer Behaviour and Economic Growth in the Modern Economy*. London: Croom Helm, 1981.

———. "Income Distribution Trends in Mexico and the Kuznets Curves." In Sylvia Ann Hewlett and Richard Weinert, eds., *Bra-*

zil and Mexico. Philadelphia: Institute for the Study of Human Issues, 1982.

————. "Income Distribution and the Quality of Life in Latin America: Patterns, Trends, and Policy Implications." LARR 18, no. 2 (1983).

Ffrench-Davis, Ricardo. *Políticas económicas en Chile, 1952–1970.* Santiago: Centro de Estudios de Planificación Nacional, Ediciones Nueva Universidad, 1973.

————. "El experimento monetarista en Chile: Una síntesis crítica." CEC 9 (December 1982).

————. "The External Debt Crisis in Latin America: Trends and Outlook." In Kwan S. Kim and David F. Ruccio, eds., *Debt and Development in Latin America.* Notre Dame: University of Notre Dame Press, 1985.

Ffrench-Davis, Ricardo, and Ernesto Tironi, eds. *Latin America in the New International Economic Order.* London: Macmillan in association with St. Antony's College, Oxford, 1982.

Fields, Gary S. *Poverty, Inequality, and Development.* Cambridge: Cambridge University Press, 1980.

Figueroa, Adolfo. *Capitalist Development and the Peasant Economy in Peru.* Cambridge: Cambridge University Press, 1984.

Filgueira, Carlos. "Acerca del consumo en los nuevos modelos latino-américanos." CEPAL (Comisión Económica para América Latina). E/CEPAL/IN.1, December 3, 1980.

Fishlow, Albert. "Brazilian Size Distribution of Income." AER 42 (1972).

————. "Some Reflections on Post-1964 Brazilian Economic Policy." In Alfred Stepan, ed., *Authoritarian Brazil.* New Haven: Yale University Press, 1973.

————. *The Mature Neighbor Policy: A New United States Economic Policy for Latin America.* Berkeley: Institute of International Studies, University of California, 1977.

————. "The Debt Crisis: Round Two Ahead?" In Richard E. Feinberg and Valeriana Kallab, eds., *Adjustment Crisis in the Third World.* New Brunswick: Transactions Books, 1984.

————. "Revisiting the Great Debt Crisis of 1982." In Kwan S. Kim and David F. Ruccio, eds., *Debt and Development in Latin America.* Notre Dame: University of Notre Dame Press, 1985.

————, ed. *Rich and Poor Nations in the World Economy.* New York: McGraw-Hill, 1978.

FitzGerald, E.V.K. *The Political Economy of Peru, 1956–77.* Cambridge: Cambridge University Press, 1980.

FitzGerald, E.V.K. "State Capitalism in Peru: A Model of Economic Development and Its Limitations." In Cynthia McClintock and Abraham Lowenthal, eds., *The Peruvian Experiment Reconsidered*. Princeton: Princeton University Press, 1983.

Forsythe, David, Norman S. McBain, and Robert F. Solomon. "Technical Rigidity and Appropriate Technology in Less Developed Countries." WD 8 (May/June 1980).

Fortín, Carlos. "The State and Capital Accumulation in Chile." In Jean Carriere, ed., *Industrialization and the State in Latin America*. Amsterdam: Center for Latin American Research and Documentation, 1979.

Foxley, Alejandro. "Stabilization Policies and Stagflation: The Cases of Brazil and Chile." WD 8 (November 1980).

———. "Stabilization Policies and Their Effects on Employment and Income Distribution: A Latin American Perspective." In William Cline and Sidney Weintraub, eds., *Economic Stabilization in Developing Countries*. Washington, D.C.: Brookings, 1981.

———. "Cinco lecciones de la crisis actual." CEC 8 (July 1982).

———. *Latin American Experiments in Neoconservative Economics*. Berkeley: University of California Press, 1983.

Foxley, Alejandro, et al., eds. *Reconstrucción económica para la democracia*. Santiago: CIEPLAN 1983.

Frenkel, Roberto, and Guillermo O'Donnell. "The 'Stabilization Programs' of the International Monetary Fund and Their Internal Impacts." In Richard D. Fagen, ed., *Capitalism and the State in U.S.–Latin American Relations*. Stanford: Stanford University Press, 1979.

Fuller, Bruce. "Is Primary School Quality Eroding in the Third World?" *Comparative Education Review* 30 (November 1986).

Furtado, Celso. *Diagnosis of the Brazilian Crisis*. Berkeley: University of California Press, 1965.

———. *Economic Development of Latin America*. New York: Cambridge University Press, 1976.

Gantt, Andrew H. II, and Guiseppe Dutto. "Financial Performance of Government-Owned Corporations in Less Developed Countries." International Monetary Fund *Staff Papers* (1968).

García, Brígida. "Desarrollo capitalista y absorción de fuerza de trabajo en México: La dimensión regional," paper presented at the Third Reunion on Demographic Research in Mexico, Mexico City, November 1986.

Geiger, Theodore. *Communism versus Progress in Guatemala*. New York: National Planning Association, 1953.

Gereffi, Gary. *The Pharmaceutical Industry and Dependency in the Third World*. Princeton: Princeton University Press, 1983.

Gereffi, Gary, and Peter Evans. "Transnational Corporations, Dependent Development, and State Policy in the Semi-periphery: A Comparison of Brazil and Mexico." LARR 16, 3 (1981).

Gil, Federico G., Ricardo Lagos E., and Henry A. Landsberger. *Chile at the Turning Point: Lessons of the Socialist Years, 1970–1973*. Philadelphia: Institute for the Study of Human Issues, 1979.

Gíl Díaz, Francisco. "The Incidence of Taxes in Mexico: A Before and After Comparison." In Pedro Aspe and Paul E. Sigmund, eds., *The Political Economy of Income Distribution in Mexico*. New York: Holmes and Meier, 1984.

Gilbert, Dennis. "The End of the Peruvian Revolution: A Class Analysis." *Studies in Comparative International Development* 15 (Spring 1980).

Gillis, Malcolm. "The Role of State Enterprise in Economic Development." *Social Research* 47 (Summer 1980).

Godfrey, Martin. "Is Dependency Dead?" Institute of Development Studies, University of Sussex, *Bulletin* 12, 1 (1980).

Goodsell, Charles T. *American Corporations and Peruvian Politics*. Cambridge: Harvard University Press, 1974.

Graham, Douglas H. "Mexican and Brazilian Economic Development: Legacies, Patterns, and Performance." In Sylvia Ann Hewlett and Richard Weinert, eds., *Brazil and Mexico*. Philadelphia: Institute for the Study of Human Issues, 1982.

de Gregorio, José. "Comportamiento de las exportaciones e importaciones en Chile. Un estudio econométrico." CEC 13 (1984).

Gregory, Peter. "An Assessment of Changing Employment Conditions in Less Developed Countries." EDCC 28 (July 1980).

———. "Employment, Unemployment, and Underemployment in Latin America" *Statistical Bulletin of the OAS* 2 (October–December 1980).

———. *The Myth of Market Failure: Employment and the Labor Market in Mexico*. Baltimore: Johns Hopkins University Press for the World Bank, 1986.

Griffin, Keith B. *Underdevelopment in Spanish America*. 2d ed. London: Allen and Unwin, 1971.

———. "Systems of Labour Control and Rural Poverty in Ecuador." In Keith B. Griffin, ed., *Land Concentration and Rural Poverty*. New York: Holmes and Meier, 1976.

Griffin, Keith B., and John Gurley. "Radical Analyses of Imperialism, the Third World, and the Transition to Socialism." *Journal of Economic Literature* 23 (September 1985).

Griffin, Keith B., and Jeffrey James. *The Transition to Egalitarian Development*. New York: St. Martin's Press, 1981.

Griffith-Jones, Stephany. *The Role of Finance in the Transition to Socialism*. London: Francis Pinter, 1981.

Grindle, Merilee. "Whatever Happened to Land Reform? The Latin American Experience." University of Texas at Austin, Institute of Latin American Studies, Technical Papers Series no. 23 (1980).

—————. *State and Countryside: Development Policy and Agrarian Politics in Latin America*. Baltimore: Johns Hopkins University Press, 1986.

Guasti, Laura. "The Peruvian Military Government and the International Corporations." In Cynthia McClintock and Abraham Lowenthal, eds., *The Peruvian Experiment Reconsidered*. Princeton: Princeton University Press, 1983.

Guzmán, Monseñor Germán, Orlando Fals Borda, and Eduardo Umana Luna. *La Violencia en Colombia*. Vol. 1. Bogotá: Ediciones Tercer Mundo, 1962.

Hamilton, Nora. *The Limits of State Autonomy: Post-Revolutionary Mexico*. Princeton: Princeton University Press, 1982.

Harberger, Arnold C. "Comments" on Foxley, "Stabilization Policies." In William Cline and Sidney Weintraub, eds., *Economic Stabilization in Developing Countries*. Washington, D.C.: Brookings, 1981.

—————. "Observations on the Chilean Economy." EDCC 33 (1985).

Hartlyn, Jonathan. "Military Governments and the Transition to Civilian Rule: The Colombian Experience of 1957–1958." JIW 26 (May 1984).

—————. "Producer Associations, the Political Regime, and Policy Processes in Contemporary Colombia." LARR 20, 3 (1985).

Hartlyn, Jonathan, and Samuel Morley, eds. *Latin American Political Economy: Financial Crisis and Political Change*. Boulder: Westview Press, 1986.

Helleiner, Gerald D. "Lender of Early Resort: The IMF and the Poorest." AER 73 (May 1983).

Henderson, James D. *When Colombia Bled: A History of the Violence in Tolima*. University, Ala.: Alabama University Press, 1985.

Hersh, Seymour. *The Price of Power: Henry Kissinger in the Nixon White House*. New York: Summit Books, 1983.

Hewlett, Sylvia Ann. *The Cruel Dilemmas of Development: Twentieth Century Brazil.* New York: Basic Books, 1980.

Hewlett, Sylvia Ann, and Richard Weinert, eds. *Brazil and Mexico: Patterns in Late Development.* Philadelphia: Institute for the Study of Human Issues, 1982.

Hirschman, Albert O. *The Strategy of Economic Development.* New Haven: Yale University Press, 1958.

———. "Land Use and Land Reform in Colombia." In Albert O. Hirschman, ed., *Journeys Toward Progress: Studies of Economic Policy Making in Latin America.* New York: Twentieth Century Fund, 1963.

———. "The Political Economy of Import-Substituting Industrialization in Latin America." *Quarterly Journal of Economics* 82 (February 1968).

———. *A Bias for Hope.* New Haven: Yale University Press, 1971.

———. "How and Why to Divest in Latin America." *Princeton Studies in International Finance* no. 76 (November 1979).

———. *Essays in Trespassing: Economics to Politics and Beyond.* Cambridge: Cambridge University Press, 1981.

———. "A Dissenter's Confession: The 'Strategy of Economic Development' Revisited." In Gerald M. Maier and Dudley Seers, eds., *Pioneers in Development.* Oxford and New York: Oxford University Press for the World Bank, 1984.

———. *Getting Ahead Collectively: Grassroots Experiences in Latin America.* New York: Pergamon Press, 1984.

———, ed. *Latin American Issues: Essays and Comments.* New York: Twentieth Century Fund, 1961.

Hoffmann, Stanley. *Duties Beyond Borders: On the Limits and Possibilities of Ethical International Politics.* Syracuse: Syracuse University Press, 1981.

Hojman, David E. "Income Distribution and Market Policies: Survival and Renewal of Middle Income Groups in Chile." *Inter-American Economic Affairs* 26 (Autumn 1982).

Holt, Pat M. *Colombia Today—and Tomorrow.* New York: Praeger, 1964.

Huberman, Leo, and Paul M. Sweezy. *Socialism in Cuba.* New York: Monthly Review Press, 1969.

Hunt, Shane. "Direct Foreign Investment in Peru: New Rules for an Old Game." In Abraham Lowenthal, ed., *The Peruvian Experiment.* Princeton: Princeton University Press, 1975.

Iguíñiz, Javier. "Basic Needs and Capitalist Production in Peru." In Claes Brundenius and Mats Lundahl, eds., *Development Strate-*

gies and Basic Needs in Latin America. Boulder: Westview Press, 1982.

Immerman, Richard H. *The CIA in Guatemala: The Foreign Policy of Intervention*. Austin: University of Texas Press, 1982.

Inter-American Development Bank. *Economic and Social Progress in Latin America, Report*, 1982 to 1985. Washington, D.C.: IDB, 1982–85.

International Labour Office. *Towards Full Employment: A Programme for Colombia*. Geneva: ILO, 1970.

International Monetary Fund. *International Financial Statistics, Yearbook*, 1983 and 1984. Washington: IMF, 1983 and 1984.

Isard, Peter. "How Far Can We Push the Law of One Price?" AER 67 (December 1977).

Isenman, Paul. "Basic Needs: The Case of Sri Lanka." WD 8 (1980).

de Janvry, Alain. *The Agrarian Question and Reformism in Latin America*. Baltimore: Johns Hopkins University Press, 1981.

Jaquette, Jane. "Belaúnde and Velasco: On the Limits of Ideological Politics." In Abraham Lowenthal, ed., *The Peruvian Experiment: Continuity and Change under Military Rule*. Princeton: Princeton University Press, 1975.

Jimenez, Emmanuel. "The Public Subsidization of Education and Health in Developing Countries: A Review of Equity and Efficiency." *World Bank Research Observer* 1 (January 1986).

Johnson, Chalmers. *MITI and the Japanese Miracle: The Growth of Industrial Policy*. Stanford: Stanford University Press, 1982.

Jolly, Richard. "Education." Part II in Dudley Seers et al., *Cuba: The Economic and Social Revolution*. Chapel Hill: University of North Carolina Press, 1964.

Jones, Leroy P. *Public Enterprise and Economic Development: The Korean Case*. Seoul: Korean Development Institute, 1975.

————, ed. *Public Enterprise in Less Developed Countries*. New York: Cambridge University Press, 1982.

Junguito, Roberto, and Diego Pisano, "Primary Products in Latin America," in Ricardo Ffrench-Davis and Ernesto Tironi, eds., *Latin America and the New International Economic Order*. London: Macmillan, 1982.

Kaufman, Robert R. *The Politics of Land Reform in Chile, 1950–1970*. Cambridge: Harvard University Press, 1972.

————. "Mexico and Latin American Authoritarianism." In José Luis Reyna and Richard S. Weinert, eds., *Authoritarianism in Mexico*. Philadelphia: Institute for the Study of Human Issues, 1977.

———. "Industrial Change and Authoritarian Rule in Latin America: A Concrete Review of the Bureaucratic-Authoritarian Model." In David Collier, ed., *The New Authoritarianism in Latin America*. Princeton: Princeton University Press, 1979.

Kay, Cristóbal. "Achievements and Contradictions of the Peruvian Agrarian Reform." *Journal of Development Studies* 18 (January 1982).

Killick, Tony, Graham Bird, Jennifer Sharpley, and Mary Sutton. "The IMF: Case for a Change in Emphasis." In Richard E. Feinberg and Valeriana Kallab, eds., *Adjustment Crisis in the Third World*. New Brunswick, Transactions Books, 1984.

Kim, Kwan S., and David F. Ruccio, eds. *Debt and Development in Latin America*. Notre Dame: Notre Dame University Press, 1985.

Kindleberger, Charles P. *The Terms of Trade: A European Case Study*. New York: M.I.T. and Wiley, 1956.

Knight, Peter T. "Brazilian Socioeconomic Development: Issues for the Eighties." WD 9 (November/December 1981).

Krasner, Stephen D. *Structural Conflict: The Third World Against Global Liberalism*. Berkeley: University of California Press, 1985.

Kravis, Irving B., and Robert E. Lipsey, "Export Prices and the Transmission of Inflation." AER 67 (February 1977).

Kravis, Irving B., A. Heston, and R. Summers. "Real GDP per Capita for More than One Hundred Countries." *Economic Journal* 88 (June 1978).

Kuczynski, Pedro-Pablo. *Peruvian Democracy under Economic Stress: An Account of the Belaunde Administration, 1963–1968*. Princeton: Princeton University Press, 1977.

Kuznets, Simon. "Economic Growth and Income Inequality." AER 45 (March 1955).

LaFeber, Walter. *The Panama Canal: The Crisis in Historical Perspective*. New York: Oxford University Press, 1978.

———. *Inevitable Revolutions: The United States in Central America*. Enl. ed. New York: Norton, 1984.

Leff, Nathaniel H. *The Brazilian Capital Goods Industry, 1919–1964*. Cambridge: Harvard University Press, 1968.

———. *Economic Policy Making and Development in Brazil, 1947–1964*. New York: Wiley, 1968.

———. "Industrial Organization and Entrepreneurship in the Developing Countries: The Economic Group." *Economic Development and Cultural Change* (July 1978).

Leff, Nathaniel H. "Entrepreneurship and Economic Development: The Problem Revisited." *Journal of Economic Literature* 17 (March 1979).

———. *Underdevelopment and Development in Brazil.* 2 vols. Boston: Allen and Unwin, 1982.

LeoGrande, William M. "Cuba: Going to the Sources." In Richard Newfarmer, ed., *From Gunboats to Diplomacy*. Baltimore: Johns Hopkins University Press, 1984.

Levy, Brian. "The Industrial Economics of Entrepreneurship and Dependent Development." Ph.D. Dissertation, Harvard University, 1983.

———. "A Theory of Public Enterprise." *Journal of Economic Behavior and Organization*, forthcoming.

Lewis, John P., and Valeriana Kallab, eds. *U.S. Foreign Policy and the Third World, Agenda 1983*. New York: Praeger for the Overseas Development Council, 1983.

Lewis, W. Arthur. "Economic Development with Unlimited Supplies of Labour." *Manchester School* 22 (1954).

———. *The Theory of Economic Growth*. London: Allen and Unwin, 1955.

———. "The State of Development Theory." AER 74 (March 1984).

Lindblom, Charles. *Politics and Markets: The World's Political-Economic Systems*. New York: Basic Books, 1977.

Linz, Juan J., and Alfred Stepan, eds. *The Breakdown of Democratic Regimes: Latin America*. Baltimore: Johns Hopkins University Press, 1978.

Lipsey, Robert, and Irving Kravis. "Export Prices and the Transmission of Inflation." AER 67 (February 1977).

Lipton, Michael. *Why Poor People Stay Poor: Urban Bias in World Development*. Cambridge: Harvard University Press, 1977.

———. "Migration from Rural Areas of Poor Countries: The Impact on Rural Productivity and Income Distribution." In Richard H. Sabot, ed., *Migration and the Labor Market in Developing Countries*. Boulder: Westview Press, 1982.

Little, Ian, Tibor Scitovsky, and Maurice Scott. *Industry and Trade in Some Developing Countries: A Comparative Study*. Oxford: Oxford University Press for the OECD, 1970.

Lowenthal, Abraham. *The Dominican Intervention*. Cambridge: Harvard University Press, 1972.

———. "Latin America and the Caribbean: Toward a New U.S. Policy." In John P. Lewis and Valeriana Kallab, eds., *U.S. Foreign Policy and the Third World, Agenda 1983*. New York: Praeger for the Overseas Development Council, 1983.

————, ed. *The Peruvian Experiment: Continuity and Change under Military Rule*. Princeton: Princeton University Press, 1975.

McClintock, Cynthia. *Peasant Cooperatives and Political Change in Peru*. Princeton: Princeton University Press, 1981.

————. "Why Peasants Rebel: The Case of Peru's Sendero Luminoso." *World Politics* 37 (October 1984).

————. "After Agrarian Reform and Democratic Government: Has Peruvian Agriculture Developed?" In F. LaMond Tullis and W. Ladd Hollist, eds., *Food, the State, and International Political Economy*. Lincoln: University of Nebraska Press, 1986.

————. "Why Peru's Alan García Is a Man on the Move." *LASA Forum* 16 (Winter 1986).

McClintock, Cynthia, and Abraham Lowenthal, eds. *The Peruvian Experiment Reconsidered*. Princeton: Princeton University Press, 1983.

MacEwan, Arthur. *Revolution and Economic Development in Cuba: Moving Toward Socialism*. New York: St. Martin's Press, 1981.

McGreevey, William Paul. *An Economic History of Colombia, 1845–1930*. Cambridge: Cambridge University Press, 1971.

————. "Population Policy Under the National Front." In R. Albert Berry, Ronald Hellman, and Mauricio Solaún, eds., *Politics of Compromise*. New Brunswick: Transactions Books, 1980.

Mallon, Florencia E. *The Defense of Community in Peru's Central Highlands; Peasant Struggle and Capitalist Transition, 1860–1940*. Princeton: Princeton University Press, 1983.

Mallon, Richard, and Juan Sourrouille. *Economic Policy Making in a Conflict Society: The Argentine Case*. Cambridge: Harvard University Press, 1975.

Malloy, James. "Generation of Political Support and Allocation of Costs." In Carmelo Mesa-Lago, ed., *Revolutionary Change in Cuba*. Pittsburgh: University of Pittsburgh Press, 1971.

Martínez, Daniel. "El agro en el Perú: 1980–1984 y perspectivas." In Germán Alarco, compilador, *Desafíos para la economía peruana*. Lima: Centro de Investigación de la Universidad del Pacífico, 1985.

Mason, Edward S. "Authoritarian Development." *World Issues* (October–November 1977).

Mason, Edward S., and Leroy P. Jones. "The Role of Economic Factors in Determining the Size and Structure of the Public Enterprise Sector in Mixed Economy LDCs." In Leroy Jones, ed., *Public Enterprise in Less Developed Countries*. New York: Cambridge University Press, 1982.

Meier, Gerald M., and Dudley Seers, eds. *Pioneers in Development.* New York: Oxford University Press for the World Bank, 1985.

Meller, Patricio. "Enfoques sobre demanda de trabajo: Relevancia para América Latina." *Estudios cieplan* 24 (June 1978).

Mellor, John W. "Food Price Policy and Income Distribution in Low-Income Countries." EDCC 27 (October 1978).

Mellor, John W., and Bruce F. Johnston. "The World Food Equation." *Journal of Economic Literature* 22 (June 1984).

Melville, Thomas, and Marjorie Melville. *Guatemala: The Politics of Land Ownership.* New York: Free Press, 1971.

Mendonça de Barros, José Roberto, and Douglas H. Graham. "The Brazilian Economic Miracle Revisited: Private and Public Sector Initiative in a Market Economy." LARR 13, 2 (1978).

Mesa-Lago, Carmelo. *The Economy of Socialist Cuba: A Two-Decade Appraisal.* Albuquerque: University of New Mexico Press, 1981.

Mesa-Lago, Carmelo, and Jorge Perez-Lopez. "A Study of Cuba's Material Product System, Its Conversion to the System of National Accounts, and Estimation of Gross Domestic Product per Capita and Growth Rates." WBS no. 770, 1986.

Mexico, Secretaria de Patrimonio y Fomento Industrial. *Plan Nacional de Desarrollo Industrial, 1979–1982.* Mexico: SEPAFIN, 1979.

Meyer, Lorenzo. "Historical Roots of the Authoritarian State in Mexico." In José Luis Reyna and Richard Weinert, eds. *Authoritarianism in Mexico.* Philadelphia: Institute for the Study of Human Issues, 1977.

Mohan, Rakesh, and Richard Sabot. "Educational Expansion and the Inequality of Pay: Colombia, 1973–1978." World Bank and Williams College (March 1985).

Morley, Samuel. *Labor Markets and Inequitable Growth: The Case of Authoritarian Capitalism in Brazil.* London: Cambridge University Press, 1983.

Muñoz Gomá, Oscar. "Hacia una nueva industrialización: Elementos de una estrategia de desarrollo para la democracia." *Apuntes cieplan* 33 (May 1982).

———. "Crecimiento y desequilibrios en una economía abierta: El caso chileno, 1976–81." CEC 8 (July 1982).

———. "Economía mixta de pleno empleo." CEC 9 (December 1982).

———. "Chile: El colapso de un experimento económico y sus efectos políticos." CEC 16 (June 1985).

———. "Hacia la reindustrialización nacional." In Alejandro Foxley et al., *Reconstrucción económica para la democracia*. Santiago: CIE-PLAN, 1983.

——. *Chile y su industrialización: Pasado, crisis y opciones*. Santiago: CIEPLAN, 1986.

Muns, Joaquin. *Industrialización y crecimiento de los paises en desarrollo*. Barcelona: Ediciones Ariel, 1972.

Murdoch, William W. *The Poverty of Nations: The Political Economy of Hunger and Population*. Baltimore: Johns Hopkins University Press, 1980.

Nelson, Lowry. *Cuba: The Measure of a Revolution*. Minneapolis: University of Minnesota Press, 1972.

Newfarmer, Richard D., ed. *From Gunboats to Diplomacy: New U.S. Policies for Latin America*. Baltimore: Johns Hopkins University Press, 1984.

Newfarmer, Richard D., ed. *Profits, Progress, and Poverty: Case Studies of International Industries in Latin America*. Notre Dame: University of Notre Dame Press, 1985.

Nurkse, Ragnar. *Problems of Capital Formation in Underdeveloped Countries*. New York: Oxford University Press, 1955.

Nyrop, Richard F., ed. *Panama: A Country Study*. Washington, D.C.: American University Foreign Area Studies, 1981.

O'Donnell, Guillermo A. *Modernization and Bureaucratic-Authoritarianism: Studies in South American Politics*. Berkeley: University of California, Institute of International Studies, 1973.

——. "Permanent Crisis and the Failure to Create a Democratic Regime in Argentina, 1955–66." In Juan J. Linz and Alfred Stepan, eds., *The Breakdown of Democratic Regimes: Latin America*. Baltimore: Johns Hopkins University Press, 1978.

O'Donnell, Guillermo, Philippe C. Schmitter, and Laurence Whitehead, eds. *Transitions from Authoritarian Rule: Comparative Perspectives*. Baltimore: Johns Hopkins University Press, 1986.

Okita, Saburo. "Causes of Rapid Growth in Postwar Japan and Their Implications for Newly Developing Countries." In Saburo Okita, *The Developing Countries and Japan: Lessons in Growth*. Tokyo: University of Tokyo Press, 1982.

Oquist, Paul. *Violence, Conflict, and Politics in Colombia*. New York: Academic Press, 1980.

Oxenham, John. "Employers and Qualifications; Brief Response." Institute of Development Studies at the University of Sussex, *Bulletin* 11, 2 (Maya 1980).

Palma, Gabriel. "Dependency: A Formal Theory of Underdevelopment or a Methodology for the Analysis of Concrete Situations of Underdevelopment?" WD 6 (December 1978).

Palmer, David Scott. "Rebellion in Rural Peru: The Origins and Evolution of Sendero Luminoso." *Comparative Politics* 18 (January 1986).

Papenek, Gustav F., ed. *Development Policy—Theory and Practice*. Cambridge: Harvard University Press, 1968.

Papanek, Gustav F., and Oldrich Kyn. "The Effects of Income Distribution on Development, the Rate of Growth, and Economic Strategy: Flattening the Kuznets Curve." *Pakistan Development Review*, forthcoming.

Parker, Phyllis R. *Brazil and the Quiet Intervention, 1964*. Austin: University of Texas Press, 1979.

Pásara, Luis. "When the Military Dreams." In Cynthia McClintock and Abraham Lowenthal, eds., *The Peruvian Experiment Reconsidered*. Princeton: Princeton University Press, 1981.

Paz, Octavio. *Posdata*. Mexico: Siglo Veintiuno, 1970.

———. *One Earth, Four or Five Worlds*. San Diego: Harcourt Brace Jovanovich, 1985.

Pearson, Scott, Walter P. Falcon, and C. Peter Timmer. *Food Policy Analysis*. Baltimore: Johns Hopkins University Press, 1983.

Pfefferman, Guy. "Some Economic Aspects of Human Development in Latin America (with Special Emphasis on Education)." In Willem Bussink et al., "Poverty and the Development of Human Resources: Regional Perspectives." WBS no. 406 (1980).

Pfefferman, Guy, and Richard Webb. "The Distribution of Income in Brazil." WBS no. 356 (1979).

Pike, Frederick B. "Guatemala, the United States, and Communism in the Americas." *Review of Politics* 17 (April 1955).

Portes, Alejandro. "Latin America Class Structures: Their Composition and Change during the Last Decades." LARR 20, 3 (1985).

Potter, Joseph, Myriam Ordóñez G., and Anthony Measham. "The Rapid Decline in Colombian Fertility." *Population and Development Review* 2 (September and December 1976).

Prebisch, Raúl. "Commercial Policy in the Underdeveloped Countries." AER 49 (May 1959).

Programa Regional del Empleo para América Latina y el Caribe (PREALC). *Mercado de trabajo en cifras, 1950–1980*. Santiago: Oficina Internacional de Trabajo, 1982.

Psacharopoulos, George. "Education, Employment, and Inequality in Less Developed Countries." WD 9, 1 (January 1981).

Ranis, Gustav. "Challenges and Opportunities Posed by Asia's Superexporters: Implications for Manufactured Exports from Latin America." In Werner Baer and Malcolm Gillis, eds., *Export Diversification and the New Protectionism*. Champaign: University of Illinois for the National Bureau of Economic Research, 1981.

―――. "Latin America: Demographic Problems and Socio-Economic Development." In Víctor Urquidi and Saúl Trejo Reyes, eds., *Human Resources, Employment, and Development*. New York: St. Martin's Press for the International Economic Association, 1983.

Ranis, Gustav, and John C. H. Fei. "A Theory of Economic Growth." AER 51 (September 1961).

Ranis, Gustav, and Louise Orrock. "Latin American and East Asian NICs: Development Strategies Compared." In Esperanza Durán, ed., *Latin America and the World Recession*. Cambridge: Cambridge University Press, 1985.

Remmer, Karen. "Public Policy and Regime Consolidation: The First Five Years of the Chilean Junta." *Journal of Developing Areas* 13 (July 1979).

―――. "Political Demobilization in Chile, 1973–78." *Comparative Politics* 12 (April 1980).

Reveíz, Edgar, and María José Pérez. "Colombia: Moderate Economic Growth, Political Stability, and Social Welfare." In Jonathan Hartlyn and Samuel Morley, eds., *Latin American Political Economy: Financial Crisis and Political Change*. Boulder: Westview Press, 1986.

Reyna, José Luis, and Richard S. Weinert, eds. *Authoritarianism in Mexico*. Philadelphia: Institute for the Study of Human Issues, 1977.

Rinehart, Robert. Chapter 1, "Historical Setting," pp. 3–70, in Harold D. Nelson, ed. *Costa Rica: A Country Study*. Washington: Foreign Area Studies, American University, 1984.

Ritter, Archibald. *The Economic Development of Revolutionary Cuba: Strategy and Performance*. New York: Praeger, 1974.

Rivera Urrutia, Eugenio. *El Fondo Monetario Internaciónal y Costa Rica, 1978–1982*. San José: Departamento Ecuménico de Investigaciones, 1982.

Rizzo, Socrates C. "Generation and Allocation of Oil Economic Surpluses." In Pedro Aspe and Paul E. Sigmund, eds., *The Political Economy of Income Distribution in Mexico*. New York: Holmes and Meier, 1984.

Roddick, Jackie. "Labour Relations and the 'New Authoritarianism' in the Southern Cone." In Jean Carrière, ed. *Industrialization and the State in Latin America*. Amsterdam: Center for Latin American Research and Documentation, 1979.

Sabot, Richard H., ed. *Migration and the Labor Market in Developing Countries*. Boulder: Westview Press, 1982.

Sachs, Jeffrey D. "External Debt and Macroeconomic Performance in Latin America and East Asia." BPEA 2 (1985).

Said, Edward W. *Orientalism*. New York: Pantheon Books, 1978.

Sánchez-Albornoz, Nicolas. *The Population of Latin America: A History*. Berkeley: University of California Press, 1974.

Sanderson, Susan R. Walsh. *Land Reform in Mexico: 1910–1980*. Orlando: Academic Press, 1984.

Saulniers, Alfred H. "The Peruvian President's Economic Dilemmas." *LASA Forum* 16 (Winter 1986).

Schlesinger, Stephen C., and Stephen Kinzer. *Bitter Fruit: The Untold Story of the American Coup in Guatemala*. Garden City, N.Y.: Doubleday, 1982.

Schoultz, Lars. *Human Rights and United States Policy Toward Latin America*. Princeton: Princeton University Press, 1981.

———. "Guatemala: Social Change and Political Conflict." In Martin Diskin, ed., *Trouble in Our Backyard: Central America and the United States in the Eighties*. New York: Pantheon, 1983.

———. "Nicaragua: The United States Confronts a Revolution." In Richard Newfarmer, ed., *From Gunboats to Diplomacy*. Baltimore: Johns Hopkins University Press, 1984.

Schuldt, Jürgen. "Política económica y restructuración social en el Perú, 1985–86: Un modelo para armar." Paper presented at the meetings of the Latin American Studies Association, Boston, October 1986.

Schultz, Theodore W. "The Value of the Ability to Deal with Disequilibria." *Journal of Economic Literature* 13 (September 1975).

Schydlowsky, Daniel M. "The Tragedy of Lost Opportunity in Peru." In Jonathan Hartlyn and Samuel Morley, eds., *Latin American Political Economy: Financial Crisis and Political Change*. Boulder: Westview Press, 1986.

Schydlowsky, Daniel, and Juan Wicht. "The Anatomy of an Economic Failure." In Cynthia McClintock and Abraham Lowenthal, eds., *The Peruvian Experiment Reconsidered*. Princeton: Princeton University Press, 1983.

Seers, Dudley. "Urban Bias—Seers versus Lipton." Institute of Development Studies at the University of Sussex. Discussion Paper no. 116 (1977).

———. "Inflation: The Latin American Experience." Institute of Development Studies at the University of Sussex. Discussion Paper 168 (November 1981).

Seers, Dudley, ed. *Dependency Theory: A Critical Reassessment.* London: Francis Pinter, 1981.

Seligson, Mitchell A. *Peasants of Costa Rica and the Rise of Agrarian Capitalism.* Madison: University of Wisconsin Press, 1980.

Selowsky, Marcelo. *Who Benefits From Government Expenditure? A Case Study of Colombia.* New York: Oxford University Press for the World Bank, 1979.

———. "Income Distribution, Basic Needs, and Trade-Offs with Growth: The Case of Semi-Industrialized Latin American Countries." WD 9 (January 1981).

Sen, Amartya K. *Resources, Values, and Development.* Cambridge: Harvard University Press, 1984.

Serra, José. "Three Mistaken Theses Regarding the Connections Between Industrialization and Authoritarian Regimes." In David Collier, ed., *The New Authoritarianism in Latin America.* Princeton: Princeton University Press, 1979.

Sheahan, John. *Promotion and Control of Industry in Postwar France.* Cambridge: Harvard University Press, 1963.

———. "Imports, Investment, and Growth—Colombia." In Gustav Papenek, ed., *Development Policy—Theory and Practice.* Cambridge: Harvard University Press, 1968.

———. "Public Enterprise in Developing Countries." In Geoffrey Shepherd, ed., *Public Enterprise: Economic Analysis of Theory and Practice.* Lexington, Mass.: Lexington Books, 1976.

———. "Aspects of Planning and Development in Colombia." Institute of Latin American Studies, University of Texas at Austin. Technical Papers Series no. 10 (1977).

———. "Market-oriented Economic Policies and Political Repression in Latin America." EDCC 28 (January 1980).

———. "Peru: Economic Policies and Structural Change, 1968–1978." *Journal of Development Studies* 7, 1 (1980).

———. "The Economics of the Peruvian Experiment in Comparative Perspective." In Abraham Lowenthal and Cynthia McClintock, eds., *The Peruvian Experiment Reconsidered.* Princeton: Princeton University Press, 1983.

Shinohara, Miyohei, Toru Yanagihara, and Kwang Suk Kim. "Jap-

anese and Korean Experiences in Managing Development."
WBS no. 574 (1983).

Sigmund, Paul E. *The Overthrow of Allende and the Politics of Chile, 1964–1976.* Pittsburgh: University of Pittsburgh Press, 1977.

Silverman, Bertram, ed. *Man and Socialism in Cuba: The Great Debate.* New York: Atheneum, 1971.

Silvert, K. H., and Gillin, John. "Ambiguities in Guatemala." *Foreign Affairs* 34 (April 1956).

Simmons, Alan B. "Social Inequality and Demographic Transition." In Archibald Ritter and David Pollock, eds., *Latin American Prospects for the 1980s: Equity, Democratization, and Development.* New York: Praeger, 1983.

Simmons, John. "Education, Poverty, and Development." WBS no. 188 (February 1974).

Skidmore, Thomas E. *Politics in Brazil, 1930–1964: An Experiment in Democracy.* New York: Oxford University Press, 1967.

—. "Politics and Economic Policy Making in Authoritarian Brazil, 1937–71." In Alfred Stepan, ed., *Authoritarian Brazil; Origins, Policies, and Future.* New Haven: Yale University Press, 1973.

Skidmore, Thomas E., and Peter H. Smith. *Modern Latin America.* New York: Oxford University Press, 1984.

Slater, Jerome. *Intervention and Negotiation: The United States and the Dominican Republic.* New York: Harper and Row, 1970.

Solari, Aldo. "Development and Education Policy in Latin America." *CEPAL Review* (1st Semester 1977).

Solís, Leopoldo. *La realidad económica mexicana: Retrovisión y perspectivas.* Mexico: Siglo Veintiuno, 1970.

—. *Economic Policy Reform in Mexico: A Case Study for Developing Countries.* New York: Pergamon, 1981.

Spalding, Rose J. *The Mexican Food Crisis: An Analysis of the SAM.* Center for U.S.-Mexican Studies, University of California at San Diego, Research Report Series, 33 (1984).

Spraos, John. "The Statistical Debate on the Net Barter Terms of Trade Between Primary Commodities and Manufactures." *Economic Journal* 90 (March 1980).

Squire, Lyn. *Employment Policy in Developing Countries.* New York: Oxford University Press for the World Bank, 1981.

Stepan, Alfred. "Political Leadership and Regime Breakdown: Brazil." In Juan J. Linz and Alfred Stepan, eds., *The Breakdown of Democratic Regimes: Latin America.* Baltimore: Johns Hopkins University Press, 1978.

———. *The State and Society: Peru in Comparative Perspective*. Princeton: Princeton University Press, 1978.

Stepan, Alfred, ed. *Authoritarian Brazil: Origins, Policies, and Future*. New Haven: Yale University Press, 1973.

Stevens, Evelyn P. *Protest and Response in Mexico*. Cambridge: MIT Press, 1974.

Story, Dale. "Sources of Investment Capital in Twentieth Century Mexico." In James W. Wilkie and Adam Perkal, eds., *Statistical Abstract of Latin America, 1984*, vol. 33. Los Angeles: University of California at Los Angeles, Latin American Center, 1984.

Sunkel, Osvaldo, and Edmundo F. Fuenzalida. "Transnationalization and Its National Consequences." In José Villamil, ed., *Transnational Capitalism and National Development*. Brighton: Harvester Press, 1979.

Tait, Alan A., Wilfrid L. M. Gratz, and Barry J. Eichengreen. "International Comparisons of Taxation for Selected Developing Countries, 1972–76." IMF Staff Paper 26 (1979).

Tanzer, Michael. *The Political Economy of International Oil and the Underdeveloped Countries*. Boston: Beacon Press, 1969.

Taylor, Lance. *Structuralist Macroeconomics; Applicable Models for the Third World*. New York: Basic Books, 1983.

———. "The Crisis and Thereafter: Macroeconomic Policy Problems in Mexico." In Peggy B. Musgrave, ed., *Mexico and the United States: Studies in Economic Integration*. Boulder: Westview Press, 1985.

di Tella, Torcuato S. "Populism and Reform in Latin America." In Claudio Véliz, ed., *Obstacles to Change in Latin America*. London: Oxford University Press, 1965.

Tello, Carlos. *La política económica en México, 1970–1976*. Mexico: Siglo Veintiuno, 1979.

———. *La nacionalización de la banca en México*. Mexico: Siglo Veintiuno, 1984.

Tendler, Judith. *Inside Foreign Aid*. Baltimore: Johns Hopkins University Press, 1975.

———. *What to Think About Cooperatives: A Guide from Bolivia*. Washington: Inter-American Foundation, 1983.

Thomas, Hugh. *Cuba: The Pursuit of Freedom: 1762–1969*. New York: Harper and Row, 1971.

Thorp, Rosemary. "The Post-Import-Substitution Era: The Case of Peru." WD 5 (January-February 1977).

———. "The Evolution of Peru's Economy." In Cynthia McClintock and Abraham Lowenthal, eds. *The Peruvian Experiment Reconsidered*. Princeton: Princeton University Press, 1983.

Thorp, Rosemary, ed. *Latin America in the 1930s: The Role of the Periphery in World Crisis*. New York: St. Martin's Press, 1984.

Thorp, Rosemary, and Geoffrey Bertram. *Peru 1890–1977: Growth and Policy in an Open Economy*. London: Macmillan, 1978.

Thoumi, Francisco E. "International Trade Strategies, Employment, and Income Distribution in Colombia." In Anne O. Krueger, ed., *Trade and Employment in Developing Countries*. Chicago: Chicago University Press for National Bureau of Economic Research, 1981.

———. "Some Implications of the Growth of the Underground Economy in Colombia." Paper presented at the meetings of the Latin American Studies Association, Boston, October 1986.

Tokman, Víctor E. "Dinámica de los mercados de trabajo y distribución del ingreso en América Latina." CEC 3 (June 1980).

Trebat, Thomas J. *Brazil's State-Owned Enterprises: A Case Study of the State as Entrepreneur*. Cambridge: Cambridge University Press, 1983.

Trejos, Juan Diego. "Costa Rica: Crisis económica y política estatal, 1978–1984." Florida International University, Latin America and Caribbean Center, Occasional Paper no. 11 (May 1985).

Tullis, F. LaMond. *Lord and Peasant in Peru: A Paradigm of Political and Social Change*. Cambridge: Harvard University Press, 1970.

United Nations. *Yearbook of International Trade Statistics, 1960*. New York: United Nations, 1962.

United Nations, Economic Commission for Latin America. *The Economic Development of Latin America and Its Principal Problems*. New York: United Nations, 1950.

———. *Towards a Dynamic Development Policy for Latin America*. New York: United Nations, 1963.

———. *Statistical Yearbook for Latin America*, 1983 and 1984. New York: United Nations, 1984 and 1985.

United Nations, Food and Agriculture Organization. *FAO Production Yearbook*, 1981, 1983, and 1984. Rome: FAO, 1982, 1984, and 1985.

United States Senate. 94th Congress, First Session. Select Committee to Study Governmental Operations with Respect to Intelligence Activities. Staff Report. *Alleged Assasination Plots Involving Foreign Leaders*. Washington, D.C.: Government Printing Office, 1975.

United States Senate. 94th Congress, First Session. Select Committee to Study Governmental Operations with Respect to Intelligence Activities. Staff Report. *Covert Action in Chile.* Washington, D.C.: Government Printing Office, 1975.

Urrutia, Miguel. "Experience with the Crawling Peg in Colombia." In John Williamson, ed., *Exchange Rate Rules.* New York: St. Martin's, 1981.

———. *Winners and Losers in Colombia's Economic Growth in the 1970s.* Oxford: Oxford University Press, 1985.

Vaitsos, Constantine V. *Intercountry Distribution of Income and Transnational Enterprises.* Oxford: Clarendon Press, 1974.

Valdés, Nelson. "Cuba Today: Thoughts After a Recent Visit." *LASA Forum* (Fall 1984).

Valenzuela, Arturo. *The Breakdown of Democratic Regimes: Chile.* Baltimore: Johns Hopkins University Press, 1978.

Valenzuela, J. Samuel, and Arturo Valenzuela. "Modernisation and Dependence: Alternative Perspectives in the Study of Latin American Underdevelopment." In José Villamil, ed., *Transnational Capitalism and National Development.* Brighton: Harvester Press for the Institute of International Studies, University of Sussex, 1979.

Vance, Cyrus R. *Hard Choices: Four Critical Years in Managing America's Foreign Policy.* New York: Simon and Schuster, 1983.

Véliz, Claudio. *The Centralist Tradition of Latin America.* Princeton: Princeton University Press, 1980.

Vernon, Raymond. *The Dilemma of Mexico's Development.* Cambridge: Harvard University Press, 1963.

———. *Storm over the Multinationals: The Real Issues.* Cambridge: Harvard University Press, 1977.

Villamil, José, ed. *Transnational Capitalism and National Development.* Brighton: Harvester Press for the Institute of International Studies, University of Sussex, 1979.

Villarreal, René. *El desequilibrio externo en la industrialización de México (1929–1975): Un enfoque estructuralista.* Mexico: Fondo de Cultura Económica, 1976.

———. "The Policy of Import-substituting Industrialization, 1929–75." In José Luis Reyna and Richard S. Weinert, eds., *Authoritarianism in Mexico.* Philadelphia: Institute for the study of Human Issues, 1977.

Villasuso, Juan Manuel. "Foreign Debt and Economic Development: The Case of Costa Rica." In Antonio Jorge, Jorge Salazar-Carillo, and René P. Higonnet, eds., *Foreign Debt and Latin American Development.* New York: Pergamon, 1983.

Vogel, Robert C. "The Dynamics of Inflation in Latin America, 1950–1969." AER 64 (March 1974).

Wachter, Susan M. *Latin American Inflation: The Structualist-Monetarist Debate.* Lexington, Mass.: Lexington Books, 1976.

Wallerstein, Immanuel. "Dependence in an Interdependent World: The Limited Possibilities of Transformation within the Capitalist World Economy." *African Studies Review* 17 (April 1974).

Wallerstein, Michael. "The Collapse of Democracy in Brazil: Its Economic Determinants." LARR 15, 3 (1980).

Webb, Richard C. "Wage Policy and Income Distribution in Developing Countries." In Charles R. Frank and Richard Webb, eds., *Income Distribution and Growth in the Less-Developed Countries.* Washington, D.C.: Brookings, 1977.

Westphal, Larry E., Yung W. Rhee, and Garry Pursell. "Korean Industrial Competitiveness: Where It Came From." WBS no. 469 (1981).

Whitehead, Laurence. "Mexico from Bust to Boom: A Political Evaluation of the 1976–1979 Stabilization Programme." WD 8 (1980).

Wiarda, Howard J., ed. *Politics and Social Change in Latin America: The Distinct Tradition.* 2d rev. ed. Amherst: University of Massachusetts Press, 1982.

Wilde, Alexander. "Conversations among Gentlemen: Oligarchic Democracy in Colombia." In Juan J. Linz and Alfred Stepan, eds., *The Breakdown of Democratic Regimes: Latin America.* Baltimore: Johns Hopkins University Press, 1978.

———. "The Contemporary Church: The Political and the Pastoral." In R. Albert Berry, Ronald Hellman, and Mauricio Solaún, eds., *Politics of Compromise.* New Brunswick: Transactions Books, 1980.

Williams, Robert G. *Export Agriculture and the Crisis in Central America.* Chapel Hill: University of North Carolina Press, 1986.

Williamson, John. "On Seeking to Improve IMF Conditionality." AER 73 (May 1983).

———. *IMF Conditionality.* Washington: Institute for International Economics, 1983.

Woodward, Ralph Lee, Jr. *Central America: A Nation Divided.* New York: Oxford University Press, 2d ed., 1985.

World Bank. *Peru: Long-term Development Issues.* Washington, D.C.: World Bank, 1979.

———. *Colombia: Economic Development and Policy Under Changing Conditions.* Washington, D.C.: World Bank, 1984.

————. *World Development Report,* annual issues. Oxford: Oxford University Press for the World Bank, 1980–1986.

————. *World Tables,* 2d and 3d eds. Baltimore: Johns Hopkins University Press for the World Bank, 1980 and 1984.

de Wylder, Steffan. *Allende's Chile: The Political Economy of the Rise and Fall of the Unidad Popular.* Cambridge: Cambridge University Press, 1976.

INDEX

NOTE: Index does not include entries for material on individual countries included in tables, or for authors in References except when discussed in text.

LIBRARY OF CONGRESS CATALOGING-IN-PUBLICATION DATA

Sheahan, John, 1923–
Patterns of development in Latin America.

Bibliography: p.   Includes index.
1. Latin America—Economic conditions—1945–
2. Latin America—Politics and government—1948–
3. Poor—Latin America. 4. Political rights—
Latin America. 5. Foreign economic relations—
Latin America. I. Title.
HC125.S498 1987   338.98   87–2853
ISBN 0–691–07735–5 (alk. paper)
ISBN 0–691–2264–X (pbk.)